Weather Reports, Forecasts & Flight Planning

Weather Reports, Forecasts & Flight Planning

Third Edition

Terry T. Lankford

McGraw-Hill

New York San Francisco Washington, D.C. Auckland Bogotá
Caracas Lisbon London Madrid Mexico City Milan
Montreal New Delhi San Juan Singapore
Sydney Tokyo Toronto

Library of Congress Cataloging-in-Publication Data

Lankford, Terry T.
    Weather reports, forecasts & flight planning
        p.   cm.
    Includes index.
    ISBN 0-07-135456-5

CIP

McGraw-Hill

A Division of The **McGraw·Hill** Companies

1 2 3 4 5 6 7 8 9 0 DOC/DOC 9 0 9 8 7 6 5 4 3 2 1 0 9

ISBN 0-07-135456-5

The sponsoring editor for this book was Shelley Ingram Carr, the editing supervisor was Sally Glover, and the production supervisor was Sherri Souffrance. It was set in Slimbach per the PFS2 design by Joanne Morbit and Michele Pridmore of McGraw-Hill's Professional Group Composition Unit, in Hightstown, NJ.

Printed and bound by R. R. Donnelley & Sons Company.

McGraw-Hill books are available at special quantity discounts to use as premiums and sales promotions, or for use in corporate training programs. For more information, please write to the Director of Special Sales, McGraw-Hill, 11 West 19th Street, New York, NY 10011. Or contact your local bookstore.

Contents

Preface

I obtained a Private Pilot Certificate in 1967 through an Air Force aero club in England—certificate because the FAA cannot spell license. Back in the states, with the G.I. Bill, I obtained the commercial and flight instructor certificates along with an instrument rating. Subsequently, as a full-time flight instructor I earned a Gold Seal. I have owned two airplanes, both Cessna 150s that have taken me across the country twice. I have also flown in Canada and Mexico.

A commercial pilot certificate and instrument rating qualified me for a position with the Federal Aviation Administration (FAA) as an Air Traffic Control Specialist (Station).

Only once as flight service specialist did I become an "air traffic controller." While at the Lovelock, Nevada FSS, a call came in from a VFR pilot caught in clouds at 13,000 ft. In such cases the control facility (approach control or center) usually provides assistance. Coordinating with Oakland Center, the controller replied: "OK, you've got 14 and below, keep me advised." Wow, instant air traffic controller!

I've been an FSS controller for 25 years, which has brought together two interests: aviation and weather. I retired from the FAA in 1998 and have been fortunate enough to obtain a position as a flight and ground instructor with Ahart Aviation at the Livermore, California, airport.

With all the books and articles written about aviation weather, it might seem everything has been said. As a flight instructor, however, I discovered that very little practical information was available for pilots on the subject of meteorology. Certain texts and periodicals contain excellent points and suggestions; most merely paraphrase government manuals; some actually include incorrect and misleading information. Many say nothing.

I find it exasperating to read an article with meteorological terms that espouses the need to understand weather then fails to include a definition or explain the application of a term. Virtually none has an understanding of information available from, or the requirements and responsibilities of, the FSS weather briefer. Nor do they present practical ways of translating, interpreting, updating, and applying information.

The *1992 National Aviation Weather Program Plan* identified a number of unmet users needs. Among these was the necessity to improve aviation weather education for pilots and weather providers. This need was reiterated in the April 1997 *National Aviation Weather Program Strategic Plan*. To date, with the exception of AOPA's Air Safety Foundation, virtually nothing has been accomplished in this area.

As an FSS controller I've become aware of requirements and procedures that the FAA seems to want to keep secret. Most requirements and procedures have to do with how FSS and air traffic controllers do their jobs. Much of this book is dedicated to points glossed over, outdated, or ignored altogether in the *Aeronautical Information Manual*.

Pilots, especially within the general aviation community, have a close relationship with the Flight Service Station. The FSS controller, whether during preflight or in-flight, has at his or her fingertips a wealth of information. The pilot, for whom the FSS exists, is an integral part of the aviation weather system. Pilots provide feedback in the form of pilot weather reports, essential for the meteorologist to verify the forecast, and for optimum system operation. When the pilot or controller forgets, or does not understand, the requirements and responsibilities of the other, the system can fail, sometimes with fatal results.

Aviation weather-related accidents continue to take their toll; analysis often reveals an inadequate, misinterpreted, or misunderstood weather briefing. With FSS automation, automated weather observations, and increased availability of direct user access terminals and other commercial weather information systems, pilots are required to read, interpret, and apply weather information on their own. A sound background in meteorology and the products available to aviation are essential to safety.

I am greatly indebted to many people for their generous help, guidance, and advice, too numerous to be listed in full. Among them are the meteorologists of the National Weather Service (NWS) at the FAA Academy in Oklahoma City, and local, regional, and center NWS offices, plus FSS controllers that I have been privileged to know, especially at the Oakland, California FSS. And the pilots who have allowed me to assist them and in turn provided me with the best education possible. This book is dedicated to these people.

Introduction

The second edition of this book was published in 1995. It contained several major and numerous minor evolutions in weather report and forecast criteria and format. Since then there has been a revolution in weather observing systems and weather report and forecast formats. Additionally, the communications revolution has made new weather products available for both preflight and in-flight use.

Rather than a revision, the third edition of *The Pilot's Guide to Weather Reports, Forecasts & Flight Planning* is the next generation. Fully automated weather observing systems are now the rule, rather than the exception. The international weather code has been adopted universally within North America for weather reports, forecasts, and notices to airmen. Real-time satellite imagery and NEXRAD radar data are routinely available. With continuing Flight Service Station (FSS) and National Weather Service (NWS) consolidation, and expansion of self-briefing systems, a pilot's ability to decode, translate, and interpret weather has taken on even greater significance.

Weather affects a pilot's flying activity more than any other physical factor. Most pilots agree that weather is the most difficult and least understood subject in the training curriculum. Surveys indicate that many pilots are uneasy with, or even intimidated by, weather. In spite of these facts, or maybe because of them, weather training for pilots typically consists of bare bones, only enough to pass the written test, while weather-related fatal accident statistics remain relatively unchanged.

Air Force pilot training contains a mere 15 hours of formal weather instruction, as compared to 50 or 60 hours in the past. Navy pilot weather training has been reduced by 25 percent to 30 hours, with no refresher. Army aviator weather training consists of about the same number of hours. My own FAA certificated primary ground school included a mere nine hours of weather. Ironically, regulations perpetuate this trend. Student, private, recreational, and commercial airplane pilots are only required to obtain and use weather reports and forecasts, recognize critical weather situations, and estimate ground and flight visibility—although windshear and wake turbulence avoidance have been added to the presolo requirement. An additional requirement of forecasting weather trends on the basis of information received and personal observations is required for an instrument rating. Only the airline transport pilot certificate requires the applicant to have any serious meteorological knowledge.

A major revision to the practical test standards in 1984 required that applicants exhibit "knowledge of aviation weather information by obtaining, reading, and analyzing..." reports and forecasts, and make "...a competent go/no-go decision based on the available weather information." The practical test standards do reference AC 00-6 *Aviation Weather* (basic meteorological theory) and AC 00-45 *Aviation Weather Services* (a basic discussion of weather reports and forecasts), but neither reference relates weather to flight situations or application to a go/no-go decision. Most flight tests are given during good weather, and pilots requesting check ride briefings, all too often, have little idea of the information required or the presentation format of the FSS briefer; this requirement would seem to have little practical consequence.

This situation evolved because when regulations were originally written, virtually all flying, except military and airline, was visual. The aircraft of the day had neither the performance nor the instruments to take on weather. When weather was encountered, pilots simply landed in the nearest field. Regulations are extremely difficult to change; take the aeronautical experience of 40 hours required for the private pilot. These hours have been woefully inadequate for years with the constant increase of additional requirements. Many of the people who write regulations and perform flight tests are former military pilots with minimal weather training, because after graduation they were under direct control of older, more experienced pilots and gained experience in a controlled environment.

Accident reports and commentaries frequently refer to a pilot's poor judgment, namely the failure to reach a sound decision. Pilot judgment is based on training and experience. Training is knowledge imparted during certification, flight reviews, seminars, and literature;

experience can be best defined as when the test comes before the lesson. Unfortunately, failure can be fatal. Pilot applicants have only their instructors to prepare them to make competent go/no-go decisions.

Odds are that little, if any, judgment training occurred unless situations were actually encountered. General aviation training runs the entire gamut from the flight school that prohibits its instrument students and instructors from flying in the clouds, to the instructor in a Cessna 182 who requested to be vectored into icing conditions to demonstrate the effects of ice on the airplane. (Neither instance seemingly exhibits sound judgment.) The fact remains that the least experienced pilots have minimum weather training. Following certification there is no requirement for additional or refresher weather instruction.

An essential part of flight preparation concerns the weather. No matter how short or simple the mission, regulations place the responsibility for flight preparation on the pilot, not the NWS forecaster, not the FSS briefer. To effectively use the available resources, a pilot must understand what weather information is available, how it is distributed, and how it can be applied to a flight situation.

This book provides information that is not only required to pass written and practical examinations, but also to prepare the dispatcher as well as the pilot—from student through airline transport, from recreational to biz-jet—to operate safely and efficiently within an increasingly complex environment.

Student, recreational, private, and commercial pilots will develop abilities to recognize and avoid critical weather situations.

Pilots will learn to obtain weather reports and forecasts, through the FAA and other sources, then interpret and apply information to flight situations.

Pilots will understand the principles of forecasting, and applying forecasts and observations to the flight environment.

Pilots will understand weather collection and distribution, symbols and contractions, charts and forecasts, and how terrain affects weather.

Pilots will recognize cloud forms, conditions conducive to icing and other meteorological hazards, and the use of pilot weather reports.

The student pilot will have access to the knowledge of the airline transport pilot.

Technical meteorological concepts and terms are translated into language any pilot can easily understand. On the other hand, such subjects as vorticity, microbursts, and upper-level weather systems will not be omitted because of complexity. Explanations of weather reports and forecast go beyond decoding and translating, to interpreting and applying information to actual flight situations. Discussions include applying weather information to VFR as well as IFR operations, and high-level as well as low-level flights.

A thorough understanding of the basics is essential: a sound foundation for the novice and a practical review for the experienced pilot. Judgment and application of judgment, plus a knowledge of the aviation weather system and its relation to air traffic control, are essential to a safe, efficient flight.

Weather reports, forecasts, and flight planning are interrelated; it might be necessary for the reader to complete the book to realize the most thorough understanding of the subject.

Chapter 1 begins with a detailed description of surface weather reports, including methods and criteria used by the weather observer—whether manual or automated. Failure to understand the observer's requirements often leads to pilot misunderstanding and unwarranted observation criticism. Limitations on observations are discussed with practical guidance on interpreting and applying information.

Surface reports are related to hazards, such as thunderstorms, turbulence, icing, low ceilings and fog, precipitation, haze, smoke, and dust, as well as winds and low-level wind shear, and high-density altitude. The advantages and limitations inherent with automated weather observing systems are presented.

Most pilots are unaware of their contributions through pilot weather reports, or the impact reports can have on the system. Inaccurate or overestimated reports of turbulence and icing cause misleading advisories to be issued. Pilots making these reports gain unrealistic confidence in their ability to handle severe conditions. Pilots receiving unwarranted advisories, based on overestimated pilot reports, might conclude all advisories are pessimistic. When severe conditions develop, these pilots can be lead down the primrose path to disaster. In chapter 2, pilot weather report criteria are discussed in detail, along with distribution and application.

Pilots now have access to real-time satellite images. Although satellite interpretation is a science in itself, many flights and all grades of pilots can benefit from these products. But, like all other weather reports and forecasts, satellite images suffer from limitations. These limitations, along with interpretation and application, are discussed in chapter 3 and presented in a manner to allow maximum application to the flight environment.

Chapter 4 begins with the methods, criteria, and limitations of the forecaster. Numerous misunderstandings and misconceptions of forecast products and terminology, potentially catastrophic to the uninformed pilot, are explained. The book tells how the pilot can interpret and apply forecasts to specific flight situations, which will become increasingly important with pilot self-briefing systems.

Approximately one dozen different forecasts are written for aviation; each has criteria, purpose, and limitations; often they overlap and might appear to be inconsistent. Analysis, however, most often reveals that the forecasts are consistent within the scope of each product. Each forecast is analyzed and put into perspective in chapters 4 through 8. The pilot can then apply the array of forecasts available, with respect to regulations, aircraft performance, and pilot ability, to efficiently operate within the system and make sound go/no-go decisions.

Beyond written weather reports and forecasts, a multitude of charts are available. Each chart has a specific purpose, use, and limitations. All charts are discussed and analyzed in chapters 9 and 10 with respect to their individual significance and application.

The weather charts discussed are available from the National Weather Service. Weather charts obtained through direct user access terminals and other private vendors are typically not as detailed, but their interpretation and application are similar.

Chapters 11 is devoted to obtaining, updating, and using weather and aeronautical information. Discussions will help the pilot efficiently obtain weather and flight planning information, which have become increasingly difficult with FSS and NWS consolidation.

Each chapter contains a discussion of the application of weather reports and forecasts to flight planning. With the addition of new technologies and products, some chapters, which appeared in previous editions, have necsssarily had to be eliminated. These chapters, VFR and IFR flight planning, and using the Air Traffic Control system, more appropriately belong in a book dedicated to mechanics of flight planning and flight plan services. Therefore, like navigational principles and techniques, these subjects are not within the scope of this book. These subjects are, however, specifically covered in other McGraw-Hill Practical Flying Series publications.

The appendixes have been significantly revised and the Glossary expanded since the second edition. Appendix A, Abbreviations, contains weather and international contractions. Weather Advisory Plotting Chart locations, and the chart itself in Appendix B, have been updated to reflect the charges that occurred on March 1, 1999.

With automated weather briefing equipment, both FAA and direct user access terminals, appropriate METAR, Terminal Aerodrome Forecast, and Winds and Temperatures Aloft Forecast locations for the pilot's defined route are automatically displayed. Therefore, these maps are no longer necessary and have been deleted. TWEB route forecast and NWS weather radar location maps have been updated. Appendix C, Area Designators, has been expanded and updated.

Text references are made to various cloud forms that frequently appear in weather reports with photographs to illustrate certain formations. An excellent, detailed, color cloud chart, The Cloud Chart is available through the National Weather Association, 6704 Wolke Court, Montgomery, Alabama 36116-2134.

The following chapters, hopefully told with a little humor, explain how to use the weather system, translate, and interpret weather reports and forecasts, then apply them to a flight situation. Sometimes we tend to take ourselves a little too seriously, so throughout the text I've poked some fun at myself and others, especially government agencies like the FAA and NWS. By doing this I've tried to inject a "reality check." However, incidents are not intended to disparage or malign any individual, group, or organization; the sole purpose is illustration.

Examples of weather reports and forecasts are real, taken from the weather circuit; none have been created.

Weather report phraseology used in the text is taken from FAA handbook 7110.10 *Flight Services*. This is the same phraseology pilots can expect in FSS radio communications and broadcasts.

Great effort has been made to ensure that information is current and accurate, as of the time of writing. However, especially in aviation and aviation weather, the only thing that doesn't change is change itself.

Surface Observations (METAR)

According to Mark Twain: "If you don't like the weather in New England, just wait a few minutes." The same can be said about the format of aviation weather reports. In less than one hundred years there have been evolutions and revolutions in the way we report the environment. Various evolutions have occurred over the years, such as the change from wind direction arrows to reporting wind in degrees (1960s), and the change from sky cover symbols to contractions (1970s). Revolutions have also taken place, such as the transmission of weather reports electronically (Teletype and radio), and the introduction of automated observations. (An automated report indicates the observation was derived without human intervention. The terms manual, augmentation, or backup refer to the fact that a person has overall responsibility for the observation, although some or all of the elements of the report are derived from automated equipment.) How has automation affect the quality of observations? More about this throughout the chapter.

The latest revolution occurred on July 1, 1996 when METAR (Meteorological Aviation Routine) replaced the North American SA (Surface Aviation) code in the United States. Mexico converted in

1995 and Canada, along with the United States in 1996. Ostensibly, METAR has standardized surface aviation reports throughout the world. However, with METAR individual member countries are allowed to change certain items in the report. For example, rather than metric the United States continues to use English units of measurement, except for temperatures.

Another revolution took place in the early 1990s. Prior to this time, when most pilots were asked about coded weather reports they'd say: "Why do I have to read the weather? When I call flight service, they read and explain the reports." Pilots have been objecting to coded weather information since its inception in the early 1930s. With Direct User Access Terminals (DUATs) and other commercially available weather systems, pilots now have to read weather on their own. Although some systems provide a plain language translation, on occasion they can be confusing and misleading. A pilot's knowledge of weather takes on greater significance with DUAT, and National Weather Service (NWS) and Flight Service Station (FSS) consolidation—with further FSS consolidation already being considered. Whether you're a beginner or an experienced hand, every pilot needs the ability to decode, translate, and interpret weather information.

Most weather reports are history by the time they are transmitted and available. In the Teletype era—prior to the late 1970s, reports were often an hour-and-a-half old. Beginning in 1978 the Federal Aviation Administration (FAA) introduced a computer system known as Leased Service A (LSAS). With this and other computerized systems, most reports are available within 20 minutes of observation. Automated observations received through DUAT or FSS are accessible within a few minutes of observation time, and are essentially real time when obtained via direct telephone or radio.

The accuracy and validity of observations, and therefore their usefulness, depend on many factors: who or what is taking the observation; the extent of the observer's training and experience; the type of equipment, if any, that is available? Automated observations have advantages and disadvantages over manual reports. Observational technique between automated and manual observations differs significantly in four major areas: visibility, weather and obstructions to vision, sky condition, and remarks. It is not a case of whether automated or manual observations are necessarily better, but they are different. How can reports be supplemented, confirmed, or refuted? Now more than ever, pilots need to use all available sources to determine weather conditions. These include adjacent weather reports, pilot weather reports (PIREPs), radar reports, satellite imagery, and forecasts.

THE COMPLETE PICTURE

Many have touted the necessity for pilots to get the "big picture." This refers to obtaining a complete weather synopsis. That is, the position and movement of weather producing systems and those that pose a hazard to flight operations. This is important, but only one element needed for an informed weather decision. I prefer the term "complete picture." As well as a thorough knowledge of the synopsis, pilots must obtain and understand all the information available from current weather, discussed in this chapter, and chapter 2, to forecast weather presented in subsequent chapters. As we shall see, each report, chart, or product provides a clue to the "complete picture." Each must be translated and interpreted with knowledge of its scope and limitations. Then, with knowledge of the "complete picture" we can apply the information to a specific flight. As observed by the United States Supreme Court: "Safe does not mean risk free." With the complete picture, knowledge of our aircraft and its equipment, and ourselves and our passengers we're ready to assess and manage risk.

The National Weather Service certifies weather observers and automated reporting equipment. The most accurate, valid, and detailed observations come from NWS, military, FSS, tower, and other observers, in that order. Why? NWS and military observers are professionals located at major airports with the latest equipment. At FSS and tower locations weather observations are a secondary duty and generally, equipment is not as sophisticated. As for the others, they are contract observers, retired air traffic controllers, local airport personnel, or even the fire department, often with little or no equipment, and the minimum of training and experience. This is not to say that many of them don't provide quality observations, but in many cases, they simply don't have the equipment, training, or experience. The FAA, NWS, and Department of Defense (DOD) are replacing manual observations with automated weather observing systems. Although many locations are augmented or backed up by human observers.

Attempts at automated weather observations have existed for more than 40 years. Automated surface observations began with the Automatic Meteorological Observing Station (AMOS). Unfortunately, this system was only capable of reporting temperature, dew point, wind direction and speed, and pressure. Occasionally, observers manually entered data to augment the report.

The Automatic Observing Station (AUTOB), a refinement of AMOS, added sky condition, visibility, and precipitation reporting. AUTOB, however, was limited to cloud amount and height measurements of 6,000 ft above ground level (AGL), and three cloud layers. Visibility values are reported in whole miles, to a maximum of seven.

In the mid-1980s, the FAA published requirements for the Automated Weather Observing System (AWOS). AWOS was originally operationally classified into four levels. These levels consisted of AWOS-A, which reports altimeter setting only; AWOS-1 (the equivalent of AMOS) reporting temperature, dew point, wind, and altimeter setting; AWOS-2 adds visibility information; and AWOS-3 reports sky conditions and ceiling along with the other elements. AWOS is a "commercially off-the-shelf" system, designed primarily for small airports with published instrument approaches, but without weather observations.

The Automated Surface Observing System (ASOS) has been developed to satisfy the requirements of both the FAA and NWS. In addition to the elements available through AWOS, ASOS will report present weather, precipitation, and include coded remarks containing climatological data. ASOS will replace the "interim" AWOS system at locations where the government has weather reporting responsibility.

Today's science strives to reach the accuracy and reliability, and reduce some of the limitations of the human observer. Manual surface observations have been decreasing on a regular basis over the last two decades, with others part-timed. An additional objective is to release air traffic control personnel for their primary duty-separating aircraft.

Approximately 1,500 FAA, NWS, DOD, and locally operated automated weather reporting locations will be operational by the turn of the century, with some 350 ASOS locations commissioned by 1999. The automated observing system routinely and automatically provides computer-generated voice directly to aircraft near airports, using FAA VHF ground-to-air radio. In addition, the same information is available through a dial-in telephone and most of the data is provided on the national weather data network.

An additional enhancement will become available during 1999. The ASOS-ATIS (Automatic Terminal Information Service) interface switch allows ASOS current weather observations to be appended to the ATIS broadcast, thereby providing real-time weather at part-time tower locations. Upon closing in the evening, the controller will have the ability to add overnight ATIS information to the ASOS automated voice message. Pilots will get normal ATIS when the tower is open and when closed, pilots will receive one-minute weather observations along with the closing ATIS information on the same frequency. This approach allows the pilot to utilize the same frequency 24 hours a day for airport information.

Most pilots are dealing with automated observations, to one degree or another, on a continuous basis. Figure 1-1 shows a typical AWOS/ASOS installation. Like manual observations, automated observations have the potential to provide an extra degree of safety, or lure the unsuspecting pilot into danger.

The new technology has its faultfinders. FSS weather briefers, NWS forecasters, weather observers, and pilots are among the critics. There is no question that automated observations, like anything new, have had "teething" problems. The two most controversial elements are visibility and sky condition. Critics cite these elements as the least accurate, they are certainly the least understood. Additionally, accommodation must be made for the lack of certain weather sensors. But we'll find that in the final analysis most criticism is due to misunderstanding, a reluctance to change, or personal prejudice.

Fig. 1-1. Automated observations have the potential to provide an extra degree of safety or lure the unsuspecting pilot to disaster.

With the preceding as a background, we can move on to the analysis of a weather observation. METAR reports appear in the following sequence:

- Type of report

- Station identifier

- Date and time of report

- Report modifier, if required

- Wind

- Visibility

- Weather and obstructions to visibility

- Sky condition

- Temperature and dew point

- Altimeter setting

- Remarks

Missing, or not reported, elements are omitted. The letter "M" means minus or less than; the letter "P" means plus or more than. Any remarks follow the contraction RMK.

Type of Report

There are two types of reports: METAR, a routine observation, and SPECI a special weather report.

METAR observations are reported each hour. Normally, elements are observed between 45 and 55 minutes past the hour. Whenever a significant change occurs a SPECI is generated. A complex criterion determines the requirement for specials. Generally, they're required when the weather improves to, or deteriorates below, Visual Flight Rules (VFR), or approach and landing Instrument Flight Rules (IFR) minimums. Specials are also required for:

- Beginning, ending, or change in intensity of freezing precipitation

- Beginning or ending of thunderstorm activity

- Tornadoes, funnel clouds, or waterspouts

- Wind shift

- Volcanic eruption

SPECIs are not available for all locations; however, these reports will carry the remark NOSPECI. In such cases, significant changes can occur without expeditious notification.

Station Identifier

METAR uses standard four-letter International Civil Aviation Organization (ICAO) location identifiers (LOCID). For the continental United States this consists of three letters prefixed with the letter "K." For example, Newark, New Jersey KEWR and Philadelphia, Pennsylvania KPHL. (Prior to the United States accepting the international standard, LOCIDs for weather reports were alphanumeric. That is, made up of letters and numbers (O45-Vacaville, California). Now, with more and more weather reports transmitted over FAA and NWS communication systems all locations will eventually use letters only (KVCB-Vacaville, California). That's why we've seen so many changes to LOCIDs recently, and why they're making even less sense than they used to!

Elsewhere in the world, the first one or two letters of the ICAO identifier indicate the region, state, or country of the station. For example, Pacific locations such as Alaska, Hawaii, and the Marianas islands start with the letter "P" to indicate the region, followed by the letter "A," "H," or "G" which represent the state within the region. Canadian station LOCIDs begin with the letter "C," Mexican and western Caribbean the letter "M," and eastern Caribbean the letter "T." A complete worldwide listing is contained in ICAO Document 7910, Location Indicators. Along with a catalogue of ICAO publications, this document is available from ICAO Headquarters:

International Civil Aviation Organization
Attention: Document Sales Unit
1000 Sherbrooke Street West, Suite 400
Montreal, Quebec
Canada H3A 2R2

LOCIDs for the United States, Canada, and Mexico are contained in FAA Handbook 7350.5 Location Identifiers, available for sale from the Superintendent of Documents. Pilots also have access to LOCIDs from aeronautical charts and through FAA Flight Service Stations, Direct User Access Terminals, and the Airport/Facility Directory—the green book.

Date/Time Group

Following observation of the last element, usually atmospheric pressure, the official time of observation is recorded. This time is transmitted as a six digit date/time group appended with a "Z" to denote Coordinated Universal Time (UTC), at times—pardon the pun—referred to as ZULU or "Z."

The first two digits represent the day of the month, the last four digits the time of observation. For example, METAR KOAK 142355Z.... This METAR for Oakland, California was observed on the 14th day of the month, at 2355 UTC.

Report Modifier

Two report modifiers may appear after the date/time group. AUTO indicates the report comes from an automated weather observation station without augmentation or backup. The absence of AUTO discloses that the report was produced manually, or that an automated report has manual augmentation or backup. When AUTO appears in the body of the report, the type of sensor equipment is contained in the remarks.

Augmented means someone is physically at the site monitoring the equipment. Augmentation requires the observer to manually add data on thunderstorms, tornadic activity, hail, virga, volcanic ash, and tower visibility, which the automated

FACT

It seems that an advisory committee of the International Telecommunications Union in 1970 was tasked with replacing the international time standard of Greenwich Mean Time (GMT). The question became whether to use English or French word order for Coordinated Universal Time—sound familiar? So, instead of CUT or TUC, UTC was adopted and became effective in the late 1980s.

equipment is not capable of reporting. Backup involves correcting nonrepresentative, erroneous, or missing data, such as wind, visibility, ceiling, temperature/dew point, or altimeter. It does not, however, necessarily mean that an observer is maintaining a continuous weather watch. The observer may not be changing, correcting, or adding information to the observation. However, the same can be true of manual reports where the weather observation has a lower priority than air traffic control duties.

COR means the METAR/SPECI report was originally transmitted with an error that has now been corrected. If a report is a correction, the time entered on the corrected report will be the same as in the original observation. The only way to identify the correction is to compare it with the original report.

Report modifiers appear in METAR/SPECI reports as follows:

METAR KFAT 150055Z AUTO...;

SPECI KFAT 150115Z COR....

Wind

Crucial for determining crosswind component, especially in areas with large magnetic variation, wind direction reported on METAR/SPECI is always reported in relations to true north, given as the direction from which the wind is blowing, and to the nearest 10 degrees. (The only time pilots can expect to receive wind direction in relation to magnetic north is from a control tower, an FSS providing Local Airport Advisory (LAA), ATIS recording, or AWOS/ASOS radio broadcast.)

Wind is reported as a two-minute prevailing wind direction and speed using a five digit group, six if the speed exceeds 99 knots. The first three digits indicate wind direction. The next two or three digits indicate speed. The units of measurement follow (KT knots, KMH kilometers per hour, MPS meters per second). In the United States, knots will continue to be used (34017KT, wind 340 degrees at 17 knots).

Gusts (G) refer to rapid fluctuations in speed that vary by 10 knots or more. Therefore, a report ...18G24KT... describes an average speed of 18 knots with fluctuations between 14 and 24 knots. Gustiness is a

Gusts are noted when winds rapidly vary by 10 kts.

measure of turbulence. The greater the difference between sustained speed and gusts, the greater the mechanical turbulence. Typically, pilots can expect light to moderate turbulence with sustained winds or gusts in the 25 to 30 knot range, and moderate or greater turbulence above 30 knots. Terrain and obstructions—such as buildings or hangers—increase turbulence intensity.

A calm wind is reported as 00000KT. If wind direction varies by 60 degrees or more with a speed greater than six knots, a variable group separated by a "V" follows the prevailing group. ..34017KT 310V010..., wind variable between 310 degrees and 010 degrees. A variable wind, especially with speeds of 10 knots or more, may indicate a rapidly changing crosswind. Pilots need to exercise additional caution during takeoff and landing with these conditions. If the wind is six knots or less, and varying in direction, it may be reported as variable "VRB" without an assigned direction. For example, ...VRB04KT..., wind variable at four. VRB may also be used in special cases at higher speeds, such as a wind shift with the passage of a thunderstorm over the station.

Wind direction, speed, and character (gusts) must be considered when determining crosswind component, or the advisability of landing at a particular airport. Since runways are identified by their magnetic orientation, METAR wind direction must be converted to magnetic to determine crosswind component. This is especially significant in areas with large magnetic variation.

Crosswind or tailwind components can be determined using a flight computer or a graph as illustrated in Fig. 1-2, Crosswind Component Chart.

Figure 1-2 allows the pilot to determine crosswind, headwind, and tailwind component. The vertical and horizontal axes represent wind speed in knots, the arc crosswind angle in degrees. Three elements are required: runway orientation (runway number), magnetic wind direction, and wind speed.

Let's say we're planning a departure from runway 25 (runway magnetic orientation 250 degrees). METAR reports surface wind from 290 degrees at 17 knots (29017KT). Local magnetic variation is 12 degrees east. Subtract easterly variation: 290 − 12 ≈ 280.

(It doesn't matter if it is a left or right crosswind; we're looking for the difference between runway heading and wind direction.) In this case, the difference is 30 degrees (28 – 25 = 30.) Enter the Crosswind Component Chart on the 30-degree radial line and proceed toward the origin of the graph—toward zero. Stop at the point where the 30-degree radial line intercepts the wind speed arc of 17 knots. Moving vertically down to the horizontal axis read nine knots, the crosswind component for this runway. By moving horizontally to the vertical axis, the headwind component is approximately 14 knots. Should the angular difference between runway and wind be more than 90 degrees but less than 180 degrees, we would have a crosswind and tailwind component.

Most airplanes have a published "maximum demonstrated crosswind component." This is not an absolute limit, but should be considered along with the pilot's training and experience. All Airplane Flight Manuals (AFMs)—also known as Pilot's Operating Handbook (POH)—contain takeoff and landing performance charts for various headwind, runway, and temperature conditions. Some AFMs also contain performance charts for takeoff with a tailwind.

Favorable conditions for turbulence exist just before, during, and after storm passage, especially when winds blow perpendicular to mountain ridges. For example, consider the following report for Mammoth Lakes, California (KMMH) that occurred just after storm passage with winds perpendicular to the rugged California Sierra Nevada Mountains.

METAR KMMH 031545Z 23045G90KT...

The KMMH runway is 09-27 and magnetic variation is 15 degrees east. To convert wind direction from true to magnetic, subtract easterly variation (east is least). Therefore, the KMMH wind is

CROSSWIND COMPONENT CHART

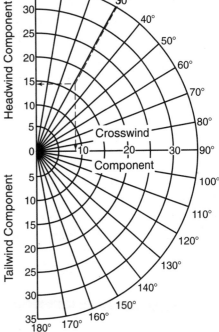

Fig. 1-2. Most airplane manuals specify maximum demonstrated crosswind component; although not absolute values, they represent a speed for which the airplane has been tested.

blowing from 215 degrees magnetic (230 – 015 = 215). At an angle of 55 degrees to the runway (270 – 215 = 55), this results in a 35-knot crosswind component for the sustained speed, and 70 knots for the gusts! This airport would not be suitable for landing. For one thing, the highway patrol closed the roads and no one could pick you up after the, umm, arrival.

One use of the remarks element in METAR/SPECI is to amplify information in the body of the report. Wind shift WSHFT or peak wind PK WND may appear in remarks of manual and ASOS observations.

Peak Winds reported > 25 KTS

Peak wind appears when speed exceeds 25 knots. The direction, speed, and time of occurrence is reported ...PK WND 3560/40..., peak wind from 350 degrees at 60 knots occurred at 40 minutes past the hour. Peak wind might substantially exceed the value in the body of the observation.

Wind shift describes a change in direction of 45 degrees or more that takes place in less than 15 minutes, with sustained speeds of 10 knots or more ...WSHFT 55..., wind shift occurred at 55 minutes past the hour. A wind shift of relative light winds might only indicate a local change; in coastal areas, the shift often signals the advance or retreat of stratus or fog. In the Midwest, the shift might precede the formation or dissipation of upslope fog. Wind shift is usually a good indicator of frontal passage. To indicate frontal passage FROPA may be included in remarks of manual or augmented stations. In Southern California a shift often indicates the advance or retreat of a Santa Ana condition—a dry, often strong, foehn-type wind over and through the mountains and passes.

FROPA = Frontal Passage

Should either the wind direction or speed sensor be out of service or unreliable, the wind group is omitted. These sensors consist of a wind vane and anomometer, or a combination known as an aerovane. (An aerovane is shown atop the instrument mast in Fig. 1-1.) Each consists of moving parts, which can fail. The next general of sensors will contain no moving parts at all—therefore becoming more reliable.

With the increased availability of automated weather observation systems, they have become a significant weather resource. This is especially true for uncontrolled fields. By monitoring the automated broadcast, as well as sky conditions, visibility, and altimeter setting, pilots receive surface wind information. From this, they can often determine favored runway. By checking the Airport/Facility Directory, and now published on aeronautical charts, pilots can establish traffic direction for that runway. This allows a more effective determination of runway in use and traffic pattern.

For airports without weather reporting service, a nearby observation may provide general weather conditions, such as wind direction and speed. A word of caution. In mountainous and hilly terrain, wind can change significantly over a very short distance.

Visibility

Visibility is a measure of the transparency of the atmosphere. During the day visibility represents the distance at which predominant objects can be seen; at night, visibility is the distance that unfocused lights of moderate intensity are visible.

> **CASE STUDY**
> One NWS observer was quite perplexed when the tower always reported increased visibility after sunset. The reason was the change in criteria. Pilots should note that daytime values do not necessarily represent the distance that other aircraft can be seen. At night, especially under an overcast, unlighted objects might not be seen at all, and there could be no natural horizon. Aviation has three distinct types of visibility: surface, slant range, and air to air.

Surface visibility represents horizontal visibility occurring at the surface-prevailing visibility or its automated equivalent. Reported surface visibility comes into play when a pilot plans to take off, land, or enter the traffic pattern VFR. Surface visibility must be at least the minimum specified for the class of airspace. If surface visibility is not reported, flight visibility is used.

Slant-range, or air to ground, visibility is the distance a pilot can see objects on the ground from an aircraft in flight. Slant-range visibility is often reduced by phenomena aloft or on the surface. It may be greater or less than surface visibility, depending upon the intensity of the phenomena aloft or the depth of the surface-based restriction.

Air-to-air, or in-flight, visibility is visibility aloft. Regulations require specific minimum in-flight visibility for VFR operations—to "see and avoid" other aircraft. Visibilities aloft are most often reduced by rain, snow, dust, smoke, and haze.

Visibility from manual observations is reported as prevailing, in statute miles "SM." For example, ...1/2SM... one-half statute mile, ...7SM... seven statute miles, or ...15SM... one five statute miles. Prevailing visibility is the greatest visibility equalled or exceeded throughout at least half the horizon circle, which need not be continuous. Figure 1-3 illustrates a reported prevailing visibility of four miles. Because one sector has a visibility of only two, which is operationally significant, remarks contain ...VIS S 2..., visibility south two. Sectors might also exist with visibility greater than prevailing. These values might or might not appear in remarks. This accounts for some apparent inconsistencies between reported values and those observed by the pilot. In Fig. 1-3, a pilot approaching the airport in the sector where the visibility is six miles may question the report. The observation, however, remains consistent within the definition of prevailing visibility.

Pilots are required to be trained in estimating visibility while in flight. Refer to Fig. 1-3. Assuming the observation was taken at an airport in controlled airspace, to legally operate VFR where the sector visibility was reported as two miles, a pilot must have flight visibility of three miles. If this cannot be done, the pilot would have to obtain an IFR, request a special VFR clearance, or depart the area. To land under the provisions of IFR, visibility must not be less than that

PREVAILING VISIBILITY

METAR: 4SM...RMK VIS S 2

Fig. 1-3. Prevailing visibility represents the greatest visibility equalled or exceeded throughout at least half the horizon circle, which need not be continuous.

CASE STUDY

At one Southern California airport, it appears local pilots estimate prevailing visibility in the following manner: "1/4 mile to the north, 1/4 mile to the east, 1/4 mile to the south, and 1/4 mile to the west—great! Prevailing visibility is one mile, it's VFR." This is not only incorrect, but also extremely dangerous.

prescribed for the approach.

Automated systems determine visibility from a scatter meter device, as illustrated in Fig. 1-4. The visibility sensor indirectly derives a value of visibility corresponding to what the human eye would see. The visibility sensor projects light in a cone-shaped beam, sampling only a small segment of the atmosphere—an area about the size of a basketball. The receiver measures only the light scattered forward. The sensor measures the return every 30 seconds. A computer algorithm—mathematical formula— evaluates sensor readings for the past 10 minutes to provide a representative value. Reported visibility is the average one-minute value for the past 10 minutes.

One misunderstanding is that automated machines extrapolate a prevailing visibility based on sensor data. This is not true. Automated visibility is not prevailing visibility and may be considerably different. The existence of fog banks and visibility in

Fig. 1-4. A scatter meter device indirectly measures how far one can see.

different sectors will not, normally, be reported. Automated visibility may not be representative of surrounding conditions. Regulations specifically consider these variables for IFR, where a suitable alternate may be required. VFR pilots must use the same caution, and though not specifically required by regulations, plan for an acceptable VFR alternate during reduced visibility or when conditions are forecast to change.

During rapidly decreasing conditions, it takes between three and nine minutes for the algorithm to generate a SPECI. During rapidly increasing conditions, the algorithm takes between six and 10 minutes to catch up with actual conditions. This feature adds a margin of safety and buffers rapid fluctuations in visibility.

Siting the visibility sensor is critical. If the sensor is located in areas favorable for the development of fog, blowing dust, or near water, it may report conditions not representative of the entire airport. Airports covering a large area or near lakes or rivers may require multiple sensors to provide a representative observation. To this end, some airports will be equipped with more than one visibility sensor. Site-specific visibility, which is lower than the visibility shown in the body of the report, will appear in remarks (VIS 2 RY11; visibility two, at runway one one).

Automated visibility values are reported from less than one-quarter (M1/4SM) to a maximum of 10 statute miles. Proponents of automated systems point out that they are more consistent, objective, standardized, continuous, and representative. This is certainly true for IFR operations, since the sensors are normally located at the approach end of the instrument runway, and are, typically, more reliable in less than VFR conditions.

Pilots and controllers have criticized automated observations because of the perceived frequency that visibilities are too high. Some pilots routinely cut the visibility in half when light precipitation is falling in the area. In the presence of rain, snow, drizzle, and fog considerable errors have been reported. Automated systems tend to be overly sensitive to ground fog. Under these conditions the human eye is affected by bright backscattered light, which sharply reduces visibility. This is comparable to the headlights of a car shining into fog or snow. The brightly reflected light may blind the observer and limit perceived visibility. Yet the lights of an approaching vehicle seem to penetrate the fog; an observer can see the approaching light source further into the fog. This is caused by light reflected back toward the observer—forward scattered. Research shows that visibility differences under these conditions between forward and back scattered light are on the order of two to one. However, there are no guarantees. For example, in low visibility conditions at Fresno and Bakersfield, in California's San Joaquin Valley, tower visibility has been reported greater than that reported by ASOS.

If conditions are bright enough to use sunglasses, expect the automated systems to report visibility about twice what the human eye perceives. At night, human observers report visibility using forward-scattered light, the same principle used by automated sensors. Therefore,

[handwritten margin note: optimism FOG/RAIN CAUSES ^errors on VIS auto reports.]

[handwritten margin note: NIGHT OBSERVATIONS MEASURE Forward Lite by manual as well as auto methods & are thus more likely in agreement than Daytime observations]

manual and automated visibilities tend to be more consistent.

Manual and automated visibility may be considerably different, especially during the day. The existence of fog banks and visibility in different sectors may not be reported. Reported visibility, manual or automated, may not be representative of surrounding conditions. Reports from surrounding locations, PIREPs, and satellite images can help fill in the gaps. The bottom line: With manual or automated reports close to VFR or IFR minimums pilots must exercise additional caution, carry extra reserves of fuel, and have a solid alternate.

Both manual and automated observations face physical limitations, such as site location, rapidly changing conditions, and contrast.

Rapidly increasing or decreasing visibility during the time of observation, with average visibility less than three miles, is reported as variable in remarks (...VIS 1 1/2V2, visibility variable between one and one-half and two). Variable visibility implies conditions rapidly changing at the airport.

METAR KLOL 021555Z ...35SM SKC...RMK VIS S 1/4

Could this observation be valid? Yes, indeed. A fog bank was south of the airport. A little while later, as the fog continued to move over the airport ...3/4SM BR SKC.../VIS NE 35 was reported.

Conditions can be quite variable and change rapidly in areas affected by stratus and fog. The following METAR/SPECI reports for Crescent City, California illustrate this point.

METAR KCEC 061755Z ...3SM...RMK VIS E35 S-N 3/4

SPECI KCEC 061805Z ...3SM...RMK VIS N-E 35 S-NW 3/4

SPECI KCEC 061810Z ...25SM...RMK VIS S-NW 1

Considering visibility alone, conditions remained technically VFR. However, a VFR pilot should consider approaching or departing the airport from the east, where remarks indicate good visibility. Regulations require VFR fuel reserves; they don't require VFR alternates, but good judgment does.

At certain tower-controlled airports, weather observers report, augment, or backup observations. These facilities are, typically, not colocated with the tower. Tower controllers report tower-level visibility when less than four miles. Because visibility can differ substantially over short distances, a complicated formula determines whether tower (TWR) or surface (SFC) visibility prevails. The remarks portion of the report contains the other value (...1SM...RMK TWR VIS 0; ...1 1/2SM...RMK SFC VIS 2). These remarks alert pilots to variable visibility over the airport. It is not unheard-of for the tower to report visibility less than three or even one mile, thus preventing VFR or special VFR operations.

Runway Visual Range (RVR) measures the horizontal distance a pilot can see high-intensity runway lights while looking down the runway—not slant range. A transmissometer transmitter projects a beam of light toward the receiver. A photoelectric cell measures the amount of light reaching the receiver. This value is electronically converted into visibility and displayed at appropriate locations (tower, FSS, weather office, or a combination of locations).

RVR is reported when prevailing VIS is <1 mile or RVR < 6000'.

RVR applies to instrument approach minimums found on IFR approach, landing, and departure procedure charts. Where available, RVR values appear in METAR/SPECI reports whenever prevailing visibility is one mile or less, or RVR is 6,000 ft or less.

RVR FORMAT

Runway Visual Range appears after visibility using the following format. The letter "R" followed by the runway number, a solidus "/," and the RVR in ft. For example: (...R29/2400FT.) (runway 29 visual range 2,400 ft). The following will be added as required:

- V variability (R32R/1600V2400FT, runway 32 right visual range variable between 1,600 and 2,400 ft)

M = less than

- M less than (R22L/M1600FT, runway 22 left visual range less than 1,600 ft)

P = MORE THAN

- P more than (R36/P6000FT, runway 36 visual range more than 6,000 ft)

If the RVR varies by one or more reportable values, the lowest and highest values are reported, separated by the letter "V." When the RVR is below the minimum value reported by the system, the letter "M" will prefix the value; when above the maximum reported by the

RVRNO means missing

system the letter "P" will prefix the value. Automated stations may report up to four RVR values. When RVR should be reported, but is missing, "RVRNO" appears in remarks.

A report indicating landing minimums does not necessarily mean that reported visibility exists at the decision height (DH) or minimum descent altitude (MDA). RVR reflects the fact that visibility can vary substantially from the normal point of observation; that is the observation point, compared to the runway touchdown zone.

Atmospheric Phenomena

Atmospheric phenomena—precipitation and obstructions to vision—follow the visibility group in METAR, using standard ICAO weather contractions contained in Tables 1-2 through 1-4. This can be the most significant portion of the report.

In METAR, precipitation and obstructions to vision may contain some or all of the following elements:

- Intensity

- Proximity

- Descriptor

- Precipitation

- Obstructions to vision

Intensity describes the rate of precipitation, including that associated with thunderstorms or showers. Intensity is entered for all types of precipitation, except ice crystals and hail. Intensity levels may also be shown with obstructions such as blowing dust, sand, or snow. As shown in Table 1-2 there are three levels of intensity:

(–) light, (no symbol) moderate, and (1) heavy.

Intensity is based on rate of fall in/hr (inches per hour), observed accumulation on the surface, and visibility. These values are summarized in Table 1-1.

Table 1-1. **Intensity of Precipitation**

PRECIPITATION	LIGHT	MODERATE	HEAVY
Rain, Freezing Rain, or Ice Pellets	.10 in/hr	.11-.30 in/hr	>.30 in/hr
Rain or Freezing rain	Scattered, Individual Drops, Easily Seen	Drops Not Identifiable; Spray Over Hard Surface	Falls in Sheets; Heavy Spray Over Hard Surface
Ice Pellets	Scattered Pellets	Slow Accumulation; VIS <7SM	Rapid Accumulation; VIS <3SM
Snow or Drizzle	VIS >1/2SM	VIS >1/4SM <1/2SM	VIS ≤1/4SM

Proximity modifies the location of a weather event in relation to the airport. Proximity applies only to weather phenomena occurring near the airport. Vicinity is defined as precipitation not occurring at the point of observation, but within 10 statute miles; or an obstruction to vision between five and 10 statute miles. When showery precipitation occurs near the station, the intensity and type are not entered.

Descriptor adds additional detail to certain types of precipitation and obstructions to vision. Although thunderstorm (TS) and showers (SH) are often used with precipitation, and may be preceded with an intensity symbol, the intensity applies to the precipitation and not the descriptor.

Intensity, proximity, and descriptor are contained in Table 1-2.

Thunderstorms have a tremendous impact on aviation operations. Thunderstorms contain every aviation hazard, form in lines or clusters, and can even regenerate.

A thunderstorm is reported when thunder is heard or when overhead lightning or hail are observed. Note that a thunderstorm may be reported without precipitation, unless precipitation is occurring at the point of observation. Thunderstorms and associated weather observed away from the station appear in remarks (RMK CB NE, cumulonimbus northeast). A report of CBs implies thunderstorm, sometimes translated by FSS briefers as "thunderstorms clouds...."

> **CASE STUDY**
> At the Ontario, California airport, the FSS was responsible for weather observations. However, because of the FSS's poor observation point, the tower reported visibility. One night while working the mid shift I thought I heard thunder. I asked the tower if they heard thunder or saw lightning. "Oh yeah," the controller said, "I've been watching it for the last couple of hours." Well, so much for the system. The FAA has taken steps, however, to ensure tower controllers immediately report this type of activity.

Convective activity reported at or near the station is a clue to possible low-level wind shear (LLWS), or microbursts. Convective LLWS and microbursts—which produce the most severe wind shear threat—are discussed in chapter 8.

When surface winds gust to 50 knots or more, or hail 3/4 in or greater accompany a thunderstorm, the storm is classified as severe. The three-quarter-inch hail criterion was established in 1954, and the wind criterion was lowered to 50 knots in 1970 for aviation purposes. Since 1996, there has not been a weather code to alert pilots to a severe thunderstorm, but the clues appear in the wind and weather phenomena groups and remarks. There is a proposal to increase severe thunderstorm criteria to winds of 52 knots (60 mph) and hail

Table 1-2 Intensity, Proximity, and Descriptor

INTENSITY		SH	Showers
–	Light	FZ	Freezing
(no symbol)	Moderate	DR	Low Drifting
+	Heavy	BL	Blowing
PROXIMITY		BC	Patches-*banc*
VC	Vicinity	MI	Shallow-*mince*
DESCRIPTOR		PR	Partial
TS	Thunderstorm		

to one inch for public use. This would substantially change the number of warnings issued; with the goal to reduce overwarning. If implemented, it would be after the year 2000.

It's important to remember that intensity refers to the precipitation not the descriptor. For example, "+TSRAGR" is a thunderstorm with heavy rain and hail. Since only one descriptor may be used TS and SH will never appear in the same group. However, FSS controllers may translate TSRA as "thunderstorm, moderate rain showers," since thunderstorms imply showery precipitation.

The weather phenomena -TSRA, sometimes translated as a light thundershower, or worse, a light thunderstorm and rain showers, is neither. The correct translation: thunderstorm accompanied by light rain or light rain showers. There is no such thing as a light thunderstorm!

Falling from stratiform clouds—stratus, altostratus, nimbostratus, or stratocumulus—precipitation is usually steady, can be widespread, and usually not heavy in intensity. Whereas, showery precipitation (SH) falls from unstable air. Showers fall from cumuliform clouds—cumulus or cumulonimbus—usually brief and sporadic, and may be heavy in intensity.

Freezing precipitation (FZ) in the form of rain (FZRA) or drizzle (FZDZ) is caused by liquid precipitation falling from warmer air into air that is at or below freezing. Droplets freeze upon impact producing structural icing. Freezing precipitation is one of the most dangerous of all icing conditions. It can build hazardous amounts of ice in a few minutes and is extremely difficult to remove. Freezing precipitation can flow back along the aircraft, beyond ice-protected areas, and covering static parts.

Aircraft without a heated pitot and alternate static source, especially in IFR conditions, would be in serious trouble. Another significant factor, especially for aircraft without ice protection equipment, is that accumulated ice could be carried all the way to the ground—making landing extremely hazardous. It cannot be over-emphasized that this hazard can affect VFR as well as IFR operations. Should this phenomena be encountered in aircraft without ice protection equipment virtually the only option, and certainly the safest, is to fly into warmer air and land. Pilots who fly into ice, with aircraft not certified for flight in icing conditions, must have the right stuff. Because, in every sense of the word, they become test pilots.

Low drifting (DR) describes snow, sand, or dust raised to a height of less than six ft above the surface. In addition to snow, sand, or dust, blowing (BL) may be applied to spray. The descriptor blowing describes a condition where the phenomena are raised to a height of six ft or more above the surface. Additionally, when applied to sand, dust, or spray, blowing implies that horizontal visibility is reduced to less than seven statute miles; applied to snow, blowing identifies snow lifted by the wind to more than six ft in such quantities that visibility is restricted at and above that level.

The descriptor patches (BC), shallow (MI), and partial (PR) are only coded with fog. Patchy fog (BCFG) and shallow fog (MIFG) indicate radiation fog extending to six ft or more above the ground; visibility in the fog area is less than 5/8SM and over other parts of the airfield greater than or equal to 5/8SM. Patchy fog randomly covers part of the airport; where as, shallow fog is more extensive and organized, but not covering the entire airfield. In both cases, visibility is not restricted by fog above the layer. Partial fog (PRFG) must meet the same height and visibility criteria as patches and shallow. However, partial fog must cover a substantial part of the station. The bottom line: All three terms describe what used to be called "ground fog;" radiation fog that reduces horizontal visibility at the surface, with little vertical extent. With the coverage of fog around the airport going from random (BC), to limited (MI), to substantial (PR).

Precipitation

Precipitation is any form of water particles, liquid or solid, that fall from the sky and reach the ground. Precipitation does not include clouds, fog, dew, frost, or virga-rain that evaporates before reaching the ground. Table 1-3 contains precipitation that may appear in the body of METAR.

Table 1-3   Precipitation

RA	Rain	GS	Small Hail/Snow Pellets-*grésil*	SG	Snow Grains
DZ	Drizzle	SN	Snow	IC	Ice Crystals
GR	Hail (≥ 1/4")-*gréle*	PL	Ice Pellets	UP	Precipitation (AUTO Obs)

Rain (RA) is liquid precipitation. The only other form of liquid precipitation is drizzle, which is distinguished from rain by droplet size.

Forward visibility is reduced when flying through precipitation, but sideward and downward visibility tend to remain relatively unaffected. The more intense the precipitation, the greater the reduction in visibility. It is possible to have VFR surface visibilities reported with flight visibility less than VFR. Figure 1-5 illustrates how precipitation, especially when heavy, can dramatically reduce visibility and obscure terrain. The heavy rain is occurring between two mountain ranges. The mountains are clearly visible in the foreground, but almost completely obscured in the background. Visibility outside the rain area is excellent. These rain showers should be avoided. Flying through steady precipitation is generally smooth, showers tend to be turbulent. Avoiding showers will not only result in improved forward visibility, but a smoother flight.

Drizzle (DZ) is liquid precipitation consisting of very small, but numerous and uniformly dispersed drops. The drops may appear to be suspended in the air. Drizzle indicates a relatively shallow cloud layer. It usually takes a cloud thickness of 4,000 ft to produce precipitation. As inferred from Table 1-1, drizzle restricts visibility to a greater degree than rain because drizzle drops are smaller and fall in stable air, often accompanied by fog, haze, and smoke.

Hail (GR) is precipitation in the form of balls or irregular lumps of ice, always produced by convective clouds, nearly always cumulonimbus. An individual ball is called a hailstone. The largest hailstones and greatest frequency occur in a mature thunderstorm cell, usually at altitudes between 10,000 and 30,000 ft. Hail usually falls in streaks or swaths beneath the thunderstorm, covering an area

Fig. 1-5. Precipitation, especially when heavy, can dramatically reduce visibility and obscure terrain; the mountains are clearly visible in the foreground, but almost completely obscured in the background.

about one-half mile long and five miles wide. However, encounters can occur in clear air outside the storm cell. Hail typically occurs in the rain area within the cloud, under the anvil or other overhanging cloud, and up to four miles from the cloud. Hail can also include other forms of frozen precipitation with differing origins, such as snow. Thunderstorms that are characterized by strong updrafts, large liquid water content, large cloud-drop size, and great vertical height are favorable to hail formation. The violent updrafts keep hailstones suspended for several up and down cycles. Each cycle adds a layer to the hailstone until it can no longer be suspended in the cloud.

Hail can cause severe damage to objects on the ground as well as aircraft in flight. Blunted leading edges, cracked windscreens, and frayed nerves are common results of a hail encounter. There have been a number of multiple turbine engine power loss and instability occurrences, forced landings, and accidents attributed to operating airplanes in extreme rain or hail. Investigations have revealed that rain or hail concentrations can be amplified significantly through the turbine engine core at high flight speeds and low engine power conditions. Rain or hail may degrade compressor stability, combustion flameout margin, and fuel control run-down margin. Ingestion of extreme quantities of rain or hail through the engine core may ultimately produce engine problems, including surging, power loss, and flameout. Pilots must be familiar with this phenomena and comply with the manufacturer's recommendations. Like most thunderstorm hazards, avoidance may be the only safe alternative.

Hail is reported in the body of METAR when hailstones are one-quarter inch or greater. Hailstone size appears in remarks (...GR...RMK GR 1/2...; hailstones 1/2 inch in diameter).

Hailstones less than one-quarter inch are reported in the body of the report as small hail (GS), with no remarks indicating size. GS is also used to report snow pellets. Snow pellets are small, white, opaque grains of ice, formed when ice crystals fall through supercooled droplets and the surface temperature is at or slightly below freezing. Snow pellets are also known as soft hail or graupel.

Snow (SN) is composed of white or translucent ice crystals, chiefly in complex branched hexagonal form and often integrated into snowflakes.

Snow can fall about 1,000 ft below the freezing level before melting. Snow can often begin with temperatures of 2°C; it's even possible to see snowflakes at temperatures around 10°C. This only occurs when the air is very dry. As snow falls into above-freezing air, it begins to melt. The water evaporates and cools the air. Evaporation cools the snow, which retards melting. Water vapor is added to the air, which increases dew point. Finally, the air cools and becomes saturated at 0°C. This is one reason why the snow level is typically below the freezing level.

Dry snow does not lead to the formation of aircraft structural ice, since the particles are dry and do not adhere to aircraft surfaces, except for heated engine inlets. However, wet snow—snow that contains a great deal of liquid water—produces structural icing. "WET SN" may appear in remarks.

Accumulations of snow on airport surfaces present an altogether different hazard. Blowing snow (BLSN) reduces visibility creating a different type of hazard, especially to the VFR pilot. Blowing snow occurs when strong winds blow over freshly fallen snow. Visibility can be reduced to near zero, but is typically restricted to within a few hundred ft of the surface. Visibility improves rapidly when the wind subsides. Drifting snow (DRSN) is raised by the wind, remains close to the surface, and does not significantly reduce visibility. Snow drifts, which can be inferred by reports of drifting snow, present an airport surface condition hazard; which typically is advertised in a Notice to Airmen (NOTAM).

Ice pellets (PL), formerly sleet, are grains of ice consisting of frozen raindrops, or largely melted and refrozen snowflakes. They fall as continuous or intermittent precipitation. Ice pellet showers are pellets of snow encased in a thin layer of ice formed from the freezing of droplets intercepted by the pellets, or water resulting from the partial melting of the pellets. Ice pellets do not bring about the formation of structural ice, except when mixed with supercooled water. Frequently, ice pellets or ice pellet showers indicate areas of freezing rain above. (On November 5, 1998, the previous international abbreviation for ice pellets was changed to "PL." It seems this was required because in certain combinations with other weather contractions it resulted in offensive language. It's nice to know our METAR and TAF reports are politically correct.)

Freezing rain (FZRA), freezing drizzle (FZDZ), and ice pellets (PL) alert pilots to significant icing conditions, and the fact that there is warmer air somewhere above the station.

Snow grains (SG), the solid equivalent of drizzle, are small, white, opaque grains of ice. Since snow grains are already frozen, they typically do not present an icing hazard.

Ice crystals (IC) might appear suspended, and fall from a cloud or clear air. They frequently occur in polar regions in stable air and only at very low temperatures. Ice crystals are not assigned an intensity. I was on watch at the Lovelock, Nevada FSS on a very cold, clear day. Ice crystals were sublimating right out of the clear air. It was a beautiful sight, but of no significance to aviation or anything else. Ice crystals do not generally result in the formation of structural icing. Ice crystals can accumulate in inlets and ducts and dislodge as a mass that can create choking and possible engine damage. A mixed condition where both ice crystals and supercooled droplets exist probably constitutes the worst condition for engine and intake icing.

Automated stations report RA (liquid precipitation that does not freeze) or SN (frozen precipitation other than hail), and intensity. Automated sites may use "UP" (unknown precipitation) to report precipitation when the precipitation discriminator cannot identify the precipitation. For example, this SPECI from Rock Hill, South Carolina.

SPECI KUZA 191942Z AUTO 36007KT 3SM UP BR BKN004 OVC009 02/01 A2976 RMK AO2 RAE11UPB35SNB11E35 P0010 TSNO

We'll use this report again, later in the chapter.

Automated sites are being equipped with freezing precipitation sensors. Additionally, the Automated Lightning Detection and Reporting System (ALDARS), which acquires lightning information from the National Lightning Detection Network, will allow AWOS/ASOS to report the occurrence of a thunderstorm. ALDARS is now operational at numerous AWOS sites and is expected to become operational with all of the FAA's commissioned ASOSs in 1999. Other forms of precipitation only appear at an augmented site.

A criticism of automated observations is the lack of specific precipitation and weather sensors; that the lack of such information might not alert the pilot to potentially hazardous conditions. Recall the "complete picture"? Automated reports can and should be supplemented with radar products. The system is now virtually complete and covers most of the country. Radar can determine the existence of rain, thunderstorms, tornadoes, snow, and hail. Radar, along with satellite imagery, is better at determining the extent of phenomena than either a manual or automated observation.

To alleviate some of the concerns with automated observations a government and industry team developed service standards for surface observations. Service standards consist of four levels, D through A.

Service Level D is a completely automated site in which the ASOS observation constitutes the entire observation; there is no augmentation or backup. This service is referred to as stand-alone D site. The FAA has determined that ASOS performance appears overwhelmingly satisfactory at locations where there has never been a human observer. Conversely, where a level D site is planned, but currently has a human observer, numerous problems and concerns have been reported—many from the observers who would lose their jobs.

Service Level C provides augmentation and backup. Service is provided under the provisions of the Limited Aviation Weather Reporting Station (LAWRS) program. Augmentation and backup is provided by tower, FSS, NWS, or Nonfederal Observation Program observers. During the hours that the observing facility is closed, the site reverts to Service Level D. In addition to ASOS data, the following elements are reported:

- Thunderstorms

- Tornadoes

- Hail

- Virga

- Volcanic ash

- Tower visibility

- Operationally significant remarks

Service level B is provided at airports that serve as small hubs, or special or remote airports that qualify for additional weather services. In addition to ASOS and level C data, the following elements are reported:

- RVR

- Freezing precipitation

- Ice pellets

- Snow depth and snow increasing rapidly

- Thunderstorm and lightning location

- Significant weather not occurring at the station

Service Level A is provided at major hubs or high-volume airports. In addition to ASOS, level C, and level B data, the following elements are reported:

- Sector visibility

- Variable sky conditions

- Cloud layers above 12,000 ft

- Cloud types

- Widespread dust, sand, and other obscurations

- Volcanic eruptions

Obstructions to Vision

Obstructions to vision, typically caused by fog, haze, dust, and smoke, are reported with visibilities less than seven miles. (Automated sites may report obstructions to vision with visibility greater than six miles.) When these phenomena exist with visibilities seven miles or greater, a remark might describe the condition (...RMK HZ ALQDS; haze all quadrants). FSS briefers sometimes use the term unrestricted to describe visibilities of seven miles or greater. This sometimes causes confusion. A pilot told visibility unrestricted might respond, "What about the haze?" Thus, the phrase visibility unrestricted does not imply that smoke, haze, dust, or even fog are not present, just that visibility is seven miles or greater.

METAR also includes five additional weather phenomena. These phenomena, along with obstructions to vision, are listed in Table 1-4.

(You've probably noticed that a number of atmospheric phenomena contractions don't make sense in English. That's because they were derived from French words—shown in italics in the previous tables. Probably the same thought process that gave us UTC!)

Fog (FG) is only reported when the visibility is less than five-

Table 1-4 Obstructions to Vision

FG	Fog (VIS <5/8SM)	SA	Sand	PY	Spray
BR	Mist (VIS (5 ≥8SM)-*brume*	DS	Duststorm	SQ	Squall
HZ	Haze	SS	Sandstorm	FC	Funnel Cloud
FU	Smoke-*fumée*	VA	Volcanic Ash	+FC	Tornado
DU	Dust	PO	Dust/Sand Whirls	+FC	Waterspout

eighths of a mile. With visibility five-eighths or greater, mist (BR) designates this phenomena. [In METAR mist (BR) refers to an obstruction to vision, not precipitation—its generic definition.]

Fog, fog modified with the descriptors patches, shallow, partial, or freezing, and mist describe the same phenomena—a cloud based on the ground. The descriptor freezing may be used with fog when the temperature is below 0°C and minute water droplets are present, whether it deposits rime or not. Freezing fog (FZFG) like most restriction to visibility is only reported when restricting visibility to less than seven statute miles.

Radiation fog tends to be patchy, shallow, or partial with lowest visibility around sunrise, usually burning off by mid morning. It tends to form in valleys after moisture has been added at the surface from passing storms. As high pressure—clear, stable conditions—builds into an area, circumstances are right for the formation of radiation fog. This condition can become persistent in California's Central Valley, the valleys of eastern Washington and Oregon, the Great Basin, and valleys of the Appalachians during winter and early spring. After frontal passage, a strong inversion locks moisture at lower levels and radiation fog forms. Zero-zero conditions over widespread areas can persist for days or even weeks, until the moisture evaporates, or another storm system moves through the area.

IFR pilots, normally, will have no difficulty operating in conditions caused by radiation fog, as long as they don't mind flying above zero-zero surface conditions. Landing minimums might not prevail until late morning or afternoon, if at all, under persistent conditions. The VFR pilot will be delayed until the condition dissipates. Many pilots routinely move their aircraft to mountain airports above the fog layer during winter months.

Advection fog forms when moist air moves over colder ground or water. The air cooled from below becomes saturated. Advection fog can form under an overcast. This is a persistent condition along the Pacific coast during the summer months. The prevailing onshore flow moves the layer into coastal sections and valleys. It is usually deepest and farthest inland at sunrise and retreats toward the ocean during the day. Winds of five to 15 knots tend to cause low ceilings rather than fog. It is typically not a factor to IFR operations. However, expect delays. Every aircraft certified for IFR and instrument qualified pilot can negotiate these conditions.

VFR pilots planning flights into or out of coastal areas should plan arrivals and departures during afternoon hours. If this is not possible, moving the aircraft to an airport a few miles inland will often allow a morning departure.

Upslope fog is typical to the western and eastern Mississippi Valley and east slopes of the Appalachians. This condition usually occurs during winter and spring. It can be widespread and will persist as long as favorable conditions continue. During upslope fog conditions, the VFR pilot is out of luck. The IFR pilot might not be much better off. They might encounter IFR landing minimums, but the condition often exists over areas the size of several states. A legal and safe IFR alternate might be beyond the aircraft's range.

Expect rain-induced fog associated with stationary, warm, or shallow cold fronts. A potential for clear icing exists in areas of rain-induced fog. Steam fog occurs in cold climates over lakes, such as the Great Lakes, in the autumn.

Haze (HZ) is caused by the suspension of extremely small, dry particles invisible to the eye, but sufficiently numerous to reduce visibility. Haze, combined with smoke (FU), often describes conditions in metropolitan areas. Large anticyclones—high pressure cells—can dominate the southeast United States trapping haze and pollutants, especially in industrial areas. Above the haze layer, visibilities are unrestricted and temperatures cool, resulting in a much more comfortable flight.

Strong inversions over cities or industrial areas can trap haze and smoke, reducing visibility to less than one mile. Landmarks are all but invisible. Dense haze often appears solid, like a cloud layer, in the distance; this occurs with high relative humidity, which can dominate the eastern two-thirds of the country. When the sun strikes the layer, light waves scatter, causing the layer to appear white. This accounts for apparent inconsistencies in surface observations. METAR might report clear or partially obscured skies with visibilities three to five miles in haze and smoke. A pilot looking into the sun often has no forward visibility or natural horizon. Pilots caught in such situations, technically VFR, have become spatially disoriented and lost control of the aircraft.

Haze and smoke are usually restricted to an area below 5,000 ft, although they can extend to well above 10,000 ft—especially in the east. During the devastating September 1987 forest fires in California, smoke tops were reported as high as 19,000 ft, with visibilities aloft zero.

Inversion-induced wind shear turbulence occurs along the boundary between cool, hazy air trapped near the surface and warm air aloft. The turbulence tends to be strongest in valleys during morning hours. Moderate or greater turbulence might be encountered penetrating the layer. After an initial outside air temperature rise during the climb through the haze, the air on top will be clear and cool. It is possible to have several haze or smoke layers trapped in inversions aloft. In the Los Angeles Basin, a haze boundary often develops with a Santa Ana condition. Warm, dry desert air overruns haze trapped in cooler, moist marine air. Moderate or greater wind shear turbulence can be expected penetrating the transition zone. Takeoff and landing can be hazardous with the boundary near the runway, often marked by a distinct transition between clear and hazy air.

Dust (DU) and blowing dust (BLDU), a combination of fine dust or sand particles suspended in the air, can be raised to above 16,000 ft by the wind. Visibilities, surface and aloft, can be at or near zero. Because of its fine particles, dust can remain suspended for days once the wind subsides.

Sand (SA) and blowing sand (BLSA), made up of particles larger than dust, usually remains within a few hundred ft of the surface. Sand can also reduce visibility to near zero. But, when the wind subsides particles fall back to the surface and visibility improves rapidly.

The descriptor drifting (DR) may be used with dust or sand. This indicates that the dust (DRDU) or sand (DRSA) has been raised by the wind to less than six ft above the ground.

Duststorm (DS) and Sandstorm (SS) report basically the same

phenomena. A dust storm is an unusual condition characterized by strong winds and covering extensive areas. In contrast to a dust storm, a sandstorm causes grains of sand to be blown into the air. Like sand, sandstorm particles usually remain within a few hundred ft of the surface. In METAR, dust storm or sandstorm are reported with visibilities equal to or greater than 5/16SM and equal to or less than 5/8SM. When visibility is less than 5/16SM with either phenomena it is reported as heavy or well developed (+DS; +SS).

Dust and dust storms can block air filters and air inlets. Sand and sandstorms, like volcanic ash—discussed next, can cause aircraft damage. This is why sand, reducing visibility to less than three miles, sandstorms, and volcanic ash warrant the issuance of a SIGMET.

Volcanic ash (VA) consists of fine particles of rock powder, blown out from a volcano. The particles remain suspended in the atmosphere for long periods, extend well into the Flight Levels, and may drift thousands of miles. Ash power, up to one-eighth of an inch in diameter, can be very abrasive. Volcanic ash can be extremely destructive to aircraft leading edges, windscreens, and engines. Turbojet aircraft engines are especially susceptible. Volcanic ash is reported in the body of METAR regardless of the restriction to visibility.

CASE STUDY

Royal Dutch airlines flight KLM867, a Boeing 747, encountered an ash cloud from the eruption of Mt. Redoubt in 1989. The aircraft lost all four engines to flameout! ATC vectored the aircraft back to Anchorage. During the descent, the crew was able to restart two of the engines and make a safe emergency landing. KLM867 was one of several aircraft damaged by the eruption. Such encounters occur every year.

Ash on the airport is another significant hazard. It can be blown into the air causing reduced visibilities and aircraft damage. Ash on the runway reduces breaking action and crews are trained to reduce or avoid the use of reverse thrust.

Volcanic ash is also a hazard to general aviation aircraft. Ash affects windscreens and leading edges. It blocks air filters and pitot systems.

The hazards of reduced visibilities and slippery runways cannot be overlooked.

Every year, pilots become lost, even lose control of the aircraft, flying in reduced visibilities. Often conditions can be improved by climbing to a higher altitude. Once above the layer, slant range visibility is usually greater with a distinct horizon preventing disorientation. The seemingly obvious assumption, the closer to the ground the better to see it, usually isn't true.

Dust/Sand Whirls (PO), commonly know as dust devils, form in dry, hot regions. They have diameters of 10 to 50 ft and extend from the surface to several thousand ft. Windspeed within the rotations vary from 25 to more than 75 knots. Dust devils are capable of substantial damage, but the majority are small.

CASE STUDY

We flew into a dust devil doing pattern work at Lancaster's Fox Field in California's Mojave Desert. The encounter was equivalent to light to moderate turbulence, it shook the Cessna 150, and the low pressure in the vortex caused both windows to pop open!

Spray (PY) consists of water droplets blown by the wind from wave crests and carried up a short distance in the air from the surface of a large body of water. Spray may be modified with the descriptor blowing (BLPY). Spray is reported in the body of METAR when it reduces visibility to less than seven miles.

A Squall (SQ) is a sudden increase in wind of at least 16 knots, sustained at 22 knots or more, for at least one minute. Usually associated with thunderstorm activity, squall implies severe low-level wind shear as well as severe turbulence.

Funnel Cloud (FC), Tornado (+FC), and Waterspout (+FC) describe tornadic activity—a small, violently spinning column of air, potentially the most destructive of all weather systems. Funnel cloud reports a tornado that has not touched the ground; tornado indicates the funnel cloud has "touched down;" waterspout represents a tornado over water in contact with the water surface.

Automated stations report FG, FZFG, BR, HZ, and SQ. Other obstructions to vision and weather phenomena will only appear at an augmented site.

Sky Condition

METAR sky condition consists of the amount of sky cover, height in ft, and under certain conditions cloud type. Heights range from the surface upward, to a maximum of 12,000 ft for automated stations. The next generation of laser CHI will report clouds to 25,000 ft. Cloud heights are reported as three digits, in hundreds of feet AGL, following sky condition (SCT030, 3000 scattered). In METAR ceiling is not designated. For aviation purposes, the ceiling is the lowest broken (BKN) or overcast (OVC) layer, or vertical visibility (VV) into a complete obscuration. (Like many specialties, aviation weather has its own language. For communication and understanding to take place, each party must understand and use the same definitions. Take the pilot that called UNICOM and asked, "What's the ceiling?" After a pregnant pause the operator replied, "I think it's oak.") A manual or augmented report will include towering cumulus (TCU) or cumulonimbus (CB) in the sky condition element of the report. For example: ...BKN035TCU..., ceiling 3500 broken tower cumulus; or ...OVC020CB..., ceiling two thousand overcast cumulonimbus.

The amount of sky cover is reported in eighths—sometimes referred to as octas—using the contractions contained in Table 1-5.

Table 1-5 Sky Cover

CLR	Clear below 12,000	Automated reports
SKC	Clear	No clouds
FEW	Few	< than 1/8 to 2/8 coverage
SCT	Scattered	3/8 to 4/8 coverage
BKN	Broken	5/8 to 7/8 coverage
OVC	Overcast	8/8 coverage

In manual observations, sky cover refers to clouds or obscuring phenomena as seen by an observer on the ground from horizon to horizon. Automated observations use a laser ceilometer Cloud Height Indicator (CHI) to determine sky cover, a distinct advantage of these systems. METAR reports sky cover as the summation of layers based on specific criteria. Conditions aloft, as seen by a pilot, can differ substantially. The summation principle with terms like obscuring phenomena and obscuration can be complex and misunderstood.

In Fig. 1-6 the observer sees 2/8 cloud cover at 1000 ft AGL and reports a few clouds at 1000 (FEW010). Another 3/8 cloud cover is observed at 1800 ft AGL. According to the summation principle a total of 5/8 (2/8 + 3/8 = 5/8) sky cover exists; ceiling 1800 broken (BKN018) is reported. The observer sees the remaining sky covered by clouds at 3000 ft AGL, and reports 3000 overcast (OVC030). The observer, unable to determine the extent of higher layers, reports them as continuous. This principle has led many a pilot to mistakenly question the accuracy of observations.

Automated stations determine sky cover and height from a laser

SUMMATION OF SKY COVER

METAR: FEW010 BKN018 OVC030
...RMK MTNS OBSCD W

Fig. 1-6. The summation principle has led many a pilot to mistakenly question the accuracy of observations.

CHI. Similar to a rotating beam ceilometer, cloud elements reflect the laser. Like visibility, a computer algorithm processes the last 30 minutes of CHI data. The computer then generates values of sky cover and cloud height for the observation. To be more responsive of the most recent conditions, the algorithm "double-weighs" the last 10 minutes of data. Up to three layers are reported.

At the transition between scattered and broken human observers often report too much cloud cover. This is known as the "packing effect," a condition where an observer does not detect the opening in the cloud deck toward the horizon. Pilots also tend to overestimate the amount of cloud cover. ASOS is not biased by these limitations.

In rapidly changing conditions, the automated system algorithm tends to lag slightly behind actual conditions. If a sudden overcast layer develops, ASOS will take 2 minutes to report a scattered layer; within 10 minutes the system will report broken conditions.

On rare occasions, ASOS may report a dense moisture layer as clouds before the layer becomes totally visible to the eye. This may occur with an approaching cold front when the sensitive laser detects the large-scale lifting of prefrontal moisture. There have been cases when ASOS reported a layer 20 minutes before an observer.

ASOS will only report conditions that pass directly over the sensor. During light wind conditions, observers have reported up to three-eighths sky cover when ASOS reported CLR. Ironically, manual observations suffer from the same limitations. Sky cover might not be representative of surrounding conditions, especially at night, or during low visibility, when the observer cannot see or evaluate the whole sky. Refer to Fig. 1-6, if the observer were unable to see the scattered layer at 1000 ft, a ceiling of 1800 ft would be reported. If the CHI or other device went through a hole in the 1800-foot layer, the observer might report a ceiling of 3000 overcast. Such errors can, and do, occur because of limitations on equipment and the observer.

Notwithstanding the previous observation, care must be exercised climbing or descending VFR through a broken deck.

FACT!

Sky cover is always an estimate from a manual station. As an FSS briefer for some 25 years, I have on occasion briefed doom and gloom only to find a bright, beautiful day. It would seem that certain tower controllers use the following criteria: They consider the roof of the tower cab as opaque; therefore, one cloud is scattered, two is broken, and three is overcast with breaks!

Although it might be possible to safely negotiate the layer, several factors must be considered. Can appropriate distance from clouds as specified in regulations be maintained? Is the weather improving or deteriorating? We don't want to get caught on top or between layers. Is the area congested with other VFR traffic or aircraft operating IFR? The criteria in the regulations are minimums; they do not necessarily equate to "safe." What alternates are available, if needed? Positive answers are required before an attempt.

For manual observation, sky cover and cloud height may only be an estimated, a more or less educated guess by the observer, based on the observer's training and experience. Like visibility, cloud cover and heights should always be viewed with caution, especially at night or close to minimums.

An estimate for the height of convective clouds can be determined from temperature/dew point. This procedure is based on surface heating of a parcel of air that rises and cools at the dry adiabatic lapse rate. When temperature reaches dew point, saturation occurs and clouds form at the Lifted Condensation Level (LCL). When a cloud layer is produced by surface heating, bases can be approximated by applying the following formula: $T - Td \times 4 \times 100 = $ Cloud Bases (AGL). $T = $ temperature in degrees Celsius, $Td = $ dew point in degrees Celsius, and 4 and 100 are constants. For example, the temperature and dew point on the METAR are 15/05. Temperature minus dew point (15 degrees C – 5 degrees C) equals 10 degrees C; apply the formula $10 \times 4 \times 100 = 4000$, and the approximate cloud bases are 4000 ft AGL.

As another example, use this observation for Denver:

METAR KDEN 182350Z ...SCT090 SCT150 BKN250 33/08...

Applying the formula to the Denver METAR, the cloud base works out to be approximately 10,000 ft AGL ($33 - 08 \times 4 \times 100 = 10,000$). This is consistent with the observer's report of 9000 scattered. An article in a popular aviation magazine claimed this procedure could be used for any cloud layer. That's not true. It's important to remember the procedure only applies to convective clouds produced by surface heating—air lifted adiabaticly.

At certain automated locations, additional sensors are used to obtain reports that are more representative. In such cases, remarks will identify site specific sky conditions that differ and are lower than those reported in the body. For example, ...RMK CIG 020 RY11..., ceiling two thousand at runway one one.

Variable describes a situation where the amount of sky cover or height changes during the period of observation, normally the 15-minute period preceding time of observation. For example, ...SCT015...RMK SCT V BKN..., scattered layer variable to broken. If more than one cloud layer is being reported, the variable layer height appears in remarks (...SCT015 SCT025...RMK SCT015 V BKN). Cloud height variability is shown as follows: ...BKN010...RMK CIG 008V012, ceiling 1000 broken...ceiling variable between 800 and 1200. A variable ceiling below 3000 ft must be reported, above 3000 only if considered operationally significant. Variability alerts pilots, briefers, and forecasters to rapidly changing conditions over the airport.

How about the following report?

METAR KMWS 131758Z 18005KT 1SM BR OVC///...

When a cloud layer develops below the point of observation, such as Mt. Wilson, 6000 ft above the Los Angles Basin, the layer is encoded "OVC///" (an overcast layer with tops below the point of observation).

A partial obscuration indicates that between one-eighth and seven-eighths of the sky is hidden by a surface-based obscuring phenomena. Precipitation—including snow, haze, smoke, and fog—usually causes this condition. Automated systems will, normally, not report this condition.

Refer to Fig. 1-7. In the example half, or four-eighths, of the sky is hidden by fog. The observer sees another one-eighth cloud cover at 3000 ft. In METAR a partial obscuration is indicated as FEW, SCT, or BKN on the surface (FEW000, between one-eighth and two-eighths of the sky obscured). In Fig. 1-7 the observer reports visibility reduced by fog (FG), four-eighths of the sky obscured, with a ceiling of 3000 broken. (The observer uses the summation principle of cloud

FACT

The FAA has conducted "blind" comparisons between manual and automated observations. At many of these locations the ASOS was installed, but not commissioned. Several of the observers complained when they were told they would not be able to use the laser CHI for cloud heights, which they had been previously using to supplement their observations.

PARTIAL OBSCURATION

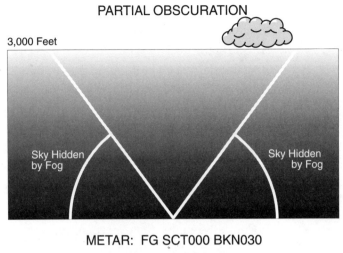

3,000 Feet

Sky Hidden
by Fog

Sky Hidden
by Fog

METAR: FG SCT000 BKN030
...RMK FG SCT000

Fig. 1-7. A partial obscuration indicates that between one-eighth and seven-eighths of the sky is hidden by a surface-based obscuring phenomena.

cover (4/8 + 1/8 = 5/8). Five-eighths is reported as a broken layer. The remark reveals that it is an obscuration (...RMK FG SCT000), not a cloud layer. What else could it be? Well, technically a layer with a base less than 50 ft would be reported as "000." This is very unlikely. If the observer did indeed mean to report a layer with a base less than 50 ft the remark ...FG SCT000... would not appear.

Figure 1-8 is a photograph illustrating the conditions described in Fig. 1-7. A fog layer obscures the sky from the horizon to about an elevation of 45 degrees. Above this point, a cloud layer is visible. At the top of what is referred to as the "celestial dome," the sky is clear.

Why such a complicated procedure? The international METAR code has no provision to report a partial obscuration. The FAA and NWS concurred—probably for the first time—and proposed that a partial obscuration be eliminated from United States reporting procedures. But, there are other players in the game, namely the Department of Defense. Within DOD is the Department of the Navy and the Marine Corps. Well, the Marines just couldn't get along without a partial obscuration. Semper fi! (As of this writing, the FAA and NWS are still attempting to eliminate partial obscurations from reporting criteria.)

Fig. 1-8. The sky from the horizon to about 45° is obscured; above a cloud layer is visible; at the top the sky can be seen.

A partial obscuration may be reported without cloud layers, for example ...3SM HZ FU SCT000...RMK HZ FU SCT000. Remarks indicate that between three- and four-eighths of the sky is hidden by haze and smoke. A partial obscuration in itself must not be confused with a ceiling. Although, with a large amount of sky hidden, cloud coverage amounts might not be representative, and slant range visibility can be less than reported surface visibility.

Normally, a pilot can expect ground contact while flying in areas with a reported partial obscuration. This is why they are not considered ceilings. Penetrating a partial obscuration VFR requires the appropriate horizontal visibility for the class of airspace. A partial obscuration with visibilities less than basic VFR can often be safely negotiated under the provisions of special VFR, discussed in chapter 12.

When the sky is completely hidden by a surface-based obscuring phenomena an indefinite ceiling (VV) is reported. An indefinite ceiling is the vertical visibility upward into a surface-based obscuring phenomena that completely conceals the sky; the distance at which a pilot can expect ground contact when looking straight down on descent, or the point at which the ground disappears on climbout. This condition is most often caused by fog, but snow, smoke, or even heavy rain can cause this condition (...+RA VV000...; heavy rain, indefinite ceiling zero).

The accuracy of an indefinite ceiling depends on the observer and available equipment. Whether the value is determined by a ceilometer or just a guess by the observer, it is reported as indefinite. In Fig. 1-9 the observer has either measured or estimated the vertical visibility as 200 ft. The sky is completely obscured. The observer, unable to determine cloud layers above, reports an indefinite ceiling 200 ...VV002....

CASE STUDY

After being briefed that his destination was reporting visibility two in mist and haze, clear below 12,000, mist and haze obscuring between four- and five-eighths of the sky (2SM BR HZ BKN000...RMK BR HZ BKN000), the Beechcraft Baron pilot emphatically demanded to know the ceiling. The pilot stated this information was required to determine IFR minimums. There was no ceiling. IFR minimums, in this case, would be based on visibility alone. The pilot could expect to maintain ground contact throughout the approach, sighting the airport at about two miles.

For automated observations total obscurations are based on visibility, temperature, and the computer cloud algorithm. Fog or precipitation may cause the CHI to report a false layer. During evaluations, automated systems reported more obscurations than the human observer did. The overreporting of obscurations has the potential of crying wolf.

Indefinite ceilings are most often associated with IFR conditions. Presume that a destination is reporting an indefinite ceiling 200 and that 200 ft is the decision height (DH) for the Instrument Landing System (ILS) approach. Assuming the observation is accurate, at DH the pilot should be able to look straight down and see the Approach

INDEFINITE CEILING

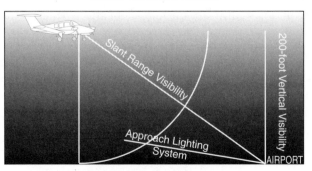

METAR: VV002

Fig. 1-9. An indefinite ceiling is the vertical visibility into a surface-based obscuring phenomena.

Lighting System (ALS). However, the pilot would not necessarily be able to see the runway due to increased slant range distance. This is illustrated in Fig. 1-9. In fact, slant range visibility could be less than vertical visibility! That's why approach lights are considered part of the ILS and minimums increase when they're out of service.

Would the conditions in the previous paragraph preclude a legal landing? Not necessarily, as long as three landing requirements are met. The aircraft must remain in a position from which a normal descent to landing can be made; the flight visibility must not be less than that prescribed for the approach; and, the runway environment (approach lights, threshold, runway, etc.) remains distinctly visible. Any requirement not met or lost after DH requires an immediate missed approach.

How about VFR with an indefinite ceiling of 1000 ft? Although ceiling and surface visibility might technically meet legal minimums, flight visibility might be substantially less. Now consider the possibility that the observer might not have ceiling height-finding equipment; the reported ceiling might only be a guess.

At Redding, California, the NWS observer made the following report:

SPECI KRDD 051650Z ...3SM FU HZ VV030....

The reported vertical visibility is 3000 ft, sky completely hidden by smoke and haze. A pilot flying in this area can only expect to maintain ground contact within about 3000 ft of the surface. This situation could be extremely dangerous for the VFR pilot. Should the pilot climb above 3000, the pilot would be in IFR conditions without ground contact, and most probably without a natural horizon. Pilots attempting to operate in similar conditions have lost aircraft control with fatal results.

Another typical situation occurs with snow. Consider the following: ...3SM -SN VV015.... The visibility is three miles in light snow, indefinite ceiling 1500. Is it VFR? Technically, yes. A pilot could expect ground contact at 1500 ft, but slant range visibility will be considerably less. Additionally, should the pilot climb above 1500 ft

AGL, the pilot may not be in clouds, but will have no visible contact with the ground and no natural horizon! This is a good example of a situation that may be legal, but not safe.

Temperature, Dew Point, and Altimeter Setting

Temperature and dew point are reported using two digits in whole degrees Celsius, separated by a solidus (/). Temperature below zero will be prefixed with the letter "M." For example, ...20/15... temperature 20 degrees C and dew point 15 degrees C, or ...08/M03... temperature 8 degrees C and dew point minus 3 degrees C. Dew point can never be higher than temperature. A reported dew point greater than temperature results from equipment malfunction, or transposition of numbers upon transmission. When the dew point is missing, temperature alone will be reported, ...M05/..., temperature minus 5 degrees C, dew point missing. When temperature is missing, both elements are omitted.

> **CASE STUDY**
> IFR pilots must also exercise caution operating close to minimums. The VOR-A approach to Ukiah, California has a Minimum Descent Altitude (MDA) of 3400 ft (2784 AGL). Ukiah was reporting SCT020 BKN050.... Sure enough, the scattered layer was at the missed approach point. During the miss the aircraft broke into the clear and was able to land. Luck: never count on this happening.

High and low temperatures affect aircraft operation and performance. Temperature also affects our operation and performance. It can get very uncomfortable on cold and windy days and normally temperature decreases with altitude. Wind chill factor is the cooling effect of temperature due to wind. Wind has the affect of lowering the apparent temperature sensed by our body. This is graphically depicted in Fig. 1-10, Wind Chill Factor.

High temperatures at high-altitude airports produce high-density altitude. Atmospheric pressure and humidity are also factors; however,

WIND CHILL FACTOR

Air Temp (°C)	10	20	30	40
20	15	13	12	12
10	1	-3	-5	-4
0	-9	-15	-19	-20
-10	-23	-32	-35	-37
-20	-35	-46	-50	-52
-30	-48	-60	-66	-69

Air Temperature Degrees Celsius (vertical axis) — Wind Speed Knots (horizontal axis)

Fig. 1-10. Wind chill factor is the apparent lowering of temperature sensed by the body.

temperature and elevation are paramount. Surface temperature forecasts are not normally available, but maximum temperatures usually occur during mid- or late afternoon. Arrival and departure times must be planned based on aircraft performance.

I have flown Cessna 150s out of Bryce Canyon, Utah (Elev. 7586), and Grand Canyon, Arizona (Elev. 6606), and a Cessna 210 out of Mammoth Lakes, California (Elev. 7128). There is no additional hazard in such operations as long as we calculate, and do not attempt to exceed, aircraft performance. Multiengine pilots must consider that airport density altitude might be above the inoperative engine ceiling.

After calculating that the aircraft has sufficient performance for conditions, which is required by regulations, it's a good idea to determine an abort point on the runway. If the aircraft is not airborne, out of ground effect, with a positive rate of climb, this point should allow the pilot to come to a safe stop on the remainder of the runway. Remember, aircraft performance data are based on a brand new airframe and engine, and perfect pilot technique.

Low temperatures cannot be ignored. Snow, snow melt, freezing rain, and frost produce structural ice that can be difficult to remove from a parked aircraft. Even a thin layer of frost can severely affect performance, and must be removed before takeoff. Expect morning frost with clear skies, close temperature/dew point spread, light surface winds, and below freezing temperatures forecast.

CASE STUDY

On most light, single-engine aircraft, cabin heat is obtained by routing outside air through a muffler shroud that surrounds the engine exhaust stacks. This raises the temperature of the air by about 20 degrees C. To illustrate, consider a trip from Reno to Lovelock in Nevada. At 7500 ft the outside air temperature (OAT) was −18 degrees C. The air entering the cabin was between 0 degrees and 5 degrees! Bring a wind breaker or jacket and dress appropriately when conditions warrant.

The solution to this problem is to hangar the aircraft, arrange for a deicing service, or plan the departure later in the day when the sun has melted the ice. During taxi, avoid areas of slush. Slush thrown into wheel wells, wheel pants, and control surfaces can freeze, resulting in locked controls and frozen landing gear.

Temperatures at or below freezing imply any precipitation will be of the freezing or frozen variety, with all of their icing implications. With a descent through an icing layer, and surface temperatures close to or below freezing, a pilot must be prepared for an approach and landing with airframe icing, possibly to an ice or snow covered runway.

If snow, ice, or slush are on the runway, aircraft control might be difficult, especially in high winds, and braking action reduced, resulting in a longer than normal ground roll. Without windscreen

CASE STUDY

Some years ago, four of us flew a Cessna 172 into the South Lake Tahoe Airport in November. After our stay, about three-quarters of an inch of ice had formed on the airplane. Being naive at the time about such conditions, I assumed it would blow off during the takeoff roll.

An experienced tower controller, however, suggested we clean the ice. It had to be scraped off with a plastic scraper! Later I calculated we had between 300 and 400 pounds of ice on the airplane. I had no experience with this condition at the time. I shudder to think what would have happened during a takeoff in a low performance airplane, 300 pounds over gross, at a high-altitude airport, with three-quarters of an inch of ice on the airfoils. This is a perfect example of where the test almost came before the lesson.

deice—that's deice, not defrost—a pilot could be faced (pardon the pun) with zero forward visibility during the landing. Regulations require the pilot to consider, "...runway lengths at airports of intended use..." Pilots operating in this environment must consider these factors when selecting destination and alternate airports, or even the advisability of making the flight.

Daytime heating causes rising air currents that produce thermal turbulence. Thermal turbulence usually occurs within 7000 ft of the surface in stable or conditionally unstable air. This means that vertical movement requires an initiating force, in this case surface heating. In stable or extremely dry air, skies remain clear. Should air parcels reach the lifted condensation level, saturation occurs, and stratocumulus or fair weather cumulus form. These clouds are most often scattered, and rarely become overcast. Should the air be conditionally unstable—a parcel of air that becomes unstable on the condition it is lifted to the level of free convection (LFC)—cumuliform clouds form, which can develop into air mass thunderstorms.

Although thermal turbulence rarely becomes severe, it can be extremely uncomfortable and annoying. Because thermal turbulence is caused by surface heating, it can usually be avoided by flying before midmorning or waiting until late afternoon. Otherwise, the only remedy is to climb above the turbulent layer, which might be marked by clouds. A word of caution to the VFR pilot: If you elect to fly above the clouds, be careful not to get caught on top. Should the air mass be conditionally unstable, clouds can build at an alarming rate and close up even faster.

When air is cooled to its dew point, moisture is added to raise the dew point, or both, fog can form. Temperature and dew point within 3 degrees C is an indicator for the possible development of fog. FSS briefers normally provide temperature/dew point under these conditions. Some FAA aviation weather broadcasts use this criteria. The formation of fog, however, requires more than just a close temperature/dew point spread.

The altimeter, in inches of mercury, follows temperature/dew point in a four-digit group prefixed with the letter "A." For example, ...A2992... altimeter two nine nine two. An extremely cold high-pressure area developed over Alaska in 1989 causing the altimeter setting to rise well above 31.00 inches, the upper limit of most aircraft instruments. Because of this situation, the FAA instituted special emergency rules. These are contained in the *Aeronautical Information Manual*.

In countries that report altimeter setting in hectopascals (millibars), the group starts with the letter "Q" rounded down to the nearest whole unit. For example, 1016.6 is reported as ...Q1016....

> **CASE STUDY**
> Flying a new Cessna 150 from Kansas to California, I found myself flying between Winslow, Arizona and Needles, California during the afternoon. Skies were clear, and winds aloft light and variable. I had to climb to 12,500 to get smooth, cool air. Descending into Needles the turbulence was continuous light to moderate below about 11,000 ft, surface winds were calm.
>
> On another occasion, I was flying one afternoon between Oklahoma City and Amarillo, Texas in air that was conditionally unstable. As is my habit, I prefer to fly above the clouds in clear, smooth, cool air. The cumulus appeared to top out at about 9000 ft. So, I thought I'd climb to a cruising altitude of 10,500. Something was strange. I was in what appeared to be level flight, but only indicating 60 knots in the Cessna 150. A scan of the instrument panel revealed the problem. I was not in level flight, but in a climb attitude above a sloping cloud deck! Topping the clouds was impossible. I was forced to descend and bounce the rest of the way to Amarillo at 4500 ft.

Remarks

The absence of operationally significant remarks is another controversial element of automated observations. The existence of weather and cloud types is paramount. The implementation of service level standards, however, has mostly elevated this concern from all but level D sites.

Remarks are divided into automated, manual, and plain language, and additive and automated maintenance date. Automated remarks indicate the type of automated station. Manual remarks amplify information already reported, describe conditions observed but not occurring at the station, or contain information considered operationally significant. Plain language remarks contain other significant data. Additive data is used by the NWS and consist of climatological information, usually in numerical code groups. Automated maintenance data reports sensor outages and maintenance requirements. Remarks use standard aviation weather contractions—contained in Appendix A, and follows the altimeter setting, separated by the contraction "RMK." Remarks can be the most important part of the report. Here again, NWS,

FSS, and military observers, because of their training and experience, tend to do a better job. Although they can get carried away.

The following observation was taken at March AFB, California METAR KRIV...RMK CREPUSCULAR RAYS SW. The Glossary of Meteorology defines crepuscular rays as, "Literally, 'twilight rays'; alternating lighter and darker bands (rays and shadows) that appear to diverge in fanlike array from the sun's position at about twilight." Towering cumulus produce this effect, especially with haze in the lower atmosphere. This would seem a rather complicated way of saying: HAZY TCU SW (hazy with towering cumulus southwest).

This observation came from an NWS observer at Denver METAR KDEN...RMK DSIPTG GUSTNADO N (dissipating gustnado north—a glorified dust devil). Well, gustnado is a local term used to describe a funnel cloud that develops along the gust front of a thunderstorm—not a tornado that would warrant a SPECI. It is believed that the gustnado receives its initial rotation from the shift in wind directions across the gust front. Cold, dense air behind the gust front lifting the warm air ahead imparts a rotating motion in the wind shear zone.

Remarks can be ambiguous, as this report taken by an FSS illustrates: KDEF ...BKN000 OVC040...RMK BR BKN000 TOPS 015. This observation would seem to indicate a 4000-foot ceiling with tops at 1500 ft, which is impossible. Could the observer have meant 400 overcast? Upon checking, 7/8 of the sky was obscured by mist and the observer could see cloud cover at an estimated 4000 ft. The remarks should have read: ...RMK BR BKN000 TOPS OBSCN 015..., tops of the obscuration 1500 ft.

The only way to clarify a report is to check with the observer. For individuals using DUAT, this will be all but impossible. An FSS will usually be able to check through its telecommunications system. But don't even ask unless some very serious—meaning emergency—operational requirement exists.

Automated, Manual, Plain Language

When used in remarks, the distance of phenomena from the station is reported as follows:

- No modifier; within five miles of the station

- Vicinity (VC); between five and 10 miles of the station

- Distant (DSNT); beyond 10 miles, but less than 30 miles from the station

- Distant (DSNT) for cloud types; beyond 10 miles.

Remarks appear in the following order.

Volcanic eruptions when first observed appear in the following sequence:

- Latitude and longitude, or approximate direction and distance from the station

- Date and time of eruption

- Size, description, height, and movement of ash cloud

- Any other pertinent information in plain language

For example: ...MT. ST. HELENS VOLCANO 70 MILES NE ERUPTED 181505 LARGE ASH CLOUD EXTENDING TO APPROX 30,000 FEET MOVING SE....

Remarks of manual and augmented observations contain details on tornadoes, funnel clouds, and waterspouts. Data include the status of the phenomena (beginning, progress, or end), location, and movement. For example: ...RMK TORNADO B13 DSNT NE, tornado began at one three minutes past the hour to the distant northeast.

Automated station type is shown as either "AO1" or "AO2" AO1 means the station does not have a precipitation type discriminator. AO2 indicates the station is equipped with a precipitation discriminator.

Next in order are:

- Peak wind

- Wind shift

- Tower or surface visibility

- Variable visibility

- Sector visibility

- Visibility at a second site

When lightning (LTG) is seen, it will appear in remarks. The frequency of occurrence and type of lightning as shown below, and location will be included.

- OCNL occasional (less than 1 flash/minute)

- FRQ frequent (between 1 and 6 flashes/minute)

- CONS continuous (more than 6 flashes/minute)

- CG cloud-to-ground

- IC in-cloud

- CC cloud-to-cloud

- CA cloud-to-air

For example: ...RMK FRQ LTGCC VC SE..., frequent lightning, cloud to cloud, near the station, southeast.

When precipitation or a thunderstorm begins or ends, remarks indicate the type of precipitation along with times of occurrence. The purpose of these remarks is climatological, but they do alert pilots, briefers, and forecasters to weather, often significant, occurring at the stations.

Recall the SPECI from Rock Hill, South Carolina.

SPECI KUZA 191942Z AUTO 36007KT 3SM UP BR BKN004 OVC009 02/01 A2976 RMK AO2 RAE11UPB35SNB11E35 P0010 TSNO

In this example, rain ended at 11 (RAE11...); unknown precipitation began at 35 (...UPB35...); snow began at 11 and ended at 35 (...SNB11E35).

In addition to beginning and ending time for thunderstorms, location and movement are included in remarks. For example, ...TS VC NE MOV NE..., thunderstorm in the vicinity northeast, moving southeast.

As previously mentioned, hailstone size appears in remarks with GR in the body of the report.

Figure 1-11 show VIRGA, precipitation falling from a cloud that evaporates before reaching the surface. At times, ice crystals or snowflakes fall from cirrus clouds. As they fall into dry air, they sublimate—change directly from a solid to a gas. These dangling white streamers are known as fall streaks, as illustrated in Fig. 1-12. Evaporative cooling turbulence develops near virga: precipitation evaporates and cools the air, causing downdrafts. A pilot penetrating these areas will encounter wind shear turbulence, which can be severe.

Next in order are:

- Variable ceiling height
- Obscurations
- Variable sky condition
- Significant cloud types
- Sky condition at a second site

Convective cloud types are reported, along with direction from the station and movement—if known. We have already touched on towering cumulus and cumulo-

Fig. 1-11. Precipitation that evaporates before reaching the surface is know as VIRGA.

nimbus, which may appear in the body of the report. What's the difference? Towering cumulus resemble a cauliflower, but with tops that have not yet reached the cirrus level. Cumulonimbus have a least part of the upper cloud smooth, fibrous, and almost flattened, often in the form of an anvil or plume, as shown in Fig. 1-11.

CBMAM (Cumulonimbus Mammatus), from the Latin word meaning udder or breast, result from severe updrafts and downdrafts. They are characterized by lobes that protrude from the bottom of the cloud. They indicate probable severe or greater turbulence, and often appear just before or at the beginning of a squall. Avoid these areas.

ACC (Altocumulus Castellanus), a midlevel cloud, indicates moisture and vertical movement. ACC might indicate thunderstorm development. VIRGA may fall from these clouds.

Fig. 1-12. Ice crystals or snowflakes that fall into dry air can sublimate, causing dangling white streamers known as fall streaks.

ACSL (Standing Lenticular Altocumulus), SCSL (Standing Lenticular Stratocumulus), and CCSL (Standing Lenticular Cirrocumulus) indicate mountain wave activity. Lenticular clouds appear smooth and remain stationary to the observer; they might develop as horizontal bands produced by long ridges, or circular and stacked from isolated peaks. Figure 1-13 shows ACSL over Maryland, downwind from the Appalachian mountains. Although these clouds imply turbulence, turbulence will not always be found.

Rotor, bell-shaped clouds that often appear as tubular lines of cumulus or fractocumulus clouds parallel to the ridge line underneath the lenticulars always imply severe or greater turbulence. One such situation occurred at Reno, Nevada where surface winds were reported gusting to 73 knots. The pilot of a corporate jet reportedly abandoned the approach when all the bottles in the cabin's liquor cabinet broke. (A new definition for severe turbulence?)

Pressure falling rapidly (PRESFR) and pressure rising rapidly (PRESRR) signify the approach or passage of a frontal system. Pressure rising rapidly accompanied by a wind shift might be reported as FROPA (frontal passage) or APRNT FROPA (apparent frontal passage).

Designated stations report sea level pressure in remarks. This three-number code follows the contraction "SLP." The code contains the last three digits of the sea level pressure to the nearest tenth of a hectopascal (hPa). Because average pressure is 1013.2 hPa, prefix the code with a 9 or 10, whichever brings it closest to 1000.0. For example, ...RMK SLP102..., sea level pressure 1010.2 hPa. A word of caution. Sea level pressure is not the altimeter setting in hectopascals (millibars).

Like SLP, designated stations report snow depth increases by one inch or more in the past hour. The remark contains the contractions ...SNINCR... in the past hour, a solidus (/), and the total snow depth on the ground at the time of the report. For example, ...RMK SNICCR 2/10..., snow increase two inches during the past hour, total depth on the ground 10 inches.

Other operational significant information is reported at this point. Below are some examples.

Fig. 1-13. Lenticular clouds appear smooth and remain stationary to the observer; they might develop as horizontal bands produced by long ridges, or circular and stacked from isolated peaks.

Figure 1-6 contains an excellent example of an operationally significant remark. The observer has reported: ...RMK MTNS OBSCD W, mountains obscured west. If an overcast ceiling of 1500 ft exists, VFR flight below the clouds could be conducted. However, due to mountain obscurement, VFR flight into or out of the valley might not be possible. Pilots accustomed to flying over flatlands need to exercise extra caution evaluating conditions in mountainous areas. Studying terrain is as important as checking the weather.

A sky condition example for Ukiah, California was presented earlier and a scattered cloud layer existed at the missed approach point. If the observation had carried the remark "...RMK MTNS OBSCD E-W," mountains obscured east through west, a pilot reviewing the approach and terrain could deduce that the scattered layer existed at the missed approach point.

This example also illustrates how observers indicate phenomena coverage. The observer starts at true north and works clockwise. If the remark read ...MTNS OBSCD E S-N, it would be translated as mountains obscured east and south through north. It's important to understand this convention to correctly relate weather in relation to the station.

CASE STUDY

I was over Palmdale on a flight to Van Nuys, California in a Cessna 150 that was not equipped for IFR. Coastal stratus obscured the mountains with Van Nuys reporting OVC030. Because of my experience and familiarity with the area, I knew where there was often a hole. On this occasion, the hole was there and I proceeded. I had plenty of fuel to return to the desert. Another pilot attempting to depart the Los Angeles Basin, under similar conditions, was not so fortunate; pilot wound through the mountains and finally into a blind canyon and the Cessna 182 came to rest on a 45-degree slope. Fortunately, the only casualty was the airplane—it was totaled.

Foehn wall describes the steep leeward boundary of flat, cumuliform clouds formed on the peaks and upper windward sides of mountains during foehn conditions—such as the Santa Ana of

Southern California and Chinook on the eastern side of the Rocky Mountains. This remark should alert the pilot to strong winds, possible turbulence, and wind shear.

BINOVC (breaks in the overcast) or the synonym HIR CLDS VSB (higher clouds visible) means from more than 7/8 to less than 8/8 of the sky is covered. Such a report should never imply VFR flight through a layer is probable or even possible. However, it might be the first indication of a layer beginning to dissipate.

Additive and Automated Maintenance Data

Additive data groups are only reported at designated stations. Groups consist of alpha/numeric codes. Since, this information does not directly relate to aviation operations they will not be discussed.

The maintenance data groups are only reported from automated stations. These consist of sensor status indicators and a maintenance indicator sign ($).

Sensor status indicators advise users that specific equipment is not available. These consist of the following:

• RVRNO Runway visual range information not available

• PWINO Present weather identifier not available

• PNO Precipitation amount not available

• FZRANO Freezing rain information indicator not available

• TSNO Lightning information not available

• VISNO Visibility sensor information not available

• CHINO Cloud height indicator information not available

When visibility or cloud height indicators at secondary sites are not available, their locations will be included. For example: ...RMK VISNO RY06..., visibility information sensor at runway six not available.

In 1997, at the direction of Congress, the FAA conducted an ASOS Operational Assessment. The report concluded that overall ASOS performs as designed. ASOS required edition/augmenting 16 percent of the time for "nonrepresentative data." Cloud height, cloud coverage, and visibility accounted for the majority of edits.

"At no point did the team consider any of the concerns significant enough to curtail the development of future ASOSs, nor did any of the concerns impact safety, efficiency of operation, or airport capacity...." ASOS availability was excellent. Sensor reliability exceeded 99 percent. "The ASOS reporting of changing cloud heights and sky coverage was the area in which most of the inconsistencies (whether perceived or real) were found." "...ASOS lagged behind the observer in reporting lowering ceilings and led the observer in reporting rising ceilings."

I must point out that human observers average visibility, sky condition, and cloud height, typically over a period of 10 to 30 minutes, just like ASOS. The addition of reporting locations and availability of weather is an undeniable advantage of automated systems. For example, a pilot might cancel a flight rather than "taking a look" with IFR or marginal VFR reported. Take the observation at Mammoth with winds gusting to 90 knots. A pilot in flight could divert before encountering severe conditions, rather than possibly arriving without enough fuel for a suitable alternate, despite best efforts to follow regulations.

Weather observations are only as useful as a pilot's understanding. This requires a knowledge of the methods of the observer, and limitations due to equipment, training, experience, and time of day. Today's pilot must not only be able to read and translate reports, but interpret their meaning and significance, then apply them to a flight situation (VFR or IFR), and the capability of the aircraft, terrain, and alternates that might be required.

The need to evaluate all available sources cannot be overemphasized—adjacent weather reports, PIREPs, radar reports, satellite imagery, and forecasts. The "complete picture" and a knowledge of weather can help with evaluation and identify erroneous observations. For example, on December 1, 1995 Fresno, California reported a tornado. The synopsis forecast high pressure, radar showed no precipitation, and the satellite indicated no cloud cover. So what happened? The observer, augmenting the report, was practicing entering supplemental data—which was inadvertently transmitted. Other manual and sensor errors can be detected in this way. Whether a manual or automated observation, pilots must remember that reported conditions may not be representative of the surrounding area.

As an old aviation axiom laments: "Aviation weather reports may not be accurate, but they're official." The question is not whether manual or automated reports are better or worse. They are different, with both having advantages and limitation that must be understood.

As far as the codes go, I think the following letter to the editor of *Flying* magazine, which appeared in the April 1997 issue, says it all:

"I am an active general aviation pilot and FSS specialist. I have learned that in aviation the only thing that doesn't change is change itself. Anyone that has a problem with change doesn't belong in Air Traffic Control or aviation. I am tired of pilots and controllers whining about the new MRTAR/TAF codes. We have some serious problems to resolve in our industry, but MRTAR/TAF codes are not one of them."

Their response: "Thanks, Terry, do you know the difference between a jet engine and a pilot (or controller)? The engine finally stops whining.—Ed."

CHAPTER 2

Pilot Weather Reports (UA, PIREPs)

Ever complain about forecasts, think they were prepared in a sterile environment, and conclude that pilots have no influence on the preparation of forecasts? If we wish to participate, pilots can and do influence forecasts. According to the National Weather Service, PIREPs are the most important ingredient for the AIRMET Bulletin, SIGMETs, Center Weather Advisories (CWA), and winds and temperatures aloft forecast amendments. In addition to the influence on forecasts, certain phenomena can only be observed by the pilot. Add the fact that over the last decade the manual observational network has dwindled and been replaced with automated systems, and the need for accurate pilot reports cannot be overstated.

Satellites, plus upper air and radar reports, supplement surface observations; satellites only observe cloud tops; upper air observations are infrequent and widely spaced; radar typically only provides precipitation information. An urgent need exists for information on weather conditions at flight altitudes, along routes between weather reporting stations—especially in mountainous areas—and at airports without weather reporting service. In many cases, the pilot is the best and only source of actual weather conditions. These phenomena include:

- Cloud layers

- Cloud tops

- Haze, smoke, dust, and sand tops

- In-flight visibility

- Slant range visibility

- Winds and temperatures aloft

- Turbulence

- Icing

- Low-level wind shear

Recognizing the importance of PIREPs, the FAA has directed air traffic controllers to actively solicit PIREPs, especially during marginal or IFR conditions, and during periods of hazardous weather. Pilots operating IFR are required to "...report...any unforecast weather conditions encountered...." These reports are not only of value to other pilots, but to controllers, briefers, and forecasters alike.

PIREPs can be provided to any air traffic facility (center, tower, FSS). Unfortunately, PIREPs reported to center and tower controllers are not always disseminated beyond the sector or control position. To ensure widest distribution, it's best to report directly to flight service, preferably Flight Watch-Enroute Flight Advisory Service (EFAS). More about Flight Watch is in chapter 11, The weather briefing.

PIREPs are transmitted under the location identifier (LOCID) for the surface report (METAR) nearest the occurrence using the file type UA (SAC UA, Sacramento pilot report). Reports may be appended, however, to major hub locations to ensure greatest prominence and widest distribution.

PIREP Format

Because of lack of direction, among both the FAA and NWS, PIREPs have appeared in confusing, misleading, and nonstandard formats. This has led to considerable misunderstanding and, in fact, has impacted the safety of our ATC system. Correctly formatted PIREPs will eliminate any confusion and increase the usefulness of this valuable product.

PIREPs are entered using the standard format illustrated in Fig. 2-1. There is no need to memorize the form because FAA/NWS specialists encode the report. However, an understanding of the format illustrates information needed, and will assist in decoding and interpreting reports. Standard contractions contained in Appendix A are used.

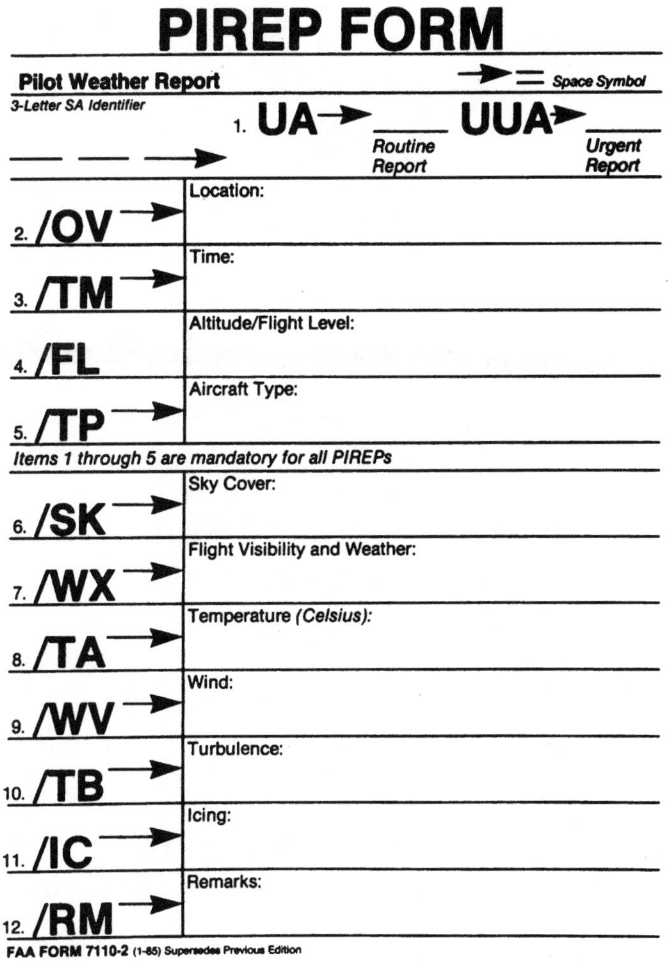

PIREP FORM

Pilot Weather Report   ➤ = *Space Symbol*

3-Letter SA Identifier

1. **UA**➤ ____ **UUA**➤ ____

— — — ➤   *Routine*   *Urgent*
                              Report   *Report*

Location:
2. **/OV** ➤

Time:
3. **/TM** ➤

Altitude/Flight Level:
4. **/FL** ➤

Aircraft Type:
5. **/TP** ➤

Items 1 through 5 are mandatory for all PIREPs

Sky Cover:
6. **/SK** ➤

Flight Visibility and Weather:
7. **/WX** ➤

Temperature *(Celsius)*:
8. **/TA** ➤

Wind:
9. **/WV** ➤

Turbulence:
10. **/TB** ➤

Icing:
11. **/IC** ➤

Remarks:
12. **/RM** ➤

FAA FORM 7110-2 (1-85) Supersedes Previous Edition

Fig. 2-1. PIREPs are encoded using the PIREP form; pilots need not memorize the form, but it does indicate information needed.

REPORT TYPE: UUA OR UA

An urgent pilot report (UUA) represents a hazard, or potential hazard, to flight operations. The message type UUA receives special handling and immediate distribution. Urgent PIREPs report the following:

- Tornadoes, waterspouts, or funnel clouds

- Hail

- Severe or extreme turbulence

- Severe icing

- Low-level wind shear when reported with an airspeed change of 10 knots or more

- Volcanic ash

- Any other phenomena considered hazardous

    Others, designated UA, receive routine distribution.

LOCATION: /OV

The location where the phenomena was observed is reported in relation to a three- or four-letter airport or radio navigational aid (NAVAID) identifier. For example: an airport (/OV HAF, Half Moon Bay airport), a fix (/OV LAX or /OV LAX060010, Los Angeles VOR, or the Los Angeles 060 radial at 10 nautical miles (nm), or between fixes (SEA-BTG, Seattle VOR and the Battleground VOR; SLC245080-JNC210040, Salt Lake City 245 radial at 80 nm and the Grand Junction 210 radial at 40 nm). Normally, if a PIREP contains conditions at an airport or specific geographical location such as a mountain pass, the code for that airport or location appears in remarks.

DEN UUA /OV DEN301021 .../TP MAN/RM OG 1V5 WND 50-80G100+ BLOWING 3/4 GRAVEL

This report contains conditions observed on the Denver 301 radial at 21 nm. The remarks (/RM) indicate the report refers to conditions on the ground (OG) at Boulder Municipal Airport (1V5). It seems the wind is gusting to more than 100 knots and blowing 3/4-in gravel around. This illustrates the importance of such reports.

Decoding reports can be difficult without a copy of FAA Handbook 7350.5 *Location Identifiers*. DUATs has a decode function; current Sectional or World Aeronautical charts contain NAVAID identifiers; and Sectional charts depict airport identifiers along with other airport data. If necessary, a pilot can always call an FSS.

TIME: /TM

Time when the phenomena was reported, referenced to Coordinated Universal Time (UTC).

ALTITUDE/FLIGHT LEVEL: /FL

The altitude, in hundreds of feet MSL, that the phenomena was encountered. DURGC (during climb) and DURGD (during descent) may appear in remarks.

TYPE AIRCRAFT: /TP

Type aircraft using standard international (ICAO) aircraft type designators. From time to time, this element will contain /TP PUP (pickup truck), /TP CAR, /TP FBO (airport Fixed Base Operator), or as reported on the Denver PIREP /TP MAN.

SKY COVER: /SK

Standard sky cover contractions (SKC, FEW, SCT, BKN, OVC) are used followed by cloud bases in hundreds of feet—like METAR, TAF, and aviation forecasts. It's important to remember that PIREP bases and tops are always reported in reference to mean sea level. Cloud tops are indicated by the word "TOP" followed by the height—similar to aviation forecasts. Additional layers are separated by a solidus (/) and clear above indicated by SKC.

For example:

.../SK FEW-SCTUNKN-TOP030/BKN060-TOP100/SKC....

Decoded: A few to scattered ($^1/_8$ to $^4/_8$ coverage) clouds with tops at 3,000 MSL; a broken layer ($^5/_8$ to $^7/_8$ coverage) bases 6,000 MSL, tops 10,000 MSL; clear above.

Recall that PIREP bases and tops are always MSL. Conditions in Fig. 1-6 were reported: ...FEW010 BKN018 OVC030.... If field elevation were 2,000 feet, a PIREP describing these conditions might read: ...FEWUNKN-TOP035/SCTUNKN-TOP043/SCTUNKN-TOP055... (tops of a few clouds 3,500, scattered 4,300 and 5,500 feet respectively). Given the summation principle the observation and pilot report are perfectly consistent.

A pilot report can be one of the most accurate means of determining cloud height, assuming the pilot actually penetrates the clouds, or climbs or descends through a scattered or broken layer. Otherwise, it's just a pilot's estimate. As pilots we should always report cloud bases and tops to the tower or FSS, especially when different from reported. But keep in mind, we reference cloud bases to a pressure altimeter set to read MSL, and the observer reports clouds AGL. (I recently passed cloud bases to a tower controller. The controller asked if they were AGL or MSL. Hum?)

WEATHER: /WX

Weather encountered and flight visibility are reported in this element.

Flight visibility is reported to the nearest whole statute mile, and encoded with the suffix SM (FV01SM, FV05SM, etc.). Unrestricted visibility appears as FV99SM. FV99SM has potential ambiguity. Does it mean visibility 99 miles or greater, or seven miles or greater? Pilots should report specific values to 98 miles to eliminate any misunderstanding.

Weather, when reported, follows visibility using standard ICAO contractions contained in Tables 1-2 through 1-4. Like METAR, should hail be reported, size appears in remarks in $1/4$ in increments (GR1/2; hail $1/2$ in).

CASE STUDY

A pilot approaching Lovelock, Nevada (elevation 3,900) skeptical of a reported visibility of two miles in blowing sand, reported flight visibility 20 miles. Upon landing, however, the pilot concurred, stating the tops of the blowing sand were at 200 feet AGL. This report would appear: ...FL075.../WX FV20SM BLSA000-TOP041....

AIR TEMPERATURE IN CELSIUS: /TA

Air temperature is reported in degrees Celsius, with negative values prefixed with letter M—like METAR.

WIND: /WV

Wind direction and speed is encoded using three digits to indicate direction, and two or three digits to indicate speed (/WV 36020KT, observed wind 360° at 20 knots). In spite of the FAA's Flight Service handbook, which states "...wind direction (magnetic)...," direction should be reported in relation to true north, which is consistent with other reports and forecasts. Speed is in knots (KT).

TURBULENCE: /TB

The intensity (NEG, LGT, MOD, SEV, EXTRM) and altitude (when different from /FL) of turbulence appears in this element. Clear Air Turbulence (CAT) and CHOP should be added when appropriate. (Both terms will be defined shortly.) When turbulence has been forecast, but reports indicate smooth /TB NEG is entered. Therefore, /TB NEG is interpreted as smooth, rather than turbulence that bounces the aircraft down.

ICING: /IC

The intensity (NEG, TRACE, LGT, MOD, SEV), type (CLR, RIME, MX) and altitude, when different from /FL, is entered in this element. Temperature should also be included with icing reports. Like turbulence, when icing is forecast but not encountered, NEG is entered; a NEG encounter is as important and useful as one reporting the phenomena!

REMARKS: /RM

This element reports low-level wind shear (LLWS), convective activity, surface conditions at airports, or other information to expand or clarify the report.

Remarks of some PIREPs have read:

/RM SMOKE OVER NWS BUILDING DRIFTING EAST-SOMEONE THINKING

CASE STUDY
The rather shaky voice that called flight service to report moderate to severe turbulence. The specialist asked the novice pilot, "Did you actually lose control of the aircraft?" The pilot replied, "Well, no." The specialist then asked, "Would it be okay if we called it light to moderate turbulence?" The pilot agreed.

/RM VFR NOT RECOMMENDED-THREE AIRCRAFT COULD NOT MAINTAIN VFR DUE TO ICING IN CLOUDS.

Something odd; oh well, I guess it is difficult to maintain VFR in the clouds when you're icing up.

/RM HAD TO CLIMB TO FL200 TO REMAIN VFR-NOW LEAVING FREQ TO CONTACT ZOA.

Because this pilot is already 2,000 feet into Class A airspace, leaving the frequency to contact ZOA (Oakland Center) seems like a "right good" idea.

Cloud bases and tops, temperatures, and even winds can be measured. Flight visibility and weather are direct observations. Intensities of turbulence and icing, however, are some of the most misunderstood quantities in aviation. That's because they're subjective, usually based on the pilot's training and experience.

Turbulence

The intensity of turbulence is, somewhat, affected by aircraft type and flight configuration. United States Air Force studies have shown the following to generally increase the effects of turbulence.

- Decreased weight
- Decreased air density
- Decreased wing sweep angle
- Increased wing area
- Increased airspeed

Classifications for the intensity of turbulence can be found in the Aeronautical Information Manual (AIM) and *Aviation Weather Services*; however, I prefer the following.

LIGHT

A turbulent condition during which your coffee is sloshed around, but doesn't spill, unless the cup's too full. Unsecured objects remain at rest; passengers in the back seat are rocked to sleep.

MODERATE

A turbulent condition during which even half-filled cups of coffee spill. Unsecured objects move about; passengers in the back seat are awakened by a definite strain against their seat belts.

SEVERE

A turbulent condition during which the coffee cup you left on the instrument panel whizzes by the passengers in the back seat. The aircraft might be momentarily out of control, but you don't let on. People not using their seat belts are peeling themselves off the cabin ceiling.

EXTREME

Usually associated with rotor clouds in a strong mountain wave or a severe thunderstorm, extreme turbulence is a rarely encountered condition where the aircraft might be impossible to control. The turbulence can cause structural damage. Your passengers are becoming concerned by the beads of sweat on your brow, your white knuckles, and new frequency and new transponder code you have just selected—121.5 and 7700.

The following reports illustrate mountain wave activity.

RNO UUA /OV FMG330025/TM 2345/FLI05/TP BE35/TB SEV/RM TMPRY LOST CONTROL...PILOT CUT ARM IN TURBC...RTNG TO RNO.

A SIGMET was in effect for severe turbulence, Reno surface winds were out of the west gusting to 27 knots, and winds across the Sierra Nevada mountains were gusting to near 50 knots. The pilot had the clues, but elected to go. From the PIREP, it would appear the pilot regretted the decision.

Another pilot caught in a mountain wave reported:

RNO UUA /OV FMG270012.../TP C404 /TB EXTREME 130-110 MOD SEV 110-090 /RM EXPERIENCING STRUCTURAL DAMAGE.

The airlines are not immune to mountain waves:

DEN UUA /OV DEN313047/TM 0158/FL350/TP L101/TB SEV/RM SEV MTN WAVE PLUS AND MINUS 6000 FPM.

This Lockheed Tristar (L101) at 35,000 feet over the Rockies experienced severe turbulence and 6,000 feet per minute updrafts and downdrafts. This illustrates the severity of mountain waves and the fact that they can extend to the stratosphere.

Mountain waves develop when strong winds, usually 40 knots or greater at crest level, blow perpendicular to a mountain range. Speed usually increases with altitude in stable air. Mountain waves can cause sustained updrafts and downdrafts occasionally reaching 3,000 feet per minute. Effects of the wave might reach from the ground to 35,000 feet, and extend hundreds of miles downstream. Altimeter errors might exceed 1,000 feet. Mountain wave activity typically can be seen on visible, and sometimes infrared, satellite imagery. With lack of adequate moisture, waves occasionally occur in clear air.

To avoid the worst conditions remain at least 5,000 feet above mountain crests. In the west, most light aircraft simply don't have that performance. This leaves three options: select a course with lower terrain, wait it out, or take a chance on getting your fillings knocked loose and maybe losing the airplane. Passenger comfort and safety should be the priority consideration.

Notwithstanding the previous example, the November 1977 Approach magazine reported: "A Navy T-39 trainer was flying a low-level, high-speed navigational training route in mountainous terrain when it encountered severe turbulence. Gust acceleration loads were so high that aircraft design limits were exceeded, resulting in separation of the tail...." All aboard were killed. The article went on to say, "Mountain waves should never be taken lightly. In addition to the T-39

CASE STUDIES

I encountered a mountain wave in California's Owens Valley while flying a Cessna 150. With cruise power and attitude, the airplane rode the wave, at the rate of 500 feet per minute, from 8,500 feet to 13,500 feet, and back down again. The ride was absolutely smooth!

crash, mountain waves were identified in the crash of a C-118 and in extensive damage to a B-52.... While this type of turbulence is obviously critical to traditional low fliers like helicopters, all aircraft are susceptible."

Turbulence encountered in clear air not associated with cumuliform clouds, usually above 15,000 feet and associated with wind shear should be reported as clear air turbulence (CAT). Slight, rapid, and somewhat rhythmic bumpiness without appreciable changes in altitude or attitude defines CHOP. Since CHOP does not cause appreciable changes in altitude or attitude, it would not be severe.

In addition to intensity, duration of turbulence should be reported.

- Briefly. Turbulence encountered for an extremely short period, usually only one or two jolts (/TB LGT /RM 2 MOD JOLTS could be reported /TB LGT BRFLY MOD).

- Occasional. Less than 1/3 of the time.

- Intermittent. Between 1/3 and 2/3 of the time.

- Continuous. More than 2/3 of the time.

Chapter 1 discusses how to use METAR to determine likely areas for turbulence. Recent and accurate PIREPs can verify or refute its presence. If reports or forecasts indicate turbulence, a pilot can minimize the hazard when encountered. Turbulence imposes gust loads that appear to be almost instantaneous. Gust loads increase with the speed of the aircraft and gust velocity.

If light or moderate turbulence is encountered or expected, avoid flight in the caution range—the yellow arc on the airspeed indicator. If severe turbulence is encountered or expected, reduce to maneuvering speed. Maneuvering speed is not printed on the airspeed indicator, although it's usually placarded near the instrument. Because gust load factor decreases as wing loading increases, maneuvering speed increases with the aircraft's gross weight. Therefore, it's often necessary to determine maneuvering speed based on gross weight.

In moderate or greater turbulence fly attitude rather than altitude. Disengage the autopilot altitude hold, if in use. The aircraft should already be slowed to turbulent air penetration speed. Don't chase airspeed or altitude. It's like riding a horse, go with it rather than fighting it. The object's to avoid imposing additional abrupt maneuvering loads. For the most part, ignore altitude unless terrain clearance becomes a problem; VFR, try to avoid IFR cardinal altitudes (4,000, 5,000, 6,000, etc.), or opposite direction VFR altitudes; IFR, inform air traffic control (ATC) of the problem and any altitude deviations required. ATC increases vertical separation during severe conditions.

Icing

As with turbulence, there is a tendency, especially with new or low-time pilots, to overestimate icing intensity. A recently rated instrument pilot, after experiencing his second encounter with icing in a Cessna 172, reported severe icing. The encounter lasted about 30 minutes, the pilot was unable to maintain altitude and forced to descend. This description, however, is only of moderate intensity. Icing intensity has been classified for reporting purposes in the AIM. Perhaps personal definitions are more descriptive.

TRACE

Ice becomes perceptible and the rate of accumulation is slightly greater than the rate of sublimation. It is not hazardous although ice protection equipment is not utilized, unless encountered for more than one hour; your spouse admires how pretty it looks on the wing; ATC has just instructed you to climb. You advise them icing is probable and request descent. The controller calmly replies that in that case "you can declare an emergency or land." Shortly, you're handed off to the next controller. You inquire about a lower altitude and the controller responds, "Is that Terry up there?" (A friend at Los Angeles Center.) A lower altitude was approved in about 15 minutes.

LIGHT

The rate of accumulation can create a problem if the flight continues for more than one hour. Occasional use of ice protection equipment removes or prevents accumulation. Ice should not present a problem if the protection equipment is used. Your student hasn't noticed the ice yet; your pilot friend in the back seat is hoping he has enough life insurance; you're negotiating with ATC for a lower altitude, which they can approve in 15 miles. This will only take about eight minutes, but each minute seems like 10.

MODERATE

The rate of accumulation, even for short periods, becomes potentially hazardous and the use of ice protection equipment or flight course diversion becomes necessary. On his second encounter with ice, a friend and his passengers, in an aircraft without ice protection equipment, survived moderate icing only because the terrain was lower than the freezing level.

SEVERE

The rate of accumulation is such that ice protection equipment fails to reduce or control the hazard. Immediate diversion is necessary. This is a situation where the person in the left seat very rapidly ceases being the pilot and becomes a passenger; the wing is an ice cube.

The type of icing has also been classified for reporting purposes.

FACT

It seems that the maximum intensity reported for icing was "heavy" until 1968. Certain pilots still insist on using this term. However, it is a misnomer because all ice is heavy! It's time to move on.

RIME ICE

Rime ice is milky, opaque, and granular, normally formed when small, supercooled water droplets instantaneously freeze upon impact with the aircraft. It is most frequently encountered in stratiform clouds at temperatures between 0°C and –20 degrees C.

CLEAR ICE

Clear ice is glossy and formed when large, supercooled water droplets flow over the aircraft's surface after impact, and freeze into a smooth sheet of solid ice. It is most frequently encountered in cumuliform clouds or freezing precipitation. Brief, but severe accumulations occur at temperatures between 0 degrees C and –10 degrees C, with reduced intensities at lower temperatures, and in cumulonimbus clouds down to as low as –25 degrees C.

RIME ICE AND CLEAR ICE (MIXED ICING)

Mixed ice is a hard, rough, irregular, whitish conglomerate formed when supercooled water droplets vary in size or are mixed with snow, ice pellets, or small hail. Deposits become blunt with rough bulges building out against the airflow.

The term ice protection equipment in the icing intensity definitions refers to aircraft and equipment certified for flight in known icing conditions. Although many aircraft have limited ice protection equipment (pitot heat, prop anti-ice, alternate static source, etc.), it should never be construed as allowable for flight in icing; their purpose is for emergency use only, should icing be inadvertently encountered. Even aircraft certified for flight in icing conditions are not designed to handle all cases. These aircraft are designed, tested, and certified for flight in moderate icing caused by cloud size droplets. They are not designed, tested, or certified for flight in severe icing or precipitation size droplets—supercooled large drops (SLD).

Icing potential exists anytime visible moisture exists—clouds or precipitation—at an air temperature of 0 degrees C or less. This contradicts the notion that icing can only occur in clouds. Chapter 1 discusses how freezing rain can be the most serious icing hazard, and the icing potential of wet snow. Both phenomena can affect the VFR pilot. The greatest icing potential occurs between the freezing level and –10 degrees C to –15 degrees C, or within a layer approximately 5,000 and 7,500 feet deep. Icing has been encountered in convective clouds at altitudes of 30,000 to 40,000 feet in temperatures less than –40 degrees C.

If the weather briefing indicates even a remote possibility of encountering ice, the pilot should accomplish several tasks. Ensure the pitot heat works with a very light touch during preflight. Check ice protection equipment for proper operation. Remember that a heated pitot is an anti-icing device, to be turned on before encountering ice; deicing equipment usually requires ice buildup before activation; improper operation can actually increase ice buildup and prevent its removal! Check alternate air or carburetor heat for an alternate source of air if the air filter ices over.

The object with ice is to minimize exposure. With temperatures 0 degrees C or less, avoid flying in clouds or precipitation. Should ice be encountered, immediately notify ATC and initiate a plan of action. The first consideration might be to climb to colder air, or above the layer based upon PIREPs and the weather briefing. Ice will slowly sublimate—change from a solid directly into a gas—when on top. Or, descend to warmer air based upon the actual freezing level on climb-out. This requires a careful check of minimum en route altitudes (MEA). Finally, if you have to, turn around because, presumably, you came from an ice-free area. The point is do something!

A popular notion in some aviation circles is that a pilot's mere mention of ice will receive emergencylike handling. Icing might be an emergency, but remember the controller's job is to separate aircraft within a finite amount of airspace. ATC might have to assign a higher altitude, but ATC cannot, and should not, be expected to fly the aircraft, or assume the responsibility of pilot in command. To paraphrase: An accurate report of actual icing conditions is worth a thousand forecasts.

The pilot had no way out because the MEA was the aircraft service ceiling. The terrain was well above the freezing level and the pilot failed to reverse course at the first sign of ice. What other options were available? The pilot could have crossed the mountains near

CASE STUDY

A nonturbocharged, nondeiced Baron departed Reno, Nevada for Southern California. Moderate icing and severe turbulence were forecast. The pilot elected to fly a direct course along the crest of the Sierra Nevada Mountains. The aircraft iced up resulting in a fatal accident.

> **CASE STUDY**
> A Bonanza pilot departed the San Francisco Bay area on a flight to Los Angeles. Icing above 7,000 feet was forecast and reported. The pilot elected to fly at 11,000 feet. The pilot's last words were, "I've iced up and stalled." The crash occurred in the San Joaquin Valley where the elevation was near sea level. Minimum altitudes near the crash were well below the freezing level. The pilot simply did nothing until aircraft control was lost.

Sacramento, minimizing exposure to ice and once over the Sierras, it was all downhill. The pilot could have flown toward Las Vegas where the weather was considerably better, or simply waited for better weather conditions. When the aircraft became ice covered, the pilot had no option but to ride the airplane to the crash site.

If a descent through an icing layer is required, remember the objective is to minimize exposure. Under such circumstances, negotiate with ATC to obtain a continuous descent. Avoid, if possible, level flight in clouds. ATC is usually very responsive to such requests.

No one has any business flying in these conditions:

FAT UUA /OV CZQ090030.../FL160-240 /TP F18/IC SEV CLR

BFL UUA /OV PMD330040.../FL100 /TP C402/IC SEV RIME/RM PUP 1 INCH CANT SEE THRU WINDSHIELD

PIREPs are the pilot's only source of reported induction system icing: iced over air intake systems and carburetor ice. Both result in loss of engine power, and left unchecked, complete power failure. The solution is to use the alternate air source on fuel injected engines, or carburetor heat on normally aspirated-carbureted engines. Induction system icing takes place anytime structural icing occurs. Symptoms are a gradual loss of power.

In addition to air intake icing, normally aspirated engines can develop ice in the carburetor throat. Known as carburetor icing, ice can form with outside air temperatures as high as 32 degrees C. As air is accelerated through the carburetor, and fuel evaporates, temperatures can be lowered as much as 33 degrees C. Whether ice

CASE STUDY

On a flight from Van Nuys, California to San Francisco in a Cessna 172 we encountered light icing after an ATC request to climb. I periodically applied carburetor heat. Something unusual occurred. With carburetor heat on, the engine ran fine: off, the engine faltered. On the ramp at San Francisco we parked next to a Navion that had also flown from Los Angeles, but at a higher altitude and encountered more ice. Sure enough, in the Navion's air filter was a large chunk of ice. I realized that the carburetor heat in the 172 was functioning as an alternate air source. I'm sure this seems ridiculously obvious; it didn't at the time, which illustrates the hazards of learning by experience.

will develop depends on the velocity of the fuel/air mixture, outside air temperature, humidity, and carburetor system. Conditions most favorable for carburetor ice are outside temperatures between –17 degrees C and 16 degrees C, high relative humidity, and low-power settings.

Carburetor ice is detected in aircraft with fixed pitch propellers by a loss of rpm, in aircraft with constant speed propellers by a loss of manifold pressure. At the first indication of carburetor ice, power loss, or engine roughness, apply full carburetor heat. Be prepared; this will result in additional power loss and engine roughness. Leave it on until the engine smoothes out, which might take several minutes. Avoid using partial heat unless the aircraft is equipped with a carburetor air temperature gauge. At times it might be necessary to leave heat on for an extended period. A flight from Page, Arizona to Las Vegas, Nevada required continuous use of heat due to carburetor icing in a Cessna 150. Don't forget to relean the mixture.

Carbureted engines are more susceptible to icing during reduced-power operation. Some aircraft and engine manufacturers recommend the use of carburetor heat during all power reductions, others only when ice is suspected. Pilots should follow the manufacturer's recommendations. If full power is required, such as a go-around, full carburetor heat and full power might cause early detonation or engine damage. It will certainly prevent the engine from developing full power,

> ## PAY ATTENTION
> I had remained overnight in Amarillo, Texas because of a line of thunderstorms that approached from the west. The Cessna 150 was parked into the wind when torrential rains moved through the area. The next morning was clear, with abundant surface moisture, temperature about 15°C, and nearly 100 percent relative humidity.

which might be critical in low-power aircraft at high-density altitudes. Again, know and follow the manufacturer's recommendations.

My first clue of trouble was the increased throttle setting required to obtain idle rpm. Engine runup also took more throttle than usual. I suspected carburetor ice and a water saturated air filter because of the conditions. I had 13,000 feet of runway.

Full throttle only gave me about 2,200 rpm. The increased ground run to rotation speed—about 7,000 feet—should have been another clue. I was off the ground and with no runway remaining and 200 feet of altitude, and the engine started losing rpm. I applied carburetor heat and the engine was running very rough producing about 1,700 rpm.

There was a tremendous psychological urge to reduce the heat and get that rpm back. I was preparing to crash straight ahead but the engine was still producing power and I decided to make a 180° turn and land on a taxiway. Then I informed a surprised tower controller of what happened; remember, a pilot's first job is to fly the airplane.

After running the engine for 20 minutes, and one aborted takeoff later, I launched into the air. The engine again performed normally above the shallow, moist layer. It was a perfect example of having the clues and ignoring them. I was extremely fortunate.

Figure 2-2 shows a composite carburetor icing probability chart. This chart was derived from FAA and Transport Canada carburetor icing probability charts. Like structural icing, carburetor icing is complex and there are few hard and fast rules. The probability chart graphically depicts carburetor icing potential previously discussed.

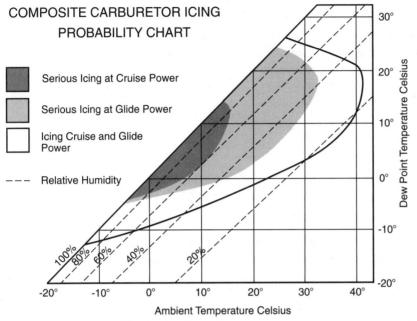

Fig. 2-2. The probability chart graphically depicts carburetor icing potential.

Remarks

Remarks amplify information or describe conditions not already reported:

SAC UUA /OV SAC/TM 1753/FL030/TP C172/TB MOD-SEV/RM LTGCG

The pilot observed lightning cloud to ground. (Pilots should use the same frequency and type descriptions for lightning as described in chapter 1 METAR remarks.)

BFL UA /OV WJF-BFL/TM 1845/FL045/TP UH60/SK OVC050/TB LGT OCNL MOD/RM THRU TSP PASS UNDER CLDS. OK FOR HELIO NOT SO HOT FOR FIXED WING

SNA UA /OV SNA-GMN/TM 2218/FL125/TP PA28/TA 00/WV 33020KT /TB MOD/RM LIKE AN E TICKET AT DISNEYLAND

An "E" ticket was for the big rides.

DEN UA /OV DEN240060/TM 1715/FL350/TP DC8/TB MOD CAT/RM MOD CAT AT 373 NEG BLO 367 (ZDV)

This report was filed by Denver Center's Weather Service Unit (ZDV). It amplifies the turbulence portion indicating that moderate CAT was encountered at 37,300 and it was smooth below 36,700.

Remarks also describe low-level wind shear, which is shear that occurs within 2,000 feet of the surface. Because of its significance, pilot reports of wind shear are extremely important. Wind shear PIREPs should include location, altitude, and airspeed changes.

RNO UA/ OV RNO.../TP DC9/RM LLWS 001-SFC +30 TO 40 KTS

The pilot experienced a 30- to 40-knot increase in airspeed between 100 feet and the surface.

STS UUA/.../FL030/TP C500/TM DURGD RY02 LLWS RESULTING IN 80 KTS CHG AIRSPEED.

Studies have shown that the great majority of nonconvective LLWS reports have in fact been triggered by low-level turbulence. Low-level turbulence was discussed in chapter 1. Many pilots lump any turbulence below 2,000 feet AGL into the category of wind shear— probably because of FAA and media emphasis on this phenomena. Both can be severe. So what's the difference? In a wind shear event a pilot can expect a sudden change in airspeed (plus or minus, but not both)—as illustrated by the preceding examples. Low-level turbulence is characterized by fluctuations in airspeed (plus and minus).

Interesting remarks abound:

/RM STRONGEST TURBC I HAVE EXPERIENCE IN 15 YEARS...; reported by a King Air.

/RM 2 PASSENGERS INJURED...HAD TO TURN BACK...; reported by a Navy P3.

/RM IFR NOT RECOMMENDED DUE TO STRONG HEAD WINDS AND 2000 FT PER MIN UP AND DOWN DRAFTS WILL NEVER DO IT AGAIN...; reported by a Cessna 182.

/RM SOME REAL GOOD JOLTS PUT KNOT ON HEAD..., aircraft type missing.

/RM ONE LARGE JOLT, STEW FELL DOWN (SHE IS OK) LOTS OF DRINKS SPILLED...; reported by a Fairchild 27.

/RM UNA TO CONTROL HELICOPTER. RETURNED. NURSES KISSED THE GROUND.

/RM WIND O/G at FCH (Fresno Chandler Airport) IS 300-330 DEGREES AT 40 KTS AND ALL THE C150'S AND C152'S ARE INTMTLY FLYING ON THEIR CHAINS.

/RM SEV LLWS AFTER 3 APCHS UNABLE TO LAND...; reported by a Lear Jet.

/RM LOTS OF BAD TURBC. THIS ISN'T THE SMARTEST THING I'VE EVER DONE. HUGHES COPTER.

/RM ROUGHER THAN A COBB...; a good old standby, but not very useful.

/OV AVX .../TP FBO/SK SKC/WX SKC/TB NEG/RM LET'S GO FLY...; AVX is Catalina Island's Airport in the Sky. If you're in the Los Angeles area, try to get out there; you may want to order a Buffalo Burger at the restaurant.

LAX UA /OV SXC213186/TM 1911/FL070/TP VYGR/SK BKNUNKN-TOP040/TB LGT /RM VOYAGER 1...; this is an actual report filed by the Voyager on their record-setting around-the-world flight.

A strong Santa Ana wind in Southern California was responsible for the conditions described in the following PIREPs at Ontario, California (ONT), surface wind was gusting to 45 knots.

ONT UUA /OV ONT/TM 1445/FL050/TP B727/TB MOD OCNL SEV 050-SFC /RM CRCLG FAP LNDG ONT

ONT UUA /OV ONT/TM 1450/FL020/TP B727/RM UNABLE TO LAND DUE TO X-WINDS

FSS and NWS specialists sometimes tend to editorialize on PIREPs, usually around the time of championship sporting events. Although, unauthorized and unprofessional, pilots can expect to see these, usually humorous, reports from time to time. Others contain comments of a personal, social, or political nature. For example:

HWD UA /OV OAK110007/TM 1600/FL060/TP BE33/SK SKC/WX FV99SM/TB NEG/RM DURC HWD NBND SEVL H LYRS AT FL015/FL042/FL060. SLANT VSBY 15-30SM. PTCHY ST OFSHR-THRU

GOLDEN GATE OVR CITY OF OAKLAND. REPORTED BY A DERANGED BONANZA PILOT

OK, I was the deranged Bonanza pilot!
Another read:

BFL UA/ OV EHF/TM 1900/FL100/TP UNKN/SK SKC/IC MOD

Could this be an example of "clear air icing?" No. A strong weather system was forecast to move rapidly into central California. As it happened, the system stalled off the coast, with weather advisories for mountain obscuration and icing continuing in effect. When it became apparent the system had stalled, I called the Aviation Weather Center and asked the forecaster to amend the advisory for mountain obscuration. I didn't mention icing; I assumed it would be amended as well. Silly me! Sure enough the forecaster amended the mountain obscuration, but left the icing advisory in effect. I stopped issuing the icing advisory, but one of my coworkers vented some frustration in the form of this PIREP.

Many years ago, I provided a PIREP to Los Angeles Flight Watch. It seems the Flight Watch specialist commented to another controller, "That pilot really knows how to give a PIREP!" The other controller responded, "He should, he works here."

PIREPs from air carriers, the military, and corporate aircraft tend to be more accurate because of the pilot's training and experience. Few student pilots fly MD11s or F18s. New and low-time pilots (inexperienced) tend to overestimate intensities of turbulence and icing, then they may think they've experienced severe conditions and might not heed reports or forecasts. This is not to say PIREPs from pilots of Cessna 150s or Piper Tomahawks are never accurate, and should be ignored.

Pilots must evaluate PIREPs within the context of surface reports, forecasts, and other PIREPs. (Part of the "complete picture.") A single report of severe turbulence from a Beech Sundowner under clear skies and light winds should be viewed with skepticism. On the other hand, a report of severe turbulence from a Cessna 172 with conditions favorable for a mountain wave, and advisories in effect, should be taken seriously. PIREPs that are not objective are worse than useless.

Not only do they give a false impression to other pilots, but also forecasters must take them as fact and issue advisories, which undermines forecast credibility.

PIREPs are an essential part of the observational program. This can be especially true at ASOS stand-alone D sites. Take for example the following METAR and PIREP for Gunnison, Colorado.

METAR KGUC 201436Z AUTO 00000KT 10SM CLR M23/M28 A3018 RMK A01

GUC UA /OV GUC/TM1520/FLUNKN/TP C310/RM PILOT REPORTS AWOS WRONG-THERE IS A LOW CIG-NEED IFR TO DEPART

The fog layer drifted over the laser CHI the next hour and a broken layer was reported at 500 feet. (Don't think this can't happen at a manual or augmented site, it does, especially at night.)

Every time we fly we become observers, but reports must be timely. Some pilots have a tendency to wait until the latter portion or end of a flight to provide a report. A pilot on a flight from Seattle to Los Angeles contacted Oakland Flight Watch and reported conditions departing Seattle two and a half hours earlier. A somewhat over-zealous briefer instructed the student to make a pilot report at the conclusion of the flight. The student calling the FSS the following day meekly apologized for failing to provide the report, then proceeded to recount in detail the conditions encountered. I'll bet this pilot doesn't forget on the next flight. Get into the habit of routinely providing timely reports. Keep in mind that reports confirming the forecast are as important as those for unforecast weather. To be of most value reports of turbulence and icing must accurately contain location, time, altitude, type aircraft, sky cover, and temperature, as well as turbulence and icing. Here again, negative reports are as valuable as those reporting severe conditions.

At present most domestic PIREPs are manually entered by FSS controllers, Center Weather Service Unit (CWSU) meteorologists, Air Route Traffic Control Center (ARTCC) weather coordinators, and military base operations personnel. To clarify any miscoded reports, pilots have only one option: Contact the local FSS. But, if the local FSS did not input the report there may be no way to verify the information.

In that case, the only option is to ignore the report.

The next time someone complains about the lack of weather information or forecast accuracy, ask if they routinely provide objective pilot reports. If you fly and just don't get around to making a report consider this:

BFL UA/OV BFL/TM 1450/FLUNK/TP ALL/RM WISH I HAD A TOP REPORT FROM BFL TO ONT.

CHAPTER 3

Satellite Images

Weather observations consist of surface observations, observations from pilots—either on the ground or during flight (PIREPs)—radar, upper air soundings, and satellite images. Our three-dimensional observational system begins with surface observations—the lower layer; next comes PIREPs, radar, and upper air observation—the middle layer; finally, satellite images provide a look from the top down.

Since April 1960, weather satellites have been orbiting over the United States. There are two main types of meteorological satellites: Polar orbiters and Equator orbiters. Pilots usually have access to the Equator orbiters or the Geostationary Operational Environmental Satellites (GOES). Our discussion will be limited to GOES. GOES satellites orbit directly over the Equator at approximately 19,000 nm. They circle the Earth once every 24 hours. From the satellites view the Earth appears to remain stationary and thus the name geostationary. Satellite images are available on many Internet sights. Most of those used here, and for our discussion, are courtesy of the National Oceanic and Atmospheric Administration (NOAA) at www.goes.noaa.gov.

Satellite interpretation is a science in itself. Therefore, we will limit our discussion to two basics images: visible and infrared (IR). Visible as the name implies is a "snapshot" of conditions on the Earth. Resolution of visible images range between one-half and two nautical miles. IR is a temperature picture. That is, the satellite senses the temperature of an area with a resolution of approximately five nautical miles. (Most of the pictures used in this chapter, and available from the NOAA web site, have a resolution of approximately five nautical miles.) Resolution deteriorates with distance from the satellite, both north and south of the equator and west and east of the satellite's position. This error is known as parallax. Because of the limitations of resolution and parallax, some clouds may be displaced several miles from their actual location and certain objects will not show accurate brightness values.

GOES east is located at approximately 75 degrees W longitude and GOES west at approximately 135 degrees W longitude. GOES east covers the eastern two-thirds of the United States, the Caribbean, and Atlantic. GOES west covers the western third of the United States, Hawaii and the eastern Pacific, and Alaska.

For visible imagery, various types of clouds and terrain reflect different amounts of sunlight. The best reflectors are large cumulonimbus clouds. Thin clouds or areas of very small clouds appear darker because less sunlight is reflected. Below is a list of the reflectivity of various surfaces, beginning with the brightest.

- Large thunderstorms

- Fresh new snow

- Thick cirrostratus

- Thick stratocumulus

- Snow, three to seven-day-old

- Thin stratus

- Thin cirrostratus

- Sand

- Sand and brushwood

- Forest

- Water surfaces

IR images begin by portraying different temperatures as black, shades of gray, and white; black is the warmest, white the coldest. Typically, black represents a temperature of about 33 degrees C and white –65 degrees C, with the gray shades representing decreasing temperature toward the white end. In fact, there are 256 distinct shades from black to white. But, warm temperatures are dark, cool temperatures gray, and cold temperatures light.

Computer technology allows the enhancement of IR images. This technique allows the operator to highlight areas of interest. Colors can be assigned to specific temperature values within the 256 shades. This results in the variety of color satellite images seen on television and available on various Internet sites. However, without knowing the exact "enhancement curve" specific interpretation is difficult. Enhancement curves allow for greater detail of certain phenomena, such as snow and ice, fog and thunderstorms, and haze, dust, and volcanic ash. These, typically, are not available for pilot use in an operational environment. Therefore, our discussion will be limited to those satellite products and phenomena for which pilots have operational access.

Like chart interpretation, best results are obtained by comparing the visible with the same time-frame IR image. Often what may be misinterpreted or ambiguous on one image can be resolved by comparing it with the other image. Unfortunately, this doesn't work at night, when only the IR image is available. (I had a pilot ask me for the visible satellite image one morning at about 6 a.m. In a feeble attempt at humor I replied, "It's not available, the flash bulb is burnt out." The pilot replied, "Yes, you've been having a lot of trouble with that satellite lately." Oh well.) Optimum interpretation results from a comparison of chart and satellite information—part of the "complete picture."

Now if we have the capability to view several images in succession—a satellite loop—we can often get a sense of weather movement, development, and dissipation. Viewing a loop will also help distinguish between terrain and surface features, and cloud cover.

In the next two sections, we will discuss the identification of geographical and weather features. In the last section of this chapter, interpretation and application are discussed. In this section, we will apply the principles of geographical and weather features identification, and include practical examples of application. Various satellite terms will be defined. Pilots can expect to see this terminology on various weather products, such as Center Weather Advisories, Alert Weather Watches, and the Convective Outlook.

Geographical Features

Typically, a distinct boundary occurs between land masses and oceans on both visual and IR satellite imagery. On visible imagery water is dark, land is gray, thick clouds are white, and thin clouds are gray. Water surfaces are the least reflective of the various surfaces and there is often a distinguishable temperature difference, especially during the time of maximum day time heating. Large lakes, bays, and rivers can usually be identified. Major mountain ranges and valleys can also be identified. Hear again, these features usually have different reflectivity and temperature ranges. Deserts are also distinguishable because of the low reflectivity of sand compared to adjacent wooded areas, mountains, and temperature contrasts, especially during the time of maximum daytime heating.

Most satellite imagery contains a grid with cultural boundaries, such as state and international borders; and often they depict large lakes for reference. A knowledge of terrain features within these boundaries is very helpful in determining the location of specific terrain features. Appendix C, Area Designators, along with aeronautical charts provide the location of various geographical features.

Snow cover is often difficult to identify. Both low clouds and snow reflect about the same amount of sunlight. This is especially true over relatively flat terrain. Differentiating between low clouds and snow can often be done be recognizing terrain features, such as unfrozen rivers and large lakes. Clouds normally obscure terrain features, but snow cover does not. Snow in mountainous country is usually easier to identify because it often forms a dendritic pattern. Mountain ridges above the tree line are essentially barren and snow is visible. In the tree filled valleys, most of the snow is hidden beneath the trees. This branchy, saw tooth, dendritic pattern identifies areas of snow cover. Figure 3-1, a visible image, shows a dendritic pattern over the southern Sierra Nevada Mountains of California and the central mountains of Idaho. Surface observations and PIREPs are helpful, especially when they confirm clear skies. Also, a comparison of earlier photos of a loop may be used. Cloud patterns typically change over time, snow cover normally changes very little from day to day. Snow cover is normally not identifiably on IR images; there is not enough temperature contrast between snow cover and adjacent surfaces.

Weather Features

On visible satellite imagery a thick cloud deck appears white, with large thunderstorms the brightest. Thin or small clouds, in themselves, do not present an aviation hazard. In an area of small or thin clouds, part of the reflected sunlight sensed by the satellite is from the tops of the clouds and part from the surface below. The resultant

Fig. 3-1. Branchy, saw tooth, dendritic patterns identify areas of snow cover over mountainous regions.

WHY DOES LAKE ERIE FREEZE?

Lake Erie often freezes in winter while the other Great Lakes remain ice free. In the autumn, surface lake temperatures decrease as air temperature lowers. Just like in the atmosphere, cooler, denser surface water sinks as warmer water from the depths rises. This mixing continues through midwinter when water throughout the lake reaches about 4 degrees C. With further cooling surface water becomes less dense that sets the sage for freezing. The other Great Lakes are much deeper and almost never reach 4 degrees C throughout their depths. Upwelling of warmer water prevents their freezing.

image is the average of the two reflectivities. The image is darker than a thick cloud and lighter than the normal surface shade. On IR imagery, thin or small clouds also create errors in shading. The imager averages surface temperature and cloud top temperature. Therefore, satellite depicted cloud height is lower than actual cloud tops. This accounts for some apparent errors between surface observation and satellite imagery.

Texture is one means of identifying cloud types. Texture appears lumpy, caused by shadows. Stratiform clouds appear flat and sheetlike because they are formed in stable air. Stratiform clouds normally show no texture. Cumuliform clouds appear rounded, billowy, and puffy on visible imagery because they are formed in unstable air. Cumuliform clouds have a lumpy texture. Cirroform clouds often have a fibrous texture. Cloud appearance is an excellent indicator of atmospheric stability.

Low clouds tops, stratus, and fog are characterized by a flat, smooth, white appearance and a lack of an organized pattern or texture. Boundaries are often sharp and defined by topography and may exhibit a dendritic pattern. It may be difficult to distinguish fog from low stratus and snow. On visible imagery they appear bright when thick; on IR images they appear dark to medium gray and may be difficult to distinguish from the surface since there is little temperature difference between the surface and cloud tops. Most types of fog show up well on visible satellite imagery. Often, the satellite is better at determining the extent of fog and stratus than surface observations.

Radiation fog is usually clearly discernible on visible imagery and at times on IR imagery, depending upon the contract between surface and cloud top temperatures. Figure 3-1 shows an extensive area of radiation fog in California's Central Valley. Note the bright, flat appearance, with sharp edges. The edges follow the contour of the valley. Although barely discernible in the picture, is what appears to be a small hole in the fog at its northern end. This is, in fact, the Sutter Butte, elevation 2,140 feet. This formation often pokes through the fog. Advection, upslope, and steam fog are usually well defined on visible imagery, except when there is a high cloud cover. In Fig. 3-3, an afternoon visible image, advection fog has cleared most of the land areas, but remains along central California's coast line. Since rain-inducted fog is caused by precipitation from a higher layer, it does not show up on satellite imagery. Fog dissipates from the edges inward.

As we shall see, weather advisory phenomena usually lie well within their designated boundaries. Satellite imagery can often further delineate these areas. Additionally, imagery may expose the fact— sorry I couldn't help it—that if weather phenomena is developing or dissipating as forecast. From Fig. 3-1, this would seem to be a good day for VFR flight along the coast and in the mountains. In the Central Valley, even IFR flights may have difficulty with extensive areas of near zero-zero conditions.

Stratocumulus clouds often appear in sheets or lines of clouds. Sometimes individual cloud elements are seen. A cloud element is the smallest cloud that can be seen on satellite imager. These clouds sometimes form in narrow bands in which individual cloud cells are connected, and are know as cloud lines, or not connected and know as cloud streets. Stratocumulus sometimes exhibit a cellular cloud pattern—that is, from a more-or-less pattern of cloud cells. They may form a closed cell or open cell pattern. Closed cell refers to the fact that cloud cover is solid, with individual convective elements rising through the layer. Open cell indicates clear air surrounding each individual convective cell. On visible imagery, cumuliform clouds typically appear rounded.

Middle clouds may appear in cellular (altocumulus) or sheet (altostratus) patterns. Like stratocumulus, altocumulus may exhibit stationary lines (altocumulus standing lenticular) indicating mountain wave activity. On IR imagery, these clouds appear lighter than low-level clouds because of their colder tops. Figure 3-2 illustrates a mountain wave as seen on visible imagery. Wave activity has developed over the northern Sierra Nevada mountains and mountains of northeast California and southern Oregon. The wave extends hundreds of miles down stream, as shown in Fig. 3-2 with wave clouds throughout northern Nevada and into northern Utah. Could wave activity be occurring south of Lake Tahoe, east of the southern Sierra Nevada Mountains? Probably. Without sufficient moisture clouds would not develop.

Figure 3-2 is a higher resolution than available from the NOAA web site. In this midday photo, terrain features are clearly visible. In fact,

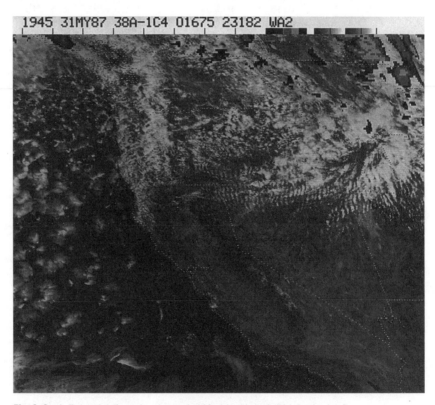

Fig. 3-2. Satellite image, in itself, cannot be used as a weather briefing; it is merely one piece of the "complete picture."

all of the terrain feature in Appendix C, Area Designators can be identified. Also, note that many smaller lakes are visible. Dendritic snow patterns of the southern Sierra Nevada Mountains are easily identifiable. It would seem to be a good flying day, except for the turbulence. All too often this is the case, clear skies and unlimited visibilities mean strong winds and lots of turbulence. Mother Nature never gives you anything for nothing. This also illustrates that the satellite image, in itself, cannot be used as a weather briefing. It is merely one piece of the "complete picture."

High clouds (cirroform) form where temperatures are very cold. Thin cirrostratus appear on visible imagery as a medium gray, on IR imagery as light or very light gray. Recall the discussion of thin clouds. Thick cirrostratus appear on visible and IR imagery as almost white. Thick cirrostratus are among the highest in reflectivity, with very cold tops. As we shall see one of the best techniques to identify cirrus is by comparing both visible and IR images of the same time frame.

Clouds with vertical development (cumulus and cumulonimbus) show up well on visible imagery. They tend to be thick, with large thunderstorms the highest on the list of reflectivity. IR imagery is a good indicator of vertical development. The closer to white, the colder, and therefore the higher the tops. Overshooting cirroform tops are also an indicator of development and severe weather potential. High clouds and those with vertical development also tend to cast shadows, especially during morning and afternoon on visible imagery.

Figure 3-3 is a late summer, afternoon visible image. As is typical this time of year air mass thunderstorms have developed over the Great Basin, and mountains of central and southern California. There are no overshooting tops, indicating storms are not severe. Typically winds at mid and upper levels are light. This is shown by no distinct cirrus blow-off, indicating little upper wind flow and little, if any, thunderstorm movement. Usually these storms are circumnavigable for both VFR and IFR operations. Notice that cirrus tops cover the storms along the southern Sierra Nevada and central California coastal mountains. Without access to real-time weather radar (storm detection equipment) or visual contact with the cells—the ability to maintain visual separation—no pilot should attempt to penetrate these areas either VFR or IFR. (Storm detection equipment refers to airborne access to real-time weather radar or lightning detection equipment. More about this subject in chapter 9.) These rules apply to any area of air mass thunderstorms.

Coastal advection fog has dissipated land areas, but remains along central California coastal sections. As previously mentioned, the visible satellite image is usually an excellent indicator of the extent and location of advection fog.

Air masses tend to show up well on satellite imagery. Large high pressure areas are often cloud-free zones. Low pressure areas, with moisture present, contain large, organized cloud patterns—with the ultimate example a hurricane. Boundaries between air masses—fronts, again with moisture present, show up well on satellite imagery.

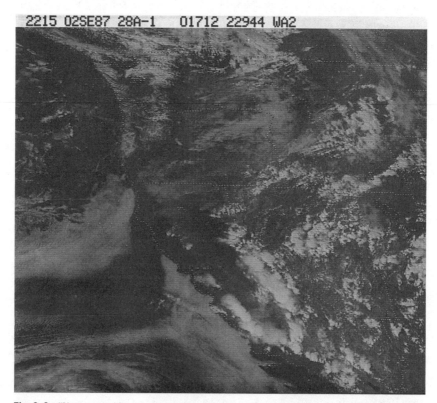

Fig. 3-3. Without access to real-time storm avoidance equipment or the ability to maintain visual separation, no pilot should attempt to penetrate an area of air mass thunderstorms either VFR or IFR.

Large weather systems often appear in the shape of a "comma." A comma cloud indicates an area of low pressure with occluded, warm, and cold fronts, and the jet stream. Maximum vorticity—upward vertical motion—occurs in the center. The surface location of fronts, especially warm and occluded, may be masked by higher clouds in the form of a cloud shield—a broad cloud pattern—or overrunning cirrus. Fronts may be indicated by cloud bands, a nearly continuous cloud formation. However, under extremely dry conditions frontal boundaries may be cloud free.

The location of the jet stream is frequently identifiable on satellite imagery. The jet stream usually crosses an occluded system just to the north of the point of occlusion. Cirrus is often associated with the jet stream and high-altitude turbulence. Cirrus that forms as transverse lines or cloud trails perpendicular to the jet stream indicates moderate or greater turbulence. These clouds might be reported as cirrocumulus. Cirrus streaks, parallel to the jet, are long narrow streaks of cirrus frequently seen with jet streams. Typically, the sharp northern edge of a cirrus cloud shield indicates the location of the subtropical jet stream, and the clouds are called jet stream cirrus.

Convective activity appears very bright on both visible and IR imagery. Often individual cells can be identified with air mass thunderstorm, previously discussed. Organized lines, produced by fronts and a squall, can also be seen. Once the cells or lines have developed the exact location of the thunderstorms may be masked by overrunning cirrus tops. Overshooting tops are most evident on visible imagery with a low sun angle. As air flows rapidly out of the storm at the surface, a line of clouds—called an arc-cloud—form along the leading edge. Arc lines (clouds) are a good indicator of severe or extreme turbulence. Out-flow boundaries are sometime depicted on the surface analysis chart. Often, new thunderstorms develop along the out-flow boundary. At a point where two or more arc lines converge, convection is strongest, producing severe weather.

Another term used with satellite imagery to identify severe convective activity is the enhanced-V. On enhanced IR imagery, a severe thunderstorm often exhibits a "V" shaped notch in the top of the cloud. The narrow end of the V points upwind. This signature frequency, but not always, is associated with tornadoes, hail, strong winds, and extreme turbulence.

Land and sea breezes, and lake effect can be detected on satellite imagery. Like mountain waves, these phenomena appear on IR, but are typically easier to see on visible imagery. Along a sea breeze front, there often exists cumulus clouds while on the seaward side of the sea breeze clear skies are typically present. Especially in the southern and eastern United States, where abundant moisture is available along with unstable air, thunderstorms can develop. These conditions also occur with large lakes. Refer to Fig. 3-4. The top image was occurred at 1515Z, or 8:15 a.m. Eastern Daylight Time (EDT). Both land and sea areas are relatively cloud free. As the land heats during the day, convection begins. Cool air over the water rushes in to replace the rising air. The middle image of Fig. 3-4 occurred at 1815Z, or 2:15 p.m. EDT. Note that cumulus clouds have developed over most of Florida, with cumulonimbus occurring along the coast, especially east of Lake Okeechobee. The bottom image in Fig. 3-4 occurred at 2015Z, or 4:15 p.m. EDT. Thunderstorms have developed over the southern three-quarters of the Florida land mass. This is an excellent example of weather development as seen on satellite imagery.

Widespread areas of haze, smoke, dust, sand, and volcanic ash can be seen on visible, and at times IR imagery. Haze on visible imagery is most easily seen over dark ocean surfaces and rarely shows up well on IR imagery. During the summer, haze boundaries may indicate frontal or air mass boundaries. Haze and smoke are most easily seen on visible imagery during the early morning or late afternoon. Smoke appears as a light gray. In Fig. 3-3, the light gray areas of the Sacramento Valley, northern California, and southern Oregon are smoke caused by the devastating fires of September 1987. (Recall in chapter 1 the example of smoke producing an indefinite ceiling at Redding, Calif. This event was produced by these fires.) Dust often shows up better on IR than visible imagery; and like haze and smoke, dust is best seen during early morning or late afternoon. How can we determine if a particular image is showing haze, smoke, or dust? By comparing the satellite image with current METARs, and along with the surface analysis and weather depiction charts, the exact phenomena can be identified.

Fig. 3-4. A sea breeze is often depicted on visible imagery as scattered cumulus over land areas, with relatively clear skies over the water.

The NWS uses various enhancements to highlight areas of haze, dust, sand, and volcanic ash for weather advisory and forecast purposes. These enhancements are normally not available to pilots in an operational environment.

Basic Interpretation and Applications

When using any satellite product a pilot's first task is to identify the image, date, and time. The image can be visible, IR, moisture, or enhanced IR. Refer to Fig. 3-5. From the bottom margin, this is a visible image with a resolution of eight kilometers (km)—about five nm. The top margin reveals the date and time, "3 10 1999 1815Z," March 10, 1999 at 1815 UTC. This is very important when comparing visible and IR images or using several images to determine weather movement, development, or dissipation. Especially for visible imagery, the time of day is important. In Fig. 3-4, 1815Z is early afternoon on the East Coast and midmorning over the Rocky Mountains. We won't expect to see as much shadowing as early morning or late afternoon images, or smoke, haze, or dust.

The grid outlines state and international boundaries, and the larger lakes. Even without the grid, the ocean and large lakes have a distinct contrast with land areas. (Before GOES 8 became operational in 1995, the grid was often hundreds of miles off—at least for FSS users of Kourvoras products.) Even at this relatively poor resolution, mountains and valleys can be seen in the southwestern states.

The upper midwest, especially Wisconsin, Illinois, and Indiana are snow covered. Note the area south of Green Bay and Lake Winnebago in Wisconsin, and the Illinois River. Even at this resolution, these land features, along with the Great Lakes, help confirm that this is a region of snow, rather than clouds. Additionally, the surface analysis and weather depiction charts can be used to confirm that this is a cloud-free area and that the image, in fact, depicts snow.

Figure 3-5 shows relatively bright clouds throughout the western portion of the Mississippi Valley, central Texas, and the Ohio River Valley. What are the cloud bases? Cloud bases for this system cannot

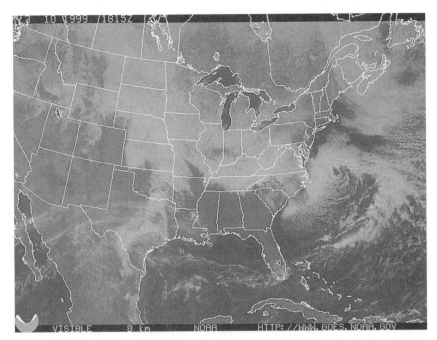

Fig. 3-5. When using any satellite product, a pilot's first task is to identify the kind of image, date, and time.

be determined from the satellite image along. For that information, we would have to consult METARs, and the surface analysis and weather depiction charts. A disorganized storm system is over the Atlantic. It still retains its more or less comma cloud appearance, with some texturing. To determine precipitation and precipitation intensity we would have to consult radar observations or the radar chart. Over northern Mexico, western Texas, and the Gulf of Mexico are darker cloud formations. From this information alone, the only deduction that can be made is that the bright clouds are relatively thick and the darker clouds are relatively thin.

To continue the analysis refer to Fig. 3-6, note that this is an IR image of the same time frame as the visible image in Fig. 3-5. Near the Great Lakes surface and water temperature are the same, as indicated by the same shade of gray. From the IR image alone, it's difficult to distinguish the snow cover of the upper Midwest from low clouds. However, by using the two images together we can conclude it is

Fig. 3-6. Recall that on IR images high clouds are cold and bright, low clouds warm and gray.

indeed snow cover. In Florida and Mexico, land temperatures are much warmer than the oceans, as revealed by much darker—warmer—land masses.

The relatively bright area over the Dakotas indicates high, cold tops. For Nebraska, Kansas, and the Ohio River Valley darker gray represents lower, warmer tops. Notice the high, cold clouds over Mexico and Texas. These clouds have an anticyclonic curvature. Since they appear dark on the visible image, we can conclude they are high, thin, cirrus clouds, and are associated with the jet stream. The jet stream runs just north of the band from central Baja California through southern New Mexico and the Texas panhandle. The clouds over the Gulf of Mexico are dark, indicating they have low, warm tops. This along with their cellular appearance in the visible image indicates stratocumulus.

Refer to the storm system off the Atlantic. The IR image shows high, cold tops along the cold front boundary, in the regions of texturing on the visible image. This indicates considerable vertical development, possibly thunderstorms. High, cold, thick clouds also exist in the area of low pressure at the comma's head. Low, thick, warm clouds are present to the southwest of the low center. From the visible image they appear to be closed cell stratocumulus, becoming open celled to the southeast. Between the stratocumulus and the cold front is an area known as the dry slot. A dry slot is an area of sinking air beneath the jet stream caused by the intrusion of dry, relatively cloud-free air.

From these satellite images we can conclude there is an upper ridge of high pressure over the southwest United States, with an upper trough of low pressure along the southeast Atlantic coast. Conditions are relatively clear in the southern tier of the state in the area of ridge-to-trough flow. However, the area of trough-to-ridge flow supports the weather system off the Atlantic coast. The jet stream runs from the Texas panhandle, then weakens over an area of relatively high pressure at the surface in the southeast United States, then curves northeast through the dry slot in the comma cloud over the Atlantic, and exits northeast over the Atlantic Ocean.

Figures 3-7 and 3-8 are visible and IR images from Goes west. Major mountain ranges and valleys are clearly distinguishable, even at this resolution. Note California's Central Valley, the deserts of southern California, and the dendritic patterns over the Sierra Nevada Mountains. Look at the white spot in southern New Mexico, just north of El Paso. You guessed it! It's White Sands.

The main feature on these images is the well-developed comma cloud off the Pacific Northwest. The low-pressure area at the center of the spiral is clearly visible. From the visible image, thick clouds are associated with the comma cloud. Distinct texturing is occurring in the region of the occluded and warm front. The exact location of these fronts is covered by the cirrus shield. However, the cold front position is distinctly visible, along with its surface frontal boundary. Ahead of the front are typical cloud formations associated with this phenomena. Behind the front is an area of open cell stratocumulus. How do we know these are stratocumulus? The IR image shows dark, warm, low tops. There are considerable, relatively thick clouds along the front in the Pacific Ocean. However, south of the latitude of San Francisco the front is weak, as revealed by the low tops in this region.

Fig. 3-7. Major mountain ranges and valleys are often clearly distinguishable on visible imagery.

Fig. 3-8. Cloud tops often reveal the strength of weather, which can be determined from IR imagery.

Note the clouds along the southern California and northern Baja coasts. By comparing the visible and IR image, we can determine that they are coastal stratus. From the visible image, the clouds are relatively thick; however, the IR reveals that their tops have temperatures the same as sea surface temperatures. Therefore, their tops are very low.

Figure 3-9 contains midday satellite images, with the visible image on the left and, a same time frame, IR image on the right. On this day lake effect snow was falling over the Great Lakes, considerable cloud cover existed over the northeast, and a line of thunderstorms had developed over the Atlantic, east of the Florida, Georgia, South Carolina coast.

The visible image shows thick cloud cover over the Great Lakes. Due to a northeasterly wind, note the clear area along the northern coast of Lake Superior, and to a lesser degree the West Coast of Lake Michigan. The IR image reveals a distinct temperature—gray shade—difference between the surface water temperature of Lake Superior and the cloud deck. This indicates some depth to the cloud layer. We would expect the greatest snow fall to the southeast of the lakes. This could be confirmed by surface observations and the radar chart. In

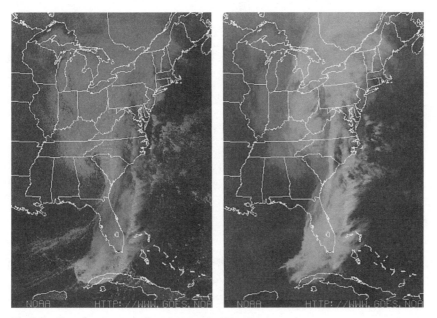

Fig. 3-9. Often a more complete picture can be obtained by comparing visible and IR imagery.

fact, this is a weak event as shown by the Radar Summary chart in Fig. 3-10. The radar chart shows an area of snow falling along the southern shore of Lake Michigan.

What is occurring over Illinois, Indiana, and central portions of Kentucky and Tennessee? The visual image indicates relatively bright reflectivity. The IR image reveals temperatures colder than surrounding clear areas to the west. The radar chart is not depicting

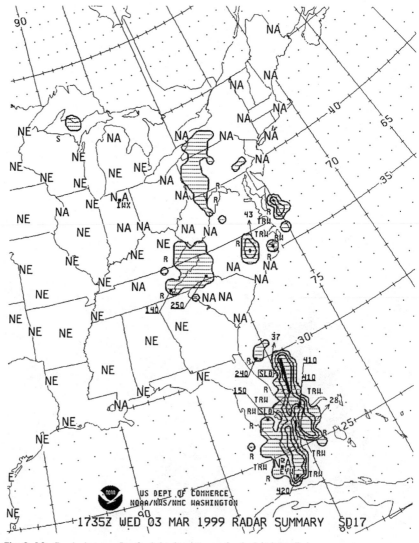

Fig. 3-10. The radar chart can usually confirm the intensity and movement of weather depicted on satellite imagery.

any precipitation echoes in these areas. From this information alone, it appears this is an area of snow cover.

Cloud cover begins over Ohio, and eastern Kentucky and Tennessee. This is revealed by the distinctly colder temperature on the IR image. The radar chart also supports this conclusion with areas of light to moderate rain in these areas. The activity is relatively benign, except in the eastern third of North Caroline and along the central Atlantic coast where thunderstorm activity (TRW) is reported.

Refer to the activity along the southeast Atlantic coast. There is a narrow, organized line with textured tops indicating thunderstorms with overshooting tops, probably into the lower stratosphere. The cirrus anvils are clearly visible on the visible image, indicating upper level winds are from the southwest. The IR image shows the highest, coldest tops along the line depicted in the visible image. The exact location, intensity, and movement of this activity can be determined from the radar chart. Refer to Fig. 3-10, the radar chart. This is in fact a solid (SLD) line of thunderstorms, with precipitation tops to 41,000 ft. The overshooting tops could be several thousand feet above this level. No aircraft, regardless of equipment should attempt to penetrate this line. Even south of the solid line, penetration will be difficult, if possible at all. The radar chart confirms the thunderstorms are moving from the southeast between 28 and 37 knots.

We have touched on the concept of the "complete picture." Notice that throughout this discussion we continually refer to other aviation weather products for additional information and verification. Satellite imagery must be used in conjunction with the surface observations, and the surface analysis, weather depiction, and radar summary charts. Satellite imagery can often reveal the extent of weather phenomena, such as stratus and fog layers, location and intensity of some types of fronts and convective activity, and regions of snow or clear skies. The combined application of satellite and observational products can confirm or refute both manual and automated weather observations.

CHAPTER 4

Weather Advisories

During the latter part of the 1950s, the United States Weather Bureau issued warnings of potentially hazardous or severe aviation weather in the form of Flash Advisories. These were subsequently divided into AIRMETs (WA) and SIGMETs (WS). AIRMETs and SIGMETs alerted pilots that significant, previously unforecast weather had developed. AIRMETs advertise conditions less severe than SIGMETs (less than VFR conditions and phenomena of moderate intensity). SIGMETs warn of severe conditions that apply to all operations. Twenty-one Weather Bureau offices routinely issued advisories. By 1970, the number of Flight Advisory Weather Service offices was reduced to nine. According to the Weather Service Operations Manual at the time: "...the Inflight Weather Advisory program is intended to provide advance notice of potentially hazardous weather developments to en route aircraft...." However, advisories were issued even when conditions were accurately portrayed in the Area Forecast (FA). To paraphrase, during this period: there were AIRMETs by the number, SIGMETs by the score. It was not uncommon to have four or more AIRMETs continuously in effect, and to this end the Continuous AIRMET (WAC) was developed. Weather advisories issued by adjacent offices were not always consistent and often overlapped. This led to confusion for pilots and briefers alike.

The Area Forecast changed in 1978 to include a HAZARDs or flight precautions section, ostensibly to reduce the number of advisories. The FA was still issued by local NWS offices.

Responsibility for issuing AIRMETs and SIGMETs for the 48 contiguous states was centralized in 1982 in Kansas City at the National Aviation Weather Advisory Unit (NAWAU).

In 1991 AIRMET criteria phenomena were removed from the Area Forecast and issued separately as the AIRMET Bulletin. The NWS Aviation Services Branch working with FAA Headquarters, industry, user groups, and—to a somewhat limited extent—input form NWS and FAA field offices initiated the change. The change was initiated to reduce the redundancy of AIRMET/Flight Precautions and correct the disappearance of AIRMETs at the next FA issuance.

SIGMETs were issued for convective activity until a DC-9 crashed in a severe thunderstorm near Atlanta in 1977. From this accident the Convective SIGMET (WST) evolved. The National Aviation Weather Advisory Unit in Kansas City had WST responsibility. Specifically assigned meteorologists issue these advisories.

In October 1995, NAWAU became the Aviation Weather Center (AWC). On Tuesday March 23, 1999, after 110 years in downtown Kansas City, AWC moved to its new quarters near the Kansas City International Airport.

Center Weather Service Units (CWSU) were established at Air Route Air Traffic Control Centers (ARTCC) in 1980. The purpose of the CWSU is to assist controllers, flow control personnel, and alert pilots of hazardous weather through a Center Weather Advisory (CWA). As is often the case with government bureaucracy, the cart came before the horse. There were no instructions for ATC personnel when CWAs first appeared. Distribution went all the way from immediate broadcast to the trash can. The FAA took months to decide that the CWA had the weight of a SIGMET and apply identical distribution and broadcast procedures.

Alert Weather Watches (AWW) and Severe Weather Watch Bulletins (WW), public forecasts, are also produced. The Severe Local

Storms office (SELS) in Kansas City issued AWWs and WWs for severe thunderstorms and tornadoes until 1997. At that time, SELS was relocated to the Storm Prediction Center (SPC) in Norman, Oklahoma.

The AIRMET Bulletin, SIGMETs, Convective SIGMETs, Center Weather Advisories, and Alert Weather Watches and Bulletins, are issued when phenomena reach specified criteria, and, like urgent PIREPs (UUA), receive priority handling and distribution.

With the number of advisories, it would seem impossible to fly into an area of hazardous weather without warning. But, this is not necessarily the case. An advisory cannot be issued for each thunderstorm, instance of turbulence, strong surface winds, icing, mountain obscuration, or IFR condition. Severe weather can develop before an advisory is written and distributed. The absence of an advisory is no guarantee that hazardous weather does not exist or will not develop.

With the preceding background we're ready for a discussion of the specifics—interpretation and application—of weather advisories. But, first let's take a general look at forecasts. The following sections apply to all forecast products, and includes a discussion of accuracy, specificity, and expectations.

Introduction to Forecasts

Sir William Napier Shaw's *Manual of Meteorology*, published in the late 1920s, nicely sums it up: "Every theory of the course of events in nature is necessarily based on some process of simplification of the phenomena and is to some extent therefore a fairy tale."

Aviation weather forecasts began with the Wright brothers' request for surface winds at Kitty Hawk, North Carolina in 1903. In the early 1920s, aviation forecast centers were established at Washington, DC, Chicago, and San Francisco. Establishment of lighted airways in the mid-1920s encouraged the Weather Bureau to begin night forecasting. Several airlines had established their own forecasting systems by the mid-1930s. Because meteorologists could, and sometimes were held responsible for weather-related accidents, forecasts tended to be pessimistic.

Forecasts were limited by lack of observational data and the complexity of the atmosphere. Meteorologists were plagued with unexpected thunderstorms, the transient nature of icing and turbulence, and the unanticipated development of fog.

Advances were made in the late 1930s and 1940s with upper air observations and facsimile transmission of weather charts. By the late 1950s, weather radar was added to the observational arsenal. Today, satellites and computers help produce forecasts. However, due to the lack of observational data and the complexity of the atmosphere, computer programs can only generate approximations.

Refer to Fig. 4-1. Observational data comes from surface, upper air, and radar reports, satellite imagery, and PIREPs. Data processing—analyzing and forecasting—is accomplished at the National Centers for Environmental Prediction (NCEP), in Washington, DC, the Storm Prediction Center (SPC) in Norman, Oklahoma, the Aviation Weather Center, in Kansas City, Missouri, Center Weather Service Units collocated at Air Route Traffic Control Centers (ARTCC), and local Weather Forecast Offices (WFO). Forecasts are disseminated through Flight Service Station, Direct User Access Terminals, and commercial vendors. Figure 4-1, the National Aviation Weather System chart, illustrates the importance of PIREPs and how they fit into the overall picture.

Meteorologists develop a forecast based on the equation:

Existing Weather + Weather Trend = Expected Weather

Trend can be the rate of change in the weather. Advection—the movement of an atmospheric property from one location to another—and development create the weather trend. Fronts and upslope fog are examples of an atmospheric property moving from one location to another, producing weather. Development is the growth of air mass thunderstorms, increase in afternoon thermal turbulence, or the dissipation of radiation fog.

Accuracy

Are aviation forecasts accurate? The FAA admits that needs, "...cannot be met by an immediate application of existing technology. The need for accurate short-term forecasts exists in every phase of flight opera-

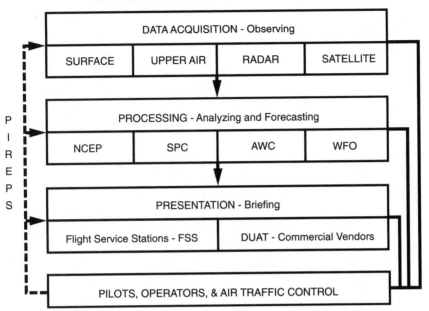

Fig. 4-1. The National Aviation Weather System chart illustrates the importance of PIREPs and how they fit into the overall picture.

tions and is critical to an efficient, smoothly operating air traffic control system." To this end the FAA and National Weather Service established Enroute Flight Advisory Service, including the implementation of high altitude Flight Watch, and Center Weather Service Units.

Forecast accuracy begins—or maybe begins to deteriorate—with observational data. The limited number of observations hinders forecast accuracy. The observational network dwindled until the introduction of automated observations. However, automated observation have their own limitations, and certain sensors (freezing rain, lightning) have yet to be fully implemented. Upper air observations, radar, and satellites help, but extensive areas remain outside the observational network. Fully half of the forecast is based on existing weather.

Available data is computer processed and analyzed. Computer equations represent the atmosphere at points approximately 125 miles apart, depending on the computer model, and at various heights. Large-scale (synoptic) weather systems are detected, but smaller-scale (mesoscale) weather systems, such as individual thunderstorms, might not be detected. Additionally, because of computer model limitations, factors such as the interaction of water, ice, and local terrain cannot be adequately taken into account. These are major limitations to the second factor in the weather equation, weather trend.

The National Weather Service monitors forecasts, but other than amendment criteria, no specific factors exist to determine forecast accuracy. Who defines accuracy? C. Donald Ahrens wrote in *Meteorology Today* (St. Paul: West Publishing Co., 1985), "At present, there is no clear-cut answer to the question of determining forecast accuracy." Few pilots and FSS controllers are aware of forecast limitations or amendment criteria. Many have developed their own perceptions that are erroneous, more often than not, due to misconceptions and misunderstandings.

Specificity

Each forecast is written for a specific purpose in accordance with specific criteria. Area Forecasts cover entire states, TWEB Route Forecasts cover routes 50 miles wide, and Terminal Aerodrome Forecasts (TAF) relate conditions within five miles of an airport. Differences are to be expected due to scale, interpretation of the weather situation, issuance times, and starting conditions. For example, localized areas of fog predicted in TWEB Route or TAFs might not appear in the Area Forecast. Or, the Area Forecast might contain a prediction for thunderstorms that might not appear in individual TAFs when the forecaster does not expect the phenomena to occur at that airport. Forecasters might legitimately differ in interpretation. The Area Forecast might predict frontal passage at one time and the TAF at another time. Forecasts are issued at different times. Therefore, information available to the forecaster, on which to base the forecast, will differ.

A thorough understanding of format, limitations, and amendment criteria are required to adequately apply a forecast, especially when using a self-briefing media. The FAA and NWS have said: "There probably is no better investment in personal safety, for the pilot as well as the safety of others, than the effort spent to increase knowledge of basic weather principles and to learn to interpret and use the products of the weather service." Then there's the legal requirement. Each pilot in command is required by regulations to become familiar with all available information concerning a flight. This includes: "For a flight under IFR or a flight not in the vicinity of an airport, weather reports and forecasts...." Even student pilots must receive instruction in the "...use of aeronautical weather reports and forecasts..." before venturing solo cross-country.

From Table 4-1, Limitations on Aviation Weather Forecasts, the following conclusions are apparent. Forecasts for good weather are more likely to be correct than forecasts for poor weather; this should be no surprise, good weather occurs more often than poor weather. Forecasts are most accurate during the first few hours of the period. Accuracy deteriorates below 80% beyond four hours when less than VFR conditions are forecast. Accurate forecasts of specific values beyond three hours is not yet possible. Forecast issuance and valid times, and amendment criteria are often based on these limitations. Forecasts are most reliable for distinct weather systems (fast moving cold fronts, squall lines, or strong high-pressure areas). Synoptic scale systems are detected within the forecast models.

Phenomena such as the time freezing rain will begin, severe or extreme turbulence, severe icing, the movement of tornadoes, ceilings of 100 ft or zero before they exist, the onset of thunderstorms that have not yet formed, and low-level wind shear, are difficult to predict with accuracy. These phenomena are often caused by mesoscale systems, or are transitory and remain undetected within the normal observational system. Computer models are of limited use. The most hazardous weather is the most difficult to forecast.

Outlook forecasts for good weather are more likely to be correct than forecasts for poor weather. Errors in timing are more prevalent than errors of occurrence. One forecaster put it this way, "We're never wrong, our timing's just off sometimes." Or forecasts are 100% correct—90% in the summer and 10% in the winter!

Unwarranted pessimism is a major forecast complaint. In a 1981 National Aeronautics and Space Administration (NASA) study pilots complained of canceling flights based on forecasts when the weather

Table 4-1 Limitations on aviation weather forecasts

1. Forecasts 12 hours and beyond for good weather (ceiling 3,000 ft or more, visibility 3 miles or greater) are more likely to be correct than forecasts for poor weather (ceiling below 1,000 ft, visibility below 1 mile).

2. Poor weather forecast to occur within 3 to 4 hours has a better than 80% probability of occurrence.

3. Forecasts for poor weather within the first few hours of the period are most reliable with distinct weather system.

4. Errors occur with attempts to forecast a specific time when poor weather will occur. Errors are less frequent forecasting poor weather within a time frame.

5. Surface visibility is more difficult to forecast than ceiling.

Forecasters can predict with 75% accuracy:

1. Within 2 hours, the passage of fast moving cold fronts or squall lines up to 10 hours in advance.

2. Within 5 hours, the passage of warm fronts or slow-moving cold fronts up to 12 hours in advance.

3. Within 1 to 2 hours, the onset of thunderstorms, with radar available.

4. Within 5 hours of the time rain or snow will begin.

Forecasters cannot predict with an accuracy that satisfies operational requirements:

1. The time freezing rain will begin.

2. The location and occurrence of severe or extreme turbulence, or severe icing.

3. The location of the initial occurrence of a tornado or low-level wind shear.

4. Ceilings of 100 ft or zero before they exist.

5. The onset of a thunderstorm which has not yet formed.

turned out to be VFR. One pilot took off in spite of the forecast and completed the flight. The report did say, however, "in this latter case...the forecast was substantially correct and the pilot was fortunate enough to find breaks in the overcast...." As we will see in subsequent chapters, forecasters are making positive efforts to improve their products. Both the NWS and FAA are working on improving forecast accuracy.

Expectations

Pilots complain equally about pessimistic forecasts and unforecast weather. Pilots, often, have an over-expectation of forecasts. Each situation is different, with many variables, and local factors. The limitations in Table 4-1 remain and forecasts are going to be missed. Errors fall into two categories: timing and the "Big Bust." The 1965 edition of *Aviation Weather* said it best: "The weather-wise pilot looks upon a forecast as professional advice rather than as the absolute truth."

PERSONAL OBSERVATION

Periodically in aviation periodicals articles are written bashing the FAA and NWS forecasters and products. I have, along with others, attempted to get details of such occurrences in order to analyze the event, only to be met with silence. It's easy to criticize, especially when there is no responsibility attached. If pilots wish, they can bring specific events to the attention of the National Weather Association's Aviation Meteorology Committee through www.nwas.org or the Aviation Weather Center at www.awc-kc.noaa.gov.

It's essential to remember these concepts during the discussion of forecasts. Forecast issuance times, purpose, conditional terms, amendment criteria, and regulations reflect the limitations on aviation forecasts. Meteorologists sometimes produce a strategic forecast. That is, a forecast with values and conditional terms that will allow conditions to go from zero-zero to ceiling and visibility unlimited without a requirement to amend. Well, that's a bit of an exaggeration, but it has occurred.

The National Weather Service's modernization and restructuring is well underway. Approximately 250 Weather Service Forecast Offices have been reduced to about 115 Weather Forecast Offices. A new computer system known as the Advanced Weather Interactive Processing System (AWIPS) is coming on line. Automated weather observing systems (AWOS/ASOS) and next generation weather radar (NEXRAD) observations are expanding the observational network.

Terminal Doppler Weather Radar (TDWR) will detect microbursts and alert pilots to low-level wind shear.

The next generation weather satellites have been launched and are operation. The wind profiler, a Doppler radar system, will replace radiosonde balloon observations at the turn of the century for upper air wind data. These technological advances promise to improve the accuracy and reliability of weather forecasts. But, for now, pilots will have to deal with today's system and its limitations.

There is not question that weather forecasts have improved dramatically since Sir William's observation some 80 years ago. But, the science of meteorology is still not exact. Several years ago during a frustrating period of unsettled weather, a NWS forecaster wrote: "Finally figured out the difference between a ridge and trough in California this month. A trough gives us cold rain; a ridge give us warm rain."

From the FAA publication *The Weather Decision*: "At the weather briefing keep in mind that: Meteorologists tend to be optimists." Say again, please....

AIRMET Bulletin (WA)

The AIRMET Bulletin is issued on a regular bases four times a day (0300Z, 0900Z, 1500Z, 2100Z), for each of the six contiguous Area Forecast (FA) areas (MIA-Miami, BOS-Boston, SFO-San Francisco, etc.) by the AWC. Issuance times change one hour during daylight savings time (0200Z, 0800Z, 1400Z, 2000Z). The Honolulu WFO issues the AIRMET Bulletin for Hawaii, with the first issuance at 0400Z. In Alaska the Anchorage, Fairbanks, and Juneau WFOs issue the AIRMET Bulletin for their respective FA areas; the product is issued with, and times coincide, to FA issuance. FA areas are depicted in Appendix C, Area Designators. The forecast is valid for six hours, with an additional six-hour outlook. Each subsequent issuance is indicated by an update (UPDT) number, beginning with the second of the Zulu date "UPDT 1." Should an amendment be issued between normal update times it will be reflected in the header (SFOS WA 251730 AMD) and given the next update number.

The Bulletin is divided into three sections designated AIRMET SIERRA, AIRMET TANGO, and AIRMET ZULU. AIRMET SIERRA describes areas of IFR conditions and mountain obscurement. AIRMET TANGO forecasts turbulence, low-level wind shear (LLWS), and strong surface winds. AIRMET ZULU shows the location and intensity of icing and includes the freezing level.

Conditions must be widespread for inclusion as an AIRMET in the AIRMET Bulletin—that is, occurring or forecast over an area of at least 3,000 square miles, approximately three times the size of Rhode Island. Localized occurrences do not warrant the issuance of an AIRMET. Failure to consider this fact has led many a pilot and briefer to unwarranted criticism of this product.

WHAT'S LOCAL?

According to Dick Williams, AWC forecaster, AIRMET Bulletins "...written on the scale of whole states do not endeavor to describe every single occurrence of IFR, icing or turbulence. The forecaster, wishing to indicate that there may be isolated observations, pilots reports, or hazardous weather, may use the term 'local.' No hard and fast rule exists for determining when 'local' becomes widespread. The forecaster relies on observations, pilot reports, satellite imagery, and his or her own judgment in determining the extent of weather features." Federal Aviation Regulations recognize the fact that every occurrence of adverse weather cannot be forecast. Regulations require that even student pilots receive instruction in, "The recognition of critical weather situations," and "estimating visibility while in flight...." In other words, the excuse, "They didn't tell me," is just that, an excuse, not a reason.

AIRMETs are issued when the following phenomena occur or are expected to develop.

- Moderate icing

- Moderate turbulence

- Sustained wind of 30 knots or more at the surface

- Ceilings less than 1000 ft and/or visibility less than three miles affecting over 50% of the area at any time.

- Extensive mountain obscurement.

Because hazards often affect more than one FA area and to provide an overview, the AIRMET Bulletin is issued using the common set of VORs depicted on the Weather Advisory Plotting Chart, Appendix B. Appendix B also contains a list of location identifiers used on the chart. Affected areas start with the most northern location and continue clockwise.

From a forecast point of view phenomena usually lies well within the delineated area. Since the AIRMET Bulletin covers a period of six hours, the phenomena may move through the area, develop, or dissipate during the forecast period. Therefore, the conditions advertised may only affect a portion of the area at any particular time. Details appear in the text of the Bulletin. For example, an icing advisory may cross several FA boundaries. Due to differing temperatures, humidity, and frontal locations specific altitudes may vary. When phenomenon is peculiar to a specific mountain range, coastal area, river basin, or valley the geographical area may be included (SNAKE RIVER VALLEY, TEXAS WEST OF THE PACOS, etc.). Appendix C contains Area Designators.

Conditional terms describe widely varying conditions over large areas. Definitions are contained in Table 4-2 Weather advisory, area forecast conditional terms. They're self-explanatory, with the exception of occasional (OCNL). Occasional describes a better than 50/50 chance of occurrence during less than half of the forecast period. OCNL often describes turbulence, icing, mountain obscurement, and IFR conditions, and reflects the transitory nature of these phenomena. A pilot may or may not encounter the condition flying through a forecast area of OCNL, but the pilot has been warned. Look at it this way: If you run into it, they're right, if you don't, they're still right! We'll discuss how to interpret and apply conditional terms throughout this chapter and chapter five, The Area Forecast.

Table 4-2. Weather Advisory, Area Forecast Conditional Terms

TERM	CONTRACTION	DEFINITION
Occasional/ Occasionally	OCNL/OCNLY	Greater than a 50% probability of occurrence/occurring for less than 1/2 of the forecast period.
Isolated	ISOLD	Affecting less than 3,000 sq. ml./events widely separated in time.
Widely Scattered	WDLY SCT	Less than 25% of area affected.
Scattered/Areas	SCT	25% to 50% of area affected.
Numerous/ Widespread	NMRS	More than 50% of area affected.

To further define the transitory nature of phenomena, the forecaster will use remarks concerning the development and dissipation of conditions. For example:

- CONDS BGNG BY...

- CONDS CONTG...

- CONDS IPVG TO...

- CONDS ENDG AFT...

- CONDS SPRDG OVR...

- CONDS MOVG...

Some of these remarks may be combined to better describe expected conditions. For example, "...CONDS BGNG BY 1200Z AND CONTG BYD 1400Z."

To alert all users that a SIGMET is in effect the AIRMET Bulletin will reference the SIGMET in the appropriate section. For example:

...SEE SIGMET XRAY SERIES FOR SEV TURBC...

Details—location, severity, and altitudes—on the phenomena would be obtained from the SIGMET text.

IFR and Mountain Obscuration

AIRMET SIERRA describes the location of ceilings and visibilities below 1,000 ft and three miles, and areas where the mountains are obscured by clouds or precipitation.

The AIRMET SIERRA portion of the AIRMET Bulletin looks like this:

SFOS WA 261345

AIRMET SIERRA UPDT 2 FOR IFR AND MTN OBSCN VALID UNTIL 262000

AIRMET IFR...CA

FROM 70 WSW OED TO ENI TO SNS TO 20W SNS TO 30W ENI TO FOT TO 70WSW OED

OCNL CIG BLO 10 VSBY BLO 3F. CONDS ENDG 17Z-19Z.

AIRMET MTN OBSCN...CA

FROM 40 W SAC TO 20 NNW RZS TO 50WNW TRM TO 40E MZB TO 10S MZB TO LAX TO 40W RZS TO 40NW OAK TO 40W SAC

CSTL MTNS OBSCD CLDS/FOG. CONDS ENDG CNTRL CA PTN AREA 19Z-20Z..CONTG SRN CA BYD 20Z THRU 02Z.

This San Francisco AIRMET SIERRA Bulletin (SFOS WA) was issued on the 26th day of the month at 1345Z. This is the third issuance for this Zulu day (UPDT 2). It is valid until the 26th at 2000Z.

IFR conditions are forecast for all or portions of California (AIRMET IFR...CA). Specifically, IFR is expected within the area from 70 nm west-southwest of Medford (OED), to Ukiah (ENI), to Salinas (SNS), to 20 west of Salinas, to 30 west of Ukiah, to Fortuna (FOT), and back to 70 west-southwest of Medford.

Within the delineated area, occasional ceilings below 1,000 ft AGL and visibilities below three miles in fog are expected. These conditions should end between 17Z and 19Z. Even if some localized areas of IFR remain beyond 19Z the forecast is correct.

The mountain obscuration is expected to end in the central California portion between 19Z and 20Z, but continue southern California beyond 20Z through 02Z-the outlook period.

Turbulence, winds, and low-level wind shear

AIRMET TANGO describes the location, intensity, and height of non-convective (thunderstorm) related turbulence. Localized or isolated moderate turbulence, not requiring the issuance of an AIRMET, also appears in this section (LGT ISOLD MOD). When turbulence is forecast that does not meet AIRMET criteria, only the general geographical area is indicated (WRN WA AND OR, etc.) Light or no turbulence is indicated by the statement: NO SGFNT TURBC EXPCTD or NO SGFNT TURBC OUTSIDE CNVTV ACTVTY.

Turbulence forecasts are based on wind flow, winds aloft, evaluation of terrain, and PIREPs. Generally, moderate intensity is forecast when the winds reach 25 to 30 knots, and severe when winds exceed 40 knots. High-level turbulence is difficult forecast.

Refer to the Chicago Area Forecast Synopsis and AIRMET TANGO portion of the AIRMET Bulletin below for the following discussion.

CHIS FA 201040

SYNOPSIS VALID UNTIL 210500

COLD FNT ALG LN MOT-LBF-ABQ AT 11Z WL MOVE TO A DLH-DSM-ALI LN BY 23Z AND DISIPT BY 210500Z.

CHIT WA 200745

AIRMET TANGO UPDT 1 FOR TURBC VALID UNTIL 201400

FROM ISN TO MQT TO COU TO ACT TO SJN TO FMN TO DEN TO ISN

OCNL MOD TURBC BLO 150 WI 100 ML OF COLD FNT. CONDS CONTG BYD 14Z THRU 20Z.

The turbulence forecast must cover the six hour forecast period—08Z through 14Z—and the outlook period—14Z through 02Z. A cold front is expected to produce occasional moderate turbulence. The CHI FA synopsis and AIRMET TANGO illustrate how a hazard can move through the delineated area, only affecting portions at any one time during the forecast period. Unfortunately, some pilots and briefers fail to understand and consider this, and accept or issue the advisory whether or not it applies, undermining the credibility of both forecast and briefing.

Frontal turbulence is caused by surface temperature differences exceeding eight degrees within 50 miles of the front, and usually occurs below 15,000 ft MSL. Since temperature is the determining factor, speed or type of front is not involved in the extent of frontal turbulence. Other types of turbulence, however, such as mechanical or wind shear, may also accompany a front. In fact, rapid changes in wind direction and speed below 3000 ft AGL within 200 miles of an advancing front may produce low-level wind shear.

The probability of moderate turbulence is better than 50%. However, it is only expected to occur for less than half of the forecast period. A pilot could expect a greater probability near the frontal zone, with its approach, and shortly after passage. This is not inconsistent but reflects the dynamic character of weather.

The following procedures can be used to avoid or minimize frontal turbulence. To avoid the phenomena, fly above the affected area or remain on the ground until frontal passage. Turbulence can be minimized by penetrating the front at a right angle, thus reducing exposure.

We know that the delineated area in the AIRMET Bulletin is usually larger than the affected area, and we must consider phenomena moving through the area during the forecast period. This explains a widely held misinterpretation. Turbulence will not necessarily occur at every location within an advisory area, during the entire forecast period. Forecasts for mechanical turbulence often cover wide areas. However, the greatest intensity will occur near mountains, leaving valleys and coastal areas relatively smooth. Often, the forecaster reflects this by stating: OCNL MOD TURBC VCNTY MTNS.

By understanding the causes of turbulence and the forecast, a pilot can determine the most likely areas and plan accordingly. This includes reducing to turbulence air penetration speed, securing objects, and briefing passengers before entering areas of probable turbulence.

Strong surface winds, for the purpose of AIRMET TANGO, are defined as sustained winds 30 knots or greater. For example:

AIRMET STG SFC WIND...MT...UPDT

FROM YXH TO BIL TO DLN TO 50N FCA TO YXH

SUSTAINED SFC WINDS GTR THAN 30 KT EPCD. CONDS CONTG BYD 21Z...ENDG BY 00Z.

Nonconvective (thunderstorm) low-level wind shear (LLWS) will be included in a separate paragraph. The paragraph will state LLWS potential, location, and cause. For example: LLWS POTENTIAL OVER MOST OF NEW ENGLAND AFTER 03Z DUE TO STG NWLY FLOW BHND CSTL LOW PRES SYS. There is a potential for LLWS over most of New England after 0300Z due to a strong northwesterly flow behind the low-pressure system over the coast. Nonconvective LLWS can be caused by:

- Fronts

- Low-level jet streams

- Terrain

- Valley effect

- Sea breezes

- Lee side effect

- Inversions

- Santa Ana or similar foehnlike winds

The occurrence, exact location, and intensity of turbulence, and LLWS is difficult to predict. The forecaster must consider the often widespread, and transitory nature of turbulence. Here again, PIREPs are the only means of validating the forecast.

"The wind bloweth where it listeth, and thou hearest the sound thereof, but canst not tell whence it cometh, and whither it goeth:..." John 3:8.

Icing and freezing level

AIRMET ZULU describes the location, intensity, and type (rime, clear, or mixed) of nonconvective (thunderstorm) icing. Layers, where significant icing can be expected, are expressed as specific values or ranges with bases and tops. This section includes forecasts for light or local moderate icing. Like AIRMET TANGO, light or local moderate icing will be described using geographical areas (NE AZ AND NW NM, etc.). Trace or no icing is indicated by the statement: NO SGFNT ICING EXPCD or NO SGFNT ICING EXPCD OUTSIDE CNVTV ACTVTY. A separate paragraph contains forecast freezing levels. Terms such as sloping or lowering describe varying levels.

Icing is as difficult to forecast as it is hazardous. Forecasters must determine which areas contain enough moisture to form clouds, which cloud areas will most likely contain supercooled droplets during the forecast period, and the freezing level. Needless to say, this is not an easy task. Pilots should consider these as forecasts of icing potential. They alert the pilot to the need to consider the possibility of icing in clouds and precipitation within the areas and altitudes specified.

With most of today's aircraft that are certified for flight into known icing capable of climbing through icing layers and flying well above potential icing areas, icing PIREPs are not as plentiful as we would like. PIREPs are the only means of validating the forecast. Some think one reason for the lack of icing PIREPs is a pilot's fear of receiving a violation. By reporting ice, they somehow ground aircraft that could handle the conditions. In reality unless an inspector's in the aircraft or emergency assistance provided, violations are rare. I would hope these individuals would be as concerned about their fellow pilots and passengers—and our insurance rates. In chapter two, we reviewed two fatal icing accidents. Had these pilots had hard evidence from a PIREP, or confessed their fate at the first indication of ice, two airplanes and five people would probably still be around.

This brings up the question: What is known icing? You won't find it in FAR Part 1 *Definitions and Abbreviations* or the Pilot/Controller Glossary. We've discussed the difficulty of forecasting and the transitory nature of icing. Do we want a forecast of icing to forbid flight? Would a report of light icing above 8500 ft, with bases 8000 and tops 9000 preclude flight for aircraft not certified for flight in known icing? What if the terrain was at 7800 and tops 15,000? Do we really want a hard answer? If some in the FAA had their way, the definition would be any time there is visible moisture and a temperature of plus five degrees Celsius or less! Should this or a similar proposal ever be adopted, it would certainly mark the end to many useful icing PIREPs. If icing is reported or forecast and we fall out of the sky and survive, or require emergency or special handling from ATC, we're a candidate for a violation. More often than not, however, ATC is so busy and so happy to get us out of their hair we'll never hear another word. No one should interpret this as meaning that I, the FAA, or ATC condone such actions. Icing for aircraft not certified for flight in icing conditions is to be avoided! At present, the decision as to whether the flight can be made safely rests solely with the pilot, where it will stay until we prove were not worthy of the responsibility. Approximately 80 to 100 icing accidents occur each year, about half from structural icing, the others involve induction system and ground icing. Most are preventable.

The following illustrates the decision-making process with forecast icing.

CASE STUDY

The aircraft was a turbo Mooney on a flight from Bakersfield, CA to Hayward, CA. The synopsis indicates moisture, but a stable air mass. Bases along the route were reported around 5000 and tops 9000 to 11,000, the freezing level 7000. Except for the coastal mountains, terrain along the route was close to sea level; terrain is a very important factor. The flight was planned at 12,000, because tops were relatively low and the aircraft had the performance to quickly climb through the potential icing layer. During the climb, trace to light icing was encountered, once on top the ice sublimated quickly. On top, there were some buildups above 12,000. Deviations to avoid these clouds were obtained from ATC. By circumnavigating the buildups, icing and turbulence were avoided. Should this be attempted in an airplane with lesser performance? Absolutely not! The bases and

> **CASE STUDY** (*Continued*)
>
> tops were known quantities. The airplane had the performance to quickly climb on top. Had that not been possible the pilot had the option to return, cloud bases were over 4000 ft above terrain and well below the freezing level. Was the icing forecast correct? Yes, remember the definition of occasional. Had the pilot required emergency assistance, he would have been a candidate for a violation. I do not intend to imply that this procedure is recommended. The decision rests solely with the pilot, based on his or her training and experience, and the capability of the aircraft.

The AIRMET ZULU portion of the AIRMET Bulletin looks like this:

SFOZ WA 141345

AIRMET ZULU UPDT 2 FOR ICG AND FRZLVL VALID UNTIL 142000

AIRMET ICG...WA OR CA

FROM YQL TO GGW TO BFF TO ALS TO 120W OAK TO 120W FOT TO 120W TOU TO YQL

OCNL MOD RIME/MXD ICGICIP BTWN 040 TO 140 WA BTWN AND 060 TO 160 OR/CA. CONDS CONTG BYD 20Z THRU 02Z.

FRZLVEL..WA W OF CASCDS..045 LWRG BY 20Z TO 035.

WA CASCDS EWD..AT/NEAR SFC WITH MULT FRZLVLS 30-35.

OR W OF CASCDS..55 NORTH TO 65 SOUTH. AFT 18Z 50 NORTH TO 75 SOUTH. OR CASCDS EWD..AT/NEAR SFC WITH MULT FRZLVLS TO 40-50

CA..AT/NEAR SFC SIERRAS AND NE PTN TIL 18Z. ELSW NEAR 70 NORTH SLPG TO 90 SOUTH. AFT 18Z 70 NORTH SLPG TO 90 CNTRL AND 100 SOUTH.

The specific area extends from Lethbridge, Alberta (YQL) to Glasgow (GGW) to Alamosa (ALS) to 120 nm west of Oakland (OAK) to 120 nm west of Fortuna (FOT) to 120 nm west of Tatoosh (TOU) and back to YQL. This area includes the coastal waters.

Intensities, type, and altitudes may differ significantly over the areas affected. Occasional moderate rime or mixed icing in clouds and precipitation is forecast from 4000 ft to 14,000 ft MSL over Washington, and from 6000 ft to 16,000 ft MSL over Oregon and California. Conditions are expected to continue beyond the end of the forecast period 20Z, through the outlook period of 0200Z. Pilots planning flight beyond the forecast period of 20Z can expect this AIRMET to be in effect at least through 02Z.

It seems a bit redundant to include the base of the icing in the icing paragraph and freezing level in the subsequent paragraph. This resulted from a pilot obtaining a briefing with icing from the FRZLVL. The base of the freezing level was not specified. Now the forecaster must enter a specific altitude in the icing paragraph. This may be in the form of BTWN as in the previous example or FRZLVL-150. FRZLVL 55-70. Pilots can expect the most significant icing within the layer specified in the icing paragraph. Trace or light icing can be expected between the freezing level and the altitude in the icing paragraph.

Next appears the freezing level paragraph (FRZLVL). Areas are defined using Geographical Area Designators, Appendix D. In Washington, west of the Cascades the freezing level is expected to lower from 4500 ft MSL to 3500 ft MSL by 2000Z. East of the Cascades, the freezing level is at or near the surface with multiple freezing levels between the surface and 3000 to 3500 ft MSL. Multiple freezing levels are caused by overrunning warm air, such as with a warm front. Freezing rain occurs in these areas. Similar conditions are expected in Oregon, but at different levels and times.

In California, the freezing level is forecast at or near the surface in the Sierra Nevada Mountains and northeast portion until 1800Z. Elsewhere the freezing level is expected near 7000 ft MSL in the north sloping to 9000 ft MSL in the south. After 1800Z, the freezing level is forecast to remain around 7000 in the north, and rise in the central and southern portions to 9000 to 10,000 ft.

In this section the forecaster has described an icing layer 6000 to 10,000 ft deep, that slopes upward about 2000 ft from north to south. The type of ice forecast, mixed, and depth of the anticipated icing layer indicate an unstable air mass. IFR pilots with aircraft certified for flight in icing conditions should have little trouble in these areas, assuming performance will allow them to climb out of the icing layer. Although, they must be prepared to contend with freezing rain east of the Cascades, and icing to the surface in parts of California. For IFR pilots of aircraft without ice protection equipment this forecast would be a very strong no-go indicator, especially east of the Cascades and the mountains of California. The VFR pilot flying in Washington or Oregon east of the Cascades will be just as susceptible to icing as an IFR pilot because of multiple freezing levels and possible freezing rain. But, as we've seen, any flight decision cannot be bases on one forecast, especially taken out of context as in this case.

Pilots planning flights below the freezing level can normally not expect to receive this advisory during an FSS preflight briefing, since icing will not affect their proposed flight. Some briefers fail to understand and consider this, and issue the advisory even through it is not a factor. This practice undermines the credibility of both the forecast and the briefing. A pilot planning a flight and briefed for low altitudes should keep this point in mind, should he or she elect, or be instructed by ATC, to climb to a higher altitude. Pilots might well consider the advisability of accepting the clearance without additional information on icing and freezing level. This point also applies to rerouting. Should the pilot or ATC reroute the aircraft advisories that were not pertinent during the briefing may now apply. We'll discuss various means to update weather in chapter eleven, The Weather Briefing.

Because of several accidents due to icing the Aviation Weather Center of the National Weather Service has revised its icing advisories—AIRMETs and SIGMETs—to imply hazards due to Supercooled Large Droplet or SLD occurrences.

SLDs are freezing drizzle or freezing-rain-size supercooled water droplets, as opposed to cloud droplets, which are much smaller. A forecast for SLDs imply rapid accumulation of mixed or clear ice, possibly forming aft of aircraft ice protected areas.

To alert pilots of potential SLD occurrences aloft, the AWC will issue advisories containing the terms mixed or clear icing in clouds or precipitation (MXD/CLR ICICIP) or clear icing in precipitation (CLR

ICGIP), which means precipitation size drops aloft. Although the rate of accumulation is only moderate, the presence of SLDs poses a significant hazard, even to aircraft with ice protection equipment.

To indicate areas of SLD there may be an AIRMET within an AIRMET, or a SIGMET within an AIRMET, to highlight the threat. For example, an AIRMET for moderate rime icing below 14,000 ft may cover a relatively large area. A second AIRMET wholly within the first AIRMET's coverage may forecast moderate mixed or clear icing in clouds and precipitation below 10,000 ft. This alerts pilots to the SLD threat within the second area below an altitude of 10,000 ft, with a potential of cloud size droplets between 10,000 and 14,000 ft.

When AIRMET phenomena is expected to develop beyond the valid time of the AIRMET Bulletin—first six hours, but within 12 hours of issuance—the details appear in the outlook section. For example:

```
CHIS WA 021945

AIRMET SIERRA FOR IFR VALID UDTIL 030200


.


NONE XPCD.


.


OTLK VALID 0200-0800Z...IFR NE KS IA MO

AFT 05Z OCNL CIGS BLO 10 VSBYS 3-5 IN PCPN/BR DVLPG NE
NRN KS NRN MO SW IA. CONDS CONTG BYD 08Z.
```

SIGMETs (WS)

SIGMETs, like the AIRMET Bulletin, often cover large areas due to the scattered and transitory nature of the phenomena they report. Therefore, the term occasional (OCNL) frequently appears. Additionally, phenomena may move through, or only affect certain geographical features within, the advisory area. In the example, strong up and downdrafts are only expected near the mountains. Failure to completely read and understand an advisory has lead many a pilot and briefer to unjustly criticize this product.

A SIGMET will only be issued when the phenomena is widespread. Local occurrences of severe turbulence and icing will appear in AIRMET Bulletin. SIGMETs are issued when the following phenomena occur or are expected to develop.

- Severe icing

- Severe or greater nonconvective turbulence

- Moderate or greater Clear Air Turbulence (CAT)

- Widespread dust storms, sandstorms, or volcanic ash reducing visibility below three miles over an area at least 3,000 square miles

For the purposes of a SIGMET, CAT is defined as nonconvective turbulence occurring at or above 15,000 ft, although it usually refers to turbulence above 25,000 ft. Because of the difficulty to forecast this phenomena, the term moderate or greater (MOGR) indicates a threat of CAT. SIGMETs contain severe or extreme only with actual reports.

In Alaska and Hawaii WFOs responsible for FAs issue SIGMETs for these conditions. These WFOs also issue SIGMETs for tornadoes, hail greater than 3/4 inch in diameter, and embedded or lines of thunderstorms.

SIGMETs are identified by forecast area, alphabetic, and product designators. The forecast area specifies within which FA the advisory applies. Next appears the alphabetic designator for the phenomena being described. (To avoid confusion with International SIGMETs, domestic SIGMET names now run NOVEMBER through YANKEE—excluding SIERRA, TANGO, and ZULU, which are reserved for AIRMETs.) The product designator (1, 2, 3, etc.) indicates the number of successive times the advisory has been issued. For example, a cold front causing severe turbulence may begin as San Francisco SFO OSCAR 1, as the front moves into the Rocky Mountains become Salt Lake City SLC OSCAR 2, and into the Plains Chicago CHI OSCAR 3. To assure continuity and alert pilots, briefers, and controllers that OSCAR 3 is the first CHI issuance, a referencing remark may be appended to the message (FOR PREVIOUS ISSUANCE SEE SLC OSCAR 2). Updates often contain changes; they must be reviewed for affected area, altitudes, and times. It's important to note both phenomena and product designators.

SFON WS 152130

SIGMET NOVEMBER 3 VALID UNTIL 160130

CA

FROM FOT TO 50NW FMG TO 50NE EHF TO RZS TO 40W RZS TO 30W OAK TO FOT

OCNL SEV TURBC BLO 100 XCP BLO 150 VCNTY SIERRAS. STG UDDFS VCNTY MTNS AND LLWS POTENTIAL BLO 20 AGL. CONDS CONTG BYD 0130Z.

In the above example, the FA designator is San Francisco ("SFO"N). The issuance date-time group follows the product designator (WS). This SIGMET was issued on the 15th day of the month at 2130Z (152130). The alphabetic phenomena designator is N (SFO"N"). SIGMET NOVEMBER is spelled out on the following line along with the product designator (3). WSs are valid for four hours as indicated by the VALID UNTIL time, the 16th day of the month at 0130Z (160130). San Francisco SIGMET NOVEMBER 3 affects all or part of California (CA). Like the AIRMET Bulletin, specific geographical areas are described using VORs on the Weather Advisory Plotting Chart Appendix B, starting with the most northern and continuing clockwise. The phenomena will usually lie well within the delineated area.

Figure 4-2 shows SIGMET NOVEMBER 3 laid out—the gray area— on a Weather Advisory Plotting Chart. Figure 4-2 also displays a portion of the Geographical Area Designators map. The gray area again shows the area covered by the SIGMET. The advisory affects a portion of northern California and most of central California. Plotting may be required to determine the extent of an advisories, and it is extremely helpful visualizing affected areas. Occasional severe turbulence is expected below 10,000 MSL, except below 15,000 MSL near the Sierra Nevada mountains. Strong up and down drafts in the vicinity of the mountains and low-level wind shear are anticipated. Conditions are expected to continue beyond the end of the advisory

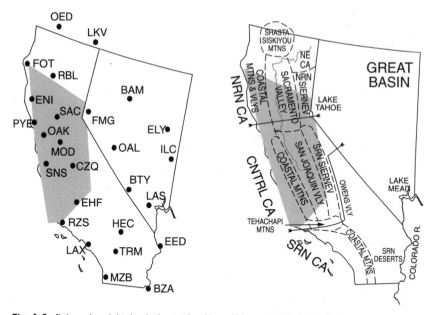

Fig. 4-2. Plotting may be required to determine the extent of an advisory, and it is extremely helpful visualizing affected areas.

period (0130Z). This means SIGMET NOVEMBER 4 should be issued prior to 0130Z. However, should factors, such as transmission trouble, delay the updated advisory, pilots should consider the advisory still in effect, unless a cancellation message is received.

> **FACT**
>
> No aircraft is tested or certified for flight in severe icing conditions, especially areas of supercooled large droplets.

Because of the hazards associated with widespread dust storms, sandstorms, and volcanic ash, a SIGMET is issued for these phenomena. To meet SIGMET criteria, dust storms and sandstorms must cause surface or in-flight visibilities to be below three miles over an area of at least 3000 sq. ml. In the case of volcanic ash, a SIGMET is issued regardless of the area affected as soon as possible after receipt of notification of an eruption. The following is an example:

ANCA WS 231604

PAZA SIGMET ALFA 39 VALID 231600/230200 PANC-

POSSIBLE VOLCANIC ASH BLW FL300 PAVLOP VOLCANO (55.4N/161.9W) WITHIN AN AREA FM 57.0N/166.0W TO 55.6N/161.7W TO 55.0N/162.0W TO 55.0N/167.0W TO 57.0N/166.0W MOVING WNW.

SATELLITE INDICATES A NEW ERUPTION OF PAVLOP VOLCANO AT ABOUT 1330 UTC ON 23 NOV 96. PLUM INITIALLY MOVING WNW.

International SIGMETs are issued for oceanic areas adjacent to the United States by a Meteorological Watch Office (MWO). The National Weather Service has MWOs at Anchorage, Alaska, Guam Island, and Honolulu in the Pacific, Kansas City, Missouri, and the Tropical Prediction Center in Miami, Florida. Criteria for domestic and international SIGMETs are similar, however the format, contractions, and wording used are different. (Contractions are contained in Appendix A, Abbreviations.)

For inclusion in a SIGMET phenomena must be widespread—affecting an area of at least 3000 sq. ml. International SIGMET are issued for the following phenomena:

- Thunderstorms

- Tornadoes

- Lines of thunderstorms

- Embedded thunderstorms

- Large areas of thunderstorms

- Large hail

- Tropical cyclone

- Severe icing

- Severe or extreme turbulence

- Dust storms and sandstorms lowering visibilities to less than 3 miles

- Volcanic ash

International SIGMETs are issued for a 12-hour period for volcanic ash events, 6 hours for hurricanes and tropical storms, and 4 hours for all other phenomena. If conditions persist beyond the forecast period, the SIGMET is updated and reissued. Below are two examples of international SIGMETs.

KNHC 021349 CCB KZNY KZMA

SIGMET ALFA 1 VALID 021335/021735 UTC KNHC-

EMBD TS OBS BY SATELLITE AND LIGHTNING DATA WI AREA BOUNDED BY 30N77W 30N75W 25.5N75.5W 25.5N77W 30N77W. CB TOPS TO FL410. MOV NE 30 KT. NC.

DGS

KNHC 021356 TJZS

SIGMET BRAVO 1 VALID 021355/021955 UTC KNHC-

VA CLD OBS FM SOUFRIERE HILLS VOLCANO MONTSERRAT 16.7N62.2W. THIN VA CLD OBS BY SATELLIE BLW 050 10 NM EITHER SIDE OF LINE 17.1N63W 17.2N63.7W. MOV NW 10-15 KT. NC.

DGS

Convective SIGMETs (WST)

Convective SIGMETs provide detailed, specific forecasts for thunderstorm related phenomena. Since thunderstorms are accompanied by severe or greater turbulence, severe icing, and low-level wind shear (LLWS), these conditions are not specified in the advisory. The Aviation Weather Center's WST unit makes extensive use of radar data to analyze thunderstorm systems. Meteorologists compare radar data with satellite imagery, lightning information, and other conventional sources to determine the need for a SIGMET. WSTs are issued when the following phenomena occur or are expected to develop and continue for more than 30 minutes within the valid period:

- Severe thunderstorms

- Embedded thunderstorms

- A line of thunderstorms

- An area of active thunderstorms affecting at least 3000 sq. ml.

WSTs for severe thunderstorms may include specific information on tornadoes, large hail, and wind gust of 50 knots or greater. An embedded thunderstorm occurs within an obscuration, such as haze, stratiform clouds, or precipitation from stratiform clouds. Embedded thunderstorms alert pilots that avoidance by visual or radar detection could be difficult or impossible. A line of thunderstorms must be at least 60 miles long, with thunderstorms affecting at least 40 percent of its length. Active thunderstorms must have a Video Integrator and Processor (VIP) level of four or greater affect at least 40 percent of an area. (Table 9-1 contains a description of radar precipitation intensity VIP levels.)

The 48 contiguous states are divided into three areas for Convective SIGMET issuance: West (MKCW WST, west of 107 degrees W longitude), Central (MKCC WST, between 107 degrees W and 87 degrees W longitude), and East (MKCE WST, east of 87 degrees W longitude). These areas are shown on the Weather Advisory Plotting Chart, Appendix B. Issued on an unscheduled basis as needed, beginning with number 1 at 0000Z, WSTs contain a forecast for up to two hours and an outlook from two to six hours.

MKCC WST 222055

CONVECTIVE SIGMET 63C

VALID UNTIL 2255Z

MO KS OK

FROM 40WNW IRK-20WNW BUM-30N TUL

LINE TS 20 NM WIDE MOV FROM 23025KT. TOPS TO FL450.

HAIL TO 1 IN...WIND GUSTS TO 50 KT POSS.

OUTLOOK VALID 222255-230255

FROM TVC-ASP-FWA-SJT-CDS-60WSW PWE-TVC

TS CONTG INVOF CDFNT THAT EXTDS FM CNTRL GRTLKS SWWD TO DPNG SFC LOW OVER N CNTRL OK. STGST STMS RMN OVER KS/MO IN AREA OF STGST LOW LVL WARM ADVCTN AND MOST FVRBL MSTR/INSTBY. STMS EXPD TO INCR IN COVERAGE AND INTSTY NEXT SVRL HRS. ADDNL STG/PSBLY SEV TS DVLPMT LKLY INVOF DRYLN THAT EXTDS SWD FM OK LOW.

PDS

This central (MKC C) WST was issued on the 22d day of the month at 2055Z (222055). It is the 63rd central issuance for this ZULU day

(CONVECTIVE SIGMET 63 C). It affects portions of Missouri, Kansas, and Oklahoma, valid for two hours (VALID UNTIL 2255Z).

Specific areas are described using the VORs on the Weather Advisory Plotting Chart. In this case from 40 ml. west-northwest of Kirksville, Missouri to 20 ml. west-northwest of Butler, Missouri to 30 ml. north of Tulsa, Oklahoma. The advisory warns of a line of thunderstorms 20 nautical miles wide moving from 230 degrees at 25 knots, tops to 45,000 ft., hail to 1 inch, and wind gusts to 50 knots possible. The black line in Fig. 4-3 encloses this area; it's nice to have the chart to visualize locations.

The WST outlook was designed primarily for preflight planning and aircraft dispatch. It normally includes a meteorological discussion of factors considered by the forecaster. It is supplemental information not required for weather avoidance, but useful to CWSU and FSS specialists for analysis and background information. Normally the outlook will not be included in broadcasts nor provided during a briefing.

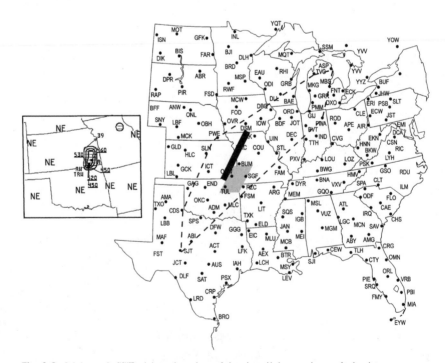

Fig. 4-3. Both the convective SIGMET and alert weather watch are perfectly consistent with the scope and purpose of each product.

The example outlook is valid for an additional four hours, covers an area from Traverse City, Michigan to Oscoda, Michigan to Ft. Wayne, Indiana, to San Angleo, Texas, to Childress, Texas, to 60 ml. west-southwest of Pawnee City, Nebraska, back to Traverse City. The broken line in Fig. 4-2 encloses this area.

The outlook translates: Thunderstorms continuing in vicinity of cold front that extends from central Great Lakes southwestward to deepening surface low over north central Oklahoma. Strongest storms remain over Kansas/Missouri in area of strongest low level warm advection and most favorable moisture/instability. Storms expected to increase in coverage and intensity next several hours. Additionally strong/possibly severe thunderstorm development likely in vicinity of dryline that extends southward from Oklahoma low. Standard contractions are contained in Appendix A.

The outlook interpretation is thunderstorms will continue due to the cold front. The strongest storms will be produced in the area of strongest low-level warm-air advection (upward moving air; a lifting mechanism), and most favorable area of moisture and instability—the three elements required for thunderstorms. Strong, possibly severe thunderstorms are likely to develop along a dryline (a lifting mechanism) that extends from the Oklahoma low-pressure area. Most meteorological terms used in the outlook discussion are contained in the Glossary.

When thunderstorms or related phenomena are the purpose of an advisory, severe or greater turbulence, severe icing, and low-level wind shear are implied. Therefore, these conditions will not be specifically addressed in the advisory or during a weather briefing.

Severe Weather Bulletins

The National Weather Service produces three severe weather bulletins that apply directly or indirectly to aviation operations. The alert weather watch (AWW) warns of severe convective weather. The severe weather watch bulletin (WW) provides details on the AWW. The hurricane bulletin (WH) advertises hazards associated with this phenomena. Both the AWW and WH are written in plane language and are primarily public forecasts.

Alert weather watches (AWW) alert forecasters, briefers, pilots, and the public to the potential for severe thunderstorms or tornadoes. Subsequent to the AWW, a Severe Weather Watch Bulletin (WW) is issued. The WW contains details on the phenomena described in the AWW. These unscheduled bulletins are primarily a public forecast, whereas the WST is a combination observation and aviation forecast.

Although Storm Prediction Center and Aviation Weather Center meteorologists coordinate their products, criteria and time frames differ. Therefore, aerial coverage might not coincide. The issuance of an AWW might precede or coincide with a WST. AWWs are numbered sequentially beginning each January 1st. The following AWW was issued just after the WST in the previous example. (Refer to the shaded area in Fig. 4-3.)

MKC AWW 222036

WW 166 TORNADO OK KS MO AR 222100Z - 230200Z

AXIS..70 STATUTE MILES EAST AND WEST OF LINE..

10S MKO/MUSKOGEE OK/ - 65NNE JLN/JOPLIN MO/

..AVIATION COORDS.. 60NM E/W /45SSE TUL - 25SE BUM/

HAIL SURFACE AND ALOFT..2 INCHES. WIND GUSTS..70 KNOTS. MAX TOPS TO 500. MEAN STORM MOTION VECTOR 25025.

When the area is described with locations not on the Weather Advisory Plotting Chart, a separate line titled ..AVIATION COORDS.. will be added. The mean wind vector is the direction and magnitude of the mean winds from 5000 ft AGL to the tropopause. It can be used to estimate cell movement. In the example 250 degrees at 25 knots.

The WST describes a developing area of interest to aviation. Inset in Fig. 4-2 is a portion of the radar summary chart observed at 2035Z. Thunderstorms have already developed along the southern portion of the line described in the WST. The area is moving toward the northeast at almost 40 knots. The WST forecaster expects the line to develop toward the northeast. Additionally, the AWW forecasts expects tornadic activity to develop along the southern portion of the line and move eastward. Expect later WSTs to cover the area toward the northeast and southwest, into the AWW, and along the area described in the WST outlook. All of this is perfectly consistent with the scope and purpose of these products.

Below is the severe weather watch bulletin (WW) corresponding to the alert weather watch in the previous example.

MKC WW 222036

URGENT - IMMEDIATE BROADCAST REQUESTED

TORNADO WATCH NUMBER 166

STORM PREDICTION CENTER NORMAN OK

336 PM CDT THU APR 22 1999

THE STORM PREDICTION CENTER HAS ISSUED A

TORNADO WATCH FOR PORTIONS OF

NORTHEAST OKLAHOMA

EXTREME SOUTHEAST KANSAS

SOUTHWEST MISSOURI

NORTHWEST ARKANSAS

EFFECTIVE THIS THURSDAY AFTERNOON AND EVENING FROM 400 PM UNTIL 900PM CDT.

TORNADOES...HAIL TO 2 INCHES IN DIAMETER...THUNDERSTORM WIND GUSTS TO 80 MPH...AND DANGEROUS LIGHTNING ARE POSSIBLE IN THESE AREAS. THE TORNADO WATCH AREA IS ALONG AND 70 STATUTE MILES EAST AND WEST OF A LINE FROM 10 MILES SOUTH OF MUSKOGEE OKLAHOMA TO 65 MILES NORTH NORTHEAST OF JOPLIN MISSOURI.

REMEMBER...A TORNADO WATCH MEANS CONDITIONS ARE FAVORABLE FOR TORNADOES AND SEVERE THUNDERSTORMS IN AND CLOSE TO THE WATCH AREA. PERSONS IN THESE AREAS SHOULD BE ON THE LOOKOUT FOR THREATENING WEATHER CONDITIONS AND LISTEN FOR LATER STATEMENTS AND POSSIBLE WARNINGS.

DISCUSSION...THREAT FOR SEVERE THUNDERSTORMS AND POSSIBLY SUPERCELLS SHOULD INCREASE ALONG COLD FRONT THIS AFTERNOON AS AIR MASS CONTINUES TO DESTABILIZE AND CAP WEAKENS. TORNADO THREAT APPEARS GREATEST IN OK IF ISOLATED CELLS CAN DEVELOP. AVIATION...TORNADOES AND A FEW SEVERE THUNDERSTORMS WITH HAIL SURFACE AND ALOFT TO 2 INCHES.   EXTREME TURBULENCE AND SURFACE WIND GUSTS TO 70 KNOTS.   A FEW CUMULONIMBI WITH MAXIMUM TOPS TO 500. MEAN STORM MOTION VECTOR 25025.

...VESCIO

Like the Severe Weather Watch Bulletin, the Hurricane Bulletin (WH) is essentially a public forecast product issued by the National Hurricane Center and written in plain language. When hurricanes are the cause for the issuance of aviation weather advisories, the hurricane will be referenced in the advisory. Below is an example of a Hurricane Bulletin.

HURRICANE GEORGES FORECAST/ADVISORY NUMBER 46

NATIONAL WEATHER SERVICE MIAMI FL   AL0798

2100Z SAT SEP 26 1998

A HURRICANE WARNING IS IN EFFECT FROM MORGAN CITY LOUISIANA TO PANAMA CITY FLORIDA. A HURRICANE WARNING MEANS THAT HURRICANE CONDITIONS ARE EXPECTED IN THE WARNED AREA WITHIN 24 HOURS. PREPARATIONS TO PROTECT LIFE AND PROPERTY SHOULD BE RUSHED TO COMPLETION.

A TROPICAL STORM WARNING AND A HURRICANE WATCH ARE IN EFFECT FROM EAST OF PANAMA CITY FLORIDA TO ST. MARKS FLORIDA. A HURRICANE WATCH IS IN EFFECT FROM WEST OF MORGAN CITY TO INTRACOASTAL CITY LOUISIANA.

HURRICANE CENTER LOCATED NEAR 26.6N 86.2W AT 26/2100Z POSITION ACCURATE WITHIN 30 NM

PRESENT MOVEMENT TOWARD THE NORTHWEST OR 305 DEGREES AT 9 KT

ESTIMATED MINIMUM CENTRAL PRESSURE 968 MB

MAX SUSTAINED WINDS 95 KT WITH GUSTS TO 115 KT

64 KT.......100NE 30SE 0SW 25NW

50 KT.......150NE 75SE 30SW 50NW

34 KT.......175NE 150SE 100SW 80NW

12 FT SEAS..300NE 150SE 150SW 275NW

ALL QUADRANT RADII IN NAUTICAL MILES

REPEAT...CENTER LOCATED NEAR 26.6N 86.2W AT 26/2100Z AT 26/1800Z CENTER WAS LOCATED NEAR 26.3N 85.8W

FORECAST VALID 27/0600Z 27.1N 87.2W

MAX WIND 95 KT...GUSTS 115 KT

64 KT...100NE 45SE 30SW 30NW

50 KT...150NE 75SE 45SW 60NW

34 KT...175NE 150SE 100SW 90NW

FORECAST VALID 27/1800Z 28.1N 88.5W

MAX WIND 100 KT...GUSTS 120 KT

64 KT...100NE 45SE 30SW 45NW

50 KT...150NE 75SE 45SW 60NW

34 KT...175NE 150SE 100SW 100NW

FORECAST VALID 28/0600Z 28.9N 89.3W

MAX WIND 100 KT...GUSTS 120 KT

64 KT...90NE 45SE 30SW 45NW

50 KT...120NE 75SE 45SW 60NW

34 KT...150NE 150SE 100SW 90NW

STORM SURGE FLOODING OF 10 TO 15 FT...LOCALLY HIGHER...ABOVE NORMAL TIDE LEVELS IS POSSIBLE IN THE WARNED AREA AND WILL BE ACCOMPANIED BY LARGE AND DANGEROUS BATTERING WAVES.

SMALL CRAFT FROM INTRACOASTAL CITY TO HIGH ISLAND TEXAS SHOULD REMAIN IN PORT. SMALL CRAFT ALONG THE

WEST COAST OF THE FLORIDA PENINSULA SHOULD REMAIN IN PORT UNTIL WINDS AND SEAS SUBSIDE.

REQUEST FOR 3 HOURLY SHIP REPORTS WITHIN 300 MILES OF 26.6N 86.2W

EXTENDED OUTLOOK...USE FOR GUIDANCE ONLY...ERRORS MAY BE LARGE

OUTLOOK VALID 28/1800Z 29.7N 89.7W...INLAND

MAX WIND 100 KT...GUSTS 120 KT

50 KT... 50NE 50SE 50SW 50NW

OUTLOOK VALID 29/1800Z 30.5N 90.0W...INLAND

MAX WIND 65 KT...GUSTS 80 KT

50 KT... 30NE 50SE 45SW 30NW

NEXT ADVISORY AT 27/0300Z

RAPPAPORT

Center Weather Advisories (CWA)

Center weather advisories, an unscheduled in-flight advisory, are issued when conditions are expected to significantly affect IFR operations and help pilots avoid hazardous weather. The advisories update or expand the AIRMET Bulletin, SIGMETs, or the Area Forecast, and might be issued when conditions meet advisory criteria. In such cases, the Center Weather Service Unit will coordinate with Aviation Weather Center forecasters for the issuance of the appropriate advisory. CWAs are also issued when local hazardous conditions develop that do not warrant other advisories. Because they often report localized phenomena, the area might be described using locations other than those on the Area Designators map, or VORs on the Weather Advisory Plotting Chart.

The CWA numbering system was somewhat complex, but has been simplified. CWAs have a three-digit number. The first digit is a phenomena number. That is, a specific weather event that required the issuance of the CWA. A separate phenomenon number will be assigned each distinct condition (turbulence, icing, thunderstorms, etc.). For example, 101 may forecast a turbulence event; 201 might be issued for icing. The second and third digits indicate the number of times a specific phenomena event has been updated. For example, 101 (first issuance), 102 (second issuance), and so on.

Below is an example of a Denver Center CWA.

ZDV CWA 101 132050-132250

CAUTION FOR MOD-SEV TURBC/MTN WAVE ACTVTY PSBL ALL FLGT LVLS OVER AND NEAR MTNS IN WY AND CO. STRONG CLD FNT MOVG THRU AREA THIS AFTN AND EVE WITH PSBL SFC WND GUSTS TO 60KT. HIGH WND WARNINGS ARE IN EFFECT FOR FNT RANGE AREA BEGINNING 14/0000Z. THIS ADVRY SUPPLEMENTS SIGMET NOVEMBER 2.

This Denver Center CWA describes phenomenon number 1. It is the first issuance for this phenomenon (ZDV CWA 101), valid from the 13th day of the month at 2050Z until 2250Z. If the advisory requires updating at 2250Z, it will become ZDV CWA 102. The CWA advises caution for moderate to severe turbulence associated with mountain wave activity for all flight levels over and near the mountains of Wyoming and Colorado. Additionally, a strong cold front moving through the area during the afternoon and evening might bring surface winds with gusts to 60 knots. High-wind warnings are in effect for the Front Range area beginning on the 14th at 0000Z. This advisory supplements SIGMET NOVEMBER 2.

This example illustrates many uses of the CWA. The advisory expands on SIGMET NOVEMBER 2 by indicating phenomena is due to mountain wave activity and mechanical turbulence. The CWA also mentions high-wind warnings for the Front Range. The Front Range, normally a local geographical reference, refers to the mountains just west of Denver, from Fort Collins to about 40 miles southwest of Denver.

ZHU CWA 101 061355-061455

FM A BPT to 40SE LFT LN..S 150 MI INTO GULF...AREA SCT LVL 3-5 TSTMS MOVG N 15 KTS. NMRS TOPS ABV 450.

The Houston Center CWSU has issued this advisory for an area of scattered VIP level 3 to 5 (see Table 9-1) thunderstorms moving north at 15 knots, with numerous tops to above 45,000 ft MSL. The area extends along a line from Beaumont, Texas to 40 miles southeast of Lafayette, Louisiana south 150 miles into the Gulf of Mexico. These locations are not on the Weather Advisory Plotting Chart. The condition has not yet met the criteria for a WST.

CWSUs also issue Meteorological Impact Statements (MIS). Strictly an in-house product, the MIS alerts controllers of weather that might affect the flow of IFR traffic. The MIS describes conditions already contained in other advisories and forecasts. From time to time overzealous FSS briefers might refer to an MIS or tower controllers record it on the Automatic Terminal Information Service (ATIS).

Dissemination

Advisories are routinely provided during FSS standard, and offered during abbreviated, briefings. (FSS weather briefings will be discussed in detail in chapter 11, The weather briefing.)

During routine FSS radio contacts, advisories within 150 miles will be offered when they affect the pilot's route. It's important to note SIGMET series and numbers to insure receipt of the latest information.

In the contiguous United States Hazardous Inflight Weather Advisory Service (HIWAS) has been commissioned. Advisories and urgent PIREPs are broadcast continuously over selected VORs. The availability of HIWAS can be determined from aeronautical charts and the *Airport/Facility Directory*.

When a WA, WS, WST, AWW, or CWA affects an area within 150 miles of a HIWAS outlet or an ARTCC sector's jurisdiction, an alert is broadcast once on all frequencies—except Flight Watch and emergency. Approach controls and towers also broadcast an alert, but it may be limited to phenomena within 50 miles of the terminal. When the advisory affects operations within the terminal area an alert message will be placed on the ATIS. Here again, overzealous controllers have been known to place SIGMET alerts for conditions hundreds of miles away on the ATIS.

In spite of criticism that advisories cover too much area, their issuance has become more conservative. Ironically, some pilots and briefers now criticize the forecast for not containing enough precautions. Virtually all criticism, however, is due to misconceptions and misunderstanding the product.

The existence of an advisory, or lack thereof, does not relieve the pilot from using good judgment and applying personal limitations. Like all pilots, I have had an occasion to park my turbo Cessna 150 and take one of American's Boeing 757s. These instances lend credence to the aviation axiom: "When you have time to spare, go by air, more time yet, take a jet." When you don't have the equipment or qualifications to handle the weather don't go! This doesn't mean every time we hear an advisory we cancel; but we do take a close look at all available information—develop the "complete picture."

CASE STUDY

For a flight from Las Vegas, Nevada to Van Nuys, California I was told by the briefer: "Well, you aren't going today!" My jaws locked up and I replied: "Oh yes I am!" I hadn't looked at the weather yet; my statement was a gut reaction to this individual's horrible technique. Advisories for turbulence, mountain obscurement, and rain showers were in effect. As is often the case in this part of the country, a direct flight was out. But, by choosing a course over lower terrain VFR is frequently possible. My decision was based on my experience, knowledge of terrain, a thorough review of all available weather reports and forecasts, and always having an out should the weather ahead become impassable. When developing the "complete picture" a knowledge of terrain is just as important as the weather.

The lack of an advisory does not guarantee the absence of hazardous weather. An unfortunate pilot learned this lesson the hard way.

CASE STUDY

The synopsis described a moist unstable air mass. Thunderstorms were not forecast for the time of flight, but were expected to develop; thunderstorms, however, were already being reported along the route. The pilot, without storm detection equipment, encountered extreme turbulence inadvertently entering a cell. The pilot, with three passengers, filed an IFR flight plan because there were no advisories. About a half hour into the flight, according to the pilot's statements to the FAA and National Transportation Safety Broad (NTSB) from the NTSB report, "...we noticed a heavy layer of clouds at and below our altitude and some 20 miles ahead....The layer in front of us seemed to be light cumulus with a heavier layer behind it (not ominous looking)." After the encounter the pilot could not understand why he was, "...never given a precaution or advisory regarding that system!" He went on to say that the accident, "Would not have happened if (the) pilot had been aware of weather conditions...." There were no advisories in effect because, at the time of the briefing, none were warranted. The pilot had the clues—moist, unstable air; thunderstorms already reported—but put complete thrust in a forecast that include no flight precautions or advisories.

The preceding examples illustrate two go decisions. One resulted in a routine flight, the other almost fatal. My intent is not to brag about my skills, or criticize another individual. I hoped to show the process, based on available information, a knowledge of weather products, and limitations, that led to the decisions.

All too often, briefers hear pilots flying aircraft without storm-detection equipment say, "Thunderstorms, ah; well I'd better go IFR." Not for me, thanks. I want to be clear of clouds where I can see and avoid convective activity. Dennis Newton, author of *Severe Weather Flying*, said: "If you are instrument-rated and are flying without radar or a Stormscope, and if you fly long enough in IFR conditions favorable to air-mass thunderstorms, sooner or later you are going to get caught."

If we wish to be accorded and exercise the privileges of pilot-in-command we have to understand the system and its limitations. We must evaluate all available information—as required by regulations—and make a flight decision based on our knowledge and limitations, and that of our aircraft and its equipment. A popular aviation saying goes: Aviation in itself is not inherently dangerous. But to an even greater degree than the sea, it is terribly unforgiving of any carelessness, incapacity, or neglect.

Those who struggle with forecasting the chaos of the weather can take solace from Galileo: "I can foretell the way of celestial bodies, but can know nothing about the movement of small drops of water."

CHAPTER 5

Area Forecasts (FA)

This chapter discusses the various written and graphic forecast products designed primarily for the en route phase of flight. Written products include domestic FAs, along with those for Alaska and Hawaii, and forecasts available for the Gulf of Mexico and Caribbean. These products are available from FAA Flight Service Station, DUATs, and via the Internet. One Internet site is the Aviation Weather Center at www.awc-kc.noaa.gov. Graphic products include significant weather prognostic charts, and the tropopause wind and wind shear and volcanic ash forecast transport and dispersion chart. These products are available on the Internet at http://weather.noaa.gov/fax/nwsfax.shtml.

Pilots, briefers, and meteorologists share misconceptions and misinterpret the purpose and scope of the Area Forecast.

CASE STUDY

A forecast for the desert portion of a fuel proficiency air race predicted scattered thunderstorms and rain showers, with wind gusts to 35 knots (SCT TSRA G35KT). Pilots criticized the forecast, complaining they didn't encounter any gusts; by avoiding the thunderstorms, they remained clear of the winds. The thunderstorms were there, and you can bet gusty winds could be found near the cells. The forecast was perfectly correct.

Others criticize an FA for being too lengthy and—ironically, in the next breath—not containing enough detail. A West Coast FSS manager was quoted (April 1986 Pacific Flyer, Lance Stalker) as saying, "Before, you had people that were familiar with the local conditions and put that into their forecasting." That's still true. Local NWS offices issue TWEB Route and Terminal Aerodrome Forecasts (TAF). The Area Forecast is not now, nor has it ever been intended to cover every single condition.

The Area Forecast predicts conditions over an area the size of several states. Due to limitations on size, computer storage, and communications equipment, the forecast cannot be divided into smaller segments, nor can it provide the detail available in other forecast products. Widely varying conditions over relatively large areas must be included, therefore small scale events are often described using conditional terms, such as occasional, isolated, and widely scattered (Table 4-2). The FA provides a forecast for the en route portion of a flight and destination weather for locations without TAFs. This contradicts a widely held notion that without a TAF there is no destination forecast. Conditions are forecast from the surface to 70 millibars (approximately 63,000 ft).

Area Forecasts in the 1960s were issued every six hours, valid for 12 hours, with a 12-hour outlook. This was time-consuming for the forecaster and, therefore, expensive. Area Forecasts in the 1970s were issued twice a day, valid for 18 hours with an additional 12-hour categorical outlook (IFR, MVFR, or VFR). Today the FA is issued three times a day, valid for 12 hours, with a six-hour outlook. The increased number of issuances and reduced valid times directly reflect forecast limitations.

Area Forecasts for the 48 contiguous states were reduced to six in 1982. Rather than being issued by local offices, responsibility was transferred to the National Aviation Weather Advisory Unit (NAWAU) in Kansas City. Appendix C, Area Designators, depicts FA coverage areas. During this period the Area Forecast was divided into five sections: HAZARDS, SYNOPSIS, ICING AND FREEZING LEVEL, TURBULENCE AND LOW-LEVEL WIND SHEAR, and SIGNIFICANT CLOUDS AND WEATHER.

In 1991 with the introduction of the AIRMET Bulletin, the FA was reduced to a SYNOPSIS and VFR CLDS/WX (VFR clouds and weather). Alaska WFO offices in Anchorage (ANC), Fairbanks (FAI), and Juneau (JNU) issue FAs three times a day; the Honolulu (HNL) WFO issues FAs four times a day. Alaskan and Hawaiian FA areas are depicted in Appendix C and use a similar format as those in the contiguous states. The Miami WFO issues a Gulf of Mexico FA for the area west of 85° West Longitude and north of 27° North Latitude which includes the coastal plains and waters from Appalachicola, Florida to Brownsville, Texas.

Table 5-1 contains FA issuance times. Note that UTC or ZULU issuance times within the 48 contiguous states change twice a year with daylight savings.

The Area Forecast begins with a heading describing the coverage of the product and valid times.

DFWC FA 210945

SYNOPSIS AND VFR CLDS/WX

SYNOPSIS VALID UNTIL 220400

CLDS/WX VALID UNTIL 212200...OTLK VALID 212200-220400

OK TX AR TN LA MS AL AND CSTL WTRS

Table 5-1. Area forecast issuance times

SFO AND SLC	CHI AND DFW	BOS AND MIA
1045/1145Z	0945/1045Z	0845/0945Z
1945/2045Z	1845/1945Z	1745/1845Z
0245/0345Z	0145/0245Z	0045/0145Z
HNL	**JNU**	**ANC AND FAI**
0345Z	0645Z	0645Z
0945Z	1345Z	1445Z
1545Z	2245Z	2245Z
2145Z		

This is the Dallas Ft. Worth FA issued on the 21st day of the month at 0945Z (DFWC FA 210945). (The C in DFW C is left over from the FAs prior to 1991. In those days, DFWC was the SIGNIFICANT CLOUDS AND WEATHER section of the FA.) The next line identifies this as the synopsis and VFR clouds and weather. The synopsis is valid until the 22nd at 0400Z (18 hours). The clouds and weather section is valid until the 21st at 2200Z (12 hours), with an outlook from the 21st at 2200Z until the 22nd at 0400Z (six hours). This FA covers the states of Oklahoma, Texas, Arkansas, Louisiana, Mississippi, and Alabama, and includes the adjacent coastal waters (OK TX AR TN LA MS AL AND CSTL WTRS). Coastal waters are defined as the area from the coastline to the Domestic Flight Information Region (FIR) boundary— typically a distance of 100 nautical miles.

Following the heading is the disclaimer paragraph.

SEE AIRMET SIERRA FOR IFR CONDS AND NTM OBSCN.

TS IMPLY SEV OR GTR TURBC SEV ICG LLWS AND IFR CONDS.

NON MSL HETS DENOTED BY AGL OR CIG.

The first sentence refers the user to AIRMET SIERRA for IFR conditions and areas of mountain obscuration. Often when IFR is forecast, the body of the FA will only contain a tops forecast. For example, AIRMET SIERRA may forecast ceilings and visibilities below 1000 ft and three miles. The FA may only contain: ST TOPS 030 (stratus tops 3000 ft). The bases of the clouds and visibilities are contained in the AIRMET Bulletin.

From AC 00-6 *Aviation Weather*, "A thunderstorm packs just about every weather hazard known to aviation into one vicious bundle." To eliminate redundancy and serve as a, we told you so, the following statement appears on every FA.

> **FACT**
> Since 1991, the Area Forecast is not a stand-alone product. For IFR ceilings and visibilities, AIRMET SIERRA must be consulted. This has led to confusion for pilots and briefers alike.

TS IMPLY SEV OR GTR TURBC SEV ICG LLWS AND IFR CONDS.

Thunderstorms imply possible severe or greater turbulence severe icing low-level wind shear and IFR conditions. A report or forecast of thunderstorms implies these and other hazards associated with thunderstorms (hail, lightning, gusty winds, and altimeter errors). The body of the FA will not specifically address these hazards, nor will briefers normally include this statement. The fact that thunderstorms are reported or forecast infers all associated thunderstorm hazards!

NON MSL HGTS DENOTED BY AGL OR CIG. This statement simply means all heights are above mean sea level (MSL), unless noted as above ground level (AGL) or ceiling (CIG). This distinction can be significant, especially in mountainous areas. Forecasts for mountain states (the west and Appalachian states) will normally reference cloud bases to MSL, while forecasts for flat terrain (midwest and east coast) will normally reference bases to AGL or CIG. When comparing the FA with METARs, this differentiation must be considered.

> **CASE STUDY**
> One evening several FSS controllers brought the East of the Cascades portion of the SFO FA to my attention. They contended the observations and the forecast had nothing in common. However, after converting the METARs to MSL heights, the observations and forecast were perfectly consistent. This example emphasizes the point that to apply a forecast a pilot or briefer must have a thorough knowledge of terrain.

Synopsis

The synopsis describes the location and movement of pressure systems and fronts, and weather patterns, usually as a brief, generalized statement. The following example is quite detailed.

COLD UPR SYS OFF WA CST AT 19Z INVOF 48N 127W MOVG EWD AT ABT 10-15 KTS. PVA INDUCED/ENHANCED CNVTV CLDS WERE ROTG ONSHR FROM NRN CA THRU SWRN WA. AMS THIS RGN APPRS QUITE MOIST AND UNSTBL AND WL SPRD ACRS NRN HLF OF FCST AREA THRU THE PD.

A cold upper-level low-pressure system is off the Washington coast at 11 a.m. PST about 100 miles west of Seattle moving east at about 10 to 15 knots. Positive vorticity advection (PVA) is inducing and enhancing convective clouds that were rotating onshore from northern California through southwestern Washington. The air mass in this region appears quite moist and unstable and will spread across the northern half of the forecast area through the period.

I prefer a detailed synopsis because my training and experience allows extra insight regarding the weather situation. This is especially important if the weather improves or deteriorates more rapidly than forecast. This synopsis would normally be summarized during FSS briefings and on broadcasts: "An upper level low off the Pacific Northwest is bringing moist unstable air over Washington, Oregon, and Northern California." Translating and summarizing in this manner is a prime function of FSS weather briefers. Pilots using DUAT will have to decode, translate, and interpret the synopsis on their own.

From this example, a conclusion might be that on a flight from northern California to Washington the best weather lies to the east, ahead of the system. The example also contradicts a widely held misconception that fronts are the only weather-producing systems.

A synopsis describes the cause of the weather, therefore language and detail will depend on the situation. The synopsis will vary from the lengthy detail in the previous example to HI PRES OVR THE ERN GLFALSK WL MOV OVR THE PNHDL AND WKN (High pressure over the eastern Gulf of Alaska will move over the panhandle and weaken).

The importance of the synopsis cannot be overemphasized. For example, the significance of a forecast for IFR conditions will depend on whether IFR is due to a coastal marine layer, upslope fog covering several states, a frontal system, or a tropical storm. Here's another example:

CHIS FA 300940

SYNOPSIS VALID UNTIL 310400

AT 10Z CDFNT FROM LS SWWD THRU NWRN IA INTO NWRN KS THEN WWD THRU CO. HI PRES OVR OH VLY AND MT. THE CDFNT WL CONT EWD AND BY 00Z WL EXTEND FROM LWR MI SWWD INTO SRN KS AS HI PRES BLDS OVR DKTS. MRNG FOG/ST OVR ERN GRTLKS WL IPV BY 16Z. AFTN/EVE TSTMS MOST ACTV ALG FNT FROM IL NEWD THRU MI...WILLIAMS...

This Chicago FA SYNOPSIS (CHIS FA) was issued on the 30th day of the month at 0940Z (300945), valid until the 31st at 0400Z. The synopsis covers the entire 18-hour forecast period. At 1000Z a cold front extended from Lake Superior southwestward through northwestern Iowa into northwestern Kansas then westward through Colorado. High pressure dominates the Ohio Valley and Montana. The cold front will continue eastward and by 0000Z will extend from Lower Michigan southwestward into southern Kansas as high pressure builds over the Dakotas. The morning fog and stratus over the eastern Great Lakes will improve by 1600Z. Afternoon and evening thunderstorms will be most active along the front from Illinois northeastward through Michigan. This forecast was prepared by Williams.

The CHIS synopsis has been plotted in Fig. 5-1. Notice the ease of visualizing conditions. A VFR flight from Green Bay, Wisconsin (GRB), to Denver, Colorado (DEN), might be well advised to delay until after frontal passage. In addition to better weather as high pressure builds into the area, the pilot could expect better tail winds in the anticyclonic circulation. An IFR flight might be planned direct to Minneapolis, Minnesota (MSP), to penetrate the front at a right angle and minimize exposure to its weather.

VFR clouds and weather

The VFR clouds and weather section includes:

- Sky condition
- Non-IFR cloud heights
- Visibility
- Weather and obstructions to visibility
- Surface winds
- Outlook

Sky condition contains cloud height, amount, and tops. Heights are normally MSL, with AGL and CIG generally limited to layers within 4000 ft of the surface. (Recall from chapter 2, Pilot weather reports, how it took several years to standardize the format for cloud bases and tops. Now all aviation forecast products report cloud bases and tops using the same format.) Cloud tops are always referenced to MSL.

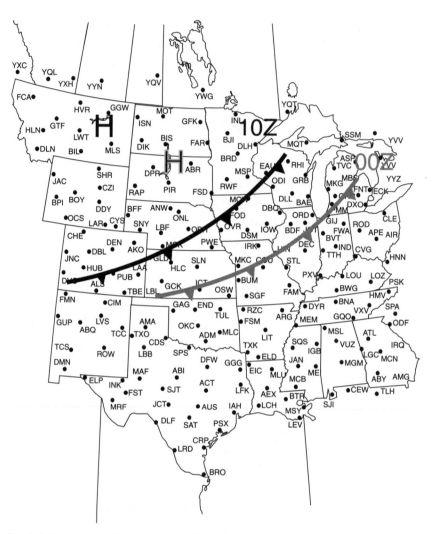

Fig. 5-1. By plotting the synopsis a pilot can better visualize conditions and the expected movement of weather systems.

Since tops of building cumulus, towering cumulus, and cumulonimbus are quite variable, only upper limits appear (CB TOPS FL300). Note that tops at or above 18,000 ft are referenced to pressure altitude or Flight Level (FL). When multiple or merging layers are forecast that would not permit VFR flight between layers, only the top of the highest layer appears (BKN- OVC080-100 LYRD TOPS TO FL200, MEGG/NMRS LYRS TOPS TO FL180). Because of its scope, FA tops cannot be more precise. TWEB Route Forecasts may contain more detail.

Surface visibility appears in the forecast when expected to be six miles or less. To be included, the area affected must be at least 3000 sq. ml. For example, 3-5SM-RA BR (visibility three to five miles in light rain and mist), or VIS 3-5SM -SHRA AND WDLY SCT - TSRA (visibility three to five miles in light rain showers and widely scattered light rain showers and thunderstorms). Table 4-2, Weather advisory, area forecast conditional terms, defines WDLY SCT as less than 25 percent of the area. Because of the scope of this product, the forecast cannot be more precise. A pilot can interpret this forecast to mean the thunderstorms should be circumnavigable.

The absence of a visibility forecast only implies general visibilities greater than six miles. Since they are not within the scope of this product, widespread visibilities of greater than six miles, or local conditions less than six miles, may exist and not be included in the FA. TWEB Route and Terminal Aerodrome Forecasts may contain greater detail, especially on local conditions.

Weather and obstructions to visibility use standard ICAO weather abbreviations. As in the preceding examples, weather and obstructions may be included with visibility.

Widespread areas of surface winds that are expected to be operationally significant appear in the forecast (20G30KT). Often associated with convective activity, TSRA G40KT translates to wind gusts of 40 knots expected to accompany thunderstorms. Direction is true, referenced to the eight points of the compass (N, NE, E, etc.). The lack of a wind forecast only implies widespread sustained speeds less than 20 knots. TWEB Route and Terminal Aerodrome Forecasts can often be used to determine winds of lesser speeds and local conditions.

The forecaster divides the FA area using standard geographical designators found in Appendix C, Area designators. The extent and detail will depend on the weather situation. The example below illustrates a standard division of the Dallas Ft. Worth FA.

SWRN TX

WEST OF PECOS RVR...SKC OR SCT CI.

EAST OF PECOS RVR...AGL SCT030 SCT100. ISOLD -RA/-TSRA.

This portion of the DFW FA covers southwestern Texas (SWRN TX). The forecaster has further divided the area into west and east of the Pacos River. This is a common feature in this FA. (If the Pecos River ever dries up, I don't think they'll be able to write a DFW FA.)

Below is another example of a VFR CLDS/WX section. The synopsis indicates midlevel moisture, with a stable air mass in the valleys. A typical situation during the winter months for Northern and Central California.

NRN/CNTRL CA

CNTRL VLYS AND CSTL VLYS SFO NWD..ST TOPS 020-025 CNTRL VLYS AND 010-020 CSTL VLYS. CONDS IPVG CSTL PTN 18-21Z.

ELSW.. SCT150 CI ABV. OCNL BKN100 TOPS 150 NRN CSTL WTRS AND CSTLN WITH SCT -RA.

In this forecast, the meteorologist has divided California, specifying this portion for northern and central sections. The forecaster has further divide the area within the text of the FA. Figure 5-2 graphically displays the forecast. Below each excerpt from the area designators map in Fig. 5-2 is a portion of the written forecast. The gray shaded area represents the affected area. The forecast for the central valleys (Sacramento and San Joaquin) and coastal valleys San Francisco northward: Ceilings below 1000 ft, visibilities below three miles in fog are contained in AIRMET SIERRA. Therefore, it is omitted from the FA. Stratus tops are expected between 2000 to 2500 ft in the central valleys, and 1000 to 2000 ft in coastal valleys; coastal valleys are forecast to improve between 18Z and 21Z. Notice how the forecaster specifies a period (18Z-21Z), rather than an exact time—another reflection on the limitations of forecasts.

Radiation fog has formed from the moisture of previous storms trapped in valleys and cooled at night under stable air. The relatively shallow layer in the coastal valleys is expected to improve by midday. Conditions in the central valleys will continue. VFR flights will be delayed until afternoon in the coastal valleys, and most probably not possible at any time in the central valleys. IFR operations will be possible assuming the pilot has takeoff, landing, and alternate

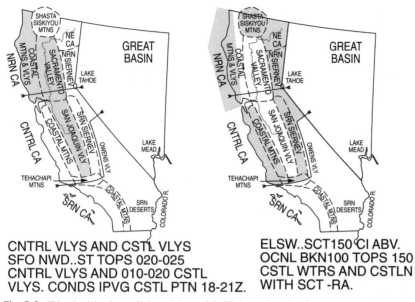

CNTRL VLYS AND CSTL VLYS
SFO NWD..ST TOPS 020-025
CNTRL VLYS AND 010-020 CSTL
VLYS. CONDS IPVG CSTL PTN 18-21Z.

ELSW..SCT150 CI ABV.
OCNL BKN100 TOPS 150
CSTL WTRS AND CSTLN
WITH SCT -RA.

Fig. 5-2. Without knowledge of geographical area designators, it is difficult to apply a written forecast.

minimums. Since ceilings less than 1000 ft, visibilities less than 3 ml are the lowest values normally found in the FA, TWEB Route and Terminal Aerodrome Forecasts should be consulted. It is not within the scope of this product to provide more detail. A pilot planning IFR into an airport without a TAF must specify an alternate. Additionally, airports within this area, without a TAF do not satisfy alternate requirements. Pilots must specify an airport with a TAF forecasting alternate minimums, or an airport out of the affected area. VFR operations above the valley fog will not be restricted. Although both VFR and IFR pilots may be flying above extensive areas of zero-zero conditions. This will pose a risk to single engine operations in case of engine failure. Pilots should weigh this danger carefully.

Elsewhere, the forecast for the coastal mountains (including northern coastal mountains above the stratus), northern mountains, Sierra Nevada Mountains, and the coast south of San Francisco is 15,000 MSL scattered with cirrus above. There will be no restrictions to either VFR or IFR operations in these areas. Landing fields in these areas would be suitable IFR alternates for valley airports. Additionally, over the northern coastal waters and coastline, due to sufficient

Table 5-2. Area forecast outlook categories

CATEGORY	CEILING (FT)		VISIBILITY (ML)
IFR	less than 1000	and/or	less than 3
MVFR	1000 to 3000	and/or	3 to 5
VFR	more than 3000	and	more than 5
WIND	sustained winds or gust of 20 knots or greater		

moisture at midlevels, occasional 10,000 MSL broken tops 15,000 MSL with a chance of light rain is expected.

Note that the area forecast may use the conditional term TEMPO, the international code for occasional; forecasters may also use BECMG to indicate a change period (BECMG 1720, becoming between 17Z and 20Z).

Outlook

A six-hour categorical outlook (OTLK) appears at the end of each 12-hour VFR CLDS/WX statement-18 hours for Alaskan FAs. Refer to Table 5-2, Area forecast outlook categories. The OTLK consists of the following categories: IFR (Instrument Flight Rules), MVFR (Marginal Visual Flight Rules), and VFR (Visual Flight Rules); these categories do not necessarily correspond to 14 CFR Part 91 definitions.

References to IFR or MVFR explain the phenomena causing the condition. For example:

- IFR CIG: ceiling less than 1000 ft.

- IFR CIG BR: ceiling less than 1000 ft and visibility less than three miles.

- MVFR HZ FU: visibilities between three and five miles in haze and smoke.

- VFR WIND: ceiling greater than 3000 ft and visibility greater than five miles; sustained surface wind or gust 20 knots or greater for the 50 percent of more of the outlook period.

A "categorical outlook" is another direct reflection on the limitations of aviation forecasts. The outlook is based on synoptic scale events and might not contain local conditions.

Pilots must carefully consider an outlook. VFR cannot be interpreted as clear, although conditions might actually be clear. VFR translates ceiling greater than 3000 ft AGL and visibility greater than five miles; how much "greater" is not specified. Often, mountain obscurement is not considered. VFR might be expected in valleys, while VFR flight through mountainous areas might not be possible. This category is an indicator that airports within the area will not require an IFR alternate.

MVFR cannot necessarily be interpreted as allowing VFR operations. If conditions were at the lower limit of the category, IFR, most often, would be required. This category is an indicator that airports will be above instrument minimums, but require an alternate. IFR indicates that VFR flight is out. The IFR pilot, however, cannot interpret this category as indicating an airport will be above instrument minimums. It indicates an IFR alternate will be required. A word of caution to the IFR pilot: outlooks are merely indicators. Categorical outlooks can never be used to determine IFR alternate requirements or suitable IFR alternate airports. FAR requirements must be met based on the latest forecasts prior to departure.

Area forecast update criteria

Weather advisories (AIRMETs, SIGMETs, CWAs, etc.) automatically amend the Area Forecast. When updated, the contraction AMD (amendment) appears in the forecast header (SLCC FA 141220 AMD). The SYNOPSIS will normally be updated with a significant change in the synoptic pattern. The CLDS/WX section is updated whenever the weather improves or deteriorates. That is when current or expected weather changes significantly from what was forecast making the FA, in the judgment of the forecaster, unrepresentative. Updated paragraphs are indicated by the contraction UPDT in the body of the forecast (ID MT...UPDT). The OTLK will be amended when a change from one or more of the categories is expected (VFR to MVFR, IFR to

MVFR, etc.). A change in the wind outlook alone, however, is not sufficient for an amendment.

These are broad statements and pilots must remember the FA describes conditions over large areas. We should not expect amendments for local or localized changes, which might be reflected in TWEB Route or TAFs, or their updates. When wide-scale changes do occur, the FA will be amended.

The following appeared in the FAA's June 1988 Air Traffic Bulletin written by forecaster Paul Smith.

A DAY ON THE FA DESK

"A typical day shift begins at 6:45 a.m. with a briefing from the midnight forecaster. We keep this as brief as possible, explaining current conditions and any expected trouble spots for the upcoming day.

"Three forecasters start the shift together, one each for the East, Central, and West. (Each forecaster is responsible for two FAs: East-BOS and MIA, Central-CHI and DFW, and West-SLC and SFO). The three forecaster's work areas are adjacent to one another to allow easy coordination.

"Several things are routine on every shift. For instance, surface maps are analyzed every two hours to keep up with current weather conditions over the area. PIREP collectives alarm at our consoles twice an hour and are displayed both in text form and graphically on a computer-generated map. (This emphasizes the importance of PIREPs.) Surface and upper-level guidance material is received from NCEP in Washington, DC.

"Many other things are not routine and occur as weather conditions warrant. When SIGMETs are in effect, or are being considered, coordination with the CWSUs occurs regularly. AIRMETs and amendments must be issued if forecast conditions go sour. When things of this type occur on a shift, the forecaster may become rushed to meet product deadlines.

"Product composition is accomplished on computer terminals. Once composed and checked, our products are transmitted to WMSC (FAA's Weather Switching Center in Kansas City, MO.) for nationwide dissemination. While we do not have backup procedures in case of computer failure, delayed FAs can and do occur due to computer or communications failure.

A DAY ON THE FA DESK (*Continued*)

"Each forecaster has a different routine in preparing a forecast. Usually, the meteorologist spends the first hour or so on shift analyzing the current weather situation and reviewing computer guidance concerning the evolution of weather systems over the following six to 24 hours. SIGMETs, AIRMETs, and forecast amendments have high priority and are issued as needed to keep briefers up to date.

"Approximately three hours prior to FA issuance, the forecasters begin work in earnest on the two FAs being written. Most forecasters draw up tentative outlines for their flight precaution areas, then consult with the person writing the adjacent forecast to develop a common set of VOR points to describe the entire area. Transmission times are staggered; the BOS and MIA FAs are transmitted first, followed an hour later by CHI/DFW and finally SLC/SF0. The issue of time differences make early coordination a necessity. Thus, for flight precaution areas extending from the Rockies to the East Coast, the west forecaster must make decisions very early concerning the aerial outline of expected weather conditions. IFR areas, because of their changeable nature, are often the last VOR outline to be "nailed down." Negotiation and point changes are made right up to our transmission deadline.

"The SGFNT CLDS AND WX (now VFR CLDS AND WX) portion of the FA is usually the last section to be composed. The forecaster makes use of many separate sources of information to develop the FA, including METARs, PIREPs, TAFs, TWEBs, satellite imagery, radar, radiosonde data, prognostic charts, standard level charts, and CSIS (the NWS) interactive computer system. During periods of extensive adverse weather conditions with multiple flight precautions and frequent conversations with CWSU meteorologists, the FA forecaster is particularly busy as transmission deadline approaches.

Alaskan, Hawaiian, and Gulf of Mexico area forecasts

In addition to the differences already mentioned between the Alaskan and contiguous states' FAs, the Alaskan FAs contain brief forecasts for designated major mountain passes. This statement will reference any appropriate AIRMET Bulletin or SIGMET and include a remark whether the passes are open (VFR), marginal (MVFR), or closed (IFR).

Below is an example of an Alaskan FA. Area Designators can be found in Appendix C.

ANCH FA 071745 AAB

AK SRN HLF EXCP SE AK...

.

AIRMETS VALID UNTIL 072100

TS IMPLY POSSIBLE SEV OR GREATER TURB SEV ICE LLWS AND IFR CONDS.

NON MSL HEIGHTS NOTED BY AGL OR CIG.

.

SYNOPSIS VALID UNTIL 080900

LOW PRES OVER THE NRN GLFALSK WKNS SLOWLY THRU THE PERIOD. A 1002 MBLOW 120 NW OF PAMY MOVES OVER NRN BRISTOL BAY BY 09Z. THE HIGH PRESRDG OVER THE CNTRL ALUTNS MOVES E TO NR PADU BY 09Z AND STARTS TOWKN. A NEW OCFNT MOVES OVER THE WRN ALUTNS BY 06Z.

.

COOK INLET AND SUSITNA VLY AB...VALID UNTIL 080300

...CLOUDS/WX...

FEW050 FEW100. SFC WNDS N G25 KT. VCY MT PASSES..HIER G40KT.

OTLK VALID 080300-082100...VFR WND.

PASSES...ALL PASSES TURBT.

LK CLARK..MERRILL..WINDY..VFR.

RAINY..VFR. WRN APCH ISOL MVFR CIG SHSN.

PORTAGE...MVFR CIG SHSN OCNL IFR CIG SHSN BLSN.

...TURB...

AIRMET TURB*OCNL MOD TURB BLW 080. VCY CHANNELED TRRN ISOL SEV

TURB WI 020 AGL. NC...

...ICE AND FZLVL...

NIL SIG. FZLVL SFC.

.

COPPER RIVER BASIN AC...VALID UNTIL 080300

...CLOUDS/WX...

FEW045 SCT-BKN100 TOPS 120. ISOL -SHSN. ISOL CIGS BLW 010 VIS BLW 3SM BR/FZFG. OTLK VALID 080300-082100...VFR.

PASS...TAHNETA...VFR TURBT.

...TURB...

NIL SIG.

...ICE AND FZLVL...

NIL SIG. FZLVL SFC.

.

CNTRL GLF CST AD...VALID UNTIL 080300

...CLOUDS/WX...

AIRMET MT OBSC*MTS OCNL OBSC IN CLDS/PCPN. NC...

SCT015 BKN060 TOPS 090. OCNL BKN012 OVC040 TOPS 160 3SM -SHSN. ISOL CIGS BLW 010 VIS BLW 3SM SN BLSN. SFC WNDS CHANNELED TRRN N 25G45KT. OTLK VALID 080300-082100...MVFR CIG SHSN WND.

...TURB...

AIRMET TURB*OCNL MOD TURB BLW 080. ISOL SEV TURB VCY CHNLD TRRN. NC...

...ICE AND FZLVL...

AIRMET ICE*OCNL MOD RIME ICEIC 045-120. FZLVL SFC....

.

KODIAK IS AE...VALID UNTIL 080300 AAA

...CLOUDS/WX...

AIRMET MT OBSC*MTS OCNL OBSC IN CLDS/PCPN. NC...

SCT015 SCT060 5SM BLSN. ISOL BKN-OVC015 TOPS 120 VIS BLW 3SM -SHSN BLSN. SFC WNDS NW 25G40 KT. HIER G65 KT OFSHR.

OTLK VALID 080300-082100...MVFR CIG SHSN BLSN WND.

...TURB...AAA

AIRMET TURB*OCNL MOD TURB BLW 080 AND FL300-360.

ISOL SEV TURB WI 020 AGL. NC...

...ICE AND FZLVL...

NIL SIG. FZLVL SFC.

.

KUSKOKWIM VLY AF...VALID UNTIL 080300

...CLOUDS/WX...

GENLY SKC.

ISOL CIGS BLW 010/VIS BLW 3SM IC BR/FG TOPS 015 VCY SETTLE-MENTS.

OTLK VALID 080300-082100...VFR.

...TURB...NIL SIG.

...ICE AND FZLVL...NIL SIG. FZLVL SFC.

.

YKN-KUSKOKWIM DELTA AG...VALID UNTIL 080300 AAA

...CLOUDS/WX...

**AIRMET MT OBSC ***SLOLY DVLPG FM W..

MTS OCNL OBSC IN CLOUDS/PCPN ABV 015. NC...

ALL SXNS..FEW015 SCT030 BKN060 TOPS 100 FEW LYRS ABV TOPS FL250. W PAEM-PAEH LN AND SPRDG SLOLY E ACRS AREA BY 03Z.. OCNL BKN015 OVC030 SCT 3SM -SHSN. OFSHR AND ALG CST ALL PDS..SFC WND SW-NW 20G35 KTS.

OTLK VALID 080300-082100...MVFR CIG SHSN.

...TURB...AAA

AIRMET TURB*PABE S..OCNL MOD TURB FL300-360. WKN...

ISOL MOD TURB SFC-050 VCY RUF TRRN.

...ICE AND FZLVL...

NIL SIG. FZLVL SFC.

.

BRISTOL BAY AH...VALID UNTIL 080300 AAB

...CLOUDS/WX...AAB

AIRMET MT OBSC*PADL W SPRDG E THRU ALL AREAS BY 21Z..MT OBSC IN CLDS AND SN. NC...

OTRW..SCT020 SCT-BKN070 TOPS 100. SPRDG FM W THRU ALL AREAS BY 21Z.. BKN015 OVC050 TOPS 130 3SM -SN. OCNL VIS BLW 3SM

-SN ISOL CIG BLW 010.

OTLK VALID 080300-082100...MVFR CIG SN. FM 15Z VFR.

...TURB...AAA

AIRMET TURB*OCNL MOD TURB FL300-FL360. WKN...

...ICE AND FZLVL...AAB

PRDG FM W THRU ALL AREAS BY 21Z..OCNL LGT RIME ICEIC 015-130. OTRW..NIL SIG. FZLVL SFC.

.

AK PEN AI...VALID UNTIL 080300 AAA

...CLOUDS/WX...

AIRMET IFR/MT OBSC*BERING SIDE..OCNL CIGS BLW 010 VIS BLW 3SM -SN BLSN. BOTH SIDES..OCNL MT OBSC IN CLDS/PCPN. NC... OTRW..SCT005 SCT025 BKN-OVC040 TOPS 090. OCNL SCT005 BKN-OVC015 3SM -SN BLSN. SFC WNDS NW G25-30 KT.

OTLK VALID 080300-082100...MVFR CIG SHSN WND.

...TURB...AAA

AIRMET TURB*OCNL MOD TURB BLW 060. NC...

...ICE AND FZLVL...

OCNL LGT RIME ICEIC 015-090. FZLVL SFC.

.

UNIMAK PASS TO ADAK AJ...VALID UNTIL 080300

...CLOUDS/WX...

SCT025 SCT-BKN050 TOPS 070. ISOL SCT005 BKN-OVC020 3SM -SN BECMG OCNL AFT 21Z. SFC WNDS W G25 KT.

OTLK VALID 080300-082100...MVFR CIG SHSN.

...TURB...

VCY RUF TRRN..ISOL MOD TURB BLW 060.

...ICE AND FZLVL...

NIL SIG. FZLVL SFC.

The following is an example of a Hawaiian FA. Area Designators can be found in Appendix C.

HNLC FA 290940

SYNOPSIS AND VFR CLDS/WX

SYNOPSIS VALID UNTIL 300400

CLDS/WX VALID UNTIL 292200...OTLK VALID 292200-300400

.

SEE AIRMET SIERRA FOR IFR CLDS AND MT OBSCN.

TS IMPLY SEV OR GTR TURB SEV ICING LLWS AND IFR CONDS.

NON MSL HGTS DENOTED BY AGL OR CIG.

.

SYNOPSIS...SFC RDG 400 NM N PHNL MOVG SOUTH SLOWLY.

.

ENTIRE AREA.

BKN-SCT250. LWR CLDS AND WX FLW.

.

WNDWD CSTL/MTN SXNS AND ADJ WNDWD CSTL WTRS OF THE BIG ISLAND.

SCT020 BKN-OVC040 TOPS 080 TEMPO BKN020 VIS 5SM -SHRA.

21Z SCT020 BKN-SCT040 TOPS 070 TEMPO BKN020 -SHRA. OTLK...VFR.

.

WNDWD CSTL/MTN SXNS AND ADJ WNDWD CSTL WTRS OF THE RMNG ISLANDS.

SCT025 SCT-BKN045 TOPS 070 ISOLD BKN025 -SHRA. OTLK...VFR.

.

KONA...KAU AND LEEWARD KOHALA SXNS.

SCT-BKN040 TOPS 080. 21Z FEW030 BKN050 TOPS 080. OTLK...VFR.

.

REST OF AREA.

SCT025 SCT045 ISOLD BKN040 TOPS 070 -SHRA. OTLK...VFR.

Two forecasts have been developed to support aviation operations in the Gulf of Mexico and Caribbean. These are the Gulf of Mexico FA and the Atlantic, Caribbean, and Gulf or Mexico FA.

The Gulf or Mexico FA is issued twice a day at 1040/1140Z and 1740/1840Z depending on whether it's standard or daylight savings time. Aerial coverage is depicted in Appendix C. The forecast has been specifically developed to support helicopter operations. It is unique in that it is a single forecast combining the FA, weather advisories, and marine precautions. Each section describes the phenomenon impacting the respective area.

The following is an example of the Gulf of Mexico FA.

TTAA00 KNHC 071830

FAGX01 KNHC 071830

FCST...071900Z-080700Z

OTLK...080700Z-081900Z

AMD NOT AVBL 0200Z-1100Z

TROPICAL ANALYSIS AND FORECAST BRANCH

TROPICAL PREDICTION CENTER MIAMI FL

GLFMEX N OF 27N W OF 85W...CSTL PLAINS AND WTRS AQQ-BRO...HGTS MSL UNLESS NOTED.

TSRA IMPLY POSS SEV OR GTR TURB...SEV ICE...LOW LVL WS AND STG SFC WND...HIGH WAVES...CIG BLW 010...AND VIS BLW 3SM.

01 SYNS...

HI PRES OVR GLFMEX THRU FCST AND OTLK PD.

02 FLT PRCTNS...

NONE.

03 MARINE PRCTNS...

NONE.

04 SGFNT CLD/WX...

CSTL PLAINS CSTL WTRS BRO-LCH...

BKN/OVC015-025 TOPS 040-060. 21Z BKN/SCT020-030. AFT 03Z AREAS VIS 3-4SM BR...AFT 06Z BKN/OVC010 WDSPRD VIS 3-4SM BR...LOC VIS BLW 3SM BR/FG. OTLK...LIFR CIG FG. 16Z MVFR CIG BR. 18Z VFR.

CSTL PLAINS CSTL WTRS LCH-AQQ...

SCT/BKN020-030 BKN050-060...ISOL -SHRA. AFT 04Z SCT/BKN010-

015 AREAS VIS 3-4SM BR...AFT 06Z BKN/OVC010 WDSPRD VIS 3SM BR...LOC VIS BLW 3SM BR/FG. OTLK...IFR CIG BR. PNS-AQQ AFT 15Z VFR. LCH-PNS AFT 16Z MVFR CIG BR.

OFSHR WTRS W OF 90W...

FEW/SCT020-030. OTLK...VFR.

OFSHR WTRS E OF 90W...

SCT/BKN020-030...ISOL -SHRA. OTLK...VFR.

05 ICE AND FZ LVL BLW 120...

NONE. FZ LVL ABV 120.

06 TURB BLW 120...

NONE.

07 WND BLW 120...

CSTL PLAINS CSTL WTRS BRO-CRP...

SFC-010 S 10-15 KT. 010-080 SW 15-20 KT. 080-120 W 15 KT. OTLK...SFC-080 SLGT INCR. 080-120 NOSIG.

CSTL PLAINS CSTL WTRS CRP-LCH AND OFSHR WTRS W OF 93W...

SFC-010 SW 10-15 KT. 010-080 SW 20-30 KT...AFT 00Z DCR SW 15-20KT. 080-120 W-NW 30-40 KT...AFT 00Z DCR NW 15-20 KT.

OTLK...NOSIG.

CSTL PLAINS CSTL WTRS LCH-AQQ AND OFSHR WTRS E OF 93W...

SFC-010 SW 10-15 KT. 010-060 SW 20-30 KT...OFSHR WTRS AFT 00Z DCR SW-W 15-20 KT. 060-120 SW-W 25-35 KT...AFT 00Z DCR W 15-25KT. OTLK...NOSIG.

08 WAVES...

CSTL WTRS BRO-PSX.....2-4 FT. OTLK...NOSIG.

CSTL WTRS PSX-BVE.....2-3 FT. OTLK...NOSIG.

CSTL WTRS BVE-AQQ.....3-4 FT. OTLK...SLGT DCR.

OFSHR WTRS............3-4 FT. OTLK...NOSIG.

The following is an example of the Atlantic, Caribbean, and Gulf of Mexico area forecast. The forecast covers the western Atlantic, Caribbean, and Gulf of Mexico and adjacent coast. Produced by the NWS's Tropical Prediction Center (TPC), this forecast covers conditions from the surface to 400 mb (24,000 ft). Refer to Appendix C for a graphical depiction of coverage.

TTAA00 KNHC 071505

TROPICAL ANALYSIS AND FORECAST BRANCH

TROPICAL PREDICTION CENTER MIAMI FLORIDA

071800-080600

ATLANTIC S OF 32N W OF 57W...CARIBBEAN...GULF OF MEXICO AND ADJCOAST N OF 23N...AND FLORIDA SFC TO 400 MB.

SYNOPSIS...

ATLANTIC DISSIPATING FRONT 21N58W 19N70W THROUGH 06Z. WEAK COLD FRONT WILL MOVE RAPIDLY ACROSS AREA N OF 30N E OF 70W THROUGH06Z. HIGH PRESSURE OVER ATLANTIC/GULF OF MEXICO NEAR 25N.

SIGNIFICANT CLD/WX...

ATLANTIC WI 30NM OF DISSIPATING FRONT

BKN/SCT025-030 BKN060-080. WIDELY SCT SHRA.

ATLANTIC N OF 30N E OF 78W

SCT/BKN030-035 BKN/OVC050-070. ISOL -SHRA.

ATLANTIC ELSEWHERE N OF 25N BTN 68W-76W

SCT/LOC BKN030 BKN/OVC060. 00Z SCT/LOC BKN035-045.

REMAINDER ATLANTIC

SCT020-030 SCT/BKN050-070.

CARIBBEAN S OF 15N E OF 75W

SCT/LOC BKN020-030 BKN/SCT050-070. ISOL -SHRA.

REMAINDER CARIBBEAN

SCT/LOC BKN030-040. ISOL -SHRA.

GULF OF MEXICO ADJ COAST W OF 93W

SCT/LOC BKN020-030. AFT 03Z AREAS BKN/OVC010-015 VIS 3SM BR.

GULF OF MEXICO ADJ COAST E OF 93W/GULF OF MEXICO N OF

28N/FLORIDA W OF 85W BKN/SCT025-030 BKN/LOC OVC070-090. ISOL - SHRA.

REMAINDER GULF OF MEXICO

SCT/LOC BKN020-030. ISOL -SHRA.

FLORIDA N OF 28N E OF 85W

FEW/SCT035-040. 00Z FEW030 SCT/BKN080-100.

REMAINDER FLORIDA

FEW/SCT035-050...EXC OVER FLORIDA KEYS SCT/LOC BKN030 WITH ISOL - SHRA.

ICE AND FZ LVL...

MOD OR GREATER IN TCU/CB TOPS ABV FZ LVL.

NONE. NE OF 32N69W 26N61W LINE FZ LVL 100-120 SLOPING TO 125-145 ELSEWHERE N OF 20N AND 150-160 S OF 20N.

TURB...

MOD OR GREATER NEAR TSRA OR +TSRA. NONE.

OUTLOOK 080600-081800...

NEXT ATLANTIC COLD FRONT WILL APPROACH FORECAST AREA W OF 75W BY18Z. HIGH PRESSURE WILL REMAIN NEAR 24N/25N. OTHERWISE LITTLE CHANGE.

Using the Area Forecast

Below is an example of a Boston AIRMET Bulletin and Boston Area Forecast used for the following discussion. It may be helpful to refer to Fig. 5-3 to better visualize conditions.

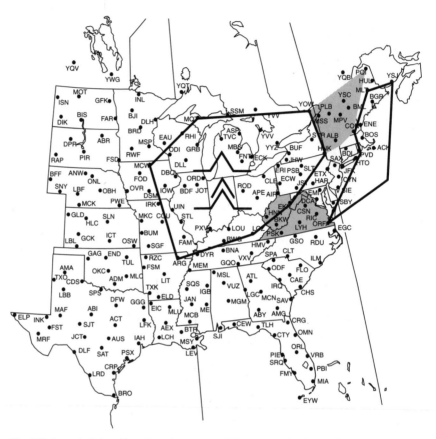

Fig. 5-3. Forecasts for distinct and fast-moving weather systems are typically more accurate than those for diffuse and slow-moving systems.

BOSZ WA 301345

AIRMET ZULU UPDT 3 FOR ICG AND FRZLVL VALID UNTIL 302000

.

ME CSTL WTRS

LGT TO LCL MOD RIME ICGIC ABV FRZLVL BTW 080 AND 150 OVER ME AND NEW ENG CSTL WTRS.

OTRW...NO SGFNT ICING EXPCD.

.

FRZLVL...50-80 ME. 80-100 NH VT MA RI CT NY LO LE OH. 100-110 NJ PA WV MD DC DE VA.

BOST WA 301345

AIRMET TANGO UPDT 3 FOR TURBC VALID UNTIL 022000

AIRMET TURBC...NY PA OH LE LO WV MD

FROM MQT TO YOW TO HNK TO EKN TO LOZ TO ARG TO MCW TO MQT

MOD TO LCL SEV TURBC 200-400. CONDS DMSHG BY 20Z.

BOSS WA 301345

AIRMET SIERRA UPDT 3 FOR IFR AND MTN OBSCN VALID UNTIL 302000

AIRMET IFR...ME NH MA RI AND CSTL WTRS

FROM MLT TO YSJ TO 150SE ACK TO ORF TO PVD TO CON TO MLT

OCNL CIG BLO 10 VIS BLO 3F. CONDS CONTG NEW ENG AND CSTL WTRS BYD 20Z THRU 02Z.

AIRMET MTN OBSCN...ME NH VT MA NY

FROM PQI TO CON TO 40SE ALB TO HNK TO YOW TO PQI

MTNS OSBCD IN CLDS. CONDS CONTG BYD 20Z IPVG BY 01Z.

OTLK VALID 2000-0200Z...MTN OBSCN WV VA

AFT 00Z MTNS OBSCD IN CLDS AND PCPN. CONTG THRU 02Z.

BOSC FA 301745

SYNOPSIS AND VFR CLDS WX

SYNOPSIS VALID UNTIL 011200

CLDS/WX VALID UNTIL 010600...OTLK VALID 010600-011200

ME NH VT MA RI CT NY LO NJ PA OH LE WV MD DC DE VA AND CSTL WTRS

.

SEE AIRMET SIERRA FOR IFR CONDS AND MTN OBSCN.

TSTMS IMPLY SEV OR GTR TURBC SEV ICG LLWS AND IFR CONDS.

NON MSL HGTS DENOTED BY AGL OR CIG.

.

SYNOPSIS...AT 18Z LOW WAS OVER LH WITH CDFNT CURVG THRU LO ERN PA CNTRL NC NRN AL BCMG STNRY TO SRN TX. BY 12Z CDFNT WILL MOVE OFF NRN AND MID ATLC CST CURVG ACRS SC NRN GA BCMG STNRY TO SRN TX.

.

ME NH

W OF MLT-CON...BKN030 BKN100 TOPS 150. AFT 01Z SCT-BKN050. OTLK...VFR.

E OF MLT-CON...OVC010-020 TOPS 150. VIS 3-5SM BR. SCT -RA. AFT 00Z SCT-BKN020 TOPS 040. VIS 3-5SM BR. OTLK...IFR CIG BR.

.

MA RI CT

CT WRN MA...BKN020-030 TOPS 060. AFT 00-03Z SKC. OCNL VIS 3-5SM BR. OTLK...IFR BR.

RI ERN MA...OVC020 TOPS 050. VIS 3-5SM BR. AFT 21-00Z SCT-BKN020. VIS 3-5SM BR. AFT 00-03Z SCT020 TOPS 040. VIS 3-5SM BR. OTLK...IFR CIG BR.

.

VT

BKN030 TOPS 080. AFT 01Z SCT040. OCNL VIS 3-5SM BR AFT 03Z. OTLK...MVFR BR.

.

NY LO

LO WRN AND NERN NY...BKN030 TOPS 060. AFT 01Z SCT040. OCNL VIS 3- 5SM BR AFT 02Z. OTLK...MVFR BR.

SERN NY...SCT-BKN030 TOPS 060. AFT 22Z SKC. AFT 02Z SKC. VIS 3-5SM BR. OTLK...IFR CIG BR.

.

NJ PA

SCT-BKN040 TOPS 060. ISOLD TSRA SRN NJ SERN PA TIL 00Z. CB TOPS FL350. VIS 3-5SM BR. AFT 00Z SKC. VIS 3-5SM BR. OTLK...MVFR BR.

.

OH LE

SCT040. AFT 00Z SKC. OCNL SCT-BKN100 WRN AND SRN PTNS OH. TOPS 150. OTLK...VFR.

.

WV

NRN 2/3...SCT050. AFT 00Z SKC. AFT 03Z SCT-BKN100 TOPS 150. VIS 3-5SM BR. OTLK...VFR BCMG MVFR CIG BR BY 10Z.

SRN 1/3...SCT-BKN050. AFT 00-03Z BKN030-040 BKN100 TOPS 180. VIS 3-5SM BR. WDLY SCT -TSRA. CB TOPS FL350. OTLK...IFR CIG TSRA BR.

.

MD DC DE VA

MD DC DE NRN VA...SCT-BKN040-050. WDLY SCT -TSRA. OCNL BKN-OVC020 CSTL SXNS. CB TOPS FL350. OTLK...MVFR CIG BR.

SRN VA...BKN040-050. WDLY SCT TSRA. OCNL OVC020 WDLY SCT TSRA ERN PTN WITH SCT SEV TSTMS. AFT 00-03Z BKN020-030. WDLY SCT -TSRA. CB TOPS FL450. OTLK...IFR CIG TSRA BR.

.

CSTL WTRS

N OF ACK...OVC010-020 TOPS 150. VIS 3-5SM BR. SCT -RA. AFT 00-03Z OVC010-020 TOPS 040. VIS 3-5SM BR. OTLK...IFR CIG BR.
S OF ACK...OVC020. VIS 3-5SM BR. WDLY SCT -TSRA. AFT 00-03Z BKN020-030 TOPS 060. OTLK...MVFR CIG.

A pilot's first task is to determine the valid time of the forecast. This Boston FA was issued on the 30th day of the month at 1745Z, becomes effective at 1800Z, and valid until the 1st at 0600Z. Old forecasts, due to late revisions or computer trouble, occasionally, remain in the system. Next, does the product cover the proposed flight. Notice the Boston FA includes Lake Erie (LE), Lake Ontario (LO), and the District of Columbia (DC). The synopsis paragraph follows the standard reference to AIRMET SIERRA, thunderstorm, and height statements. The main weather feature, a cold front forecast to move through the FA area. Notice the 18-hour valid time, through the outlook period.

Refer to AIRMET ZULU. Light to locally moderate rime icing in clouds from 8000 to 15,000 ft MSL over Maine and New England coastal waters is forecast. The forecaster does not expect extensive moderate icing. This is an example of icing that does not meet "AIRMET criteria." Otherwise, no significant icing—trace or no icing—is expected. From the freezing level paragraph we see the freezing level is expected to slope from around 5000 in northern Maine to 8000 ft in the south. This condition would be a definite consideration for aircraft without ice protection equipment.

Next, refer to AIRMET TANGO. Moderate to locally severe turbulence is forecast between 20,000 and 40,000 ft within the delineated area (see Fig. 5-3). Notice that only portions of New York and Pennsylvania are affected, with turbulence expected to diminish by 2000Z. This is an example of a condition dissipating during the forecast period. Since severe turbulence will be localized, a SIGMET has not been issued. Should a SIGMET be in effect a statement following the paragraph will refer to the advisory (...SEE SIGMET OSCAR 1 FOR SEV TURBC...). Is this the only area where significant turbulence can be expected? No, remember that thunderstorms imply moderate or greater turbulence and low-level wind shear, which are not addressed separately.

Now refer to AIRMET SIERRA. Occasional ceiling below 1000 visibilities below three in fog is forecast. The outlined section in Fig. 5-3 over New England and the coastal waters represents this area. Conditions will continue beyond 2000Z through 0200Z. The gray shaded areas of Fig. 5-3 depict mountain obscurement. The mountains of New York and New England are expected to be obscured in clouds. Here, conditions are expected to improve by 0100Z. A second mountain obscuration paragraph provides details on conditions in West Virginia and Virginia. Mountains are expected to become obscured in clouds and precipitation after 0000Z, and continue through 0200Z—the end of the outlook period. This is an example of a condition developing during the period.

Generally, advisories for IFR and mountain obscurement are synonymous. They represent low ceilings and visibilities that will preclude VFR flight within all or part of the affected area. Pilots, especially those used to flying over flat terrain, must use caution with mountain obscurement forecast. Weather reports from valley stations may indicate VFR flying conditions, but VFR flight through passes and over the mountains may be impossible. Again, it's imperative for the pilot to have a sound knowledge of terrain. When the forecast indicates the phenomena will be occasional, for example the IFR paragraph in the BOS AIRMET Bulletin, the probability of occurrence is greater than 50 percent, but expected to occur for less than half the forecast period. A forecast for occasional phenomena should not of itself warrant the cancellation of VFR flight. All available information, however, must be considered and caution exercised, with suitable alternates available—the "complete picture." The absence of a conditional term indicates the phenomena will be widespread— for example, the BOS AIRMET SIERRA mountain obscurement paragraphs. This means a greater than 50 percent probability occurring for more than half the forecast period. VFR flight probably will not be possible, but there could be areas where the phenomenon does not exist. This is not an error, but a limitation of the forecast product.

VFR CLDS-WX paragraphs describe expected weather for the forecast area. Areas are usually described using Area Designators, Appendix C. In Maine and New Hampshire west of a MLT CON line—

the mountains—BKN030 BKN100 TOPS 150 (These heights are all MSL) are expected from 1800Z until after 0100Z. With mountain peaks in the 3500 to 5000-foot range, they will be obscured as advertised in AIRMET SIERRA; where minimum en route altitudes (MEA) are above 5000, icing in clouds can be expected. After 0100Z conditions are forecast to improve to SCT-BKN050, consistent with AIRMET SIERRA. General visibilities through the period will be six miles or greater, with no significant precipitation. The outlook is VFR, but remember its definition.

East of MLT-CON line—the coastal plain—OVC010-020 TOPS 150, VIS 3-5SM BR, SCT -RA (These are again MSL), with occasional IFR conditions (AIRMET SIERRA). The forecaster expects conditions to begin to improve, but not until after 0000Z. VFR will be iffy. MEAs are lower and, with flights below 5000, ice should not be a factor. After 0000Z conditions will improve somewhat, but remain marginal to IFR. Tops will lower significantly in the coastal areas. The outlook indicates the ceilings below 1000 and visibilities below three miles in mist will persist.

Moving to the New Jersey, Pennsylvania paragraph (NJ PA), notice that isolated thunderstorms and rain showers are forecast for southern NJ and southeastern PA. Since they're expected to be isolated, circumnavigation should be possible. Although, we wouldn't want to be poking around in clouds without storm detection equipment. Under the circumstances, climbing above the lower layer where visual separation from convective activity can be maintained would be a prudent procedure. What about turbulence and icing? They're implied with any forecast of thunderstorms. The outlook, MVFR BR, indicates visibilities will be between three and five miles in mist. The ceiling? Well, greater than 3000 ft.

Refer to the Maryland, District of Columbia, Delaware, Virginia (MD DC DE VA) paragraph. Notice for southern VA the forecast indicates, OCNL OVC020 WDLY SCT TSRA ERN PTN WITH SCT SEV TSTMS. Over the eastern portion of southern VA, a chance of severe thunderstorms is expected. The outlook, IFR CIG TSRA BR, indicates ceiling less than 1000 ft, visibilities less than three in mist, rain showers, and thunderstorms.

The final paragraph forecasts conditions for the CSTL WTRS. The area is divided into north and south of Nantucket, MA (ACK).

This FA describes a distinct weather system. Notice how the AIRMET Bulletin, synopsis, and VFR clouds and weather are all tied together. FAs will not always be this detailed or consistent, but the example has provided most variables used in this product.

Both the Area Forecast and AIRMET Bulletin must be carefully reviewed to determine conditions en route.

The following case study is based on data from the 1145Z FA and the 1445Z AIRMET Bulletin. The following discussion reflects the limitations and scope of these products, which must be understood for correct interpretation and applications.

CASE STUDY

FA:

SAN JOQUIN VLY...BKN010-020 SCT-BKN120. VIS 3-5SM BR. 17-20Z BKN025-035 BKN100. TOPS FL180....

WA:

AIRMET IFR...CA

FROM 30NE CZQ TO 40SE EHF TO 40SW EHF TO 40W CZQ TO 30NE CZQ

OCNL CIGS BLW 010 VIS BLW 3SM BR. CONDS ENDG 18-20Z....

At first glance, it may seem as if these forecasts are contradictory—it did to the FSS controllers who brought it to my attention. The FA appears to predict VFR, the AIRMET IFR. Let's analyze these products. The FA forecasts conditions for the San Joaquin Valley, which consist of California's Central Valley Stockton southward. The WA forecasts conditions for the San Joaquin Valley Fresno/Madera southward. This distinction will be important.

For the San Joaquin Valley the FA predicts a greater than 50 percent probability for greater than 1/2 of the forecast period (12Z to between 17-20Z) for broken clouds based between 1000 and 2000 ft MSL. This translates to between 500-1000 and

> **CASE STUDY** (*Continued*)
> 1500-2000 ft AGL; because of terrain elevations, the lower conditions will be in the southern portion of the valley. A higher scattered to broken layer based at 12,000 ft MSL, visibilities 3-5SM in mist is also forecast. Between 17-20Z conditions are forecast to become: 2500- 3500 ft broken, 10,000 ft broken.
>
> For the southern half of the San Joaquin Valley the WA predicts a greater than 50 percent probability for less than 1/2 of the forecast period (15Z to between 18-20Z) ceilings below 1000 ft, visibilities below 3SM in mist.
>
> These forecasts are perfectly consistent within the scope and purpose of each product.

Significant weather prognostic charts

On October 27, 1997 the Significant Weather (SIGWX) Graphics Unit of the Aviation Weather Center took over the production of the 12/24-hour low-level significant weather prognoses chart and all high-level charts for the Atlantic and Pacific Oceans. The low-altitude charts provide outlook guidance for flights below 24,000 ft over the contiguous United States. They are not a substitute for a standard preflight briefing. High-altitude charts are designed to provide the en route portion of international civil aeronautical operations above 24,000 ft; these charts must be used along with any valid domestic or international weather advisories.

The 12–24 hour low-level significant weather prognostic (prog) chart is issued four times a day, valid at 0000Z, 0600Z, 1200Z, and 1800Z depending on issuance time. Because it takes approximately six hours to prepare and distribute the chart, by the time it becomes available valid times are only up to 18 hours. If a pilot calls just prior to the next issuance, only a 12-hour forecast would be available. The 12–24 hour prog consists of four panels. The two upper panels forecast significant weather from the surface to 400 mb (24,000 ft). The lower panels depict the location, intensity, and coverage of precipitation, and the location of surface features—fronts and pressure systems. Significant weather prog chart symbols are contained in Fig. 5-4.

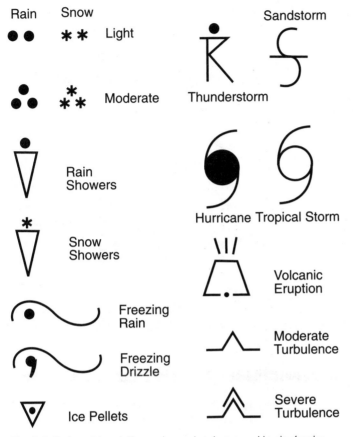

Fig. 5-4. Weather symbols on significant weather prog charts denote type and intensity of weather.

Forecast weather categories (VFR, MVFR, and IFR) have the same definitions and limitations as the area forecast outlook categories and the weather depiction chart.

Turbulence is depicted within dashed lines, with turbulence symbols indicating intensity. In Fig. 5-5 at 0000Z, over the southern Rockies, moderate turbulence is forecast below 24,000 ft MSL. Moderate to severe turbulence below 14,000 ft is expected over portions of California, Arizona, Utah, Colorado, and New Mexico. Note the turbulence symbols representing moderate and severe.

Although icing is not directly forecast, it's implied in clouds and precipitation above the freezing level. Supercooled, large drops are inferred in areas of forecast freezing precipitation. Freezing level is

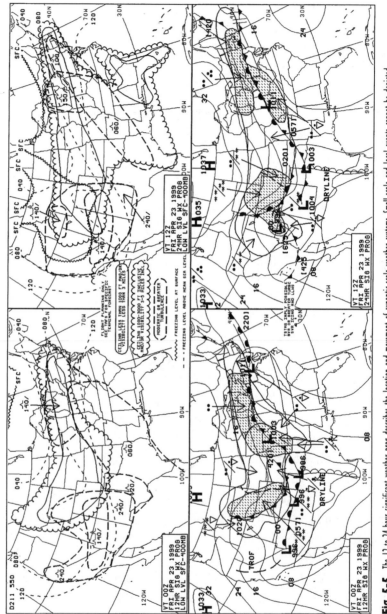

Fig. 5-5. The 12-to-24-hour significant weather prog describes the location and movement of synoptic-scale weather systems. Small-scale and local events cannot be depicted.

represented by short, dashed lines, and the freezing level at the surface denoted by a zigzag line and the contraction SFC. During the forecast period in Fig. 5-5 freezing levels range from around 4000 ft in the north to 12,000 ft in the south. In the early morning hours of April 23rd freezing temperature at the surface are expected over the northern Rockies and Great Basin.

Fronts and pressure systems use standard symbology contained in chapter 10. Central pressure is also noted. For example, in the 12Z panel the central pressure of the high over southern Canada is 1037 mb, the low over Texas is 1003 mb. Front type, intensity, and character are also depicted. Table 10-1 contains the code. For example, the frontal system in southern California [425]. This decodes as a cold front at the surface, weak, little or no change, forming or existence expected. The warm front aloft symbol in Texas is used to depict a DRYLINE, or temperature/dew point front.

Lines on the lower panels enclose areas of precipitation. Hatching indicates the precipitation is expected to cover half or more of the area. For example, in Fig. 5-5 is a large enclosed area, with an area of hatching within the overall area. In the outer-non-hatched-area precipitation is forecast over less than half the area depicted. In other words, scattered. The hatched area represents precipitation covering more than half the area, or widespread. Precipitation type and intensity are depicted using the symbols in Fig. 5-4.

In preparing this chart, forecasters cannot consider mesoscale features; the chart is a synoptic depiction. Local conditions might not be accurately portrayed. These progs tend to underestimate convective activity in the west, along with the intensity of Pacific storms and the forecaster tends to smooth over local variations due to terrain. Therefore, these charts are most useful in the Midwest and East.

The chart in Fig. 5-5 is valid at 0000Z Friday, April 23rd and 1200Z Friday, April 23rd. Be careful converting to local time, for example, 0000Z Friday translates to 5 p.m. Thursday, Pacific Daylight Time.

Let's say we're planning a flight from, Kansas City to St. Louis. Refer to the Thursday evening (00Z FRI APR 23 1999) panel of Fig 5- 5. A surface low and associated stationary front are forecast over Missouri.

MVFR ceilings and visibilities in widespread light to moderate rain and thunderstorms are expected. Moderate turbulence is forecast below 14,000 ft, with the freezing level high at 12,000 ft.

VFR flight may be possible and an IFR flight below 12,000 ft should not have to contend with icing. However, both VFR and IFR flights will have to deal with thunderstorms. With organized weather systems and thunderstorms, it does not appear that flight above the clouds for light aircraft will be possible. Without storm detection equipment, an IFR flight does not appear practical. Although VFR ceilings and visibilities are forecast, avoiding thunderstorms will be chancy.

Refer to the Friday morning (12Z FRI APR 23 1999) panel of Fig 5-5. The low-pressure system and associated front are forecast to move eastward. MVFR is still forecast, with scattered rain or rain showers. No significant turbulence is expected; the freezing level remains around 12,000 ft. Both VFR and IFR operations appear practical under these conditions. However, a flight decision must also be based on our personal minimums. More about personal minimums in chapter 11.

Strictly a surface prog, the 36–48 hour significant weather prog is issued twice daily, valid at 0000Z and 1200Z. By the time the chart becomes available, valid times only provide a 30- and 42-hour forecast. Should a pilot call a Flight Service Station or download the product just prior to the next issuance, only a 30-hour forecast would be available.

Refer to Fig. 5-6, the 0000Z, and 1200Z Saturday forecast. The front is forecast to continue to move slowly southward as high pressure builds into the upper Midwest. Scattered rain and rain showers are expected to persist through the forecast period.

What can be concluded about clouds, visibilities, turbulence, and icing? Drawing on our knowledge, we can make the following assumptions. High pressure generally means fair weather. Weak pressure gradients and the absence of convective activity indicate no significant turbulence. These conditions are not conducive to icing. However, conditions could be right for extensive areas of radiation fog causing IFR weather.

Using progs, remember the limitations on aviation forecasts, especially timing. Then, when requesting outlooks, review issuance

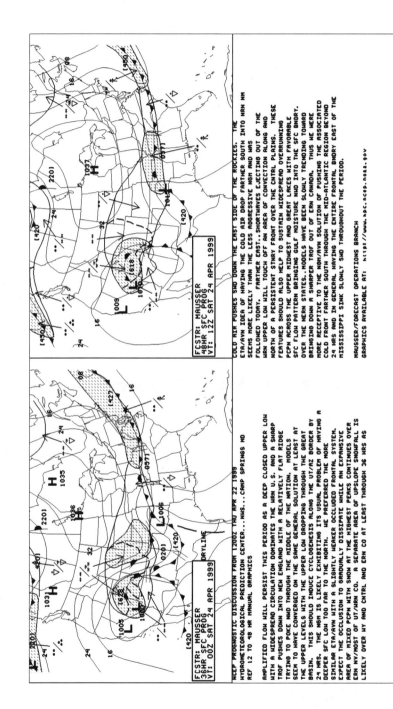

Fig. 5-6. The 36-to-48-hour significant weather prog only provides the location and movement of weather systems and areas of precipitation.

and valid times to obtain the latest forecasts. Keep in mind that these forecast progs are not available beyond about forty-two hours.

The High-Altitude Significant Weather Prog

The high-altitude significant weather prog provides a graphic view of forecast weather from 400 mbs (millibars) to about 70 mbs, approximately 24,000 through 60,000 ft. All heights are pressure altitudes (flight levels). These charts depict:

- Thunderstorms and cumulonimbus clouds
- Tropical cyclones
- Severe squall lines
- Moderate or severe turbulence
- Moderate or severe icing
- Widespread sandstorms or dust storms
- Surface fronts
- Tropopause height
- Jet streams
- Volcanic eruptions

Charts are valid at 0000Z, 0600Z, 1200Z, and 1800Z.

Scalloped lines enclose areas of forecast cumulonimbus development, divided into three categories: isolated (ISOL) less than one-eighth coverage, occasional (OCNL) one-eighth to four-eighths coverage, and frequent (FRQ) five-eighths to eight-eighths coverage. Cumulonimbus clouds imply hail, and moderate or greater turbulence and icing. Bases and tops are shown by numerical figures below and above a short horizontal line. Bases below 24,000 ft are indicated by XXX below the line. For example, in Fig. 5-7, through northeast Mexico, Texas, and Louisiana, the forecast indicates an area of isolated (less than one-eighth coverage), embedded cumulonimbus with tops to 42,000 ft, bases below 24,000 ft (XXX). Clear Air Turbulence, not associated with cumulonimbus clouds, is indicated by a dashed line containing a turbulence intensity symbol and forecast height. In Fig. 5-7, off of Chile, South America, moderate turbulence is expected between 28,000 and 40,000 ft.

The expected location of jet streams is indicated by long black lines. Figure 5-7 implies the turbulence off Chile is due to a jet stream at 40,000 ft (FL400), with a core speed of 90 knots, indicated by one flag and four barbs (each flag represent 50 knots, each barb 10 knots). The double-hatched line to the right or left of the maximum speed indicates a change in speed of 20 knots. For example, the jet stream over the North Atlantic has a core speed of 90 knots, then increases to 120 knots east of Newfoundland.

The chart also contains the expected height of the tropopause—the boundary between the troposphere and stratosphere. The height of the tropopause over the West Coast is indicated by numerals enclosed in a box and forecast around 50,000 ft off northern California. A five-sided polygon indicates areas of high or low tropopause heights. For example, in Fig. 5-7 off the southern California coast is a high point in the tropopause, forecast to be at 54,000 ft.

Significant frontal boundaries are depicted using standard symbols, with system movement indicated by an arrow and speed printed by the arrowhead. For example, the cold front in the central Mississippi Valley depicted in Fig. 5-7, is expected to move to the south at 10 knots.

The names of tropical cyclones are entered next to the symbol. In Fig. 5-7, hurricane Danielle is located off the Florida coast, tropical storm Bonnie off New Brunswick, and tropical depression Howard in the central Pacific.

Severe squall lines are depicted within areas of cumulonimbus clouds by the symbol: - V - V - V. Widespread sandstorms or dust storms are enclosed by scalloped lines, labeled with the appropriate symbol.

Volcanic activity is indicated by a trapezoidal figure depicting an eruption. The symbol and any known information concerning the name of the volcano, latitude and longitude, the date and time of the first eruption, and a reminder to check SIGMETs will be included in the legend of the chart. Figure 5-7 shows the Popocatepetl eruption in central Mexico.

The chart is often an excellent place to begin planning a high altitude flight (above FL 240). For example, a pilot might plan to

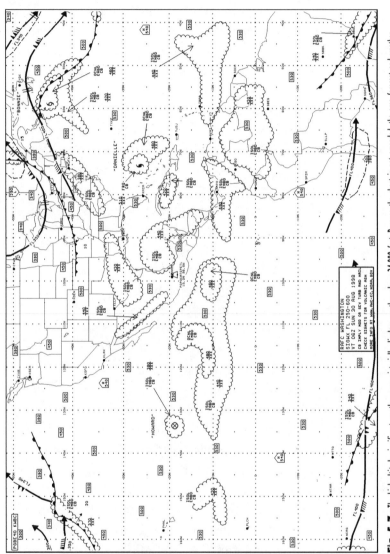

Fig. 5-7. The high-altitude significant weather prog pictorially displays weather above 24,000 feet. Because the chart is not amended, the area forecast and weather advisories must be consulted to complete the forecast weather picture.

follow the jet stream to take advantage of tail winds. If turbulence, for example a lifeguard flight, were a significant factor, the pilot might plan a route to avoid wind shear turbulence. A flight from east to west might also select a route to avoid maximum jet stream head winds. The chart can also be used to determine areas of cumulonimbus, cloud tops, and tropopause heights. If aircraft equipment (storm detection equipment) or performance does not allow the pilot to climb above thunderstorms, the pilot may wish to avoid areas where coverage is expected to be occasional or frequent. The pilot should note the expected height of the tropopause. If thunderstorms develop, the isothermal layer of the tropopause caps all except severe activity.

Pilots, like FSS briefers, can use the chart for the en route portion of a high-altitude weather briefing, but pilots, as well as briefers, must not substitute the chart for the area forecast and weather advisories. The chart is not amended and severe weather might develop that is not depicted. The area forecast is also needed to provide weather details for climbout and descent.

Additional data related to the jet stream may be obtained from the domestic tropopause wind and wind shear prog. This two-panel chart depicts the forecast winds at the tropopause, and tropopause height, and vertical wind shear. An example is contained in Fig. 5- 8.

The left panel in Fig. 5-8 forecasts winds at the tropopause. Wind speed is shown by isotachs at 20 knots intervals. Areas of wind speeds between 70 and 110 knots, and between 150 and 190 knots are shaded to help locate the jet core. Horizontal wind shear can be determined from the spacing of the isotachs. Expect moderate or greater turbulence when winds exceed 18 knots per 150 miles. In Fig. 5-8 significant horizontal wind shear turbulence is indicated north of the jet core over the eastern Pacific and western states, and again north of the jet core off eastern Canada.

The right panel in Fig. 5-8 depicts tropopause height and vertical wind shear. Heights are pressure altitudes or flight level (F450, 45,000 ft). Vertical wind sheer is in knots per 1000 ft and depicted by dashed lines at 2 knot intervals. Wind shear is averaged through a layer from about 8000 ft below to 4000 ft above the tropopause. Vertical wind

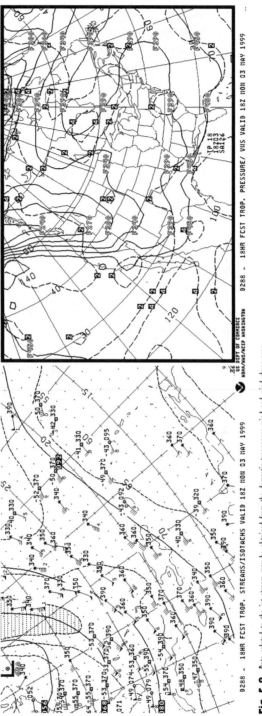

Fig. 5-8. Data related to the jet stream may be obtained from the domestic tropopause wind and wind shear prog.

shear can be determined directly from the dashed lines in Fig. 5-8. The vertical shear critical for probable turbulence is from 4 to 6 knots per 1000 ft. This value is shown from southeast Colorado to east of Florida, and associated with the jet over eastern Canada.

The National Weather Service produces an experimental Volcanic Ash Forecast Transport and Dispersion chart (VAFTED). Figure 5-9 contains and example.

Each complete chart consists of 8 panels. The 4 panels in any column are for a single valid time after eruption. In the example valid times are 12Z 19 APR 96 (eruption + 12H) and 00Z 20 APR 96 (eruption + 24H). Individual panels are for layers applicable to aviation operations and are identified at the side of a panel with upper and lower flight levels (FL) in hundreds of ft. In the example: surface to FL200, FL200 to FL350, and FL350 to FL550, the bottom panel is a composite from the surface to FL550. For each column, the forecast valid time separates the upper three panels from the composite panel. Volcano eruption information is at the lower left. A description of the input meteorology is at the lower right with a message to SEE CURRENT SIGMET FOR WARNING AREA. The visual ash cloud symbol and run description are at the lower center. Upper half and lower half panels are included for viewing detail. Volcanic ash cloud charts for Hazards Alert Volcanoes are always listed first. Charts for volcanoes of interest (TEST- volcanoes) will then be listed. Only upper half and lower half panels are included for TEST-volcanoes. TEST-volcanoes are usually updated on a daily basis. (If the same volcano is listed first as a Hazards Alert Volcano and then below as a TEST-volcano, the Hazards Alert Volcano listed first takes precedence.)

There's no question that the FA has improved. The NWS's decision to consolidate in Kansas City and the commitment of Aviation Weather Center forecasters has resulted in standardization and consistency. The FA is a valuable and useful tool as long as pilots, briefers, and dispatchers understand its purpose, format, conditional terms, and limitations. The forecasters at AWC request positive user feedback. That is, constructive criticism of their products. But, they need to know the date and time of the occurrence,

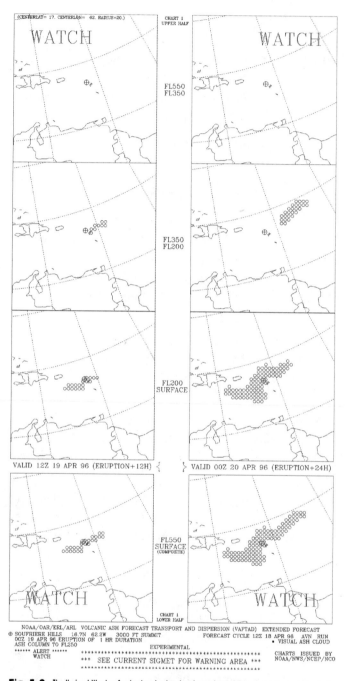

Fig. 5-9. The National Weather Service has developed and experimental Volcanic Ash Forecast Transport and Dispersion chart (VAFTED) to assist pilots in avoiding ash hazards.

and specific user comments. These can be sent to AWC via their Internet site or writing to:

Aviation Weather Center

7220 NW 101st Terr., Rm105

Kansas City, MO 64153-2371

Take, for example, the following case study.

> ### CASE STUDY
>
> An AIRMET Bulletin forecast IFR conditions in stratus and fog for the San Joaquin Valley. Rather than forecasting stratus tops, which were only about 2000 ft, and a high layer based about 12,000 ft in the area forecast, it simply read ST BR TOPS FL200. This would indicate that VFR flight was not possible below 20,000 ft! The problem? There was about two miles of clear air between the tops of the stratus and the next layer. We had a chat about this and it hasn't occurred since.

As promised from chapter 1: Never rely on a single piece of data. The FA is only one product, one piece of the "complete picture." Localized conditions may not be included. Flight decisions should never be based solely on this or any other product. The FA must be used along with all available information. Forecast limitations cannot be overemphasized along with using all available sources.

"Whatever may be the progress of the sciences, never will observers who are trustworthy and careful of their reputations venture to forecast the state of the weather."

Dominique Argo, French Astronomer-Physics (1786-1853)

CHAPTER 6

TWEB Route Forecasts

TWEB route forecasts were developed as scripts for the FAA's Transcribed Weather Broadcast (TWEB) and Pilots Automatic Telephone Weather Answering Service (PATWAS). With few exceptions, TWEB broadcasts over low-frequency radio beacons and very high-frequency omnidirectional radio ranges (VOR) have been decommissioned. TWEBs may be used for the en route-forecast portion of the Telephone Information Briefing Service (TIBS). These forecasts can also be used during Flight Service Station weather briefings. Telephone numbers for PATWAS and TIBS can be found in the Telephone Numbers section of the *Airport/Facility Directory*. As of this writing, TWEBs are not available through DUATs or other commercial weather providers. TWEBs are, however, available from the Aviation Weather Center's Internet page (www.awc-kc.noaa.gov) and many local Weather Forecast Office sites. TWEB route numbers and locations are contained in Appendix B, Report and Forecast Locations.

Like most forecast products, TWEBs have been revised over the years, and issuance and valid times standardized. The most recent revisions occurred in 1997 when the FAA and NWS eliminated many routes in the southeastern United States. TWEBs are issued four times a day and are valid for 12 hours, as shown in Table 6-1.

Table 6-1 TWEB issuance times and valid periods

ISSUANCE TIME (Z)	VALID PERIOD (Z)
0200	0200-1400
0800	0800-2000
1400	1400-0200
2000	2000-0800

TWEB forecasts are divided into route forecasts and local vicinity forecasts. TWEB route forecasts are valid for a corridor 25 nm either side of the route centerline, and a 25-nm radius semicircle around the end points. Local vicinity forecasts are, typically, valid for a 50-nm radius, except for certain irregularly shaped areas. Additionally, designated Weather Forecast Offices write a TWEB synopsis.

Refer to the 420 TWEB route forecast heading below for the following discussion.

420 TWEB 061402 KOAK-KACV. ALL HGTS MSL XCP CIGS.

TWEB route forecasts are numbered as shown in Appendix B. Following the route numbers are the valid period and the route end anchor points. In the example this is the 420 TWEB route, valid on the sixth day of the month from 14Z until 02Z, route end anchor points are Oakland and Arcata in California (420 TWEB 061402 KOAK-KACV). This is followed by a height statement similar to that used on the area forecast: All heights mean sea level except ceilings.

The loss of reporting stations has caused revisions to the TWEB network resulting in the issuance of certain routes on a part-time basis. In such cases the notation NIL TWEB is used.

426 TWEB 250520 TSP MTNS SOLEDAD-CAJON-BNG PASSES AND ADJ MTNS. NIL TWEB.

This evening issuance of the 426 route, for the Tehachapi Mountains, Soledad, Cajon, Banning Passes and adjacent mountains will be delayed due to lack of observations. Additionally, amendments might not be available for selected routes, which will contain a remark, (NO AMDTS AFT 04Z). Significant changes can occur without an amendment, so this serves the same purpose as NOSPL on METAR. It's a warning that caution must be exercised, especially during marginal and deteriorating conditions.

Pilots, FSS controllers, and forecasters have been instrumental in revising TWEB routes. For example, the 420 route at one time forecast conditions from Concord to Arcata to Crescent City, California (KCCR-

KACV-KCEC). However, with the loss of 24-hour observations at Crescent City and only part-time observations at Concord, the forecast was suspended during the night. But, by changing the anchors—end points on the route—to Oakland and Arcata (KOAK-KACV), with 24-hour observations, the route once more became available full-time. Other routes in the area have also been revised, as a direct result of pilot input. This is an excellent example of how pilots, FSS controllers, and forecasters, working together, can improve the system. In recent years automated weather observations have almost eliminated this type of problem.

Synopsis

The synopsis contains a brief description of fronts, pressure systems, and local climate or terrain factors affecting the routes, valid for the same period as the route forecasts. The TWEB synopsis often contains more detail than is possible in the area forecast. Therefore, the TWEB synopsis might be of more value describing local conditions. More detail is possible because the TWEB synopsis only covers about one-fifth the area of the FA. Refer to Appendix B for TWEB synopses locations.

LAX SYNS 191402 UPR RDG ALG W CST WITH NLY FLO ALF. SFC HI CONTS TO BLD OVER GT BASIN FOR CONTG SANTA ANA CONDS.

This Los Angeles (LAX) synopsis covers the routes issued by the Los Angeles WFO. An upper level ridge is along the west coast with a northerly flow aloft. Surface high pressure continues to build over the Great Basin—the high plateau generally consisting of Nevada, Utah, and southern Idaho—for continuing Santa Ana conditions— strong, sometimes warm, northeasterly winds over Southern California.

The detail of a TWEB synopsis depends on the weather pattern.

ATL SYNS 302008 STNRY FNT NR MYR-ABY-PAM. HI PRES CNTRD OH DRFTG SEWD.

This Atlanta (ATL) synopsis describes a stationary front from Myrtle Beach, South Carolina (MYR) to Albany, Georgia (ABY) to Panama City, Florida (PAM). High pressure centered over Ohio is drifting southeastward. A more complex weather system is reflected in a longer synopsis.

IND SYNS 042008 CD FNT XTNDS FRM NRN LK ERIE THRU CNTRL OH INTO NRN AL. WK TROF EXTNDS FRM SFC LO SW LWR MI THRU W CNTRL IN. UPPR LVL LOW OVER NRN IL WL BRNG SCT TRW MAINLY OVR WRN AND NRN RTES THIS AFTN AND EVE. PRZYBYLINSKI

In this Indianapolis synopsis a cold front extends from northern Lake Erie through central Ohio into northern Alabama. A weak trough extends from a surface low in southwest Lower Michigan through west central Indiana. The upper level low over northern Illinois will bring scattered rain showers and thunderstorms mainly over the western and northern routes this afternoon and evening. The synopsis was prepared by Przybylinski.

> **CASE STUDY**
> Pilots using the Internet will have to contact an FSS for clarification of contractions or phrases they do not understand or are not decoded through the systems decode function. One evening I had a pilot call the FSS with such a question. He didn't understand the last word of the synopsis. I explained it was the name of the meteorologist who wrote the forecast.

Earlier it was mentioned how personal comments sometimes get into weather products.

SFO SYNS 091402 SFC HI PRES OFSHR WITH LWR PRES OVER INTR CA. THIS IS MY LAST SET OF TWEBS.....EVER. SHORTY THOMAS.

On one synopsis the forecaster signed his name: SENYOR CHEWBACCA. Then, every once in a while something gets transmitted that shouldn't have.

SFO SYNS 032121 THE QUICK BROWN FOX JUMPED OVER THE LAZY DOG BECAUSE THERE WAS NO WEATHER OF ANY MERIT TO TALK ABOUT.

I'll leave the names off this one.

Significant Clouds and Weather

TWEBs use the same terminology and contractions as the area forecast. Forecasts contain significant clouds and weather, with significant defined as phenomena affecting at least 10 percent of a route, or in the forecaster's judgment important to flight planning.

In the body of the forecast all time references are UTC, abbreviated Z. The forecast is in the following order: locations, time, conditions. Conditions may be modified using the conditional terms in Table 6-2.

TWEB forecasts consist of:

- Surface winds
- Surface Visibility
- Weather and obstructions to visibility
- Sky condition
- Mountain obscurement
- Nonthunderstorm low-level wind shear

Sustained surface winds are normally forecast when expected to be 25 knots or greater. Format is the same as used on METAR and TAF. For example, SFC WND 34025G35KT (surface winds 340 degrees at 25 gusting to 35 knots). Wind gust associated with thunderstorms may also be included (SFC WND G40KT). The lack of a wind forecast only implies sustained speeds less than 25 knots over 90 percent of the forecast area.

Table 6-2 TWEB route forecast conditional terms

TERM	CONTRACTION	DEFINITION
Isolated	ISOLD	Single cells or localized conditions (No percentage), implies circumnavigable.
Widely scattered or local	WDLY SCT/LCL	Less than 25% or area/route affected.
Scattered or areas	SCT/AREA	25% to 54% of area/route affected.
Numerous or widespread	NMRS/WDSPRD	More than 54% of area/route affected.

Surface visibilities are always included. To indicate unrestricted visibility P6SM is used (greater than 6 statute miles). Care is taken to avoid crossing categories in the forecast—IFR-MVFR, or IFR-VFR, and so on.

Significant weather is included using standard weather contractions described in chapter 1. Obstructions to visibility are included when visibility is expected to be less than 6 ml.

Cloud heights are based on a standard reference: ALL HGTS MSL XCP CIGS (all heights mean sea level except ceilings) or ALL HGTS AGL XCP TOPS (all heights above ground level except tops). The use of AGL and CIGS are normally limited to layers within 4000 ft of the surface. TWEBs were basically a low-altitude forecast—below 15,000 to 18,000 ft. That no longer necessarily applies, but forecasters emphasize cloud conditions below 12,000 ft. With no clouds, or scattered clouds above approximately 12,000 ft, the forecaster might use the phrase NO SGFNT CLDS/WX (no significant clouds or weather); this translates as any clouds present should be easily circumnavigable. Like other reports and forecasts sky cover used standard contractions (SKC, FEW, SCT, BKN, OVC). Again, the forecaster will attempt to avoid crossing categorical boundaries. CLR BLO 120 or AOA BKN120 may be used based on automated observations when the forecaster considers them representative for the route.

When forecast, tops will normally only be included for layers with tops below 15,000 ft. Like the FA, for multiple or merging layers, that would not permit VFR flight between layers, only the top of the highest layer appears. However, because of the local nature of the product, tops are often more specific and, therefore, useful. Cloud tops may also be indirectly specified. For example, CIGS BKN020 OBSCG TRRN BLO 030.... Cloud tops are expected to be 3000 ft.

Mountain obscurement has been added (MTNS OBSCD ABV..., MTN RDGS OBSCD, or ALL PASSES OBSCD), and geographical features might be specified (TSP-Tehachapi-MTNS, CSTL MTNS). Because of the local nature of the forecast, not all locations appear on the area designators maps in Appendix C. Pilots unfamiliar with locations on TWEB forecasts will have to consult an FSS.

Nonconvective low-level wind shear is included when expected. The extent of coverage will be included.

Icing and turbulence information are not included in TWEB forecasts. This information is available from appropriate weather advisories.

The following is the complete 420 TWEB previously introduced.

420 TWEB 061402 KOAK-KACV. ALL HGTS MSL XCP CIGS. KOAK-KUKI P6SM SCT015 AREAS CIGS BKN015...AFT 20Z P6SM SKC-FEW250. KUKI-KACV P6SM SCT020 BKN040 LCL 5SM -SHRA BR CIGS BKN020 MTNS OBSCD TOPS BLO 080...AFT 20Z P6SM SCT-BKN040 BKN150

The route forecast begins with the segment from Oakland to Ukiah: Visibility unrestricted; 1500 ft MSL scattered, areas of ceilings 1500 ft broken; after 20Z conditions improving to clear to a few clouds at 15,000 ft.

The forecast for the segment from Ukiah to Arcata: Visibility unrestricted; 2000 ft MSL scattered, 4000 ft MSL broken; local areas of visibility 5 ml in light rain showers and mist, with ceilings 2000 ft broken, mountains obscured, tops below 8000 ft MSL; after 20Z 4000 ft MSL scattered to broken, 15,000 ft broken.

> **CASE STUDY**
>
> As an FSS supervisor, I counsel specialists to keep briefings clear and concise. One area of verbiage is high, thin cirroform clouds; all cirroform clouds are high! But leave it to the National Weather Service when sure enough, one day I find 426 TWEB...HI THIN CIFM CLDS. What can you do?

The length and detail of TWEB forecasts vary widely. Some are one-liners, others take up a half of a page. Just try getting that and a half-dozen more like it on a three-minute tape for the broadcast and you get some idea why FSS specialists speak so fast.

Local Vicinity Forecasts

Local vicinity forecasts have been developed to cover metropolitan areas; locations are contained in Appendix C. They normally cover a radius of 50 nm.

358 TWEB 061402 PGTSND WITHIN 25NM RDS KSEA. ALL HGTS
MSL XCP CIGS. P6SM SCT050 BKN100 OVC200...17Z P6SM -RA
SCT025 OVC040...19Z P6SM -RA SCT-BKN015 BKN025 OVC040...LCL
VIS 3-5SM -RA...21Z P6SM - SHRA SCT-BKN030 BKN050.VC KPAE AFT
21Z AREAS VIS 3-5SM -RA CIGS BKN-OVC009.

This is an example of the Seattle local vicinity forecast. It covers the Puget Sound area within a 25-nm radius of the Seattle-Tacoma (KSEA) airport.

Exceptions to the 50-mile radius occur in Southern California and Arizona where large, irregular, homogeneous geographical areas exist. These routes are depicted in Fig. 6-1. The 431 TWEB covers the Los Angeles Basin, from the San Fernando Valley along the San Gabriel and San Bernardino Mountains to Hemet, and back to Santa Ana. The 432 Route from Santa Ana to San Diego also predicts conditions for the adjacent mountains—shown in gray in Fig. 6-1. The 426 Route forecasts conditions over the Tehachapi Mountains, and mountains and passes north and east of Los Angeles—shown in gray in Fig. 6-1. This includes a specific forecast for the SOLEDAD, CAJON, and BNG (Banning) PASSES. The 429 Route includes the Southern California deserts, south of a Palm Springs-Needles line, and the 425 route the southwestern Arizona deserts south of a Phoenix-Needles line—shown in gray in Fig. 6-1.

Amendment Criteria

Table 6-3 contains TWEB amendment criteria. When phenomena occurs, is expected to develop, or is no longer anticipated, an amendment will be issued. Amendments are also required for thunderstorms and low-level wind shear. Routes will also normally be amended when trends indicate, in the forecaster's judgment, that the forecast will be substantially in error or unrepresentative. FSS controllers make inquiries when discrepancies develop, or significant differences occur between FA and TWEB forecasts. Amendments can originate in this manner. Pilots have no direct way of resolving FA and TWEB forecast discrepancies. Their only option would be to consult with the Flight Service Station.

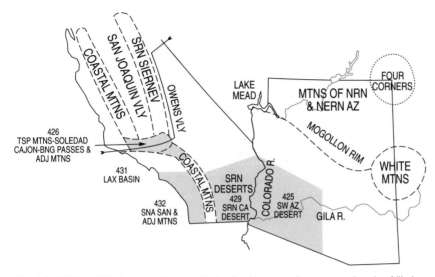

Fig. 6-1. TWEB local vicinity forecast normally covers a 50-mile radius of large metropolitan areas, except in southern California and southwest Arizona where large, irregular homogeneous geographical areas exist.

Forecasters consider issuance times in the decision to amend. Because it takes time to write and distribute an amendment, if the next issuance is in less than two hours, the forecaster might elect to delay and issue the new forecast, rather than amend. As can be seen from Table 6-3, amendments are directed at low-altitude changes. If these criteria are not met, the forecast is considered accurate, and will not be amended.

Using the TWEB Route Forecast

Flight Service Station controllers in the western third of the United States use TWEB forecasts more often than in other parts of the country. This is due to the effect of terrain on weather. Often the TWEB is more representative because it covers a smaller area in more detail than is possible with the area forecast. With the Internet these TWEB forecasts are becoming more available to pilots. Pilots should not overlook this valuable, but underused product.

Below are examples of the San Francisco area forecast synopsis and Seattle TWEB synopsis for the same period.

Table 6-3 TWEB forecast amendment criteria

CEILING		VISIBILITY	
With a forecast of:	Amend if:	With a forecast of:	Amend if:
<3000 ft	>3000 ft	<5 ml	>5 ml
≥3000 ft	≤3000 ft	≥5 ml	<5 ml
3000 to 1000 ft	>1000 ft	3 to 5 ml	>3 ml
>1000 ft	≤1000 ft	>3 ml	≤3 ml

SYNOPSIS AND VFR CLDS/WX

SYNOPSIS VALID UNTIL 070500 CLDS/WX VALID UNTIL 062300...

OTLK VALID 062300-070500 WA OR CA AND CSTL WTRS.

SEE AIRMET SIERRA FOR IFR CONDS AND MTN OBSCN.

TS IMPLY SEV OR GTR TURB SEV ICE LLWS AND IFR CONDS.

NON MSL HGTS DENOTED BY AGL OR CIG..

SYNOPSIS...AT 10Z CDFNT WAS OFF WA OR CST. BY 05Z CDFNT WILL LIE FROM XTRM NRN ID TO NWRN NV. ASSOCD UPR TROF OFFSHR WILL MOV TO WA OR..

SEA SYNS 061402 CDFNT OFSHR RCHG WA CSTLN ARND 17Z...KBLI-KSEA-KPDX LN 19Z-21Z...IDAHO BDR NR 02Z. SWLY FLOW ALF. AMS MOIST STBL AHD OF FNT WRN WA...STBL WITH INCRG MID/HI LVL MSTR ERN WA AFT 18Z. VERY COLD/UNSTBL AMS MOVG OVR WA BHND FNT WITH PSCZ DVLPG VC KPAE AFT 20Z. OUTLOOK 02Z-12Z UPR LVL TROF OFSHR RCHG CSTLN ARND 12Z.SWLY FLOW ALF CONTG. AMS MOIST/UNSTBL. PSCZ DSIPTG 06Z-10Z. DF

The FA reports a cold front, with an associated upper trough, offshore moving through Washington and Oregon. The TWEB synopsis reports the front reaching the Washington coastline around 17Z, a Bellingham, Seattle, Portland line between 19Z and 21Z, and the Idaho border near 02Z. This is certainly more precise and detailed than the FA. There is a southwesterly flow aloft. The air mass is moist, stable ahead of the front in western Washington, and stable with increasing mid- to high-level moisture over eastern Washington after

18Z. A very cold and unstable air mass is moving over Washington behind the front with the Puget Sound Convergence Zone (PSCG) developing near Paine after 20Z.

PUGET SOUND CONVERGENCE ZONE

According to Brad Colman, Seattle-Tacoma National Weather Service:

"A wind-borne rain band often keeps Seattle wet. When a west wind blows into Washington state and across Puget Sound, Seattle or one of its suburbs more often than not has a cloudy and rainy day. But the whole area doesn't get soaked. Typically, a narrow band of clouds and rain often parks over one place while a neighboring locale remains dry, sometimes sunny. Only those places that fall victim to the Puget Sound convergence zone stay wet."

Since TWEBs are issued two hours after terminal aerodrome forecasts (TAF), an outlook may be included to coincide with the end of the TAF valid time. This has been done with the Seattle TWEB synopsis. The outlook (02Z-12Z) forecasts the upper level trough offshore reaching the coastline around 12Z, the southwesterly flow aloft continuing, the air mass remaining moist and unstable, and the PSCZ dissipating between 06Z and 10Z. What about the letters DF? In this case they are the forecaster's initials.

The considerable difference between FA and TWEB synopsizes will not always be this extreme. But, the example dramatically shows how a local synopsis can paint a much more detailed, specific picture of the weather situation.

Below is an excerpt from the SFO FA for Washington state. Figure 6-2 graphically compares and contrasts the areas covered by the FA and the TWEB routes.

SFOC FA 061045

WA CASCDS WWD

CSTL SXNS...SCT050 BKN100. 12-15Z BKN015-030 OVC060. OCNL VIS 3-5SM RA. TOPS FL200. OTLK...MVFR CIG.

INTR SXNS...SCT-BKN120. 14-18Z BKN020-030 OVC060. OCNL VIS 3-5SM RA. TOPS FL200. OTLK...MVFR CIG..

208

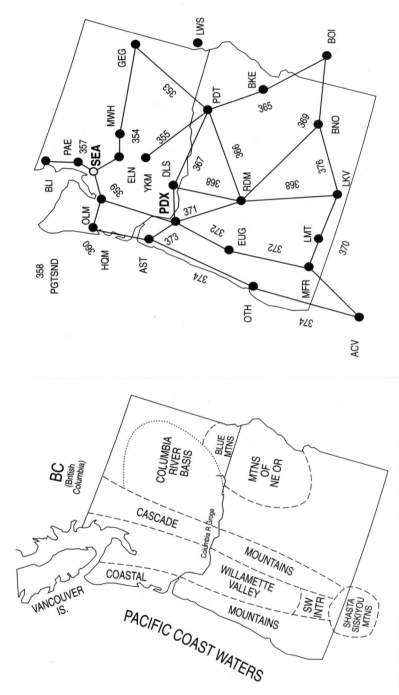

Fig. 6-2. TWEB forecasts often contain more detail than is possible in the FA, although they are usually perfectly consistent within the scope of each project.

WA E OF CASCD

WRN PTN...SCT140. CI ABV. 15Z BKN120. 20Z SCT-BKN060 BKN100.
ISOL SHRA. TOPS FL200. OTLK...VFR.

ERN PTN...SKC OR SCT CI. 15Z SCT140. 18Z SCT080 BKN120. 22Z
SCT- BKN060 BKN100. ISOL SHRA. TOPS FL200. OTLK...VFR SHRA..

The forecaster has divided the area west of the Cascades into
coastal sections and interior sections, east of the cascades into
western and eastern portions. The 359 TWEB, Seattle-Olympia-
Portland route corresponds to the interior sections (INTR SXNS) of the
FA. The 353 TWEB, Spokane-Pendelton route corresponds to the
eastern portion (ERN PTN) of the FA.

359 TWEB 061402 KSEA-KOLM-KPDX. ALL HGTS MSL XCP CIGS.
KSEA-KTDO P6SM SCT050 BKN100 OVC200...17Z P6SM -RA SCT025
OVC040...19Z P6SM - RA SCT-BKN015 BKN025 OVC040...LCL VIS 3-
5SM -RA...21Z P6SM -SHRA SCT-BKN030 BKN050. KTDO-KPDX P6SM
SCT100 BKN200...16Z P6SM SCT- BKN040 BKN100 OVC200...LCL -
RA...20Z P6SM -RA SCT-BKN025 OVC040...00Z P6SM -SHRA SCT025
BKN040.

353 TWEB 061402 KGEG-KPDT. ALL HGTS MSL XCP CIGS. P6SM
SCT150 SCT- BKN250...17Z-24Z P6SM SCT080 BKN200...AFT 00Z
P6SM SCT-BKN070-080 BKN200 WITH SCT -SHRA.

The TWEB forecaster has further subdivided the 359 TWEB area into
the leg from Seattle to Toledo and Toledo to Portland. To help visualize
expected conditions Table 6-4 breaks down the forecasts into visibility,
sky condition, and weather for two specific times, 14Z and 19Z.

CASE STUDY

Among the various opportunities that I have had with the FAA
was to serve as an expert witness. The plaintiff's attorney was
quite perplexed that I testified that different forecasts for the
same area were essentially the same although they were not
identical. The fact is different forecasts may appear to be
substantially different, without any significant operational impact.
Weather forecasting is not an exact science.

Table 6-4 Area forecast/TWEB comparison

14Z	Area Forecast	TWEB SEA-TDO	TWEB TDO-PDX
Visibility	P6SM	P6SM	P6SM
Sky Condition	SCT-BKN120 TOPS FL200	SCT050 BKN100 OVC200	SCT100 BKN200
Weather	NIL	NIL	NIL
19Z			
Visibility	OCNL 3-5SM	LCL 3-5SM	P6SM
Sky Condition	BKN020-030 OVC060 TOPS FL200	SCT-BKN015 BKN025 OVC040	SCT-BKN040 BKN100 OVC200
Weather	OCNL RA	–RA	LCL –RA

Back to Table 6-4. At the first time period, 14Z, both visibility and weather are the same for each forecast. Although sky condition appears at first glance to be very different, there is not any significant operation difference. Both forecast midlevel scattered to broken clouds. The SEA-TDO TWEB does predict a local scattered layer at 5000 ft. This should have no significant impact on either VFR or IFR operations.

The second time, 19Z, predicts lowering conditions with both forecasts. The TWEB forecast, because of its scope, can better define the time that conditions will deteriorate. Otherwise, again, forecasts for visibility, sky conditions, and weather are essentially the same.

We come to the same conclusions reviewing the ERN PTN and the FA and the 353 TWEB route forecast. The visibility forecast is the same (P6SM). The FA forecasts lowering clouds and precipitation earlier than the TWEB. Since the FA must cover a larger area than the TWEB, and the TWEB route is in the extreme eastern portion of the FA area, this is perfectly consistent. Both forecasts accurately represent expected weather conditions with the scope and purpose of each product.

TWEBs do not directly forecast turbulence or icing. However, turbulence, and strong updrafts and downdrafts are implied by weather associated with these phenomena. For example, strong winds and mountain wave activity indicate turbulence. Icing can be expected above the freezing level where visible moisture exists, or in areas of freezing precipitation. Like the FA, thunderstorms imply severe or greater turbulence and icing, and low-level wind shear. Specific forecasts for turbulence and icing must be obtained from the FA and weather advisories.

TWEB routes and synopses often provide more precise timing and detail than is possible in the FA. They provide additional specific information on visibility, surface winds, timing, and local conditions that is not possible in the FA. But, like other forecast products, TWEBs cannot cover every instance of hazardous weather. Although the number of TWEB routes is extensive, many areas are not covered. Never extrapolate nor extend the forecast beyond its defined area.

Revised TWEB standards were adopted to standardize the product. However, as is often the case, interpretation of the new instructions was not consistent. Just after implementation, this message appeared from one weather service office: TWEB ROUTES DELAYED DUE TO RIDICULOUS NEW FORMAT.

CHAPTER 7

Terminal Aerodrome Forecast (TAF)

Some think the only place a pilot will actually see a Terminal Aerodrome Forecast (TAF) is on an FAA exam. This might have been true in the past, but with FSS consolidation, DUAT, and other commercial vendors, responsibility for decoding, translating, and interpreting this product will rest with the pilot. Incorrect interpretation could lead to anything from an embarrassing chat with a Flight Standards District Office (FSDO) inspector to an aircraft accident.

Like METAR, the United States adopted the international TAF code on July 1, 1996. According to sources within the National Weather Service, "A few of the changes seem to defy logic—in fact they are illogical." At first glance the format appears confusing, but actually the basic forecast remains the same.

TAFs are issued four times a day (0000Z, 0600Z, 1200Z, 1800Z) valid for 24 hours. This has answered the criticism that terminal forecasts be written more often and be valid for a longer period. Forecasts using TAF (World Meteorological Organization—WMO) codes are also issued by local base weather offices for many military locations. Military TAFs have different criteria than those issued by the NWS, therefore, some differences in format and content will occur.

The meteorologist must, normally, have at least two consecutive METARs before issuing a TAF. As a minimum, these observations must, usually, contain wind, visibility, and obstructions to visibility, weather, sky condition, temperature, dew point, and altimeter setting. However, after analyzing available data, if in the forecaster's judgment, a missing observation or element will have no impact on the quality of the forecast, it may be issued or continued.

Airports with part-time weather observations normally require three hours after the first observation for the TAF to be written, distributed, and become available. The TAF may not be issued if an observation or element is missing. For example, with a missing dew point, pilots could expect to see KXYZ TAF 071919 TAF NIL DUE MSG DEW PT. Likewise when the observation ceases the forecast will contain the statement AMD NOT SKED AFT 03Z. This alerts the user that amendments are not available after 0300Z.

Automated observations are allowing more TAFs to be written on a 24-hour basis. However, should certain sensors be unavailable a remark will indicate the TAF status—for example, AMD LTD TO CLD VIS AND WIND (amendments limited to clouds, visibility, and wind). This indicates that weather phenomena such as thunderstorms and freezing precipitation can occur without generating a TAF amendment.

Prepared by local Weather Forecast Offices (WFO), Terminal Aerodrome Forecasts contain specific information for individual airports. TAFs are issued in the following format:

- Type
- Location
- Issuance time
- Valid time
- Forecast

There are two types of TAF issuance, a routine forecast issuance TAF and an amended forecast TAF AMD. TAFs may be corrected (COR) or routinely delayed (NIL). TAF location is identified by the four-letter ICAO station identifier. Issuance date and time consists of a six-digit group. The first two digits represent the day of the month and the last four digits UTC issuance time. The valid period is a four-digit group, usually 24 hours, in UTC. The forecast group is divided into body and remarks. Remarks amplify or describe conditions that differ from that in the body of the forecast group. Conditional terms describe variability.

In the United States TAFs cover a five-statute mile radius of the center of an airport's runway complex. Vicinity (VC) is defined as an area from beyond five miles to 10 statute miles from the center of the runway complex.

A word of caution, it's dangerous to extrapolate the TAF beyond five miles. Over flat terrain, such as the Midwest, chances are that nearby airports might have similar conditions. This does not relieve the pilot, however, of checking appropriate FA or TWEB forecasts. In hilly or mountainous terrain this practice can be disastrous. For example, afternoon surface winds during the summer are routinely strong and gusty at San Francisco International Airport, whereas, at other Bay Area airports, winds remain relatively calm due to wind direction and terrain.

Conversely, an airport in the middle of a valley might have benign surface winds; however, at a nearby airport below a canyon, surface winds can prevent landings altogether. This is not uncommon in the Los Angeles Basin when Santa Ana winds blow; winds at the Ontario, California airport might be out of the west less than five knots, but at Rialto, only about 10 miles away, winds might be out of the north gusting to more than 40 knots. Rialto lies just below the Cajon Pass.

Terminal forecasts should be written as simply and straightforward as possible. To describe significant changes during the forecast period the forecast is subdivided into one or more smaller time segments. Changes or expected changes in ceiling and visibility that cross a flight category threshold are considered operationally significant. These categories are defined in Table 5-2, Area forecast outlook categories, with the addition of low IFR (LIFR: ceiling less than 500 ft and/or visibility less than 1SM). Additional ceiling and visibility thresholds correspond to IFR alternate requirements and approach and landing minimums. Other elements that are considered operationally significant are:

- Thunderstorms
- Low-level wind shear
- Freezing precipitation
- Ice pellets
- Moderate or greater rain
- Snow expected to accumulate
- Sustained winds greater than 15KT
- Wind direct changes of 30 degrees or more with speeds of 12KT or more
- Wind gust value changes of 10KT or more

The body of the TAF uses the following format:

- Wind
- Visibility
- Weather
- Sky condition
- Wind shear, when applicable

Like the METAR code, wind is forecast as a five or six digit group when considered significant to aviation. The contraction KT follows the wind forecast and denotes the units as knots. Gustiness is a forecast for rapid fluctuations of 10 knots or more indicated by the letter G following the wind group: 34025G40KT (mean wind speed 25 knots with gusts to 40 knots), or VRBG50 (wind gusts to 50 knots). Unlike the FA or TWEB, the TAF does provide a specific wind forecast.

A popular aviation magazine reported that winds received from a tower were miles per hour and on TAFs winds were knots. Let's settle the matter: wind direction true or magnetic, blowing from or toward the reported direction, speed knots or miles per hour. All official—for some reason the FAA in Washington hates the word "official," therefore I use it as often as possible—aviation wind observations and forecasts are reported in relation to true north, given as the direction from which the wind is blowing, with speed in knots. The only time a pilot will receive winds in relation to magnetic north is from a tower, ATIS or AWOS broadcast, or as part of a local airport advisory because runway numbers are magnetic.

Prevailing visibility up to and including six statute miles is forecast. Visibility greater than six miles is indicated by the letter P for plus (P6SM—visibility greater than six statute miles). Military and many international TAFs forecast visibility in meters.

Weather and obstructions to vision use the same format and codes as METAR. With no significant weather expected, the weather group is omitted. When significant weather is forecast, then expected to change to no significant weather, the contraction NSW (No Significant Weather) appears. NSW will not appear when any of the following phenomena are expected to occur.

- Freezing precipitation
- Moderate or heavy precipitation
- Drifting or blowing dust, sand, or snow
- Dust storms or sandstorms
- Thunderstorms
- Squall
- Tornadoes
- Phenomena expected to cause a significant change in visibility

Tornadic activity, including tornadoes, waterspouts, and funnel clouds will normally not appear in terminal forecasts since the probability of occurrence at a specific location is extremely small. Volcanic ash will always be forecast when expected.

Sky condition uses the same format and contractions as METAR, cloud heights are always reported above ground level (AGL). That is: amount, height, cloud type, or vertical visibility. This is important when using a TAF product or comparing it with observations, PIREPs, or other forecasts. The ceiling is always the first broken or overcast layer, or vertical visibility into a complete obscuration. TAFs are specifically intended for arriving and departing aircraft, therefore cloud layers above 15,000 feet might not be included when a lower ceiling appears. When cumulonimbus clouds are expected CB is appended to the cloud layer. CB is the only cloud type forecast in TAFs. NWS prepared terminal forecast will not include forecasts of partial obscurations.

Low-level wind shear (LLWS) on Terminal Aerodrome Forecasts refers to nonthunderstorm shear, within 2000 ft of the ground. Wind direction, speed, and height are included. LLWS appears when PIREPs report an airspeed gain or loss of 20 knots or more, or vertical shears of 10 knots or more per 100 feet are expected or reported. Low-level wind shear, when forecast, will appear following sky condition on domestic TAFs, in the following format: ...WS015/24035KT...

- WS: wind shear
- 015: height in hundreds of feet (above ground level) of the wind shear (1500 ft AGL)
- /24035: wind direction and speed (knots) above the wind shear (240 degrees at 35 knots)

Since turbulence and icing forecasts are contained in the AIRMET Bulletin and SIGMETs, United States domestic TAFs will not include these phenomena.

Conditional Terms

In the body of the TAF prevailing conditions have a greater than 50 percent probability of occurrence, are expected to last for more than one hour during each occurrence, and cover more than half of the forecast period. This explains a major TAF misconception. Conditions may differ in the body of the forecast from actual conditions, but the forecast is considered accurate as long as conditions fall within the prescribed parameters. More about this when we discuss amendment criteria.

TAF conditional terms consist of temporary (TEMPO) conditions and probability (PROB) forecasts. TEMPO and PROB are considered remarks to the body of the forecast. TAF terms are defined in Table 7-1. When determining minimums (approach and landing, or alternate) the lowest conditions within the appropriate time must be considered. Therefore, if conditions are lower in the TEMPO group, those conditions must be applied.

TEMPO indicates that temporary conditions are expected to occur during the forecast period. TEMPO describes any condition with a 50 percent or greater probability of occurrence, expected to last for generally less than an hour at a time, and to cover less than half of the forecast period. The time during which the condition is expected to occur is indicated with a four-digit group giving beginning and ending times UTC. For example, SCT030 TEMPO 1923 BKN030; three thousand scattered temporarily between 1900Z and 2300Z ceilings three thousand broken. A ceiling of three thousand broken is expected to exist for periods of less than one hour during the 1900Z to 2300Z time frame. TEMPO is equivalent to, and may be translated by FSS controllers as, occasional (OCNL).

A PROB group indicates the probability of occurrence of thunderstorms or other precipitation events. PROB 40 indicates a 40-percent probability; PROB 30 indicates a 30-percent probability. This

Table 7-1 Terminal aerodrome forecast conditional terms

No conditional term	A greater than 50-percent probability of occurrence, expected to last for more than one hour during each occurrence, and cover more than half of the forecast period.
TEMPO	A 50-percent or greater probability of occurrence, expected to last for generally less than an hour at a time, and to cover less than half of the forecast period.
VC (Vicinity)	An area from beyond 5 miles to 10 statute miles from the center of the runway complex.
Probability of precipitation	
PROB 40	A 40-percent probability.
PROB 30	A 30-percent probability.

is followed by a four-digit time group giving beginning and ending times. PROB40 is the equivalent of chance (CHC), and PROB 30 slight chance (SLT CHC).

Forecast Change Groups

Forecast change groups consist of from (FM) followed by a time group (tttt) FMtttt, and becoming (BECMG) followed by a time group (TTtt) BECMG TTtt. The FMtttt group is used when a rapid change is expected, usually within less than one hour. For example, BKN020 FM1630 SKC—before 1630Z ceiling two thousand broken, around 1630Z the sky condition will change to clear. The BECMG TTtt group indicates a more gradual change in conditions over a longer period. The BECMG group indicates a change in conditions that are expected to occur at either a regular or irregular rate at an unspecified time, but within the period.

Figure 7-1 illustrates the operational impact of a BECMG group. If conditions are expected to deteriorate during the BECMG period, those conditions must be considered to exist at the beginning of the period. Conversely, if conditions are expected to improve during the BECMG period, the lower conditions must be considered to exist to the end of the period. The first example in Fig. 7-1 shows the ceiling deteriorating during the BECMG period. From an operational perspective pilots and dispatchers must consider the lower condition (OVC005) to exist any time after 18Z. The second example in Fig. 7-1 shows the visibility improving during the BECMG period. Again, from an operational perspective the lower condition (1SM BR) must be considered to exist through 22Z.

Although weather typically behaves in this manner, the BECMG group can have significant operational impact. In response to user requirements, the NWS has agreed to use the BECMG group sparingly, and when used not to exceed two hours. Additionally, forecasters will avoid using a BECMG group to forecast minimum conditions, especially visibility less than 1/2 statute mile.

Let's decode, translate, and interpret the following TAF for New York's Kennedy International Airport.

TAF KJFK 191130Z 191212 08023G33KT 5SM -RA BR OVC007 WS020/11045KT TEMPO 1212 2SM RA BR OVC005 BECMG 1618 07028G38KT WS020/11050KT BECMG 1921 06023G45KT WS020/10055KT

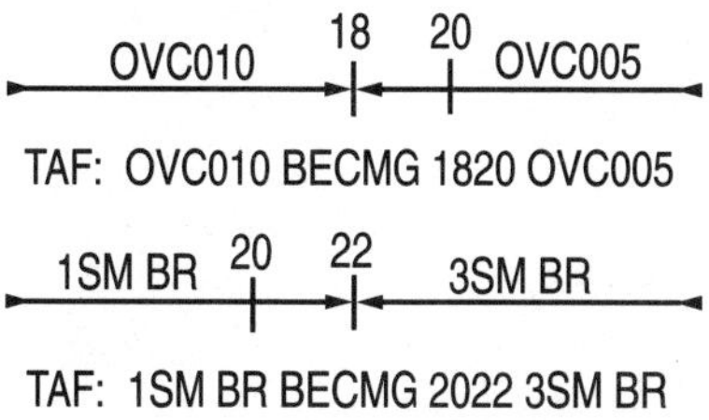

	18	20	
OVC010			OVC005

TAF: OVC010 BECMG 1820 OVC005

	20	22	
1SM BR			3SM BR

TAF: 1SM BR BECMG 2022 3SM BR

Fig. 7-1. The BECMG group can have significant operational impact; the NWS has agreed to use the BECMG group sparingly, and when used not to exceed two hours.

This forecast was issued on the 19th day of the month at 1130Z. It is valid from the 19th at 1200Z until the 20th at 1200Z. Note that the first element contains all the forecast categories. The wind is from 080 degrees at 23 gusting to 33 knots; visibility is 5 statute miles in light rain and mist; ceiling 700 ft overcast; wind shear at 2000 ft, wind at that altitude 110 degrees at 45 knots. (There is a greater than 50 percent probability of occurrence, expected to last for more than one hour during each occurrence, and cover more than half of the forecast period.) Occasionally (TEMPO) between 12Z and 12Z—the entire forecast period—visibility 2 statute miles in moderate rain and mist, ceiling 500 ft overcast. Since the wind group is omitted from the TEMPO group, it is expect to remain 08023G33KT. (There is a 50 percent or greater probability of occurrence, expected to last for generally less than an hour at a time, and to cover less than half of the forecast period.) Since the remarks in the TEMPO group are lower than the body, for flight planning purposes they must be applied through the entire period. That is, for determining IFR alternate requirements for the entire period of the forecast (12Z to 12Z) visibility 2SM and ceiling OVC005 must be applied.

Wind and wind shear are expected to become between 16Z and 18Z 070 degrees at 28 gusting to 38 knots. What about the other elements of the forecast? In a BECMG group only the elements expected to change are included. Therefore, visibility, weather, and sky condition forecast in the body and remarks are expected to continue. This is one difference between a BECMG and FM group. In a FM group all elements of the forecast, even if they are not expected to change, must be included. Because higher winds are forecast in the second part of the BECMG group they must be applied beginning at 16Z. For example, if the wind conditions in the BECMG group (07028G38KT) exceed our maximum crosswind component, the forecast would preclude our landing at any time after 16Z. The same interpretation applies to the second BECMG group, where wind and wind shear are expected to increase.

Pilots can expect to see differences in domestic TAF codes and those used on military forecasts. Military forecasts may include temperature, turbulence, and icing, in addition to visibility in meters. Table 7-2 decodes temperature, turbulence, and icing codes. Table 7-3 converts meters to statute miles.

This is a TAF for Travis Air Force Base, California.

KSUU 101111 24010G15KT 9999 BKN070 BKN180 QNH3020INS

BECMG 1415 22010G15KT 9999 VCRA SCT050 BKN070 OVC180 620507 QNH3018INS

BECMG 1718 22010G15KT 9000 -RA BR SCT030 BKN050OV100 62048 51005 QNH3014INS WND 20012G18KT 21003

BECMG 0405 20010G15KT 8000 -RA BR BKN030OVC050 62408 51005 QNH3005INS T11/23Z T08/13Z

The forecast was issued on the 10th day of the month and is valid from the 10th at 1100Z through the 11th at 1100Z.

The initial period, 1100Z, forecasts winds 240 at 10 gusting to 15 knots, visibility 9999 meters, ceiling 7000 ft broken 18,000 ft broken, altimeter setting 30.20 in. From Table 7-3 we see that 9999 translates to more than 6 statute miles (P6SM). Note that the altimeter setting (QNH) is also forecast. Another difference between domestic and military TAFs.

Conditions are forecast to change between (BECMG) 1400Z and 1500Z to wind 220 at 10 gusting to 15 knots, visibility 9999 meters, rain in the vicinity, 5000 ft scattered ceiling 7000 ft broken 18,000 ft overcast, icing 620507, altimeter setting 30.18 in. Rain in the vicinity translates to rain occurring beyond 5 statute miles and 10 statute miles of the airport. Notice this period contains an icing group 620507.

Decode the icing group using Table 7-2. The numeral 6 tells us it is an icing group. The next digit (2) represents icing intensity— light icing in cloud. The next three digits (050) represent the base of the icing layer in hundreds of feet MSL-5000 ft. The last digit (7) indicates the thickness of the icing layer in thousands of feet—7000 ft or tops of the icing layer at 12,000-ft MSL.

Table 7-2 Terminal aerodrome forecasts

Temperature:	TT_iT_i/tt
	T - Temperature Group
	T_iT_i - Temperature Celsius
	tt - Time UTC
Turbulence:	5ihhhd
	5 - Turbulence Group
	i - Turbulence Intensity
	hhh - Base height hundreds of feet
	d - Thickness in thousands of feet
Turbulence Intensity:	
0	None
I	Light turbulence
2	Moderate turbulence in clear air, infrequent
3	Moderate turbulence in clear air, frequent
4	Moderate turbulence in cloud, infrequent
5	Moderate turbulence in cloud, frequent
6	Severe turbulence in clear air, infrequent
7	Severe turbulence in clear air, frequent
8	Severe turbulence in cloud, infrequent
9	Severe turbulence in cloud, frequent
Icing:	6ihhhd
	6 - Icing Group
	i - Icing Intensity
	hhh - Base Height hundreds of feet
	d - Thickness in thousands of feet (0 indicates to top of clouds)
Icing Intensity:	
0	No icing

Table 7-2 Terminal aerodrome forecasts *(Continued)*

1	Light icing
2	Light icing in cloud
3	Light icing in precipitation
4	Moderate icing
5	Moderate icing in cloud
6	Moderate icing in precipitation
7	Severe icing
8	Severe icing in cloud
9	Severe icing in precipitation

The next change group occurs between 1700Z and 1800Z. The forecast expects wind 220 at 10 gusting to 15 knots, visibility 9000 meters in light rain and mist, 3000 ft scattered ceiling 5000 ft broken 10,000 ft overcast, icing 620408, turbulence 51005, altimeter setting 30.14 in., wind between 21Z and 03Z 200 at 12 gusting to 28 knots. Visibility is expected to decrease to 6 statute miles in light rain and mist. Light icing in clouds is expected between 4000 and 12,000 ft MSL.

Decode the turbulence group using Table 7-2. The numeral 5 tells us it is a turbulence group. The next digit (1) represents turbulence intensity—light turbulence. The next three digits (000) are the base of the turbulence layer in hundreds of feet MSL—0000 ft or the surface. The last digit (5) indicates the thickness of the turbulence layer in thousands of feet—5000 ft or top of the turbulence layer at 5000-ft MSL.

The next change is expected between 0400Z and 0500Z. The forecast expects wind 220 at 10 gusting to 15 knots, visibility 8000 meters in light rain and mist, ceiling 3000 ft broken 5000 ft overcast, icing 620408, turbulence 51005, altimeter setting 30.05 in., temperature T11/23Z T08/13Z. Visibility is expected to decrease to 5 statute miles. Icing and turbulence are expected to continue.

Again, decode the temperature group using Table 7-2. The maximum temperature of 11 degrees C is forecast to occur at 2300Z, minimum temperature of 8 degrees C at 1300Z.

Whether international or military, TAFs suffer from the same limitations as any other forecast. It really can't be said that a domestic TAF or military TAF is necessarily more accurate. However, by comparing a domestic TAF with a nearby military TAF, one could get a "second opinion."

Amendment Criteria

The NWS forecast manual states: "Amendments shall be issued when expected or observed conditions:

1. Meet amendment criteria for the specified forecast elements
2. Are expected to persist, and
3. In the forecaster's judgment, there is sufficient, reliable information,...on which to base a forecast."

Table 7-3 Visibility in meters

Meters	Statute ML	Meters	Statute ML
0000	0	2200	1 3/8
0200	1/16	2400	1 1/2
0300	1/8	2600	1 5/8
0400	3/16	2800	1 3/4
0500	5/16	3000	1 7/8
0600	3/8	3200	2
0800	1/2	3600	2 1/4
1000	5/8	4000	2 1/2
1200	3/4	4800	3
1400	7/8	6000	4
1600	1	8000	5
1800	1 1/8	9000	6
2000	1 1/4	9999	6+

Amended TAFs contain the contraction AMD. For example:

TAF AMD

PDX 101440Z 101512...

This amended forecast for Portland International Airport was issued on the 10th at 1440Z and is valid from 1500Z on the 10th until 1200Z on the 11th.

Amendment criteria have changed significantly in the 1990s. Even with these changes, reviewing Table 7-4, Terminal aerodrome forecast amendment criteria, we see the reason for some of the criticism of this product. Ceilings above 3000 ft and visibilities more than six miles must decrease below these value before an amendment is required. Amendments are not required, for example, for a forecast ceiling of 10,000 decreasing to 5000 ft. Although, the forecaster has the authority to amend the forecast when forecaster considers it operationally significant. As conditions lower, becoming more significant, amendment criteria intervals decrease. The forecast is considered accurate as long as the criteria in Table 7-4 are met.

The new amendment criteria reflect operations needs. Note that a decrease or increase from basic VFR (1000 and 3), nonprecision approach minimums (600 and 2), and precision approach minimums (200 and 1/2) require an amendment. As we will see, however, this does not mean that at the moment these criteria are met, an amendment will be issued.

From Table 7-4, changes in wind speed less than 12 knots do not require an amendment. At speeds of 12 knots or greater the speed must differ by 10 knots or more. Therefore, a forecast of 20 knots would have to decrease to 10 or increase to 30 before an amendment is required. Basically, TAF wind speeds are considered accurate when within 10 knots of forecast. A pilot competent to handle 20 knots must consider that with a forecast of 20 knots, actual winds could increase to almost 30 knots without a requirement to amend. Within these parameters the forecast is considered correct.

The only weather phenomena requiring amendments are thunderstorms, freezing precipitation, ice pellets, and LLWS. The unforecast occurrence or ending of rain or snow does not require an amendment. This fact has led both pilots and briefers to erroneously criticize the forecast.

When phenomena described in VC moves, or is expected to move, within five miles of the airport an amendment is required. The phenomena can appear in the body or remarks of the amendment. But, it must be phenomena described in the weather section of Table 7-4.

At locations with part-time observations the remark NIL AMDTS AFT (time)Z will appear. As used in TWEBs, this serves as a warning that significant changes can occur without an amendment. Extra caution must be exercised operating into these airports, especially during marginal or deteriorating conditions.

A forecast of landing minimums, VFR or IFR, is no guarantee those conditions will exist at our estimated time of arrival. An IFR alternate affected by the same weather pattern as the destination may satisfy regulations, but leave a pilot on the proverbial limb with a busted

Table 7-4 Terminal aerodrome forecast amendment criteria

FORECAST	AMEND IF:
Wind (KT)	
≤ 12	Direction differs by 30°; speed differs by 10 kt
Gusts with mean speed ≤12	Gusts 10 above forecast
Visibility (SM)	
> 5	≤ 5
3 to 5	> 6 or < 3
2	≥ 3 or < 2
1 to 1 1/2	≥ 2 or < 1
1/2 to 3/4	≥ 1 or < 1/2
< 1/2	≥ 1/2
Weather	
Thunderstorms, freezing precipitation, or ice pellets	Does not occur or no longer expected
No thunderstorms, freezing precipitation, or ice pellets	Occurs or is expected
Ceiling (ft)	
< 3000	> 3000
2000 to 3000	> 3000 or < 2000
1000 to 1900	> 1900 or < 1000
600 to 900	> 900 or < 600
200 to 500	> 500 or < 200
< 100	≥ 200
Low-level wind shear	
LLWS	No LLWS expected
No LLWS	LLWS occurs or is expected

forecast. For example, if a pilot's destination was Fresno, in California's Central Valley, Bakersfield may qualify as a legal alternate. However, with Tule Fog—a local name given to a condition of extensive wintertime fog—in California's Central Valley a viable alternate might be along the coast, not affected by this phenomena. This would also apply to airports affected by up-slope fog or frontal systems. If at all possible, a pilot should select an alternate not affected by the weather pattern affecting the destination. At the risk of being redundant, we're back to knowing the synopsis and continually updating weather en route, the "complete picture."

Using the Terminal Aerodrome Forecast

Apparent inconsistencies arise because different forecasts serve different purposes. The following example compares FA and TWEB forecasts with TAFs.

Below are excerpts from the Chicago AIRMET Bulletin and FA, the 216 TWEB route forecast from Chicago, Illinois to Burlington, Iowa, and the Chicago O'Hare International and Burlington Regional TAFs.

CHIS WA 121945

AIRMET SIERRA UPDT 4 FOR IFR VALID UNTIL 130200

AIRMET IFR...MN IA MO WI IL

FROM 100NE GFK TO INL TO BDF TO FAM TO SGF TO 100NE GFK

OCNL CIG BLW 010/VIS BLW 3SM PCPN/BR. LTL MOVMT EXP OVR NRN SXNS OF THE AREA..SHFTG SLOLY EWD SRN SXNS. CONDS CONTG BYD 02Z THRU 08Z.

CHIC FA 121845

SYNOPSIS AND VFR CLDS/WX

SYNOPSIS VALID UNTIL 131300

CLDS/WX VALID UNTIL 130700...OTLK VALID 130700-131300

IL

NRN...CIG BKN-SCT020-030 BKN080. TOPS 140. OCNL VIS 3-5SM

-SHRA. SCT TSRA. CB TOPS FL400. OTLK...MVFR CIG SHRA BR.

216 TWEB 122008 KCHI-KBRL. ALL HGTS AGL XCP TOPS. KCHI-50SM
SW KCHI P6SM BKN100 WDLY SCT 2SM TSRA OVC040-050...AFT
05Z 4SM -RA BR OVC020-030. 50SM SW KCHI-KBRL 5SM -SHRA
OVC010-020 SCT 2SM TSRA OVC010-020...AFT 06Z 5SM BR WDLY
SCT 2SM TSRA OVC010-020.

TAF

KORD 121730Z 121818 07012KT P6SM BKN100 TEMPO 2024 3SM
TSRA

OVC045CB

FM0000 08015G25KT P6SM OVC040 TEMPO 0004 3SM TSRA

OVC025CB

FM0400 08012KT 4SM -RA BR OVC022=

TAF AMD

KBRL 122122Z 122118 32013KT P6SM FEW020 BKN050

FM2130 30012KT 5SM -SHRA OVC035

TEMPO 2202 3SM TSRA OVC015CB

FM0200 34008KT 5SM BR OVC010 TEMPO 0618 -SHRA

PROB40 0610 3SM TSRA OVC015CB=

Figure 7-2 depicts these forecasts on excerpts from the Weather
Advisory Plotting chat and TWEB Route chart. Chicago AIRMET
SIERRA has been plotted in gray on Fig. 7-2, occasional ceilings and
visibilities below 1000 ft and 3 ml. The AIRMET covers the western
half of the 216 TWEB route, including Burlington, Iowa.

The 216 TWEB divides the route into two segments, Chicago to 50
ml southwest of Chicago, and 50 ml southwest of Chicago to
Burlington. Note how the TWEB has divided the route into segments
and two distinct times.

216 TWEB 122008 KCHI-KBRL. ALL HGTS AGL XCP TOPS. KCHI-50SM
SW KCHI P6SM BKN100 WDLY SCT 2SM TSRA OVC040-050...
50SM SW KCHI-KBRL 5SM -SHRA OVC010-020 SCT 2SM TSRA
OVC010-020...

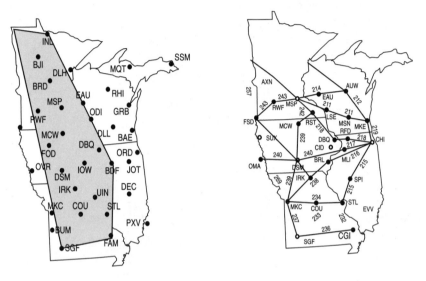

IL
NRN...CIG BKN-SCT020-030 BKN080. TOPS 140. OCNL VIS 3-5SM
-SHRA. SCT TSRA. CB TOPS FL400. OTLK...MVFR CIG SHRA BR.

Fig. 7-2. Apparent inconsistencies arise because the FA, TWEB, and TAF forecasts serve different purposes.

The TAFs are further able to be divided into specific times. To help visualize forecast conditions Table 7-5 provides a comparison of these products. A time frame of 2000Z to 0000Z has been selected with appropriate forecasts covering the 216 TWEB route.

The TAF provides much more detail on surface winds than is available with either the FA or TWEB. Typically, the FA does not forecast visibility or ceiling less than 3 ml or 1000 ft. How much less? We don't know. This makes the FA all but useless for determining IFR approach and landing, or alternate requirements. Therefore, the TWEB is much more helpful in forecasting conditions at airports not served by a TAF, but within the area of coverage of the TWEB. This is especially true for the second half of the TWEB route. From Table 7-5 we see that expected weather is consistent within each forecast.

Table 7-5 FA, TWEB, TAF forecast comparison

2200Z-0000Z			
	FA	TWEB CHI-50 SW CHI	ORD TAF
Wind	< 20KT	< 25KT	07012KT
Visibility	3SM	2SM	3SM
Weather	–SHRA/TSRA	TSRA	TSRA
Ceiling	2000 ft	4000 ft	4500 ft
2200Z-0000Z			
	FA	TWEB 50 SW CHI-BRL	BRL TAF
Wind	< 20KT	< 25KT	30012KT
Visibility	< 3SM	2SM	3SM
Weather	–SHRA/TSRA	–SHRA/TSRA	–SHRA/TSRA
Ceiling	< 1000 ft	1000 ft	3500 ft

Let's say we're planning an IFR arrival to an airport beyond five miles from the Burlington airport, but within the area served by the TWEB. In accordance with FARs, we must determine if an alternate airport is required, and, if so, select a suitable alternate. Our ETA is 2300Z. From the TWEB we see the forecast for one hour before until one hour after our estimated time of arrival (ETA) is visibility 2SM ceiling 1000 ft. Therefore, an alternate is required.

The preceding comparison contradicts a common misconception that in the absence of a TAF there is no forecast on which to base destination, alternate, and fuel requirements. If not TWEBs, the FAs are always available—maybe not as detailed as we might like, requiring additional alternates and fuel, but nonetheless available.

Forecasters consider four elements when writing TAFs:

1. Expected weather
2. Local effects
3. Climatology
4. Amendment criteria

Attention to detail places a premium on the forecaster's time and judgment.

In addition to the new TAF amendment criteria several other changes have improve the terminal forecast. The NWS recommends that forecasters restrict the use of conditional terms and keep TEMPO restricted to short periods. Forecasters are encouraged to amend when conditions do not materialize, even when amendment criteria have not yet been met.

Due to a number of factors, inconsistencies with reported conditions are to be expected. The forecaster might not believe observations are representative or the forecaster might expect conditions to change rapidly. Even in the body of the forecast there is only a greater than 50 percent probability of occurrence, during more than one-half the forecast period. Amendment criteria give the forecaster some latitude. The forecaster might be waiting until TAF amendment criteria are reached—reported or expected. The time required to write and distribute an amendment is also a consideration; saturated computer and communications systems can hinder timely updates. If there is less than two hours between the time an amendment is required and a new forecast becomes effective or the next portion of the forecast becomes effective, an amendment might not be issued. Time parameters on domestic TAFs, even with a FM group, usually indicate phenomena will change within two hours of the specified time. Additionally, forecasters have other duties that might hinder timely amendments.

FAs, TWEBs, and TAFs are usually perfectly consistent given their individual purpose and criteria. Apparent inconsistencies arise because cloud heights in the FA are generally MSL, whereas in the TAF cloud heights are always AGL; TAFs can consider local effects not within the scope of other products—or a pilot attempts to extrapolate a TAF beyond five miles. When inconsistencies develop, FSS controllers and forecasters coordinate to resolve differences. Pilots using DUAT will have to consult an FSS for resolution.

Domestic TAFs do not directly forecast turbulence or icing. However, like METAR, these phenomena are implied. Strong surface winds, LLWS, and thunderstorms indicate turbulence—surface temperatures close to freezing with cloud layers, freezing precipitation, and thunderstorms imply icing.

Pilots continually demand to know exactly when an airport will improve to IFR landing minimums or VFR conditions. This accuracy simply is not yet possible, but both the FAA and NWS are working on these issues. Alternate airport and fuel reserve requirements take these limitations into consideration. However, departing with appropriate alternates and adequate fuel does not relieve the pilot from updating weather information, and when necessary revising the flight plan, en route.

CHAPTER 8

Winds and Temperatures Aloft Forecasts (FD)

A Navion pilot called flight service with a request for "winds aloft." The specialist asked, "...for what altitudes?" The pilot rather indignantly replied, "Whatever's best for my direction of flight!" Well, let me tell you it's 53,000 ft every time.

Winds and temperatures aloft forecasts (FD) for the contiguous United States, Alaska, and many oceanic areas are computer generated at the National Centers for Environmental Prediction (NCEP) outside Washington, D.C. FDs for the Hawaiian islands are produced by the Honolulu Weather Forecast Office. Based on the twice daily radiosonde balloon observations (balloon with a radiosonde attached) are normally released at 1100Z and 2300Z daily. Launch sites can be found in the Airport/Facility Directory, on the page opposite the inside back cover. Because these sites and times are published, pilots cannot expect to receive balloon launch warnings in the form of NOTAMs or broadcasts, except for unscheduled releases.

A computer program known as the Nested Grid Model (NGM) analyzes data. NGM is one of the latest forecast models and has replaced the Limited Fine Mesh (LFM) for FD-tabulated forecasts; with a smaller grid, better resolution, and terrain taken into account to a greater degree than the LFM, the NGM has improved forecast accuracy. However, the NGM can only consider synoptic (large-scale) weather systems. The computer projects system movements and produces a forecast. Although large-scale terrain, to some extent, is considered, local features are not. Therefore, FDs tend to be less accurate in the western states, especially below 12,000 ft.

Approximately 750 upper air stations worldwide—about 120 in the United States—take observations. Stations are generally located on land, leaving great expanses of ocean without observations, although satellite and aircraft reports help fill in the gaps. The computer must interpolate for locations without observations and sparse observational data hinders the accuracy of the forecast.

Winds and temperatures aloft forecasts can be obtained from a number of sources: Flight Service Stations (FSS), Pilots Automatic Telephone Weather Answering Service (PATWAS), Telephone Information Briefing Service (TIBS), Direct User Access Terminals (DUAT), and commercial vendors.

Tabulated Forecasts

FDs normally become available after their scheduled transmission times of 0440Z and 1640Z. They consist of three forecast periods: six, 12, and 24 hours. These periods are labeled FD1, FD2, and FD3 for levels through 39,000 feet, and FD8, FD9, and FD10 for 45,000 and 53,000 feet (Table 8-1).

> **CASE STUDY**
>
> My student and I had planned a cross-country flight using FDs obtained from DUATs. We then called flight service and filed our flight plans. I had my student obtain a standard weather briefing to compare the information from an FSS briefing with that received from DUATs. The FDs provided in the FSS briefing were significantly different from those received from DUATs. Why? Between the time we obtained the DUAT briefing, completed the calculations, and called flight service, new FDs had become available.

FAA Automated Flight Service Stations display levels 3000 through 53,000 ft. Although the 45,000- and 53,000-foot levels are not

Table 8-1 Winds and temperature aloft forecast schedule

FILE TYPE	VALID	FOR USE
Forecasts based on 0000Z data, available at 0440Z		
FD1 FD8	0600Z	0500-0900Z
FD2 FD9	1200Z	0900-1800Z
FD3 FD10	0000Z	1800-0500Z
Forecasts based on 1200Z data, available at 1640Z		
FD1 FD8	1800Z	1700-2100Z
FD2 FD9	0000Z	2100-0600Z
FD3 FD10	1200Z	0600-1700Z

available for all standard FD locations. Other FSSs usually post levels through 39,000 ft; the two higher levels are available on request. FSSs usually post the 6- and 12-hour forecasts (FD1 and FD2), with the 24-hour forecasts (FD3) available on request.

FD3s and FD10s are plagued with the same limitations as other forecasts and must be viewed with skepticism and used only for advanced planning, then updated with the latest forecasts prior to departure—recall the previous Case Study. This requires the pilot to become familiar with the issuance times in Table 8-1. For example, a pilot planning a 1900Z departure might obtain the FD3s, based on 0000Z data, the evening before departure. The FD1s, based on 1200Z data, become available at 1640Z. If the pilot fails to update the forecast, he or she could be wide open to a violation in case of a problem.

```
DATA BASED ON 301200Z
VALID 301800Z       FOR USE 1700-2100Z.      TEMPS NEG ABV 24000

FT    3000    6000    9000    12000   18000   24000   30000

SFO   3513   3316+10  3220+06 3224+01 3138-11 3148-24 325539
RNO           0605    3308+02 3217-02 3134-16 3052-28 316542
```

```
        34000      39000

        315846     315954
        316848     316853

        DATA BASED ON 301200Z
        VALID 301800Z     FOR USE 1700-2100Z.     TEMPS NEG ABV 24000

        FT    45000     53000

        SFO  314961    304263
```

This example contains the FD1 and FD8 forecasts, based on the 30th day of the month 1200Z radiosonde data (DATA BASED ON 301200Z). The DATA BASED ON must always be checked. From time to time old FDs fail to be purged and remain in the system. It's possible to receive data that is 24 hours old. The next line states VALID 301800Z FOR USE 1700-2100Z. These FDs are for use between 1700Z and 2100Z. The computer does not forecast an average; the model predicts winds and temperatures for one specific time, in this case 1800Z (VALID 301800Z).

Forecasts based on expected movement of synoptic systems explain one reason for apparent errors. With rapidly moving or intensifying systems, FDs can change significantly during the FOR USE period. This would be especially true for flights at the beginning or end of the FOR USE period.

Forecast levels are True Altitude—true height above sea level—through 12,000 ft. From 18,000 through 53,000 ft, levels are Pressure Altitude—height as indicated with an altimeter setting of 29.92 inches (1013.2 mb). The example shows FDs for SFO (San Francisco, California) and RNO (Reno, Nevada).

Levels within the area of frictional effect between the wind and the Earth's surface are omitted. Therefore, forecast levels within approximately 1500 ft of the surface, and temperatures for the 3000-foot level, or levels within 2500 ft of the surface, do not appear.

Refer to the SFO 12,000-foot winds. The first two digits of a wind group represent true direction, from which the wind is blowing, to the nearest 10 degrees ("32"24+01); the third and fourth digits indicate speed in knots (32"24"+01); and the last two digits are temperature in degrees Celsius (3224"+01"). Temperatures, plus or minus, are indicated through 24,000 ft; all temperatures above 24,000 are below 0 degrees C and the minus sign is omitted. Therefore, 3224+01 is wind blowing from 320 degrees true at 24 knots, temperature +01 degrees C.

Forecast speeds less than five knots are encoded 9900, and referred to as light and variable.

CASE STUDY

Briefers are periodically asked, "What's the direction and speed of the light and variable winds?" In one extreme case a rather irate pilot demand to know what was "actually written on the paper." The specialist replied, "niner-niner-zero-zero!"

Pilots must interpolate—compute intermediate values—to determine direction, speed, and temperature between forecast levels and reporting locations. Plan to fly from Oakland to South Lake Tahoe at 13,500 feet; use the SFO and RNO FDs. Average the 12,000- foot and then the 18,000-foot levels. At 12,000 ft, direction is the same. A difference in speed of seven knots results in an average of 21 knots (7/2 = 4; 17 + 4 = 21). The average temperature is zero. At 18,000, again the direction is the same. A difference in speed of four knots results in an average of 36 knots (4/2 = 2; 34 + 2 = 36). The difference in temperature is five, resulting in an average of −14 (−5/2 = −3; −11 + (−3) = −14). Be careful with the algebraic sign. The result: 12,000 ft, 320 degrees at 21 knots −01 degrees C, and at 18,000 ft, 310 degrees at 36 knots −14 degrees C.

The 13,500 level is one-quarter of the way between 12,000 and 18,000 feet. Therefore, divide the difference between levels by four and add the result to the 12,000-foot values. Wind direction is 320 degrees, speed 25 knots (15/4 = 4; 21 + 4 = 25) and temperature −04 degrees C (−13/4 = −3; −1 + (−3) = −4). Because direction is to the nearest 10 degrees, speed in whole knots, and temperature in whole degrees Celsius, the result cannot have a value in smaller increments than the original data; values are rounded off. As already noted, be careful of the algebraic sign. FAA exams might require calculating wind direction to the nearest five degrees; however, for practical purposes this is not necessary.

Is a forecast of 701548 a misprint or garbled in transmission? With forecast winds of 100 knots or more, five is added to the first digit of the wind direction group. Therefore, to decode, subtract five from the first digit of the wind direction, and add 100 to speed. In this example wind direction, speed, and temperature are:

DIRECTION	SPEED	TEMPERATURE
70	15	48
–5	110	
20	115 knots	–48 degrees

(No mathematical sign [+ or –] was specified, so the temperature must be negative.) Maximum speed for FD tabulated forecasts is 199 knots.

Forecast Charts

Forecast winds and temperatures aloft are also available in graphic form, issued twice daily, and valid at 1200Z and 0000Z. FD charts are excellent for determining forecast winds for long distance flights. By visually depicting winds at various levels, favorable routes and altitudes can be determined. The eight panels contain forecast levels from 6000 through 39,000 ft. The winds aloft chart is illustrated in Fig. 8-1. Because of valid times and computer models, some differences between the chart and tabular forecasts are to be expected.

Plotted data are standard. Wind direction is forecast to the nearest 10 degrees and speed five knots. Arrows with pennants and barbs are similar to those on other charts. The first digit of the wind direction is obtained from the general direction of the arrow. Pennants (50 knots), barbs (10 knots), and half barbs (five knots) denote speed.

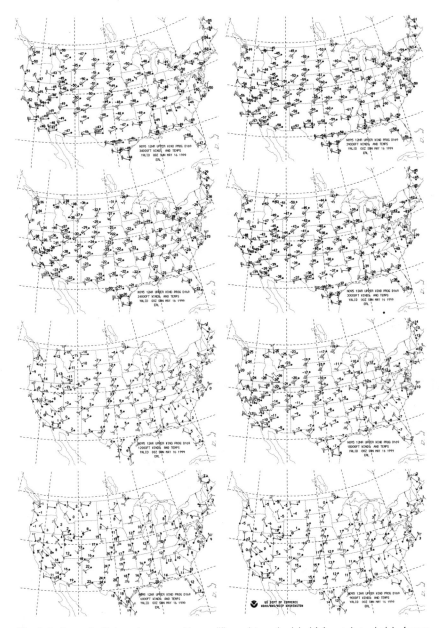

Fig. 8-1. Because of valid times and computer models, some differences between the winds aloft forecast chart and tabular forecasts are to be expected.

Amendment Criteria

Although FDs are generated in Washington, regional NWS offices are responsible for amendments. FDs are amended when, in the forecaster's judgment, there is a change or an expected change in the wind or temperature that would significantly affect aircraft operations. Amendment procedures are complex. (In some 30 years, I can count the number of FD amendments that I have seen on one hand.) Table 8-2 contains amendment criteria.

Reviewing Table 8-2, there must be a considerable difference between forecast and actual winds to require an amendment. In general, forecasts within 30 degrees of direction, and plus or minus 20 knots are considered accurate. As with turbulence and icing, the only way to verify the forecast is through pilot reports.

Using the FD Forecast

FDs provide the pilot with two valuable pieces of information: wind direction and speed, plus temperature. Both significantly affect aircraft

Table 8-2 Winds and temperatures aloft amendment criteria

WITH A FORECAST OF:	AMEND IF:
Wind direction	
Speed 5 knots < 30 knots	Direction change ≥ 45 degrees
Speed ≥ 30 knots	Direction change ≥ 30 degrees
Wind speed	
Speed < 70 knots	Speed change ≥ 20 knots
Speed 70 to 100 knots	Speed change ≥ 30 knots
Speed 100 to 135 knots	Speed change ≥ 40 knots
Speed > 135 knots	Speed change ≥ 50 knots
Temperature	
Observed or forecast change	≥ 5 degrees Celsius

operation and performance. Failure to properly consider and apply either can be potentially hazardous.

In spite of its limitations, the FD can never be ignored. Pilots are required by regulations to consider "...fuel requirements..." and are prohibited from beginning a flight either VFR or IFR "...unless (considering wind and forecast weather conditions)..." the aircraft will have enough fuel to fly to destination, an alternate if required, and still have appropriate fuel reserves. Fuel reserve minimums, which do not necessarily equate to "safe," in no way relieve the pilot from keeping careful track of ground speed, and revising the flight plan accordingly.

When reserves are marginal, good operating practice dictates the careful tracking of position and ground speed. Marginal is not necessarily synonymous with legal; in sparsely populated areas, a fuel reserve of 30 minutes with clear weather reported and forecast might be sufficient. But with marginal weather or thunderstorms, and the nearest suitable alternate 35 minutes away, a 30-minute reserve doesn't make any sense. Chapter 7 discusses how legal alternates might not be satisfactory with a busted forecast. The same is true for legal fuel reserves.

This leads directly to personal minimums. My flight school requires a minimum one-hour fuel reserve for all flights. Additionally, we don't depart without a minimum of two-hour fuel for local flights; for cross-country or instruments flights, fuel must be topped off. Why? Because it's safe. In the following case studies, compliance with these personal minimums would have prevented these incidents.

The venturi effect at mountains and mountain passes accelerates winds over ridges and through passes. Stronger than forecast winds should be expected in these areas, especially within 5000 ft of terrain.

Low-level jet streams can develop under certain meteorological conditions. A clue to their existence can be obtained by comparing surface winds and winds aloft forecasts. Such a low-level jet occurs during the spring months in California's San Joaquin Valley. On one such occurrence surface winds were reported calm, winds at 3000 ft were 080 degrees at 30 knots! Such reports are strong indicators of moderate or greater nonconvective low-level wind shear.

Conversely, after strong afternoon mixing surface winds within the mixing layer—a layer several thousand feet deep—can develop to

CASE STUDIES

The following situation illustrates how a series of small, at the time, seemingly insignificant factors have the potential to lead to disaster. The flight from Van Nuys, California, to Tonopah, Nevada, was based on four hours of fuel and a 10-knot head wind; time en route estimated 3:15. My Cessna 150 was fueled Friday when I arrived at Van Nuys. During the preflight Sunday morning, I noticed the fuel was not at the top of the fuller neck—factor one. This was not unusual because the airplane was parked on a slight incline, and some fuel tends to vent overboard. The departure required an IFR climb to on top conditions, which added about 15 minutes to time en route—factor two.

Over Trona, California, about halfway, ground speed checks indicated winds were as forecast. Calculations indicated adequate fuel for Tonopah based on four hours of fuel and ignoring the extra time required for departure.

The Cessna 150 climbs like a wet mop, so I decided not to land at Trona—factor three. The fuel gauges were bouncing on zero, I still had 30 minutes to destination, and there were no suitable alternates—factor four. I made a straight-in approach and had everything stowed ready to crash, but landed safely in spite of some extremely poor planning. By the way, they put 22.6 gallons in my 22.5-gallon-usable airplane. Never again.

A Grumman Tiger pilot—instructor with student—was not so fortunate. On a flight from Salt Lake City to Tonopah, they crashed short of the airport, out of fuel. The pilot couldn't understand why, after calculating that the airplane had 2:45 fuel, the engine quit after only 2:31. Needless to say, the FAA wanted to have a little chat with this person.

altitudes higher than normal. Under such conditions the lower-level winds aloft forecasts can be erroneous. On low-level flights, especially within about 3000 to 5000 ft of the surface pilots are usually better off using surface wind observations and forecasts, rather than FDs. This would also be a turbulent layer.

Aircraft performance charts are based on the Standard Atmosphere, more precisely the International Standard Atmosphere (ISA). Standard atmosphere temperature and pressure at sea level are 15 degrees C and 29.92 inches of mercury. The standard lapse rate—decrease of temperature with height—in the troposphere is approximately 2 degrees C per thousand feet. Temperature decreases to a value of –57 degrees C at the tropopause—the boundary between the troposphere and the stratosphere—at approximately 36,000 feet for midlatitudes. An isothermal lapse rate occurs in the stratosphere to about 66,000 feet. This is illustrated in Fig. 8-2.

Altitudes on the ISA chart are pressure altitudes. Pilots using the local altimeter setting fly indicated altitude for levels through 17,500 feet, and pressure altitude at 18,000 feet and above. Winds aloft forecasts are true altitude through 12,000 feet, so there will be a slight difference between the altitudes in the forecast (true altitude) and those flown by the pilot (indicated altitude). However, unless

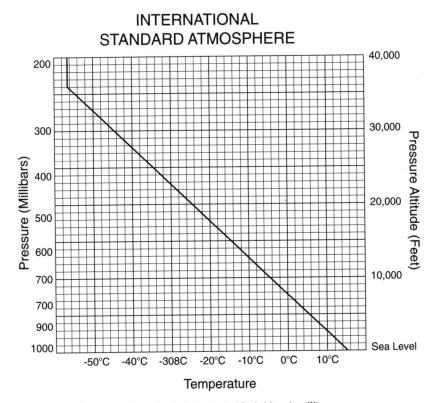

Fig. 8-2. Aircraft performance charts are based on the International Standard Atmosphere (ISA).

atmospheric pressure is extremely high or low, the difference is negligible. A variance of one inch of mercury from standard would only result in a 1000-foot altitude difference. Temperature is the biggest factor.

Standard conditions rarely occur in the real world and performance charts are based on standard conditions; accommodation must be made for a nonstandard environment, usually a temperature correction. Manufacturers sometimes provide an ISA conversion with cruise power setting charts for high, low, and standard temperatures or simply note that performance is based on standard conditions. The aircraft doesn't understand any of this and performs based on the environment-pressure altitude and temperature.

Nonstandard conditions affect true air speed (TAS) and performance, as well as power settings. (TAS is calibrated, or equivalent, airspeed corrected for air density-pressure altitude and temperature. TAS is used on flight plans, and is independent of wind direction and speed.) An aircraft with an advertised service ceiling of 13,100 ft is based on standard conditions. Differences are usually not significant unless the pilot is operating at the limit of the aircraft's performance. Unfortunately, this occurs every year with pilots that attempt to cross the Sierra Nevada or Rocky Mountains in conditions well above standard. Some pilots can't understand why an aircraft with a service ceiling 13,100 ft can't climb above 12,000 ft with an outside air temperature of 0 degrees C. Density Altitude, which is pressure altitude corrected for temperature, at 12,000 ft and temperature 0 degrees C is 13,100. And, this is an ideal case. A runout engine, poor leaning technique, over gross weight, and the possibility of turbulence and downdrafts would further decrease performance. You can't fool Mother Nature; attempts can be fatal.

All aircraft have limitations, including turbojet aircraft that often fly at the edge of their performance envelope where nonstandard conditions critically affect performance. The pilot's task is to determine aircraft performance based on forecast temperatures aloft. This requires the information in Fig. 8-2, The International Standard Atmosphere. From the previous discussion, the average temperature from Oakland to South Lake Tahoe at 13,500 ft was −04 degrees C. Figure 8-2 indicates that the

CASE STUDIES

My 1966 Cessna 150 had a book ceiling of 12,650 ft. We planned to traverse the 9941-foot Tioga Pass in California's Sierra Nevada range. The winds were out of the northeast at only 10 knots, resulting in a slight downdraft from the wind flowing up the east slopes and down the west slopes as we approached the pass. Temperature was slightly above standard, and in combination with the wind, the airplane wouldn't climb out of 9500 ft. We had to proceed north along the west slopes of the mountains to Ebbett's Pass at 8732 ft, where we were able to safely cross the mountains. Gain the required altitude prior to reaching the crest, and with sufficient room to make a comfortable 180, if required.

On another occasion, we had filed for an IFR flight from Lancaster Fox Field in the Mojave Desert to Ontario, California. I requested 7000 ft and planned to go through the San Fernando Valley because of lower minimum altitudes. The clearance came back, "cleared via the Cajon two arrival; climb and maintain 11,000." The surface temperature was 30 degrees C and the Cessna 150 was not going to 11,000 that day. After negotiating with a rather perturbed ground controller, I received my requested routing. Pilots must know their aircraft's performance and not allow ATC, or anyone else for that matter, to push them into an untenable—in this case unobtainable—position.

standard temperature for 13,500 ft is –10 degrees C. The forecast temperature is 6 degrees warmer, which is above standard. The air is less dense than standard, so aircraft performance will be less than performance charts advertise for standard conditions. Based on the above conditions, density altitude is about 15,000 ft.

Certain performance charts require the pilot to determine temperature at altitude relative to ISA. For example, the forecast temperature over Reno at Flight Level 300 (30,000 ft) is –42 degrees C. Figure 8-2 indicates that the standard temperature for that pressure altitude is –45 degrees C. Certain flight computers can be used to determine ISA temperatures; the Jeppesen CR-3 has a true altitude computation window. With the scales aligned (10 on the outer scale with 10 on the inner scale), standard temperature is read under pressure altitude. Under 30,000-ft pressure altitude, –45 appears. Therefore, the forecast temperature is ISA +3.

FDs are a source of forecast freezing level. They should be in general agreement with the FA because they're based on the same data. Differences result from FD freezing levels representing only one point in time, whereas FA forecasts take into account changes during the period. However, if a significant difference occurs, be alert for other possible forecast errors. FSS controllers coordinate with forecasters under such circumstances. Pilots using DUAT would normally have to consult an FSS for resolution. From the example FDs, the expected freezing level at 1800Z over SFO is approximately 12,500 ft, lowering to 11,000 ft in the RNO area.

FDs can be used to determine the approximate height of the tropopause. Winds are strongest just below the tropopause. Checking the example FDs, SFO winds at 39,000 feet are 59 knots and at 45,000 feet have decreased to 49 knots. Also note that speed continues to decrease at 53,000 feet and temperature remains almost constant. Therefore, the tropopause is between the 39,000 and 45,000-foot pressure levels.

FD forecast limitations and amendment criteria must be understood for effective flight planning. Product preparation, plus the advantages—and to some extent, the limitations—of computer models have already been discussed. Surface heating, as well as terrain affect winds aloft. Today's technology cannot account for the effects of land/sea and mountain/valley winds, nor frictional effects between wind and the surface. Other forecast problems include the extent and availability of data, and timing.

FDs are based on the expected movement of weather systems, so errors result when weather systems move faster or slower than forecast. This is one reason why Flight Watch specialists are required to continually solicit reports of winds and temperatures aloft. Specialists are specifically trained to recognize these situations and provide updated information. Careful tracking of position and ground speed will verify the accuracy of the FDs.

Inertial navigation, LORAN, Global Positioning System (GPS), and other computerized navigation systems can provide immediate wind readouts. Anyone remember how to calculate winds with the E6B flight computer? Electronic flight computers make the calculation easy. This is a reminder for pilots to become actively involved in the system with PIREPs. Observed winds aloft, whether they confirm or contradict the forecast, should be routinely passed to Flight Watch. Only two upper air observations are made each day, so PIREPs are the only other direct source of observed winds, and the only way to verify the forecast.

The situation might change in the future with wind profilers that will automatically and almost continuously provide high-resolution upper-air wind measurements. Naturally, the closer to observation time, the more accurate the forecast. Accuracy normally deteriorates with time— the FD2s and especially the FD3s. Since the evening forecast becomes available after 0440Z, it doesn't make much sense to request winds any earlier for the following day. Flights departing after 1640Z must consult the new FDs. Weather patterns can change significantly in 12 hours.

The pilot has no option but to use FDs in flight planning by regulation. Local or short flights might mean nothing more than an eyeball interpolation. Exams and flight tests require computer calculations. Flights toward the limit of aircraft range will require a careful interpolation and calculation.

With the general criticism of winds aloft forecasts, it's amazing how many pilots call and must absolutely have winds two or even three days in the future. Then there's the guy who calls Flight Watch and can't understand why the winds are 20 degrees and five knots off forecast. Oh well, you can't please everyone. By now, we should have some insight into FD limitations, the causes of inaccuracies, and perceived errors of this valuable, but often maligned product.

CHAPTER 9

Radar and Convective Analyses Charts

"A disastrous thunderstorm accident close to Bowling Green, Kentucky, in 1943 that involved an American (Airlines) DC-3 started a chain of events that eventually led to the first systematic research into thunderstorm behavior. The plane crashed onto the ground either near or under a severe thunderstorm. Buell (C. E. Buell, chief meteorologist, American Airlines 1939–1946) initiated a letter to the Civil Aeronautics Board pointing out the appalling dearth of understanding of what actually occurs inside a thunderstorm, as evidenced by the accident investigation. He recommended a massive research effort be organized to probe into thunderstorms and document their internal structure," according to Peter E. Kraght in Airline Weather Services 1931–1981.

Radar was one of many projects, and played a significant role, in the early 1950s. Early airborne radars had many technical problems, but by the beginning of the 1960s, most airliners were equipped with airborne weather radar. Ground-based radar was also developed.

Access to radar information has increased over the years. Until the mid-1990s, NWS radars in the east and FAA radars west of the Rockies, supplemented by a few NWS sites, were used to compile a national radar summary chart. An NWS network in the west was originally thought unjustified because severe weather is relatively rare in that area. Radar weather reports (RAREPs) and convective analysis charts are routinely transmitted on NWS and FAA circuits, and available through many private services. Many twin, and more and more, single-engine aircraft are being equipped with airborne weather radar or lightning detection systems, and there have been several attempts to place ground-based radar displays in the aircraft.

By 1997, the last of the old WSR-57 weather radars had been decommissioned; these were replaced by the next generation (NEXRAD) weather radar (WSR-88D). NEXRAD is a Doppler radar system that, with a few minor exceptions, provides coverage from coast to coast in the contiguous United States, Hawaii, Alaska, and the Caribbean. Each system, product, or service has its own particular application and limitations that must be thoroughly understood for safe and efficient flight.

Radar

Although an oversimplification, radar displays an image dependent on reflected energy or backscatter. Intensity depends on several factors; among them are particle or droplet size, shape, composition, and quantity. NEXRAD radars are capable of displaying both precipitation as well as cloud size particles. However, most displays available to pilots display precipitation-size particles only. Therefore, a precipitation-free area does not translate into a cloud-free sky. Droplets reflect more energy than snow. There is almost no relation between the intensity of snow and backscatter. Therefore, an intensity is not assigned a radar report of snow. On the other hand hail, coated with water, produces the best backscatter and the notation hail shaft may appear on reports and charts.

Pilots have access to NWS radar and airborne weather radar, and to a limited extent ATC radar. The FAA is currently providing Air Traffic Controllers with either separate or overlay NEXRAD products. Each system has a specific purpose and its own application and limitations.

ATC radar is specifically designed to detect aircraft; a narrow fan-shaped beam reaches from near the surface to high altitudes. ATC radars have a wavelength of 23 centimeters (cm), ideal for detecting aircraft, but which reduce the intensity of detected precipitation; additional features reduce the radar's effectiveness to see weather.

To efficiently detect aircraft, and eliminate distracting targets, ATC radars use circular polarization (CP), moving target indicator (MTI), and Sensitivity Time Control (STC).

CP results in a low sensitivity to light and moderate precipitation. MTI only displays moving targets; unless droplets have a rapid horizontal movement they remain undetected; even rapidly moving precipitation will not be observed when advancing perpendicular (tangentially) to the radar beam. STC further eliminates light and decreases the intensities of displayed precipitation. Naturally, controllers, especially at approach facilities, engage these features during poor weather to accomplish their primary task-aircraft separation.

NWS radars, on the other hand, with a narrow linearly polarized beam, are ideal for detecting precipitation-size particles. Sensitivity Time Control on NWS radars compensates for range attenuation, which is loss of power density due to distance from echoes. STC-displayed intensity remains independent of range, and therefore targets with the same intensity, at different ranges, appear the same to the radar specialist. NWS radars can detect targets up to 250 nautical miles (nm), however, due to range and beam resolution, which is the ability of the radar to distinguish individual targets at different ranges and azimuth, an effective range of 125 nm is used.

NEXRAD is a quantum leap in providing early warning of severe weather. NEXRAD will be the standard for the next 20 to 25 years with a wavelength of 10 cm. The WSR-88D network will consist of up to 195 units, 113 NWS sights in the contiguous United States, with additional sites in Alaska, Hawaii, the Caribbean, and western Europe, and 22 Department of Defense (DOD) units. The NEXRAD network fills the radar gaps in the West.

Since NEXRAD is a Doppler radar, it detects the relative velocity of precipitation within a storm. It has increased the accuracy of severe thunderstorm and tornado warnings, and has the capability of detecting wind shear. Figure 9-1 shows a NEXRAD weather radar transmitter site. The radar specialist using a WSR-88D will have Radar Data Acquisition,

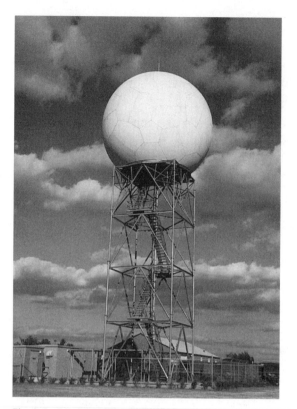

Fig. 9-1. National Weather Service and military NEXRAD radars cover most of the continental United States.

Radar Product Generation, and Display units, as shown in Fig. 9-2. NEXRAD provides hazardous and routine weather radar data typically above 6000 ft east of the Rockies and above 10,000 ft in the western United States. It can also be made available in the aircraft through Mode S transponders with automatic data link capability.

Airborne weather radars are low power, generally with a wavelength of three centimeters. Precipitation attenuation, which is directly related to wavelength and power, can be a significant factor. Precipitation attenuation results from radar energy being absorbed and scattered by close targets and the display becomes unreliable in close proximity to heavy rain or hail. Intensity might be greater than displayed, with distant targets obscured. An accumulation of ice on the radome causes additional distortion.

Fig. 9-2. The NEXRAD radar provides the radar specialist with a computer display of radar echoes, including the relative motion within a storm system.

Figure 9-3 illustrates the effects of precipitation attenuation, showing how a heavy precipitation pattern with a very strong gradient might appear on an NWS 10-cm radar, compared with the same weather system as seen as 3-cm aircraft units. A pilot seeing the pattern on a 3-cm set might elect to penetrate the weather at what appears to be the weakest point only to find the most severe part of the storm, or find additional severe weather where the radar indicated clear.

When using an airborne weather radar, it is imperative to understand the particular unit, its operational characteristics, and limitations. "Just reading through the brochure that comes with the equipment is certainly not enough to prepare a pilot to translate the complex symbology presented on the [airborne] scope into reliable data. A training course with appropriate instructors and simulators is strongly recommended," according to the March–April 1987 FAA Aviation News.

ATTENUATION

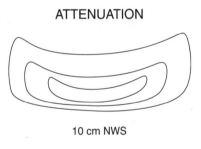

10 cm NWS

3 cm Aircraft

Fig. 9-3. Precipitation attenuation, caused by close targets absorbing and scattering the radar's energy, can be a serious problem with low-power, short-wave-length sets.

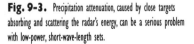

CASE STUDIES

According to the National Transportation Safety Board (NTSB), precipitation attenuation was a contributing factor in the crashes of a Southern Airways DC-9 in 1977 and an Air Wisconsin Metroliner in 1980. Precipitation attenuation is not significant with NWS 10-cm high-power units, however, it can be a serious problem with units of five centimeters or less, especially in heavy rain. The NTSB recommends: "...in the terminal area, comparison of ground returns to weather echoes is a useful technique to identify when attenuation is occurring. Tilt the antenna down and observe ground returns around the radar echo. With very heavy intervening rain, ground returns behind the echo will not be present. This area lacking ground returns is referred to as a shadow and may indicate a larger area of precipitation than is shown on the indicator. Areas of shadowing should be avoided."

In August 1985 a Delta Air Lines L-1011 crashed at the Dallas/Fort Worth Airport. The NTSB was unable to determine if the crew had been using airborne weather radar at the time of the crash. The NTSB report did state however: "The evidence concerning the use of the airborne weather radar at close range was contradictory. Testimony was offered that the airborne weather radar was not useful at low altitudes and in close proximity to a weather cell...;" although, "At least three airplanes scanned the storm at very close range near the time of the accident." The accident was probably caused by a microburst from a single severe storm cell, which illustrates how weather can develop rapidly, often without any severe weather warning.

Flight Service Stations (FSS) and Center Weather Service Units (CWSU) have access to real-time weather radar. Controllers and specialists are specially trained to interpret information for preflight briefings and in-flight weather updates. FSS and Flight Watch specialists translate radar echo coverage into the following categories:

- Widely Scattered—Less than 1/10

- Scattered—1/10 to 5/10

- Broken—6/10 to 9/10

- Solid—More than 9/10

Limitations exist. West of the Rockies, sites suffer from extreme ground clutter—interference of the radar beam due to objects on the ground. Implementation of the NEXRAD network has helped to eliminate many limitations.

Private vendors also have access to radar data. Information from radars is coded and transmitted. When using radar information it's important to know how the unit displays information such as intensity, and if it is indeed a real-time observation, or a freeze or memory display.

The violent nature of thunderstorms causes gust fronts, strong updrafts and downdrafts, and wind shear in clear air adjacent to the storm out to 20 miles with severe storms and squall lines. Precipitation, which is detected by radar, generally occurs in the downdraft, while updrafts remain relatively precipitation free. Clear air or lack of radar echoes does not guarantee a smooth flight near thunderstorms.

Lightning detection equipment

Lightning detection equipment, trade named Stormscope, was invented in the mid 1970s by Paul A. Ryan as a low-cost alternative to radar. Stormscope and similar lightning detectors sense and display electrical discharges in approximate range and azimuth to the aircraft. Stormscope also has limitations. One misconception proclaims that in the absence of dots or lighted bands there are no thunderstorms. However, NASA's tests of the Stormscope differed. Precipitation intensity levels of three and occasionally four (VIP levels) would be indicated on radar without activating the lightning detection system. A clear display only indicates the absence of electrical discharges. This does not necessarily mean convective activity and associated thunderstorm hazards are not present. Even tornadic storms have been found that produced very little lightning. The lack of electrical activity, as with the absence of a precipitation display on radar, does not necessarily translate into a smooth ride.

Many authorities agree that a combination of radar and Stormscope is the best thunderstorm detection system. It cannot be overemphasized that these are avoidance, not penetration devices. Thunderstorms imply severe or greater turbulence and neither radar nor Stormscope, at the present, directly detect turbulence.

Automated radar weather reports (RAREPs)

The National Weather Service routinely takes radar observations from NWS at 35 minutes past the hour. These observations are coded and transmitted over the FAA's weather distribution system and are available on DUAT and the Internet from the AWC's Web site. Locations are contained in Appendix B, Forecast and Report Locations. Aerial coverage is graphically depicted in the *Aeronautical Information Manual* (AIM). The radar report or SD (storm detection) is now automatically generated by NEXRAD radars, which explains some apparent inconsistencies. For example, in the west ground clutter is sometimes reported as weather echoes. SDs contains the following information:

1. The location of the radar.
2. The time of observation.
3. The configuration of echoes.
4. The coverage of echoes.
5. The type of precipitation.
6. The intensity of precipitation.
7. The location of echoes.
8. The movement of echoes.
9. Height of echoes.

The following illustrates a coded SD report. All reports begin with the radar site. This is a report for Davenport, Iowa (DVN). Note that location identifiers do not necessarily correspond to LOCID used with airports and navigational aids (NAVAID). This is the 1535Z observation.

```
DVN 1535 LN 9TRWXX 95/72 119/119 10W C2237
AREA 1TRW++4R- 288/127 91/114 155W C2239 MT 450 AT 108/99
AUTO
```

^IJ10112 JI32222222 KI322213332 LI324212344
MHI2220001456 NH4302 NQ266 OH45 ORI4 PI1 RN1

ECHO CONFIGURATION AND COVERAGE

Echo configuration falls into three categories: cell, area, and line. A single isolated area of precipitation, clearly distinguishable from surrounding echoes, constitutes a cell. The following illustrates how cells are indicated on a RAREP.

FWS 1035 CELL TRWXX 323/95 D30 C2730 MT 550 HOOK 321/91...

This Fort Worth, Texas (FWS) 1035Z special observation reports a cell with a 30-nm diameter (D30) exhibiting a hook echo. Cell diameter refers to precipitation, not necessarily the diameter of the cloud, which could be considerably larger. A hook echo is the signature of a mesolow, often associated with severe thunderstorms that produce strong gusts, hail, and tornadoes. An area consists of a group of echoes of similar type that appear to be associated. A line (LN) defines an area of precipitation more or less in a line—straight, curved, or irregular—at least 30 miles long, five times as long as it is wide, with at least 30-percent coverage. Echo coverage is reported in tenths. In DVN example, the line has 9/10 (LN "9" TRWXX) coverage and the area 1/10 (AREA "1" TRW++4R-) coverage of thunderstorms with very heavy rain and 4/10 (AREA 1TRW++"4"R-) light rain.

PRECIPITATION TYPE AND INTENSITY

SDs, at least at this writing, use the old, pre-1996, aviation weather symbols. These are contained in Table 9-2. In the DVN example the line and the area contain thunderstorms and rain showers (TRW). Following precipitation type, one of the six standard Video Integrator and Processor (VIP) levels describe intensity. VIP level definitions and descriptions are contained in Table 9-1. The line is extreme (TRW "XX") and the area very strong (TRW "++"), with weak rain (R"-").

ECHO LOCATION AND MOVEMENT

The RAREP defines the location of precipitation by points, azimuth (true), and distance (nm) from the reporting station. The line in the

Table 9-1 Radar precipitation intensity levels

VIP LEVEL	SYMBOL	ECHO INTENSITY	PRECIPITATION INTENSITY	RAINFALL RATE (IN) STRATIFORM	RAINFALL RATE (IN) CUMULIFORM	ASSOCIATED WEATHER
1	—	Weak	Light	> 0.1	> 0.2	LGT-MOD TURBC PSBL LTNG
2	(no symbol)	Moderate	Moderate	0.1 to 0.5	0.2 to 1.1	LGT-MOD TURBC PSBL LTNG
3	+	Strong	Heavy	0.5 to 1.0	1.1 to 2.2	SEV TURBC & LTNG
4	++	Very strong	Very heavy	1.0 to 2.0	2.2 to 4.5	SEV TURBC & LTNG
5	X	Intense	Intense	2.0 to 5.0	4.5 to 7.1	SEV TURBC LTNG WIND GUST HAIL
6	XX	Extreme	Extreme	> 5.0	> 7.1	SEV TURBC LTNG EXTENSIVE WIND GUST HAIL

Table 9-2 RAREP/Radar summary chart plotted data

SYMBOL	MEANING	SYMBOL	MEANING
PPINE	No echoes	PPINA	Not available
NE	No echoes	NA	Observation unavailable
LEWP	Line echo wave pattern	BWER	Bounded weak echo pattern
WER	Weak echo region	MLT LVL	Melting level
T	Thunderstorm	RW	Rain showers
R	Rain	S	Snow

DVN report extends from a point 95° at 72 nm (95/72) to a point 119° at 119 nm (119/119), 10 nm wide (10W). The points 288/127 91/114 155W encompass the area. Cell movement indicates short-term motion of cells within the line or area. Cell movement within the line is from 220° at 37 knots (C2237) and area is 220 at 39 knots (C2239).

ECHO HEIGHT

Maximum heights are reported in relation to azimuth and distance from the reporting station, with approximate elevation in thousands of feet MSL (MT 450 AT 108/99). Tops within a stable air mass are usually uniform indicated by the letter U (MT U120, uniform tops to 12,000 ft MSL). It's important to remember these are precipitation tops, not cloud tops. Precipitation tops will be close to cloud tops within building thunderstorms. However, precipitation in dissipating cells will normally be several thousand feet below cloud tops.

RAREP digital data appears at the bottom of the report. A grid centers on the reporting station. Each block, 22 nm on a side, is assigned the maximum VIP level observed. When 20 percent of a block contains VIP level one, that level is assigned. Therefore, from digital data alone, all that can be concluded from VIP level one is that at least 20 percent of that grid contains weak echoes.

Letters represent coordinates; numbers indicate the maximum VIP level for that and succeeding coordinates to the right. These numbers are a prime ingredient in Convective SIGMETs. From the Davenport example we see that strong activity is relatively isolated. It appears that most significant cells can be circumnavigated with storm detection equipment, with only isolated thunderstorm activity within the AREA. We should be able to confirm this with actual real-time radar imagery and the radar summary chart.

Below is another example of a RAREP from the Sacramento, CA (DAX), NWS site. Sacramento radar was not showing any significant weather prior to the following observation.

```
DAX 0135 CELL TRW++ 349/80 D9 C2920 MT 250
AREA IR- 10/115 46/30 80W C2920 MT 130 AT 33/79
IN41 KM101=
```

Look what popped up, a level four (very strong) cell. Thunderstorms were not forecast. This single cell with a diameter of nine miles and approximate precipitation tops to 25,000 ft "didn't read the forecast." The cell should be easily circumnavigable, and only present a hazard if it occurred near the departure or destination airport. A pilot should not fly into, close to, or under this cell.

```
DAX 0235 CELL RW 346/81 D6 C2820 MT 170
AREA IR- 6/95 87/15 80W C2820 MT 120 AT 22/89
IN21 LOI=
```

One hour later the cell has deteriorated to moderate rain showers and continues to decrease in intensity, with maximum precipitation tops down to 17,000 ft MSL. Convective activity can develop and dissipate, often unforecast, at an alarming rate.

Radar Summary Chart

The radar summary chart graphically displays a computer-generated summation of RAREP digital data. The date and time of the observation (time is important because the transmission system might make the report several hours old) appear on the chart. Figure 9-4 illustrates a May 17, 1999 summary based on 1435Z data. [Note that this is the same day and same time frame as the Davenport, Iowa (DVN) RAREP in the previous section.] Similar to the RAREP, the chart contains

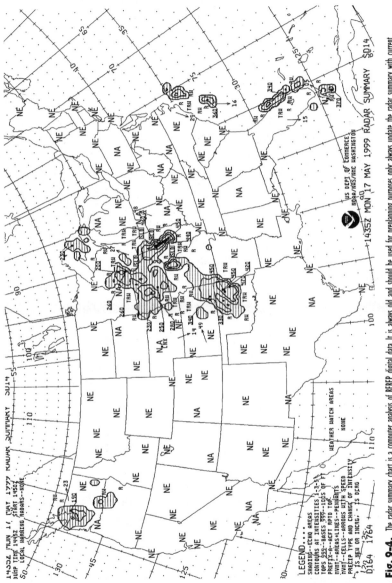

Fig. 9-4. The radar summary chart is a computer analysis of RAREP digital data. It is always old and should be used for preplanning purposes only; always update the radar summary with current observations.

information on precipitation type, intensity, configuration, coverage, tops and bases, and movement.

Echo movement and tops are depicted using symbology similar to the RAREP. An arrow with the speed printed at the arrowhead represents echo or cell movement. Echoes within the line in Illinois (Fig. 9-4) are moving from the southwest at 27 knots at the northern edge and from the southwest at 48 knots central and southern portions. Maximum tops are to 46,000 ft. When bases can be determined, the height MSL will appear below the line.

Echo configuration is graphically depicted. Echoes reported as a line are drawn and labeled solid (SLD) when at least 8/10 coverage exists, such as the line in Illinois. From the REREP data, we can determine that this line has 9/10 coverage. The computer plots lines of equal value to indicate echo coverage and intensity. However, unlike the RAREP, the chart only displays three levels. The first contour includes VIP levels one and two (echoes in central Nebraska and eastern Washington state), the second contour depicts levels three and four (echoes in western Washington state), and the third contour levels five and six (echoes in Iowa, northeast Missouri, and around the line in Illinois).

AC 00-45 Aviation Weather Services states: "When determining intensity levels from the radar summary chart, it is recommended that the maximum possible intensity be used." Precipitation type uses the same symbology as the RAREP.

Using RAREPs and the Radar Summary Chart

Pilots can expect to find holes in what the RAREP or radar summary chart portray as an area of solid echoes. This apparent inconsistency is due to several factors. Targets farther from the antenna might be smaller than depicted due to range and beam resolution. NWS weather radars, at a range of 200 miles, cannot distinguish between individual echoes less than seven miles apart. A safe flight between severe thunderstorms requires 40 miles, so this provides adequate resolution to detect a safe corridor. Recall that as little as 20 percent coverage of VIP one requires the entire grid to be encoded, so holes also occur with isolated and scattered precipitation. On the radar summary chart, large areas might be enclosed by relatively isolated echoes.

For example, in Washington state west of the Cascades, the chart depicts a large area of light to moderate rain and rain showers, precipitation tops to 19,000 ft, moving to the east-northeast at 23 knots. We would suspect this area to only contain scattered precipitation, except along the west slopes of the Cascades where orographic effect has resulted in heavy to very heavy precipitation, although the chances of very heavy precipitation are low. How far south does this activity extend? Be careful. The chart shows that the Portland, Oregon radar is not available (NA).

Assumptions can never be made with RAREPs or the Radar Summary Chart. Can a pilot fly from Oklahoma City and Kansas City avoiding severe weather by at least 20 miles? Not without weather avoidance equipment, contact with a facility with real-time weather radar, or visual contact with the convective activity. Why? RAREPs and the Radar Summary Chart are observations, not forecasts. They report what occurred in the past, and convective activity, as we've seen, can develop and move at an astonishing rate. Time of observation is an important consideration. RAREPs might be as much as two hours old and the radar summary chart from two to four hours old. On the other hand, reports from air traffic controllers with access to NEXRAD observations are usually real-time.

Even though the NEXRAD radar network is complete, there are still a few gaps in the west, coverage is only designed for precipitation above 10,000 ft, and ground clutter is still a problem. Although coverage should be adequate for most severe weather, there is no guarantee of complete coverage. Additionally, pilots must be careful to observe the notation NA, which means radar data is not available. This is especially true when using products from commercial vendors. What appears to be a hole in convective activity, might only be missing data. When using such services be sure you know how the vendor displays missing data.

A pilot can never assume there are holes in the solid line in Illinois. The chart can only be interpreted as 8/10 or more coverage within the line. In fact, as we've seen, the Davenport REREP for about the same time frame showed 9/10 coverage! A pilot could expect to see something similar to Fig. 9-5. By reviewing RAREP digital data, a pilot

Fig. 9-5. A pilot should never attempt to negotiate a line of convective activity without airborne storm detection equipment or direct access to real-time ground-based weather radar information.

can quickly assess echo intensity and coverage. For example, review the digital data for the Davenport RAPEP. Most of the activity is VIP level 2 or lower. But, again without storm detection equipment, access to real-time radar information, or visual contact with convective activity penetrating the area should not even be considered.

The radar summary chart provides general areas and movement of precipitation for planning purposes only, and must be updated by hourly RAREPs or real-time weather radar. Chart notations, such as OM (Out of Service for Maintenance) or NA (Not Available) must be considered. The chart must always be used in conjunction with other charts, reports, and forecasts—the "complete picture." Once airborne, in-flight observations—visual or electronic—and real-time weather radar information from air traffic controllers must be used.

Precipitation should not of itself be cause to cancel a flight. For example, the returns in Washington and Oregon in Fig. 9-4—mostly light to moderate activity. Chances are the Cascades and high mountains will be obscured. Again, without further information a flight decision cannot be made with the information available. A flight decision must be made with the following considerations. What is the coverage and intensity of precipitation? What is the weather expected to do (improve/deteriorate)? What is the pilot's experience level, the capability of the aircraft, and the time of day? It can be difficult to see clouds at night, although lightning flashes are visible, distances can be difficult to judge. How familiar are we with the terrain and weather patterns over the intended route? Is an alternate available if the planned flight cannot be completed? Are we mentally prepared to divert, should it become necessary? What about the our physical condition? Tired and anxious to get home is a potentially fatal combination.

Convective Outlook and Severe Weather Outlook Charts

The convective outlook (AC) is prepared by the Storm Prediction Center at 0700Z, 1500Z, and 1930Z daily. The 0700Z issuance covers a 24-hour period from 1200Z to 1200Z, and the 1500Z and 1930Z ACs update the original issuance. The AC describes the potential for thunderstorm activity and describes areas where thunderstorms might approach severe limits. Risk categories are defined: slight risk 2 percent to 5 percent coverage, moderate risk 6 percent to 10 percent coverage, and high risk more than 10 percent coverage.

```
MKC AC 222001
CONVECTIVE OUTLOOK...REF AFOS NMCGPH94O.
VALID 222000Z - 231200Z
THERE IS A SLGT RISK OF SVR TSTMS TO THE RIGHT OF A LINE
FROM 40 E IND 30 NE OWB PAH 35 ESE FYV MKO 45 WSW TUL 25
SE PNC 30 ENE EMP 30 NE MKC BRL 25 NE MMO 15 WNW SBN 30
W FWA 40 E IND. GEN TSTMS ARE FCST TO THE RIGHT OF A LINE
FROM 20 ESE NEL 25 WSW ABE PIT BWG JBR 10 SSE FSM 25 NNW
MLC 30 NE OKC PNC 10 NNW EMP 20 W 3OI 10 NNW DBQ 30 SE
OSH 20 ENE OSC 30 SSW ART 15 SSE PVD.
GEN TSTMS ARE FCST TO THE RIGHT OF A LINE FROM 30 S MTJ
GUP PRC 30 NE DAG 40 SSE BIH 50 ESE NFL 55 S EKO 20 SSE VEL 30
S MTJ.
...SEVERE THUNDERSTORM FORECAST DISCUSSION...
SURFACE LOW CENTER REMAINS OVER SERN KS AT THIS
```

TIME...WITH STATIONARY FRONT EXTENDING NEWD INTO NERN MO AND NRN IL AND TRAILING COLD FRONT MOVING ACROSS WRN OK/NWRN TX. EXTENSIVE SURFACE HEATING HAS OCCURRED INTO NERN OK/FAR SERN KS/SWRN MO EARLY THIS AFTERNOON...THOUGH AMOUNT OF LOW LEVEL WAVE CLOUDS ON VISIBLE IMAGERY SUGGESTS STRONG LID/CAP REMAINS OVER THIS REGION. HOWEVER LARGE SCALE LIFTING ALONG NOSE OF MID/UPPER LEVEL SPEED MAX AND ASSOCIATED WITH SHORT-WAVE TROUGH LIFTING ACROSS ERN KS...SHOULD ALLOW STORMS TO INCREASE ALONG FRONT INTO MO OVER THE NEXT FEW HOURS. AXIS OF MODERATE INSTABILITY WITH SURFACE-BASED CAPES TO 1500 J/KG SHOULD ALSO CONTINUE AHEAD OF FRONT AND...COMBINED WITH INCREASING DEEP LAYER SHEAR...WILL SUPPORT A THREAT OF ISOLATED SEVERE THUN-DERSTORMS. FORECAST SOUNDINGS INDICATE WIND FIELDS WILL REMAIN MORE THAN SUFFICIENT FOR SUPERCELLS...HOW-EVER STRONG CAP MAY LIMIT ACTIVITY TO A LINE OF STORMS FORCED ALONG COLD FRONT WITH MAIN THREATS OF ISO-LATED LARGE HAIL/DAMAGING WINDS. OTHER STORMS MAY INCREASE INV OF STATIONARY FRONT OVER NRN MO INTO NRN IL DURING THE EARLY EVENING...THOUGH 18Z SOUNDING FROM ILX SUGGESTS BEST SEVERE POTENTIAL INTO THIS REGION MAY WAIT UNTIL LATER THIS EVENING WHEN STRONGER MID/UPPER LEVEL SPEED MAX LIFTS NEWD AND SURFACE LOW MOVES ACROSS. ACTIVITY SHOULD INCREASE IN COVERAGE INTO THE EVENING ALONG LOW LEVEL JET AXIS INTO THE MID MS RIVER VALLEY...THOUGH SEVERE POTENTIAL WILL LIKELY DIMINISH LATER TONIGHT AS INSTABILITY AND LAPSE RATES WEAKEN. ..EVANS.. 04/22/99

This AC was issued on the 22nd day of the month and valid from 222000Z until 231200Z. The time frame for this AC is the same as the example WST and WW discussed in chapter 4, weather advisories. There is a slight risk of severe thunderstorms to the right of a line described by the location identifiers. General thunderstorms are forecast to the right of a line specified by the location identifiers. General thunderstorms are those not expected to reach severe limits. This is followed by a severe thunderstorm forecast discussion. This narrative falls into the same category as the outlook portion of Convective SIGMETs, providing synoptic details in meteorological terms directed toward forecasters more than pilots. Although the discussion often provides insight into the overall weather picture.

A surface low center remains over southeastern Kansas at this time, with a stationary front extending northeastward into northeastern Missouri and northern Illinois, with a trailing cold front moving across western Oklahoma and northwestern Texas. Extensive surface heating has occurred into northeastern Oklahoma, far southeastern Kansas, and southwestern Missouri early this afternoon, although the amount of low-level wave clouds on visible imagery suggests a strong lid or cap remains over this region. However, there is large-scale lifting along the nose of a mid- to upper-level speed max and associated with short-wave trough lifting across eastern Kansas should allow storms to increase along the front into Missouri over the next few hours. An axis of moderate instability with surface-based caps to 1500 joules/kilogram should also continue ahead of the front and combined with increasing deep layer shear, will support a threat of isolated severe thunderstorms. Forecast soundings indicate wind fields will remain more than sufficient for supercells. However, strong caps may limit activity to a line of storms forced along the cold front with the main threats of isolated large hail and damaging winds. Other storms may increase in the vicinity of the stationary front over northern Missouri into northern Illinois during the early evening, although the 18Z sounding from ILX suggests that best severe potential into this region may wait until later this evening when stronger mid- to upper-level speed max lifts northeastward and surface low moves across. Activity should increase in coverage into the evening along low-level jet axis into the mid-Mississippi river valley, although severe potential will likely diminish later tonight as instability and lapse rates weaken.

The severe weather outlook chart provides a preliminary 48-hour thunderstorm probability potential. The left panel gives a 24-hour outlook for general and severe thunderstorms. Figure 9-6 is valid for the same time frame as the AC in the previous discussion. From Fig. 9-6, there is a slight risk of severe thunderstorms in the central Mississippi and Ohio River valleys. The right panel, for the next 24 hours, shows the severe activity moving southeastward.

This chart indicates areas where conditions are right for the development of convective activity sometime during the period. The manually prepared chart is a pictorial display of the AC, however, it is not amended nor updated.

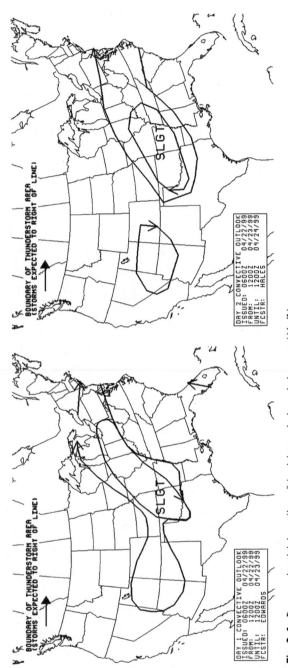

Fig. 9-6. The severe weather outlook chart provides a preliminary look at general and severe thunderstorm potential for 48 hours.

A potential for thunderstorms exists within depicted areas. This does not necessarily mean thunderstorms will develop. The chart, like the AC, is strictly for advanced planning to alert forecasters, pilots, briefers, and the public to the possibility of future storm development. Appropriate FAs, TAFs, WSTs, and severe weather watches must be consulted just prior to and during flight for details on convective activity.

Moisture/Stability Charts

Moisture/stability charts consist of the lifted index analysis, precipitable water, freezing level, and average relative humidity charts. Available twice daily, the charts are computer-generated from radiosonde data. Notice in Fig. 9-7 and 9-8 that the analysis is based on the 0000Z observation, Thursday April 22, 1999. This is the same general time frame as the WST and WW in chapter 4 and AC previously discussed. Due to computation and transmission times this chart is about four-and-a-half hours old by the time it becomes available.

The Lifted Index provides an indication of atmospheric moisture and stability—thunderstorm potential at the time of observation. The Lifted Index compares the temperature that a parcel of air near the surface would have if lifted to the 500-mb level and cooled adiabatically, with the observed temperature at 500 mbs. The index indicates stability at the 500-mb level. The index can range from +20 to –20, but generally remains between +10 and –10 (the figures are strictly an index, not a representation of temperature). A positive index indicates a stable condition, high positive values very stable air. A zero index indicates neutral stability. Values from zero to minus four indicate areas of potential convection. Large negative values from minus five to minus eight represent very unstable air, which could result in severe thunderstorms—should convection develop.

The K Index evaluates moisture and temperature. The higher the K Index the greater potential for an unstable lapse rate and the availability of moisture. The K Index must be used with caution; it is not a true stability index. Large K Indexes indicate favorable conditions for air mass thunderstorms, during the thunderstorm

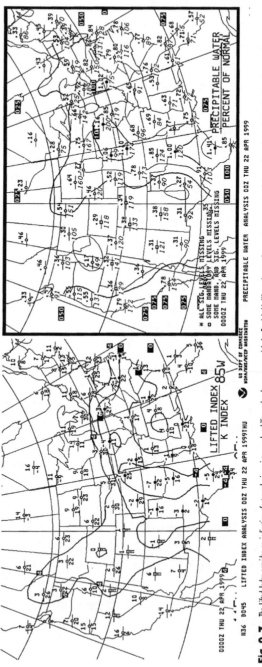

Fig. 9-7. The Lifted Index provides an indication of atmospheric moisture and stability—thunderstorm potential; the Precipitable Water analyzes water vapor content between the surface and the 500-mb level.

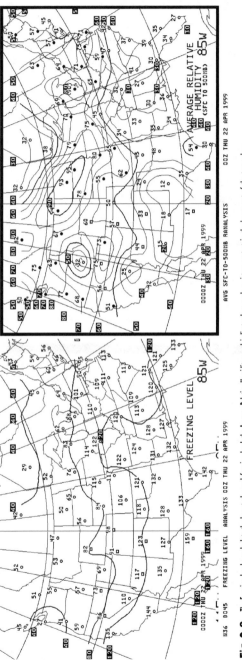

Fig. 9-8. The Freezing Level panel plots the lowest observed freezing level; the Average Relative Humidity panel indicates large-scale moisture content in the lower part of the troposphere.

season. K values can change significantly over short periods due to temperature and moisture advection.

Refer to the Lifted Index panel, left panel Fig. 9-7. The Lifted Index appears above the K Index in the plotted data. Isopleths— lines equal in number or quantity—of stability are plotted beginning at zero, then for every four units (plus and minus). Negative Lifted Indexes and large K values exist over southern Mississippi Valley and into the Ohio River Valley. The chart would, therefore, indicate a potential for thunderstorms in those areas— no surprise. Conversely, positive Lifted Indexes and small K values were observed over the southwest indicating little moisture and a stable lapse rate.

The precipitable water panel, right panel of Fig. 9-7, analyzes water vapor content from the surface to 500 mbs. Darkened station circles indicate large amounts of available water. Isopleths of precipitable water are drawn at one-quarter intervals. The panel is more useful for meteorologists concerned with flash floods. The chart can be used to determine if the air is drying out or increasing in moisture with time by looking at the wind field upstream from a station. Therefore, a pilot can get an excellent indication of changes in moisture content. For example, considerable moisture exists over southern Mississippi Valley and into the Ohio River Valley. Elsewhere in the United States, the air is relatively dry this day.

By applying wind flow from observed and forecast charts, we can obtain a general sense of movement. For example, from the thunderstorm discussion in the AC we would expect the moisture and instability to be advected to the southeast. Which, in fact, the convective outlook chart indicates.

The freezing level chart, left panel of Fig. 9-8, plots the lowest observed freezing level. These are plotted in hundreds of feet mean sea level above the station circle. Lines connecting equal values of freezing level are drawn at 4000-ft intervals. Below freezing temperatures at the surface are indicated by a dashed line labeled 32F. For this observation surface temperatures across the United States are above freezing. (Below freezing surface temperatures are indicated by the contraction BF.) Freezing levels range from around 4000 ft in the north to well above 12,000 ft in the south. Multiple entries indicate inversions, and above-freezing temperatures, aloft (none exist on this particular observation). Keep in mind this is observed data and must be used with forecast information contained in the AIRMET Bulletin, SIGMETs, and other forecasts for flight planning.

Two crossings of the freezing level can occur with surface temperature below freezing. For example, should a station report 68 above 39; temperatures are below freezing from the surface to 3900 ft MSL, with a layer above freezing air from 3900 to 6800 ft.

Figure 9-9 pictorially illustrates three crossings of the freezing level. Note first surface temperature is above freezing. The first crossing occurs at 2200 feet MSL (22 below the station circle), the second crossing occurred at 3200 feet MSL (32), and the third at 7600 feet MSL (76). In this example, air temperature that is above freezing occurs from the surface to 2200 feet, and again between 3200 and 7600 feet—the gray shaded area to the right of the 0 isotherm. This could be significant should an altitude be required to shed ice. A word of caution. Don't bet your life that these conditions will exist. Hoping an inversion aloft will be available should never be your only escape plan.

Freezing level data (RADAT) in the past appeared in remarks on 00Z and 12Z surface observations associated with radiosonde (upper air) observation sites. The RADAT has been removed form these observations in the contiguous United States. At the present, RADAT information is only available from an FSS. In the future, DUAT or the Internet may make this data available. Radiosonde release sites can be found in the back of the appropriate *Airport/Facility Directory*.

The data consists of the freezing level in hundreds of feet MSL, and relative humidity at that level. For example,.../RADAT 32078; the first two digits represent relative humidity (32 percent) at the freezing level of 7800 MSL. With multiple freezing levels, the highest relative humidity is indicated by the letter "L" lowest, "M" middle, or "H" highest crossing of the zero degree temperature. For example, the RADAT for the station in Fig. 9-9 might appear: .../RADAT98M022032076. In this example, the highest relative humidity is 98 percent, which occurred at the middle (M) 3200-foot crossing.

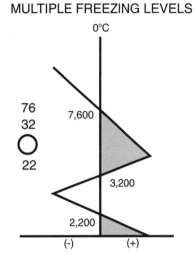

MULTIPLE FREEZING LEVELS

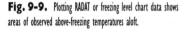

Fig. 9-9. Plotting RADAT or freezing level chart data shows areas of observed above-freezing temperatures aloft.

High relative humidity indicates moisture and the possibility of icing at and above the freezing level. This is similar to the information available on the Freezing Level chart, except that relative humidity is not plotted on the chart.

Other RADAT and chart symbols indicate the sounding was missed (M), due to equipment trouble or other factors, or delayed (NIL). If the entire sounding is below 0°C, RADAR ZERO or BF will be reported.

The average relative humidity panel, right panel of Fig. 9-8, analyzes the average relative humidity from the surface to 500 mbs. Darkened station plots indicate high humidity—50 percent or greater. Isohumes—lines of equal relative humidity—are drawn at 10-percent intervals. The chart indicates large-scale moisture content in the lower part of the troposphere. Frequently clouds and precipitation are indicated by relative humidity of 50 percent or greater. Clouds and precipitation are indicated in the northern Mississippi Valley and Great Lakes regions with a lifting mechanism available and 70 to 90 percent relative humidity. Little, if any, clouds or precipitation would be expected in the desert southwest with humidity of 40 percent or less.

Figure 9-8 indicates several likely areas for significant convective activity. The central Mississippi Valley and Ohio River Valley are prime candidates, due to abundant moisture and instability.

These charts are useful in determining the characteristics of a particular weather system in terms of stability, moisture, and possible aviation weather hazards. Although these charts are hours old by the time they become available, the weather systems will tend to move these characteristics with them. Although, caution should be exercised as characteristics may be modified through development, dissipation, or the movement of weather systems.

The lifted index analysis is only one element used to develop the AC, severe weather outlook chart, and other forecasts. Instability below 500 mbs might not be indicated. The chart is several hours old when received, and the Lifted Index does not consider a lifting mechanism, nor can it consider modifications by the development, dissipation, and movement of systems. AC 00-45 Aviation Weather Services states: "It is essential to note that an unstable index does not automatically mean thunderstorms."

Certain pilots have attached great significance to the AC and lifted index analysis. They infer some additional insight into thunderstorm activity and severity from these products. The lifted index is an observation and only one element used to prepare the AC and other products. The convective outlook and severe weather outlook chart are just that, an outlook. They merely provide a statement of potential and must never be used in place of weather advisories, the area forecast, or terminal aerodrome forecasts.

Microbursts and Low-Level Wind Shear

As aircraft instruments and navigational system capabilities improved, pilots began taking on more and more weather. Hazards of fog and low clouds were solved with the Instrument Landing System (and increased fuel reserves). Icing was overcome in the 1930s and, for the most part, turbulence and thunderstorms were mastered with high-cruise altitudes and radar. With these hazards solved, major air carrier accidents most often fall into the categories of mechanical failure, pilot error, and wind shear.

The hazards of wind shear can be even more critical to general aviation. Wind shear, a rapid change in wind direction or speed, has always been around. Convective activity produces severe shear, which is defined as a rapid change in wind direction or velocity causing airspeed changes greater than 15 knots or vertical speed changes greater than 500 feet per minute. The microburst produces the most severe wind shear threat.

Rain-cooled air within a thunderstorm produces a concentrated rain or virga shaft less than one-half mile in diameter, which forms a downdraft. The downdraft or downburst has a very sharp edge, forms a ring vortex upon contact with the ground, and spreads out— causing gust fronts that are particularly hazardous to aircraft during takeoff, approach, and landing. Reaching the ground the burst continues as an expanding outflow.

A microburst consists of a small-scale, severe storm downburst less than two-and-a-half miles across. This flow can be 180 degrees from the prevailing wind, with an average peak intensity of about 45 knots.

Microburst winds intensify for about five minutes after ground contact and typically dissipate about 10 to 20 minutes later. Microburst wind speed differences of almost 100 knots have been measured. On August 1, 1983, at Andrews Air Force Base, indicated differences near 200 knots were observed. Some microburst events are beyond the capability of any aircraft and pilot to recover. Although normally midafternoon, midsummer events, microbursts can occur any time, in any season.

The FAA, along with a group of aviation specialists, has developed AC 00-54 *Pilot Windshear Guide*. Although, primarily for the airlines, much of the information can be applied to general aviation. Avoidance is the best defense against a microburst encounter. When the possibility of microbursts exists, the pilot must continually check all clues. Therefore, he or she must learn to recognize situations favorable to this phenomenon.

Wind Shear Recognition

The following discussion is based on *AC 00-54, Pilot Windshear Guide* and a Department of Commerce publication, *Microbursts: A Handbook for Visual Identification*. The latter publication is for sale by the Superintendent of Documents. It contains an in-depth, technical explanation of the phenomena along with numerous color photographs depicting microburst activity. It should be part of every pilot's library.

Microbursts can develop any time that convective activity, such as thunderstorms, rain showers, or virga occur, associated with both heavy and light precipitation. Approximately five percent of all thunderstorms produce microbursts. And, more than one microburst can occur with the same weather system. Therefore, pilots must be alert for additional microbursts—if one has already been encountered or reported—and be prepared for turbulence and shear as subsequent microbursts interact. Microbursts are characterized by precipitation or dust curls carried back up toward the cloud base, horizontal bulging near the surface in a rain shaft forming a foot-shaped prominence, an increase in wind speed as the microburst expands over the ground, and abrupt wind gusts.

Microbursts can occur in extremely dry, as well as wet, environments. The lack of low clouds does not guarantee the absence of shear. Microbursts can develop below clouds with bases as high as 15,000 feet. As virga or light rain falls, intense cooling causes the cold air to plunge, resulting in a dry microburst. Evaporative Cooling Turbulence, associated with this phenomena, has already been discussed. Anvils of large dry-line thunderstorms can produce high-level virga and result in dry microbursts. High-based thunderstorms with heavy rain should be of particular concern. This was the type that produced intense wind shear in the 1985 Delta accident in Dallas/Fort Worth.

Embedded microbursts are produced by heavy rain from low-based clouds in a wet environment. A wet microburst might first appear as a darkened mass of rain within a light rain shaft. As the microburst moves out along the surface, a characteristic upward curl appears.

The potential for wind shear and microbursts exists whenever convective activity occurs. Pilots should review forecasts (FAs, TAFs, WSTs, and AWWs) for thunderstorms (thunderstorms imply low-level wind shear) or the inclusion of LLWS. Check surface reports and PIREPs for wind shear clues: thunderstorms, rain showers, gusty winds, or blowing dust. Dry microbursts are more difficult to recognize. Check surface reports for convective activity (VCRA, CBs, or VIRGA) and low relative humidity (15 degrees C to 30 degrees C temperature/dew point spread).

The Low-Level Wind Shear Alert System (LLWAS) has been installed at 110 airports in the United States. The system detects differences between wind speed around the airport and a reference center-field station. Differences trigger an alert. Sensors are not necessarily associated with specific runways, therefore descriptions of remote sites are based on the eight points of the compass: "Center field wind three one zero at one five. North boundary wind zero niner zero at three five."

The *Airport/Facility Directory* advertises the availability of LLWAS under Weather Data Sources. The lack of an LLWAS alert does not necessarily indicate the absence of wind shear. LLWAS has limitations. Magnitude of the shear might be underestimated. Surface obstructions can disrupt or limit the airflow near the sensor and due to location of sensors, microburst development might go undetected, especially in the early stages. Sensors are located at the surface, therefore, microburst development that has not yet reached the surface will be undetected and because coverage only exists near the runways, microbursts on approach will not be observed. Even with these limitations, LLWAS can provide useful information about winds near the airport.

Development and installation continues on an automated Terminal Doppler Weather Radar (TDWR) system that is based on the same principle as NEXRAD. TDWR will provide wind shear and microburst warnings to controllers.

Airborne radar returns of heavy precipitation indicate the possibility of microbursts. Although potentially hazardous dry microbursts might only produce weak radar returns. Strong wind shear might occur as far as 15 miles from storm echoes. Radar echoes can be misleading by themselves, and it might require a Doppler radar to spot the danger of a dry microburst. The southwest edge of an intense storm can appear weak both visually and on radar, however, this area is known to spawn tornadoes and severe wind shear. Convective weather approaching an airport, the downwind side, tends to be more hazardous than activity moving away.

No quantitative means exist for determining the presence or intensity of microburst wind shear. Pilots must exercise extreme caution when determining a course of action. Microburst wind shear probability guidelines have been developed by the FAA, and apply to operations within three miles of the airport, along the intended flight path, and below 1000 feet AGL. Probabilities are cumulative, therefore when more than one point exists, probability increases.

The following indicate a high probability of wind shear with the presence of convective weather near the intended flight path.

1. Localized strong winds reported, or observed blowing dust, rings of dust or tornadolike features.

2. Visual or radar indications of heavy precipitation.

3. PIREPs of airspeed changes 15 knots or greater.

4. LLWAS Alert or wind velocity change of 20 knots or greater.

A pilot must give critical attention to these observations. A decision to avoid, divert, or delay, is wise.

The following indicate a medium probability of wind shear with the presence of convective weather near the intended flight path.

1. Rain showers, lightning, virga, or moderate or greater turbulence reported or indicated on radar.

2. A temperature/dew point spread of 15°C to 30°C.

3. PIREPs of airspeed changes less than 15 knots.

4. LLWAS Alert or wind velocity change less than 20 knots.

A pilot should consider avoiding these conditions. Precautions are indicated.

The FAA states: "Pilots are...urged to exercise caution when determining a course of action." Probability guidelines "...should not replace sound judgment in making avoidance decisions." In aviation weather, there are no guarantees. The lack of high or medium probability indicators in no way promises the absence of wind shear when convective weather is present or forecast. Avoidance is the best precaution.

Review the following Colorado Springs (COS) METAR and UUA for wind shear probability indicators.

METAR KCOS 202150Z 36012G24KT 45SM -TSRA BKN090 OVC250 23/08 A3019 RMK TS OVH MOV E OCNL LTGCG SW E

COS UUA /OV COS/TM 2156/...TP PA60/RM AIRSPEED +– 40 KTS, THOUGHT I WAS IN THE TWILIGHT ZONE

A thunderstorm with rain showers, a 15-degree temperature/dew point spread, strong, gusty surface winds, and lightning is being reported. Add the PIREP and there are two high and two moderate probability indicators. This is an example of the dry environment. A pilot must be watchful for visual microburst and LLWS clues.

This METAR indicates a wet microburst environment.

METAR KPHL 032250Z 36018G24KT 1SM +TSRA BR VV006...RMK FQT LTGICCG

A thunderstorm with heavy precipitation, strong, gusty winds, and lightning is being reported. There is certainly a high probability of wind shear and microbursts.

Takeoff, Approach, and Landing Precautions

Select the longest suitable runway for takeoff. Determine at what point the takeoff can be aborted with enough runway to stop the aircraft. Certain manufacturers provide tables for takeoff calculations, otherwise, the pilot will have to base this distance on landing roll tables and experience. Use the recommended flap setting for gusty wind or turbulent conditions, if available. Use maximum-rated takeoff power. This reduces takeoff roll and overrun exposure. Consider increased airspeed at rotation to perhaps improve the ability of the airplane to negotiate wind shear or turbulence after liftoff. Do not use a speed reference flight director. Be alert for airspeed fluctuations that might be the first signs of wind shear. Should shear be encountered with sufficient runway remaining, abort the takeoff. This decision, however, can only be made by the pilot, based on training and experience. After takeoff, use maximum rated power and rate of climb to achieve a safe altitude, at least 1000 ft AGL.

Select the longest suitable runway to land. Consider a recommended approach configuration with a higher than normal approach speed. Turbulent air penetration or maneuvering speed should be considered. Establish a stabilized approach at least 1000 ft AGL with configuration, power, and trim set to follow the glide slope without additional changes. Any deviation from glide slope or airspeed change will indicate shear. The autopilot, except for autoflight systems, should be disengaged, with the pilot closely monitoring vertical speed, altimeter, and glide slope displacement. Ground speed and airspeed comparisons can provide additional information for wind shear recognition. Increased approach speed, while providing an extra margin for safety, will require longer than normal landing distance.

Wind Shear Recovery Technique

Wind shear recovery technique has not yet been developed for small aircraft. The following wind shear recovery technique, developed for airline aircraft, has been adapted from AC 00-54. It is, however, logical and applicable to most wind shear encounters in practically any aircraft.

Wind shear recognition is crucial to making a timely recovery decision. Encounters occur infrequently with only a few seconds to initiate a successful recovery. The objective is to keep the airplane flying as long as possible in hope of exiting the shear. The first priority must be to maintain airplane control. The following guidelines were developed for the airlines, exact criteria cannot be established. Whenever these parameters are exceeded, recovery and/or abandoning the takeoff or approach should be strongly considered. It must be emphasized that it is the responsibility of the pilot to assess the situation and use sound judgment in determining the safest course of action. It might be necessary to initiate recovery before any of these parameters are reached.

1. Plus or minus 15 knots indicated airspeed.

2. Plus or minus 500 feet per minute vertical speed.

3. Plus or minus one dot glide slope displacement.

4. Unusual throttle position for a significant period.

If any condition is encountered, aggressively apply maximum rated power. Avoid engine overboost unless required to avoid ground contact. While on approach, do not attempt to land. Establish maximum rate of climb airspeed. As with any turbulent condition, pitch up in a smooth, steady manner. Should ground contact be imminent, pitch up to best-angle-of-climb airspeed, being careful not to stall the airplane. Controlled contact with the ground is preferable to an uncontrolled encounter. When airplane safety has been ensured, adjust power to maintain specified limits. When the airplane is climbing and ground contact is no longer an immediate concern, cautiously reduce pitch to desired airspeed.

The key to the thunderstorm and LLWS hazard is avoidance. A superior pilot uses superior knowledge to avoid having to use superior skill. At the first sign of severe shear reject the takeoff or abandon the approach. It is easier to explain an aborted takeoff or missed approach to passengers rather than to explain an accident to the FAA and insurance company—assuming you're still around to do so.

Avoidance is the operative word with thunderstorms, microbursts, and wind shear. A pilot's proper application of many resources—training, experience, visual references, cockpit instruments, weather reports and forecasts—make avoidance possible.

CHAPTER 10

Air Analysis Charts

Considerable misunderstanding arises because many aviation weather texts fail to adequately describe and explain nonfrontal weather-producing systems. A pilot presented with such a situation will commonly ask the briefer, "Where's the front?" Only to be told, "There is no front." Weather occurs at all altitudes within the troposphere; the surface analysis chart often cannot solely explain the weather, even weather occurring at or near the surface.

Surface and upper-air analysis charts graphically display a three-dimensional view of the atmosphere based on selected locations at the time of observation. These charts provide a primary source for locating areas of moisture and vertical motion. The following products are normally available to aviation.

- Surface analysis

- Weather depiction

- 850-mb constant pressure chart

- 700-mb constant pressure chart

- 500-mb constant pressure chart

- 300-mb constant pressure chart

- 200-mb constant pressure chart

Each provides details on phenomena occurring at that level. The most complete description of the atmosphere can only be obtained from a combined analysis, which should include the radar summary chart.

Surface Analysis Chart

The surface analysis chart provides a first look at weather systems. Sea-level pressure is the key element. Observed station pressure, converted to sea level, allows analysis from a common reference. The sea-level conversion introduces errors, especially in mountainous areas. The data is computer analyzed for a first guess at isobars—lines of equal sea-level pressure. NWS meteorologists manually correct the chart before transmission and annotate the position of fronts based on pressure patterns, wind shifts, the previous chart, and satellite imagery. The chart also contains wind flow, temperature, and moisture patterns, providing a primary source for the synopsis.

The surface analysis chart has come a long way since its inception. Figure 10-1 shows a Daily Weather Map circa 1918. These maps were first drawn by hand by individual weather stations, then were transmitted by facsimile. Now charts are computer generated and distributed.

Often the exact location, and sometimes even the presence, of fronts are a matter of judgment (a front can be a zone several hundred miles across). Additionally, fronts do not necessarily reach the surface; they might be found within layers aloft. This is especially true in the western United States and the Appalachians where mountain ranges break up fronts. Therefore, there might be differences between the charted position of fronts and their location as described in the FA or TWEB synopsis. In such cases, it would be advisable to compare chart, FA, and TWEB analysis, and the time of each product.

The surface analysis chart is prepared and transmitted every three hours and is available at Flight Service Stations and through most commercial vendors with graphics capability. The amount of detail

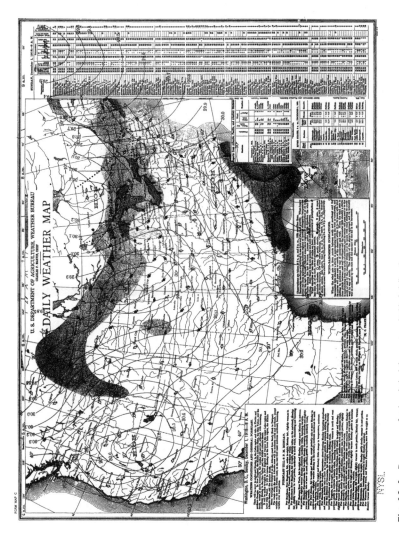

Fig. 10-1. These maps were first drawn by hand, then were transmitted by facsimile, and are now computer generated and distributed.

available will depend on the vendor. Observed data must be plotted and analyzed, so the chart is always old, sometimes several hours, by the time it becomes available. The chart should always be updated with current reports.

An overall perspective of the history of system movements can be obtained by reviewing previous charts. Even though, care must be used with the apparent movement of low-pressure centers, fronts, and troughs, especially across the western United States. Their movement is subjectively analyzed by the meteorologist.

Surface Analysis Station Model

Most pilots have forgotten how to read station models. But, with commercial weather vendors, pilots might need to brush up on this skill. Flight Watch specialists, trained in their interpretation, use surface analysis chart station models when METARs are not available. Pilots don't need to decode the entire model, just the details significant to aviation.

Figure 10-2 provides an explanation of the station model. Information on the right is primarily for the meteorologists. Above and below the model are cloud types. On the left is information most significant to aviation. This includes temperature and dew point (degrees Fahrenheit), present weather (symbols similar to Fig. 5-4), total sky cover (Fig. 10-3), and wind direction and speed—each barb represents 10 knots, half barb 5 knots, and a flag 50 knots.

From Fig. 10-3, total sky cover contains more detail than METAR reports. There is a general correlation, but heights are not provided, and it is the summation of all cloud layers. Automated sites are depicted with a square. A diagonal line in the upper left corner of the square indicates CLR BLO 120. Figure 10-3 also decodes cloud-type symbols used with station models. Considerable information can be deduced from reported cloud types. A pilot should have a general understanding of the codes. Unfortunately, cloud-type codes will disappear with many automated observations.

Meteorologists divide clouds into four main groups:

• Low clouds (bases near the surface to about 6500 feet)

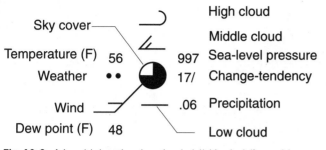

Fig. 10-2. Surface analysis chart station modes contain much valuable information significant to aviation.

Total Sky Cover

Clear	less than 1/10	1/10-5/10	6/10-9/10	10/10 BINOVC	10/10	☓

vv

Clouds

1 CU		1 AS		1 CI	
2 CU		2 AS		2 CI	
3 CB		3 AC		3 CI	
4 SC		4 AC		4 CI	
5 SC		5 AC		5 CS	
6 ST		6 AC		6 CS	
7 FC		7 AC		7 CS	
8 CU/SC		8 AC		8 CS	
9 CB		9 AC		9 CC	

Fig. 10-3. Considerable information can be deduced from reported cloud type.

- Middle clouds (bases from 6500 feet to 20,000 feet)

- High clouds (based at or above 20,000 feet)

- Clouds with vertical development (based near the surface, tops of cirrus; Cu and Cb)

Notice that in Fig. 10-3 Cu and Cb are listed with low clouds, associated with their bases.

The following discussion, based on the cloud types in Fig. 10-3, might refer to a code number (1 through 9) to the left of the contraction and symbol.

The code starts with low clouds with vertical development. Cumulus (1) describes fair weather Cu, seemingly flattened, with little vertical development: no significant weather, turbulent below the bases and smooth on top. Cumulus (2) contains considerable vertical development, generally towering. This type precedes the development of cumulonimbus and thunderstorms. METAR may contain TCU (towering cumulus). This refers to growing cumulus that resembles a cauliflower, but with tops that have not yet reached the cirrus level. Cumulonimbus (3) exhibit great vertical development with tops composed, at least in part, of ice crystals. Tops no longer contain the well-defined cauliflower shape. Cumulonimbus (9) have clearly fibrous (cirroform) tops, often anvil shaped. (You may have heard the saying, "I'm on cloud nine." This was its origin.) Regardless of vertical development, a cloud is classified as cumulonimbus only when all or part of the top is transformed, or in the process of transformation, into a cirrus mass. Any cumulonimbus cloud should be considered a thunderstorm with all the ominous implications.

Stratocumulus (4) and (5), and cumulus and stratocumulus (8) represent a moist layer with some convection. Stratocumulus (4) forms from the spreading of Cu, which indicates decreasing convection. Stratus indicates low-level stability. Fractostratus and fractocumulus (scud) are normally associated with bad weather.

Middle clouds fall into two general types: altostratus and altocumulus. Altostratus indicates a stable atmosphere at mid levels. Altostratus (1) is thin, semitransparent, while altostratus (2) is thick enough to hide the sun or moon. Rain or snow, even heavy snow, can fall from altostratus. When the cloud layer thickens and lowers it becomes nimbostratus (Ns).

Altocumulus indicates vertical motion at mid levels. Altocumulus (3) is thin, mostly semitransparent. Altocumulus numbers (5), (6), and (7) describe cloud thickness, development, and altocumulus associated with other cloud forms.

High clouds are known as cirrus, cirrostratus, and cirrocumulus. Cirrus (1) consists of filaments, commonly known as mares' tails. Cirrus (2) and (3) are often associated with cumulonimbus clouds. Cirrus (4) usually indicates a thickening layer, which might be associated with the approach of a front. Cirrostratus (5 through 8) describe sheets or layers of cirrus. Sun or moon halos often appear in these layers. Cirrocumulus indicate vertical motion at high levels and might indicate high-altitude turbulence.

Cirrus, of itself, has no significance to low-level flights. However, cirrus is often associated with the jet stream and high-altitude turbulence. Cirrus that forms as transverse lines or cloud trails perpendicular to the jet stream indicates moderate or greater turbulence. These clouds might be reported as cirrocumulus.

Cirrus streaks, parallel to the jet, are long narrow streaks of cirrus frequently seen with jet streams. Jet stream cirrus and cloud trails are easily identified from satellite imagery.

Selected present-weather symbols are contained in Fig 5-4. The station model in Fig. 10-2 shows two rain symbols. Symbols can be combined to indicate more than one phenomenon occurring. Precipitation representations will appear above the thunderstorm symbol to indicate type and intensity of precipitation accompanying the "thunder bumper." Unknown light precipitation from automated sites is indicated by:

"?-."

Temperature and dew point, in degrees Fahrenheit, appear to the left of the station model. Wind is indicated as the direction (true) from which the wind is blowing, with barbs, half barbs, and flags representing speed in knots.

Information to the right of the station model is less significant to the pilot. Sea-level pressure, in millibars, is decoded the same as METAR; Fig. 10-2 shows 997, therefore the sea-level pressure is 999.7 millibars. The pressure change, during the past three hours, in 10ths of millibars, and its tendency—increasing, decreasing, steady—appear below sea-level pressure. Any precipitation during the past six hours, to the nearest hundredth of an inch, appears in the lower right.

Let's decode, translate, and interpret the station model in Fig. 10-2. Total sky cover is broken (6/10 to 9/10). Cloud bases are not provided, but they can be inferred from cloud type. The low clouds consist of fractostratus, or scud. Thick altostratus and cirrus are also being reported, so the scud can't be too extensive. The higher cloud types might indicate an approaching front. Wind is out of the southwest at 15 knots. Visibility, which does not directly appear, is probably good in spite of a relatively close temperature/dew point spread (8 degrees F). Moisture is being added by rain, however. If the wind remains constant, additional moisture could increase the amount of fractostratus. But if the wind subsides, fog and reduced visibility might result. Except for low-level mechanical turbulence due to wind, the atmosphere appears stable from the cloud types reported. Therefore, mostly smooth flying conditions and light icing in clouds and precipitation above the freezing level are indicated.

Surface Chart Analysis

Figure 10-4 contains front symbols, provides a description of the front, and defines suggested hues used for color displays. Semicircles and triangles are normally omitted with a color display. Open semicircles and triangles indicate the location of a front aloft. Frontogenesis, the initial formation of a front or frontal zone, is depicted by a broken line with the appropriate front-type symbol. Frontolysis, the dissipation of a front or frontal zone, is represented by a broken line with the appropriate front-type symbol on every other line. As previously mentioned, frontal zones can occur in layers aloft. Hollow semicircles and triangles indicate the location of a frontal boundary aloft.

Refer to Fig. 10-5, which is the 1500Z, February 24, 1998 surface analysis chart.

Pressure patterns indicate areas at the surface that are under the influence of high or low pressure, troughs, or ridges. The terms high and low are relative. A high is defined as an area completely surrounded by lower pressure. Conversely, a low is an area

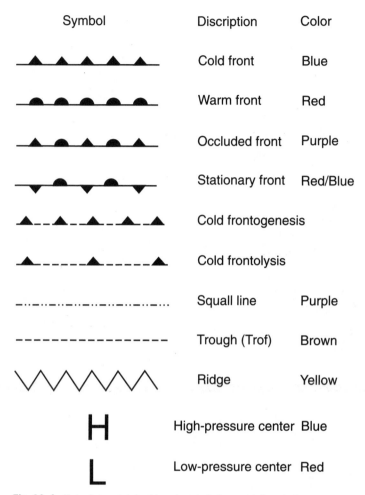

Symbol	Discription	Color
	Cold front	Blue
	Warm front	Red
	Occluded front	Purple
	Stationary front	Red/Blue
	Cold frontogenesis	
	Cold frontolysis	
	Squall line	Purple
	Trough (Trof)	Brown
	Ridge	Yellow
H	High-pressure center	Blue
L	Low-pressure center	Red

Fig. 10-4. Weather charts use standard symbols or colors to describe front type and other weather features.

surrounded by higher pressure. Lines known as isobars connect areas of equal sea-level pressure. Beginning with 1000 mbs, lines are drawn at four millibar intervals (00, 04, 08, etc.). Weak pressure gradient may be drawn at two-mb intervals using dashed isobars. Pressures at each pressure center are indicated by a three- or four-digit number. For example, the high center over Iowa has a central pressure of 1019 mbs, the low over southern Nevada, 997 mbs.

A trough consists of an elongated area of low pressure. Figure 10-5 shows that a trough extends southwest from the low in Nevada through southern California. A ridge, the opposite of a trough, is an

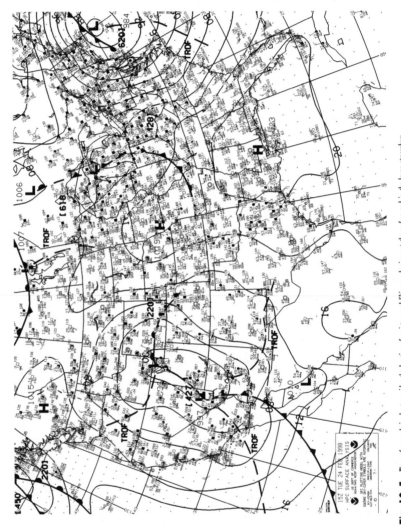

Fig. 10-5. The surface analysis chart provides the location of moisture and lifting mechanisms at the surface and in the lower atmosphere.

elongated area of high pressure, almost always associated with anticyclonic (clockwise in the northern hemisphere) wind flow. Figure 10-5 shows that a ridge extends from the high center over Iowa into south-central Canada.

Wind blows across isobars due to friction between the wind and surface, causing convergence and divergence; convergence—upward vertical motion—destabilizes the atmosphere, which increases relative humidity, clouds, and precipitation. Divergence—downward vertical motion—stabilizes the atmosphere, which decreases relative humidity and clouds. Convergence of itself does not necessarily produce poor weather, nor does divergence produce good weather. Other factors, such as moisture, must be considered. Surface convergence and divergence only affect the atmosphere below about 10,000 ft, but they are a major factor in the "weather machine"—vertical motion.

Convergence occurs along curved isobars surrounding a low or trough. Maximum convergence takes place at the low center or along the trough line. Figure 10-5 shows surface winds blowing into the low in northern Utah.

Troughs are not fronts, although fronts normally lie in troughs. A front is the boundary between air masses of different temperatures, whereas, a trough is simply a line of low pressure. Both phenomena produce upward vertical motion.

Note the anticyclonic, outward flow from both high centers in Fig. 10-5. Maximum divergence takes place at the high center. The symbol for a ridge is a continuous zigzag line, normally not depicted on the surface analysis. A high or ridge implies surface divergence.

There is a misconception that high pressure always means good flying weather. Although good weather often occurs, there are exceptions. Strong pressure gradients at the edge of high cells can cause vigorous winds and severe turbulence. Near the center of a high, or with weak gradients, moisture and pollutants can be trapped at lower levels, causing reduced visibilities and even producing zero-zero conditions in fog for days or even weeks.

A three-digit code entered along the front specifies its type, intensity, and character (Table 10-1). For example, the type, intensity, and character of the front over Lake Superior is [618. The type is 6 (occlusion), intensity 1 (no specification), and character 8 (diffuse). Two short lines crossing a front indicate a change in classification.

Frontal intensity is based on frontal speed. That is the temperature gradient in the cold sector, the region of colder air at a frontal zone. A front with waves indicates weak low-pressure centers or portions of the front moving at different speeds. A front with waves needs to be watched. The weak low-pressure areas can intensify and cause significant weather.

The position of the isobars represents pressure patterns or gradients that determine wind flow. Surface wind blows at an angle to the isobars from high to low pressure. Station models show this flow for moderate or strong gradients. However, in mountainous areas, and with weak gradients, the pattern might be confused by terrain or local surface temperature differences.

The isobar pattern represents the relative strength of the wind. Closer spacing of the isobars means stronger pressure gradient force,

Table 10-1 Front type, intensity, and character

CODE	TYPE	INTENSITY	CHARACTER
	(first digit)	(second digit)	(third digit)
0	Quasi-stationary surface	No specification	No specification
1	Quasi-stationary aloft	Weak, decreasing	Frontal area activity, decreasing
2	Warm front surface	Weak, little/no change	Frontal area activity, little change
3	Warm front aloft	Weak, increasing	Frontal area activity, increasing
4	Cold front surface	Moderate, decreasing	Intertropical
5	Cold front aloft	Moderate, little/no change	Forming or existence expected
6	Occlusion	Moderate, increasing	Quasi-stationary
7	Instability line	Strong, decreasing	With waves
8	Intertropical front	Strong, little/no change	Diffuse
9	Convergence line	Strong, increasing	Position doubtful

therefore, stronger wind. Wider spacing of the isobars means weaker wind. Figure 10-5 shows a weak gradient in New Mexico accompanied by light winds and a stronger gradient over New England with stronger winds.

The surface analysis chart can be used to determine vertical motion at and near the surface. Convergence and divergence have been discussed. Fronts also produce vertical motion. Figure 10-4 and Table 10-1 describe how these phenomena are depicted on the surface analysis chart.

A front is generally the zone between two air masses of different density. Temperature is the most important density factor, therefore fronts almost invariably separate air masses of different temperatures. Other factors can distinguish a front, such as a pressure trough, change in wind direction, moisture differences, and cloud and precipitation forms.

Norwegian meteorologist Vilhelm Bjerknes, and his son Jakob, developed the polar front theory at the beginning of the twentieth century. World War I had begun and it was popular to use the language of the conflict. Thus, weather was described using words like fronts, advances, and retreats. The weather did resemble a war between air masses.

The Earth's atmosphere is a giant heat exchanger, moving cold air down from the arctic and warm air up from the tropics. Typically in the northern hemisphere the cold air pushes down from the northwest, lifts, and replaces the warm air. The boundary where this action takes place is known as a cold front. However, to accomplish this, at some point, warm tropical air must replace the colder air to the north. This typically takes place ahead of the cold front as the warm air, moving from the south, rises above and replaces the colder, retreating air; this boundary is known as a warm front. Cold fronts move faster than warm fronts; sometimes the cold front will overtake the warm front and an occlusion occurs and the front is known as an occluded front. When frontal speed decreases to five knots or less it is labeled stationary. This action is more or less continuous around the world at middle latitudes. Fronts produce vertical motion from the surface to about the middle troposphere.

The intensity and movement of fronts is affected by many factors, such as, temperature, moisture, stability, terrain, and upper-level systems. Another factor is slope; the average cold front slope is one mile vertically for every 100 miles horizontally. The closer the front is to the jet stream the steeper the slope, and typically the stronger the front.

Fronts run the spectrum from a complete lack of weather, to benign clouds that can be conquered by the novice instrument pilot, to fronts that spawn lies of severe thunderstorms that no pilot or aircraft can negotiate. Each front—for that matter any weather system—must be evaluated separately, then a flight decision can be made based on the latest weather reports and forecasts, and the pilot's and airplane's capabilities and limitations.

The surface analysis chart may depict a dryline. A dryline, or temperature-dew point front, marks the boundary between moist, warm Gulf air and dry, hot air from the Southwest. If usually develops in New Mexico, Texas, and Oklahoma during the summer months. A dryline can trigger thunderstorms and tornadoes.

The surface analysis chart may depict an outflow boundary. An outflow boundary is a surface boundary left by the horizontal spreading of thunderstorm cooled air. The boundary is often the lifting mechanism needed to generate new thunderstorms.

Upslope and downslope flow causes vertical motion. This can be determined from the chart when familiar with the terrain. Upslope produces the same characteristics as convergence and downslope divergence. Strong downslope flows are sometimes given local names, such as the Chinook (Indian for snow eater) that develops along the eastern slopes of the Rockies and the Santa Ana of southern California. The Chinook has been known to raise temperatures as much as 22 degrees C in 15 minutes, and melt and evaporate a foot of snow in a few hours. The strong winds can exceed 85 knots, causing extreme damage.

Forecast synopses often include "upslope" and might contain "Chinook" or "Santa Ana" when these conditions occur. In Fig. 10-5, upslope is occurring over the eastern Rockies of Colorado and Wyoming, associated with circulation around a low, and eastern Texas, associated with circulation around a high. Note that around the low, upslope with convergence is producing precipitation; around the high with divergence aloft, fog has developed. Conversely, over Alabama and Georgia there is a downslope, offshore flow, with associated clear skies.

Onshore and offshore flows of moderate or greater intensity can be determined from the chart. An onshore flow can translate into advection fog, upslope, or convection with the development of thunderstorms—depending on conditions, and an offshore flow can produce clear skies. An onshore flow can be seen in Fig. 10-3 along the Texas Gulf Coast.

Temperature and moisture patterns are determined by analyzing station model temperatures and dew points. Considerable moisture at the surface exists along the Texas Gulf coast with an onshore flow that has caused fog to develop.

The Weather Depiction Chart

Figure 10-6 shows the 1600Z February 14, 1998 weather depiction chart. The weather depiction chart is computer generated, analyzed, and transmitted every three hours, as a record of observed surface data. Frontal positions are obtained from the previous surface analysis. The information is hours old by the time the chart becomes available: Data should always be updated with current reports. The chart is analyzed into three categories—IFR, MVFR, and VFR—the same as the area forecast outlook and the low-level significant weather prog.

The chart is computer analyzed, so it cannot consider terrain, nor is it intended to represent conditions between reporting locations. Gross errors between depicted categories and actual weather can occur. It may be helpful to compare the weather depiction chart with a current satellite image. The rather significant difference between the coverage are due to the limitations of the weather depiction chart. Conditions could improve or deteriorate. The weather depiction chart is not a substitute for current observations.

Weather Depiction Station Model

Station models on the weather depiction chart plot cloud height in hundreds of feet AGL, beneath the station circle. When total sky cover

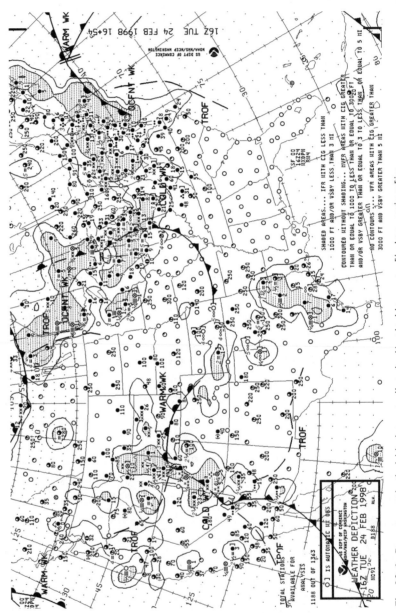

Fig. 10-6. The computer-generated weather depiction chart cannot consider terrain and is not intended to represent conditions between reporting conditions.

has few or scattered clouds, the base of the lowest layer appears. Visibilities of six miles or less, and present weather, are entered to the left of the station. Sky cover and present weather symbols are the same as used on the surface analysis. Automated sites are indicated by a bracket "]" to the left of the station model.

Refer to Fig. 10-6. The station model in south central Texas shows the sky obscured ("X" in the station circle), cloud base at 100 feet AGL (1, underneath station circle). Visibility is reduced in fog to one-quarter mile (1/4, left of fog symbol). The bracket to the left of the station model indicates this is an automated observation. Because the number of stations analyzed exceeds the number plotted, contoured areas might appear without station models. For example, the depicted area of MVFR in southern California.

Weather Depiction Chart Analysis

The weather depiction chart provides a big, simplified picture of surface conditions. It alerts pilots and briefers to areas of potentially hazardous low ceilings and visibilities. The chart is a good place to begin looking for an IFR alternate.

Figure 10-6 was generated one hour after the surface analysis chart in Fig. 10-5. Widespread IFR conditions exist over the Great Lakes and northeast. The chart could be used to determine likely locations for a suitable alternate for an IFR flight into the New York area. With an occluded front moving into New England an alternate to the south, such as Virginia, would be indicated.

Caution is indicated along the east slopes of the Rockies in Colorado and Wyoming. Although the weather depiction indicates only isolated areas of IFR, with upslope occurring conditions could deteriorate rapidly. Appropriate TAFs must be consulted. To find a suitable IFR alternate a pilot may have to go all the way to central Nebraska, an area not under the influence of upslope conditions.

The weather depiction chart confirms our analysis of the surface chart. IFR and MVFR due to upslope fog is depicted in eastern Texas; clear skies and unrestricted visibilities are reported over the southeast United States.

Upper-Air Analysis Charts

Weather exists in the two lower layers of the atmosphere—the tropo-sphere and the stratosphere—and the boundary between them, the tropopause.

Pilots fly and weather occurs in three dimensions, so a need exists to describe the atmosphere within this environment. The National Weather Service prepares several constant pressure charts. These computer-prepared charts are transmitted twice daily based on 0000Z and 1200Z upper-air observations. Each level has a particular significance. Table 10-2 describes the general features of each level.

To decode station height, prefix 850 mb with a 1, prefix a 2 or 3 to the 700-mb height—whichever brings it closer to 3000 meter, add a 0 to the 500-mb and 300-mb heights, and for 200 mb, prefix with a 1 and add a 0. For the 300-mb and 200-mb charts, the temperature/dew-point spread is omitted when the air is too cold to measure dew point (less than −41 degrees C).

Each chart represents a constant pressure level, so it is analyzed for altitude or height in meters above sea level. Lines, known as contours, connect areas of equal pressure surface height. Contours are analyzed in the same way as isobars, the closer the spacing of the contours, the stronger the wind. However, wind blows parallel to the contours, due to the lack of friction; only pressure gradient and Coriolis forces are present.

Constant Pressure Analysis Station Model

Constant pressure analysis charts depict radiosonde data. Figure 10-7 illustrates standard station plots. Wind direction and speed use stan-dard symbology, except for the contraction LV, which indicates light and variable.

Temperature is plotted in degrees Celsius. However, unlike surface station plots, the temperature/dew point spread, or dew point depression, appears instead of the dew point temperature. For example, in Fig. 10-7, the 850-mb station model has a temperature of minus one, and a dew point depression is two; therefore, the dew point temperature is minus three. Darkened station circles are plotted when

Table 10-2 Constant pressure chart analysis

PRESSURE LEVEL (MB)	PRESSURE ALTITUDE (FT)	TEMP/DEW POINT SPREAD	ISOTACHS	CONTOUR INTERVAL (METERS)	HEIGHT METERS PLOTTED/DECODE	PRIMARY USES
850	5000	Yes	No	30	585/1585	Synopsis
						Advection
						Convergence
						Divergence
700	10,000	Yes	No	30	928/2928	Synopsis
						Advection
500	18,000	Yes	No	60	572/5720	Synopsis
						Advection
						Troughs/ridges
300	30,000	Yes	Yes	120	911/9110	Synopsis
						Jet stream
200	39,000	Yes	Yes	120	192/11,920	Synopsis
						Jet stream

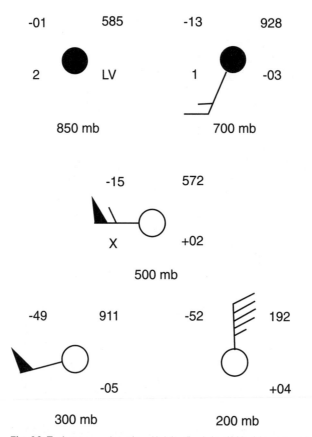

Fig. 10-7. Constant pressure chart station models depict radiosonde data of height, wind, temperature, and moisture for various pressure levels.

the temperature/dew point spread is five degrees or less, indicating a moist atmosphere at that level. This alerts pilots and forecasters to potential clouds, precipitation, and icing depending on temperature. An X indicates a temperature/dew point spread greater than 29 degrees, for example in Fig. 10-7, the 500-mb plot. With temperatures less than –41, air is too dry to measure dew point, and dew point depression is omitted on the 300-mb and 200-mb plots in Fig. 10-7.

The upper right corner of the plot contains the height of the constant pressure level. Table 10-2 decodes these values. The number in the lower right corner represents height change during the past 12 hours, in tens of meters. For example, in Fig. 10-7, the height of the 700-mb surface has lowered 30 meters (–03). In general, lowering heights indicate deteriorating weather and rising heights indicate improving weather. The greater the fall or rise, the more rapid the change. Weather systems tend to move in the direction of greatest height change.

Note that the constant pressure charts in the following sections correspond to the same time frame and the surface analysis and weather depiction charts previously discussed.

850-mb and 700-mb Constant Pressure Charts

Table 10-2 shows that the 850-mb and 700-mb charts represent the lower portion of the troposphere, approximately 5000 and 10,000 ft, providing a synopsis for these levels. The 850-mb chart might be more representative of surface conditions west of the Rockies than the surface analysis. In the west, areas of frictional convergence/divergence can be located. For example, from the 850-mb chart in Fig. 10-8, a downslope condition exists over South Carolina, Georgia, and Alabama, where the air is dry as indicated by the open station models. However, in the extreme southwest and New England the air at this level is moist, as indicated by the solid station models. A weak upslope can be seen along the eastern slopes of the Rockies.

These charts are particularly useful in monitoring cold and warm air advection. When isotherms—dashed lines of equal temperature—cross contours at right angles the temperature properties of the air mass are advected (moved) in the direction of the winds. At the 850-mb and 700-mb levels, warm air advection produces upward motion and cold air advection downward motion. Therefore, warm air advection destabilizes conditions, whereas, cold air advection tends to stabilize the weather. Figure 10-8 shows warm air advection on the east side of the low in Nevada. Conversely, cold air advances toward Florida. Note that these patterns fit the analysis of the surface and weather depiction charts. Warm air advection might be all that's needed to trigger thunderstorms.

Areas of moisture can be determined by examining station models for temperature/dew-point spread. Icing is implied in areas of visible moisture with temperatures between 0 degrees C and –10 degrees C. The 700-mb chart, Fig. 10-9 shows temperatures within this range, at

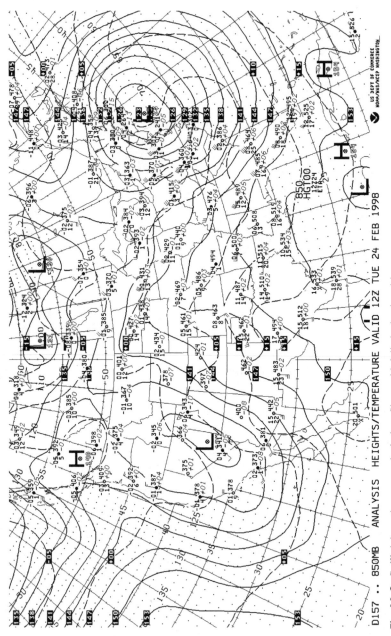

D157 .. 850MB   ANALYSIS   HEIGHTS/TEMPERATURE   VALID 12Z TUE 24 FEB 1998

Fig. 10-8. The 850-mb chart may be more representative of surface conditions west of the Rockies than the surface analysis.

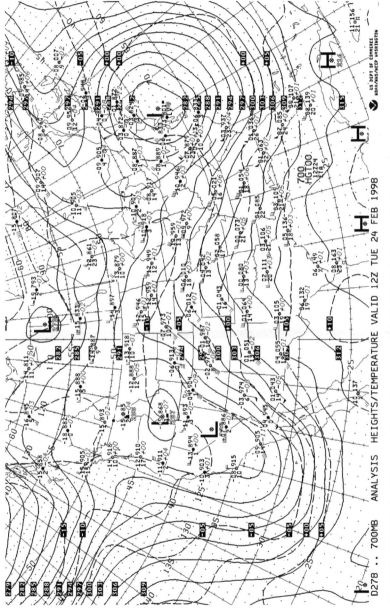

Fig. 10-9. The 700-mb chart is usually the reference level for mountain waves, and along with the 850-mb chart, describes the atmosphere in the lower troposphere.

this level, over most of the United States. The air is moist in the western states and New England, implying a potential for icing, however, over the southeast there is little moisture present indicating little icing potential.

These charts can be used to determine the potential for turbulence and mountain wave activity. The 700-mb chart is usually the reference level for mountain waves. Winds in excess of 40 knots imply moderate or greater mechanical turbulence. When winds of these speeds blow perpendicular to a mountain range, accompanied by cold-air advection (a stabilizing condition), a strong potential for mountain waves and associated turbulence exists.

Air mass thunderstorms tend to move with the 700-mb winds. In midlatitudes, a 700-mb temperature of 14 degrees C or greater tends to inhibit convection at this level. If convection occurs below, clouds tend to stop rising and spread out at about the 700-mb height.

500-mb Constant Pressure Chart

Probably the most important and useful chart—maybe even more important to meteorologists than the surface analysis—the 500-mb chart describes the atmosphere in the middle troposphere, which is an altitude of approximately 18,000 feet. This chart provides important pressure, wind flow, temperature, and moisture patterns, and can be used to determine areas of vertical motion at this level.

Troughs and ridges are easily seen in Fig. 10-10. Unlike the surface analysis chart, where upward vertical motion takes place along a trough line, upward vertical motion at the 500-mb level takes place between the trough and ridgeline. In Fig. 10-10 upward vertical motion is occurring from the trough over California to the ridge over the Midwest. Troughs transport cold air down from the north and warm air up from the south. Warm air rides northward on the east side of the trough—trough to ridge flow—so the air is lifted as it moves northward, producing upward vertical motion. When moisture is present, such as the area over the Great Basin and northern Rockies, clouds and precipitation in the midtroposphere develop. Conversely, in the ridge-to-trough flow from the Midwest to the east coast, cold air sinks southward, producing downward vertical motion with clear, dry

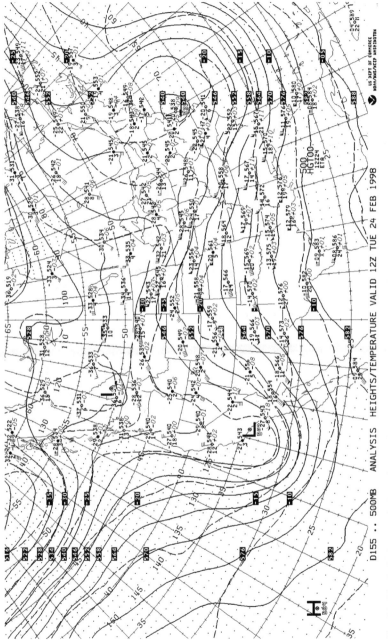

Fig. 10-10. The 500-mb chart describes the atmosphere in the middle troposphere and might be more important to meterologists than the surface analysis.

309

conditions in the midtroposphere. Clouds and precipitation frequently accompany upper-level lows and troughs, even without surface frontal or storm systems.

Three to seven major waves in each hemisphere circle the globe. These global, or long-wave, ridges and troughs extend for thousands of miles. Long-waves move generally eastward at up to 15 knots, but can remain stationary for days or even retreat.

Short waves, embedded in the overall flow, tend to pass through the long wave pattern at speeds of 20 to 40 knots. Most surface lows and frontal systems are associated with upper-level short wave troughs. Figure 10-10 illustrates a short wave trough from the low over Idaho to the Texas panhandle. This feature enhances the vertical motion at this level. Although usually best seen on the 700-mb chart, significant waves usually extend to the 500-mb level. Upper troughs are a key to the evolution of weather systems.

When a short wave trough moves through a long wave trough, upward vertical motion is amplified. Short wave trough can even create upward vertical motion as they move through a ridge. Short waves can be strong vertical-motion producers. Information on short waves often appears in FA and TWEB synopses.

Cold air advection destabilizes and warm air advection stabilizes the atmosphere at the 500-mb level. This is opposite to the effects of cold and warm air advection near the surface. Rising air will be warmer than surrounding air, so cold air advection enhances thunderstorms by promoting vertical development, sometimes referred to as a cold low aloft. A cold low aloft tends to be slow and move erratically. Warm air advection at this level strengthens high-pressure ridges and diminishes low-pressure troughs. In Fig. 10-10, cold air advection is occurring in the trough-to-ridge flow from the west coast to the upper Midwest.

Moisture at the 500-mb level can be determined by darkened station models. In Fig. 10-10, darken station models occur over the Great Basin and northern Rockies and over New England. These indicate areas where the temperature/dew point spread is five degrees or less. This chart is a good indicator of high level icing in summer months and with storms that are either well developed or contain tropical moisture.

Surface weather systems tend to follow the 500-mb flow and organized thunderstorms tend to move in the direction of the 500-mb winds. The 12-hour height change provides a general trend for system movement. Rising heights indicate a building ridge or weakening trough, and lowering heights indicate a deepening trough or weakening ridge.

At the 500-mb level, the shape of the contours rather than wind speed determines the potential for turbulence. At this level, wind shear turbulence occurs as an airplane flies through an area of changing wind direction or speed. Therefore, the greater the curvature, or direction change, the greater the potential for, and intensity of, turbulence. The horizontal distance where this change occurs is critical. The greater the curvature of contours, the greater the probability of turbulence. Therefore, more turbulence potential exists in the trough over the west coast than over the Plains states (Fig. 10-10). The probability of turbulence also exists in the sharp ridge over western Canada. Developing low-pressure troughs moving from the northwest are particularly dangerous.

Areas of potential turbulence occur in merging flows or the neck of a cutoff low. In Fig. 10-10, a merging flow exists over south, central Canada. Turbulence could also be expected in the neck of the cutoff lows over Nevada and New England.

FSS controllers have been criticized for not appreciating the importance of, or providing information from, the 500-mb chart, and even discarding the product. I know of no FSS that does not have access to the 500-mb chart. However, like pilots, some controllers are better schooled than others are. Translation and interpretation of the chart over the telephone is difficult. The best answer is direct access, which is available through DUAT and other commercial vendors with graphics capability.

300-mb and 200-mb Constant Pressure Charts

The 300-mb and 200-mb charts provide details of pressure, wind flow, and temperature patterns at the top of the troposphere and occasionally into the lower stratosphere. The charts indicate the strength of features in the lower atmosphere. Strong storm systems on the surface are reflected in the 300-mb and 200-mb patterns, whereas weaker systems lose their identity at these levels. The 500-mb low over Idaho in Fig. 10-10 has lost its identity at the 300-mb and 200-mb level. (Rather than a closed low—surrounded by a closed contour—it has weakened into a trough.) But, the low over New England retains its identity through the 300-mb level (Fig. 10-11 and Fig. 10-12). This indicates that the relative strength of the low over New England is greater than the low over Idaho.

At midlatitudes, such as the United States, the jet stream can usually be found on the 300-mb and 200-mb charts. Wind speeds and curvature of contours provide a clue to clear air turbulence (CAT). Because wind speed and direction is of primary importance, areas with observed wind speeds of 70 to 110 knots are indicated by hatching. A clear area within the hatching identifies speeds of 110 to 150 knots. If speeds exceed 150 knots, a second hatched area appears. Areas of potential turbulence occur in:

- Sharp troughs (Fig. 10-11 along the west coast and over New England).

- In the neck of cutoff lows (Fig. 10-11, over the New York state).

- In a divergent flow (Fig. 10-11), over the northern Rockies).

Turbulence in these areas can exist despite relatively low wind speeds.

Remember that these are observed data charts, not forecasts. The forecast locations of upper air phenomena, such as turbulence, thunderstorms, and the location and strength of the jet stream must come from the FA, high altitude significant weather prog, and the tropopause wind and wind shear prog discussed in chapter 5.

Jet Stream

The jet stream was virtually unknown until World War II when pilots flying at high altitudes reported turbulence and tremendously strong winds. These winds blew from west to east near the top of the troposphere. Not until 1946 was the jet stream fully recognized as a meteorological phenomenon.

As can be seen in Fig. 10-13, sharp horizontal temperature differences cause the jet stream; across strong temperature gradients,

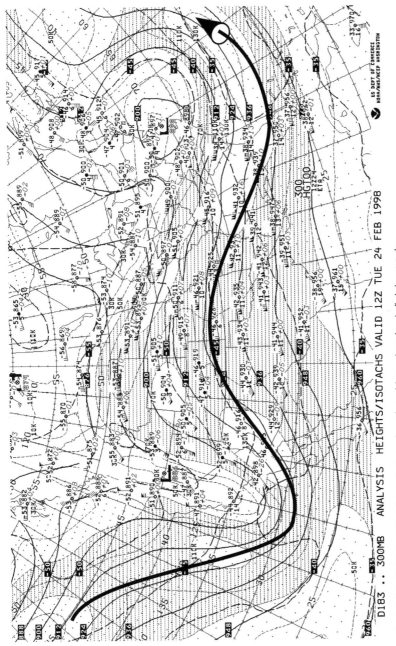

D183 .. 300MB   ANALYSIS   HEIGHTS/ISOTACHS VALID 12Z TUE 24 FEB 1998

Fig. 10-11. The 300-mb and 200-mb charts describe the atmosphere at the top of the troposphere and occasionally the lower stratosphere.

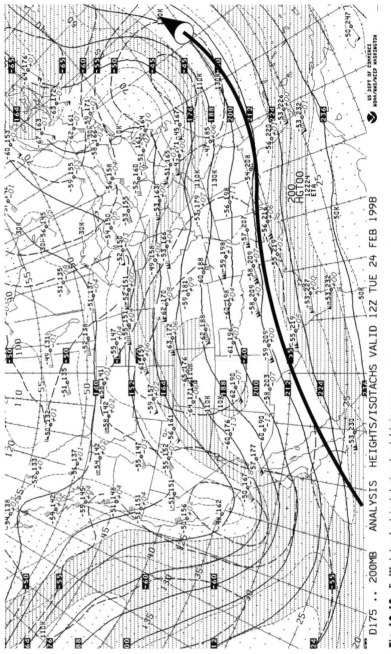

Fig. 10-12. The 200-mb chart often depicts the location and speed of the jet stream.

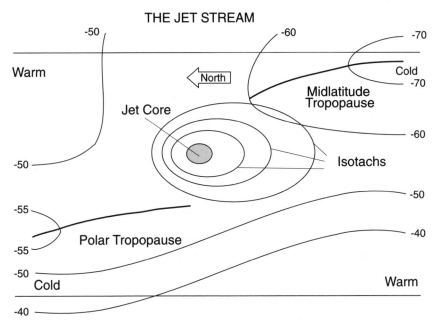

Fig. 10-13. Sharp horizontal temperature differences cause strong pressure gradients that result in the jet stream.

temperature changes rapidly with height. In such zones, the slope of constant pressure surfaces increases with height. The 500-mb slope is greater than that at 700-mb, and the 300-mb slope is greater than that at 500 mb. The slope of the pressure surface determines approximate wind speed. When pressure surface slope increases with height, wind speed increases with height. This is the general case in the troposphere. Winds are light or calm in areas of little or no horizontal temperature difference. And, in some cases, winds can decrease with height in the troposphere. This tends to occur within large high-pressure areas. Since fronts lie in zones of temperature contrast, the jet is closely linked, or associated with frontal boundaries. When wind speed becomes strong enough, the flow is termed a jet stream.

A jet stream is a narrow, shallow, meandering area of strong winds embedded in breaks in the tropopause. Two such breaks occur in the northern hemisphere: the polar jet located around 30 degrees-60 degrees N at an approximate height of 30,000 ft, associated with the polar front, and the subtropical jet around 20 degrees-30 degrees N at approximately 39,000 ft. To be classified a jet stream, winds must be

50 knots or greater, although winds generally range between 100 and 150 knots; winds can reach 200 knots along the East Coast of North America and Asia in winter when temperature contrasts are greatest.

A "jet" is most frequently found in segments 1000 to 3000 miles long, 100 to 400 miles wide, and 3000 to 7000 feet deep. The strength of the jet stream increases in winter in mid and high latitudes when temperature contrasts are greatest, and shift south with the seasonal migration of the polar front. The troposphere varies in depth from an average 55,000 ft at the equator to 28,000 ft at the poles, deeper in summer than in winter. The 300-mb and 200-mb charts are ideal for locating the jet. Jet cores are shown by thick black lines in Fig. 10-11 and Fig. 10-12.

As a rule, locations north of a jet stream associated with a surface front are likely to be cold and stormy; locations south of this boundary tend to be warm and dry. A jet embedded in a long wave can remain relatively stationary for weeks; this usually brings long periods of bad weather to the north of its location and good weather to the south. The movement of surface high- and low-pressure areas and fronts is related to the movement of the jet stream. Low-pressure areas tend to move with the jet stream flow. As the wave with the jet passes, a ridge builds aloft usually bringing high pressure and good weather. However, as high pressure builds, surface pressure gradients are often strong, causing powerful, sometimes destructive, surface winds.

The presence of jet streams has a significant impact on aircraft operations. The jet stream can cause a significant head wind component for westbound flights, increasing fuel consumption and requiring additional landings.

Another factor associated with the jet is wind shear turbulence (CAT). With an average depth of 3000 to 7000 ft, a change in altitude of a few thousand feet will often take the aircraft out of the worst turbulence and strongest winds. Maximum jet stream turbulence tends to occur above the jet core and just below the core on the north side. Additional areas of probable turbulence occur where the polar and subtropical jets merge or diverge, such as off the southeast coast of the United States as illustrated in Figs. 10-11 and 10-12. In this area the polar jet, as seen in Fig. 10-11, merges with the subtropical jet depicted in Fig. 10-12.

CASE STUDIES

In December 1998, a passenger aboard a United Air Lines Boeing 747 died as the result of head injuries suffered when the aircraft flew into an area of severe CAT over the Pacific Ocean. The passenger was not wearing a seat belt. Other less severe injuries have resulted from CAT, again mostly due to the failure to wear seat belts.

In November 1997, I was riding "jump seat" on a Delta Air Lines Boeing 737 from Oakland to Salt Lake City. At flight level (FL) 370, the ride was smooth to occasional light turbulence. Over the radio, we could hear a Delta Boeing 757 constantly complain to ATC about the moderate turbulence at FL390. As chance would have it, I flew on that airplane, with that crew, from Salt Lake City to Washington's Dulles airport. It turned out they flew their first leg from San Jose to Salt Lake City, almost the same route I had flown at FL370 in the Boeing 73. This illustrates how the intensity of the jet stream CAT can change significantly over a relatively short distance.

Observed Winds Aloft Chart

The observed winds aloft chart, which is transmitted twice daily, plots radiosonde data. This four-panel chart provides observed winds at four levels:

- Second standard level

- 14,000 feet (600 mb)

- 24,000 feet (400 mb)

- 34,000 feet (250 mb)

The second standard level (lower left panel Fig. 10-14) occurs between 1000 and 2000 feet AGL. The chart provides observed winds above the surface, but within the frictional layer. This chart supplements the constant pressure charts by providing observed wind and temperatures between constant pressure levels. Observed winds are, therefore, available for the following heights:

- Second standard level
- 5000*
- 10,000*
- 14,000
- 18,000*
- 24,000
- 30,000*
- 34,000
- 39,000*

* Obtained from constant pressure charts

Station models are similar to those on the winds and temperatures aloft forecast chart, chapter 8. Refer to the San Diego plot at the 34,000-ft level in Fig. 10-14. The small number 6 adjacent to the wind pennant indicates the second digit of the wind direction (260 degrees); wind barbs indicate the speed is 45 knots; temperature is –49 degrees C. Note the station circles for Las Vegas, Nevada and Salt Lake City; they indicate the wind speed is less than 5 knots or light and variable.

The chart portrays the state of the atmosphere in the past—like constant pressure charts, about two-and-a-half hours old by the time the chart becomes available. Observed winds should not be substituted for winds aloft forecasts. However, should gross differences occur between observed and FD forecasts, a pilot may wish to consult an FSS or Flight Watch; both have direct access to NWS forecasters.

Vorticity

Any nonmeteorologist pilot who wishes to better understand atmospheric phenomena will require a basic knowledge of vorticity. Although some pilot-meteorologists feel this subject far too technical for pilots, I disagree. At the very least, pilots, especially those using DUAT, will come across this term in synopses, Convective SIGMETs, and the

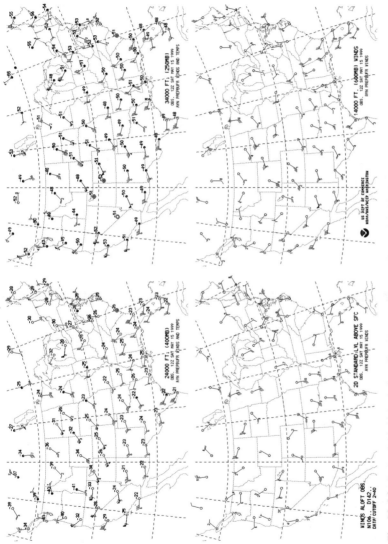

Fig. 10-14. The observed winds aloft chart describes conditions that existed in the past; it should not be substituted for winds aloft forecasts.

convective outlook. An understanding of vorticity will help relate the fact that not all weather occurrences can be attributed to pressure and frontal systems alone, as displayed on weather charts. However, for those "bottom-liners" that only wish to know the implications of vorticity, skip to the last few paragraphs of this section of the chapter.

Anything that spins has vorticity, which includes the earth. Vorticity is a mathematical term that refers to the tendency of the air to spin; the faster air spins, the greater its vorticity. A parcel of air that spins counterclockwise—cyclonically—has positive vorticity; a parcel that spins clockwise— anticyclonically—has negative vorticity.

The Earth's vorticity is always positive in the northern hemisphere because the earth spins counterclockwise about its axis. An observer, standing on the north pole, will have maximum vertical spin, one revolution per day. An observer's vertical spin will decrease when moving toward the equator, becoming zero at the equator. (Coriolis force is maximum at the poles and zero at the equator.) The rate, or value, of the vorticity produced by the Earth's rotation is, not surprisingly, known as the Earth's vorticity.

Now consider the atmosphere, which is usually in motion, and generally will have its own vorticity relative to the Earth, or relative vorticity. The sum of the Earth's vorticity plus relative vorticity equals absolute vorticity. The value of absolute vorticity at midlatitudes usually remains positive because of the Earth's rotation.

Air moving through a ridge, spinning clockwise, gains anticyclonic relative vorticity. Air moving through a trough, spinning counterclockwise, gains cyclonic relative vorticity. Therefore, there tends to be downward vertical motion in ridge to trough flow, and upward vertical motion in trough to ridge flow.

Absolute vorticity is analyzed at 500 mbs. Although normally not available to the pilot, 500-mb heights/vorticity charts are routinely available from weather chart sources. High values of absolute vorticity (greater than 16) have strong cyclonic rotation, indicating strong upward vertical motion, and low values (less than 6) have anticyclonic rotation, indicating strong downward vertical motion.

Vorticity is advected like other atmospheric properties. Therefore, the pilot can expect to see the terms Positive Vorticity Advection (PVA) and Negative Vorticity Advection (NVA) (referring to relative vorticity).

Positive Vorticity Advection indicates:

1. A trough or low moving into an area.

2. A ridge or high moving out of an area.

3. Upward vertical motion probably occurring.

4. Increasing cloud cover and precipitation.

Negative Vorticity Advection indicates:

1. A ridge or high moving into an area.

2. A low or trough moving out of an area.

3. Downward vertical motion probably occurring.

4. Decreasing cloud cover.

Regions of PVA are swept along within the overall flow. They represent microsystems that can rotate around synoptic scale highs and lows. These areas can be referred to as A VORT MAX or VORT LOBE. If an area of PVA moves over a stationary surface front, a wave can form and a storm can develop. An area of PVA might be all that's required (a lifting mechanism) to trigger thunderstorms when moisture and instability are available. On the other hand, NVA might prevent thunderstorm development.

An additional discussion of vorticity is contained in McGraw-Hill's companion book, *Cockpit Weather Decisions*.

Upper-Level Weather Systems

This chapter's introduction mentions the fact that many aviation weather texts fail to adequately describe nonfrontal weather producing systems. We've looked at warm and cold air advection in the lower troposphere and aloft, orographic lift (upslope/downslope), and convergence and divergence. We discussed the 500-mb wave and its significance. Short waves, vorticity, and the jet stream were described along with their effects on surface and high-altitude weather.

Upper-level weather systems tend to modify and direct surface weather. They can intensify or stabilize conditions at the surface, trigger thunderstorms, and enhance or retard the intensity of frontal zones.

Difluence, divergence aloft, develops when contours diverge or move apart as seen on the 300-mb chart to cause surface convergence and increased cyclonic vorticity. Surface lows can develop in this way.

Figure 10-15 illustrates the effects of an upper-level weather system. The 1300Z weather depiction chart shows no major weather systems, but almost one-quarter of the country is covered by snow producing IFR and MVFR weather. The 1200Z 500-mb chart reveals the culprit, a strong upper-level low over the Ohio Valley. The FA synopsis read:

DEEP UPR LOW OVER SRN IL AT 10Z MOVG SEWD. LARGE TROF AND CYCLONIC FLOW FROM THE IL LOW SWD THRU GLFMEX....

This weather event closed airports for days, and was blamed for the deaths of dozens of people.

Lifting mechanisms have a cumulative effect. Upper-level troughs perpendicular to and behind a front intensify the storm. These fronts tend to be fast moving. Conversely, fronts parallel to an upper-level trough tend to be weak and slow moving.

Upper-level lows occur when cold air at the base of the trough is cut off from the cold air to the north. This closed circulation can lead to a circular jet stream. The weather remains moist and unstable although the surface front has passed.

With the approach of an upper-level trough, a period of eight to 12 hours of poor weather can be expected. The surface front will precede

CASE STUDY

A perfect example occurred one afternoon with scattered thunderstorms forecast for northern California, northern Nevada, and eastern Oregon. No weather systems were depicted on either the surface analysis or 500-mb chart. However, thunderstorms did occur, right along a line of difluence. The difluence caused just enough surface convergence to trigger thunderstorms.

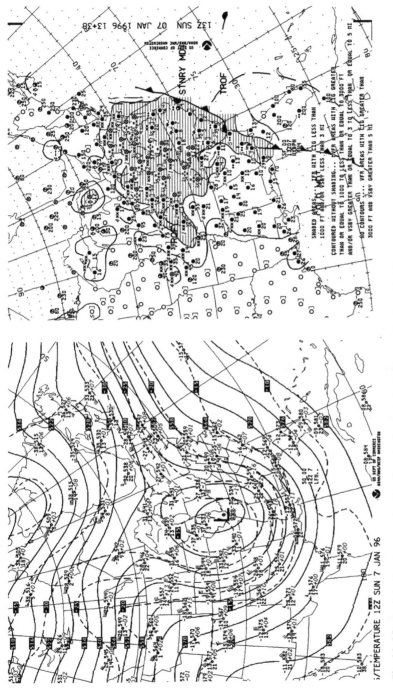

Fig. 10-15. Upper-level weather systems can cause devastating surface weather, often without a clue about the cause on the surface analysis chart.

the trough, usually bringing IFR weather. However, without a front, the upper trough or low might only bring marginal VFR conditions with localized areas of IFR. Under these conditions, VFR flight might be possible, except in mountainous areas that remain obscured in clouds and precipitation.

Closed upper-level lows tend to remain stationary. A closed low reflected vertically through the atmosphere tends to move erratically. These systems can cause poor weather and precipitation to linger for days. Off the West Coast, the systems can bring bands of moist unstable air from the Pacific. The weather deteriorates as a band moves through, then improves, only to deteriorate with the next band. The Area Forecast cannot, and does not, consider this. Under these conditions, a pilot must be careful not to be suckered by a temporary improvement.

During one episode, an upper low meandered over Red Bluff, California for five days. Pilots would call day after day wanting to know when the weather would clear. After awhile, the common response became, "The low is forecast to move east out of the area tomorrow, but that's what they said yesterday."

During winter months, upper lows can form over the Great Basin of Nevada and Utah. Known as the Ely Low, they can persist for days bringing snow and IFR conditions over extensive areas. Over the Midwest and eastern United States, deep upper lows can form over surface frontal systems. When this occurs, surface fronts tend to move slowly, bringing days or even weeks of snow and poor weather, closing airports for hours, or even days, at a time. During summer months, closed lows aloft support the development of thunderstorms, once surface lifting begins.

On the other hand, the absence of an upper-level trough will tend to weaken and slow a front's progress. A ridge aloft even with a surface front will not tend to produce thunderstorms or severe weather because the ridge prevents the required vertical development. A temperature difference may mark the frontal boundary, but without sufficient moisture and lifting to produce clouds. It is not unusual to have cloud tops below 10,000 feet with weak fronts.

These examples illustrate how upper-level weather systems can cause severe conditions at the surface, or dampen or cancel out the

Fig. 10-16. The hurricane is the ultimate example of a nonfrontal weather-producing system.

vertical motion required to produce weather. The point that not all weather is caused by frontal systems has been a theme of this chapter. In fact, nonfrontal weather producing systems have considerable influence on surface conditions. As shown in Fig. 10-16, the hurricane is the ultimate example. Hurricanes produce just about every kind of nasty weather extending over thousands of square miles, for days or even weeks.

The Weather Briefings

Because all flights were local, little need existed for meteorological information in the early days of aviation. Nor was aeronautical information, Notices to Airmen (NOTAMs), necessary because pilots departed and landed at the same field, assuming the engine didn't quit. By the spring of 1918, the United States Post Office Department began working on a transcontinental airmail route. A combination rail/air route between New York and Chicago was established by July and a month later extended to San Francisco. Authorization was granted in August 1920 for the establishment of 17 Airmail Radio Stations. Personnel originally were to load and unload mail. However, as traffic increased, the need for weather information became apparent. Airmail radio personnel soon began taking weather observations and developing forecasts. The information was relayed via radiotelegraph to adjacent stations. In-flight weather reports were heavily relied upon for the weather briefing.

Postal personnel soon became involved in air traffic as well as postal services and in July 1927 were transferred to the Department of Commerce, Bureau of Lighthouses, along with their facilities, now known as Airway Radio Stations. The stations were transferred in August 1938 to the Civil Aeronautics Authority and they became Airway Communication Stations. Finally, these facilities became

Flight Service Stations (FSSs) with the establishment of the Federal Aviation Agency in 1958. The Weather Bureau became increasingly responsible for the collection and distribution of aviation weather and forecasts. Pilots obtained briefings from the Weather Bureau, filed flight plans, and acquired aeronautical information from the Flight Service Station.

Due to the increase in air commerce, and other factors, in 1961 the Weather Bureau began the certification of FSS personnel as pilot weather briefers. The Federal Aviation Agency and the Weather Bureau mutually signed a Memorandum of Agreement in 1965 delegating responsibility for pilot weather briefing to the FAA. FSS briefers had little in the way of guidelines during this period regarding the structure of the briefing; they basically read weather reports and forecasts verbatim as requested by the pilot.

A Field FSS Pilot Briefing Deficiency Analysis group began a special evaluation of pilot briefing services in 1975. The group sighted deficiencies in the use of a standardized briefing format. (The standardized format had been taught at the FAA Academy for some time, however, it had yet to be incorporated in the FSS handbook.) Other areas identified were the reading of weather reports and forecasts verbatim as opposed to interpreting, translating, and summarizing data. A poor level of proficiency in reading, understanding, and employing facsimile charts was noted. Briefers failed to obtain sufficient background information to tailor the briefing to the type of flight planned.

From this study came the Agency's emphasis on an extremely rigid briefing format and an ambitious refresher training program. Unfortunately, the Agency did little to inform pilots or other offices within the Agency of this change in policy. This led to a good deal of friction between briefers and pilots.

Over the years, however, through mostly local efforts, pilots have become acquainted with the standard briefing format. The refresher training was to be a continuing program conducted at least every five years. However, with few exceptions, this program has been abandoned presumably due to fiscal constraints.

The National Transportation Safety Board (NTSB) also conducted a special investigation into Flight Service Station weather briefing inadequacies. In six of 72 accidents involving fatalities, the Safety Board determined that pertinent meteorological information was not passed to the pilot during the weather briefing. Basically, these deficiencies consisted of failure to pass weather advisories and icing forecasts, and downplaying forecasts of hazardous weather. The result of which has led to what many pilots consider overdoing dissemination of these advisories.

A major change occurred in 1983 when the extremely rigid format was relaxed somewhat. Three types of briefings emerged:

- Standard briefing.

- Abbreviated briefing.

- Outlook briefing.

- Requirements for in-flight briefings were also specified.

Almost from the time the FAA took over pilot briefing responsibility in 1965, the Service A (weather) teletype system was obsolete. Since that time, proposal after proposal was made to update weather distribution. Even by the early 1980s, most Flight Service Stations still used the 100 word per minute electromechanical teletype equipment. Briefers had to sift through mountains of paper to provide a briefing with weather reports as much as one-and-a-half hours old by the time they were relayed and available. Figure 11-1 shows a typical teletype-era briefing position.

The FAA approved what was termed the interim Service A system in November 1978 that had been tested at the Chicago FSS. Subsequently the Service B teletype system for the transmission of flight plans and other messages was incorporated. Referred to as the Leased A and B System (LABS), it is in use at nonautomated FSSs. LABS was designed to update FSS Service A until a complete computer system could be developed and installed. LABS eliminates the need for the briefer to sort and post specials, PIREPs, NOTAMs, and most amended forecasts. These housekeeping chores, which took considerable time, have been eliminated. With this system, most weather reports are available within five to 15 minutes of observation. Development of Model 1, a so-called completely computerized

Fig. 11-1 In the Teletype era, briefers had to sift through mountains of paper, and weather reports were often one-and-a-half hours old.

system, began in 1982 and came on line in 1985. Automated Flight Service Stations (AFSSs) use this equipment. Figure 11-2 shows a typical Model 1 briefing display.

According to the FAA, "The primary benefit of the (FSS automation) program is improved productivity through automation of specialist's access to detailed briefing information and flight plan filing. To some extent the improved quality of pilot briefings reduces the need for multiple briefings as in the past." Model 1 is in the same evolutionary category as ARTCC flight data processing was in the early 1970s. It takes care of many of the data processing functions, such as flight plan transmission and tracking.

From a weather-briefing point of view, however, it presents the same information that was available from teletype and LABS. With Model 1 amendments are more timely, but this won't be directly obvious to the pilot. Model 1 does not necessarily improve pilot briefing productivity, in fact productivity in certain cases is reduced. Model 1 is truly "user hostile," and presents information in much the same way as DUATs and other commercial briefing systems.

In the late 1990s with the loss of the Miami AFSS due to hurricane Andrew and the St. Louis AFSS due to floods, Model 1 equipment was not only becoming unsupportable, but none existent. Model 1's replacement will be OASIS (Operational and Supportability Implementation System). OASIS will essentially provide the same data, but now with its own weather graphics system. OASIS, like Model 1, will allegedly increase the quality and quantity of FSS briefing services. Although, OASIS does provide some very important ergonomic advances, don't count on improved quality or quantity unless the FAA decides to do some serious FSS controller training. To date the system continues to be plagued with problems and delays. Project initial installation has now been pushed back to 2000.

Regulations require each pilot in command, before beginning a flight, to become familiar with all available information concerning that flight. This information must include: "For a flight under IFR or a flight not in the vicinity of an airport, weather reports and forecasts...and any known traffic delays of which the pilot has been advised by ATC."

Fig. 11-2 Much of the flight data processing at Model 1 facilities has been automated, but a weather briefing remains essentially the same.

Additional regulations specify fuel and alternate airport requirements. The regulations do not, however, require that meteorological and aeronautical information be obtained from the FAA.

Standard Briefing

The standard briefing is designed for a pilot's initial weather rundown prior to departure. Standard briefings are not normally provided when the departure time is beyond six hours, nor current weather beyond two hours. It is to the pilot's advantage to obtain a standard briefing, or update the briefing, as close to departure time as possible.

Background information

1. The type of flight planned. Always advise the briefer if the flight can only be conducted VFR, or that an IFR flight is planned, or can be conducted IFR. Normally, the briefer will assume a pilot is planning VFR, unless stated otherwise. Student pilots should always state this fact to help the briefer provide a briefing tailored for a student's needs. Also, new or low-time pilots and pilots unfamiliar with the area will receive better service if they advise the briefer. This alerts the briefer to proceed more slowly, with greater detail.

2. The aircraft number or pilot's name. This is evidence that a briefing was obtained, as well as an indicator of FSS activity. In the absence of an aircraft number, the pilot's name is sufficient. (At the briefer's request for an aircraft number the pilot replied, "I don't have one." When asked for a name, the pilot again replied, "I don't have one." One thing for sure, the briefer can't get in trouble on that briefing.) Most briefings are recorded and reviewed in case of incident or accident; it's in the pilot's interest to get "on the record" as having received a briefing.

3. The aircraft type. Low-, medium-, and high-altitude flights present different briefing problems. This information allows briefers to tailor the briefing to a pilot's specific needs. By knowing the aircraft type, the briefer, many times, can estimate

general performance characteristics such as altitude, range, and time en route.

4. The departure airport. Pilots must be specific, they know the airport, but the briefer usually doesn't. Some use generalities such as Los Angeles when their actual departure airport is Oxnard, more than 50 miles away; and there is always the ever-popular: "Here." This is important with FSS consolidation, "800" telephone numbers, and in metropolitan areas.

5. The estimated time of departure. The estimated time of departure is essential, even if general. Briefer: "When are you planning on departing?" Pilot: "Well, that depends on the weather." This response tells the briefer nothing. In such a situation a pilot could respond, "I'd like to go this afternoon, but I can put the flight off until tomorrow."

6. The proposed altitude or altitude range. This information is needed to provide winds and temperatures aloft forecasts. If an altitude range is specified, for example 8000 to 12,000 feet, the briefer can provide the most efficient altitude for direction of flight.

7. The route of flight. The briefer will assume a pilot is planning a direct flight, unless otherwise stated. If not, a pilot must provide the exact route or preferred route, and any planned stops. Total time is essential when stops or anything other than a direct flight are planned; for IFR flights, the estimated time of arrival is required to determine alternate requirements. This will assist the briefer in providing weather for the planned route.

8. The destination airport. Again, pilots must be specific. If not, a pilot might not receive all available weather and NOTAM information. A Piper Cub pilot on one occasion requested a briefing to Los Angeles. The briefer asked if his intended destination was Los Angeles International. It was! Another pilot obtained a briefing from Chino, California to the stated destination Stockton, California and was told there were no NOTAMs for the

route. At the end of the briefing the pilot matter-of-factly said the actually destination was going to an airport about 20 miles east of Stockton, Columbia. Now there were a few NOTAMs!— the airport would be closed during certain hours, a temporary tower was in operation, and acrobatic flight and parachute jumping were being conducted.

9. Estimated time en route. Many briefers can estimate time en route based on aircraft type. This information is needed to provide en route and destination forecasts. Total time en route is essential when stops or anything other than a direct flight are planned; for IFR flights, the estimated time of arrival is required to determine alternate requirements.

10. Alternate airport. If you already have an alternate in mind, provide it at this time. FSS equipment will automatically display alternate airport current weather, forecast, and NOTAMs to the briefer.

This might seem like a lot of information, but it really isn't. The briefer must obtain this information before or during the briefing. Providing background information will allow briefers to do a better job, which is provide the pilot with a clear, concise, well-organized briefing, tailored to pilot's specific needs.

Briefing Format

All right, the background information has been provided; what can a pilot expect in return? The briefer is required, using all available weather and aeronautical information, to provide a briefing in the following order. Pilots should be as familiar with this format as the mnemonic C-I-G-A-R (Controls, Instruments, Gas, Attitude, Runup), or the IFR clearance format.

1. Adverse conditions. Any information, aeronautical or meteorological, that might influence the pilot to cancel, alter, or postpone the flight will be provided at this time. Items will consist of weather advisories, major NAVAID outages, runway or airport closures, or any other hazardous conditions.

The adverse conditions provided should only be those pertinent to the intended flight. This is one reason why the pilot must provide the briefer with accurate and specific background information. The briefer should then only furnish those conditions that affect the flight. There is, unfortunately, some paranoia among briefers where they provide anything within 200 miles of the flight, whether it's applicable or not.

2. VFR flight is not recommended (VNR). Undoubtedly the VNR statement is the most controversial element of the briefing; nevertheless, the FAA requires the briefer to: "Include this recommendation when VFR flight is proposed and sky conditions or visibilities are present or forecast, surface or aloft, that in (the judgment of the specialist), would make flight under visual flight rules doubtful."

   This leaves considerable leeway for the briefer; some use this statement more than others. The inclusion of this statement should not necessarily be interpreted by the pilot as an automatic cancellation, nor its absence as a go-for-it day. Notice that VNR applies to sky condition and visibility only. Such phenomena as turbulence, icing, winds, and thunderstorms, of themselves, do not warrant the issuance of this statement. And, it is important to remember that this is a recommendation. Why then such a statement? It's simple, every year pilots insist on killing themselves and their passengers at an alarming and relatively constant rate by flying into weather where they have no business. This statement was instituted in 1974, presumably because the last person a pilot would talk to was usually the briefer.

   A logical, although alarming, result of the VNR statement is the increasing number of pilots who, in the absence of VNR, ask, "Is VFR recommended?" Others criticize a perceived overuse of the statement as reducing its effectiveness. This is certainly true in many cases. But, for now the bottom line remains: The decisions as to whether the flight can be safely conducted rests solely with the pilot.

According to the Flight Services handbook, the reason for VNR must be provided. For example, "VFR is not recommended into the Monterey area because of visibilities one-half mile and ceilings 200 ft; conditions are not expected to improve until around noon." Briefers have been known to use some exceeding poor technique in this area. One briefer told a pilot, "The San Fernando Valley is still VNR." Oh well.

Some pilots say never say never. Here is the exception that proves the rule. Never let the briefer make the go/no-go decision. The briefer is a resource, and some are better than others. This applies equally to optimistic and pessimistic briefers and briefings.

3. Synopsis. The synopsis is extracted and summarized from FA and TWEB route synopses, weather advisories, and surface and upper-level weather charts. This element might be combined with adverse conditions and the VNR statement, in any order, when it would help to more clearly describe conditions.

These three elements should provide us with the "big picture," part of the "complete picture." The synopsis should indicate the reason for any adverse conditions, and tie in with current and forecast weather. During this portion of the briefing, pay particular attention for clues of turbulence and icing, even if a weather advisory is not in effect. For example, areas of locally moderate turbulence and icing may be overlooked.

4. Current conditions. Current weather will be summarized: point of departure, en route, and destination. Relevant PIREPs and weather radar reports will be included. Weather reports will not normally be read verbatim, and might be omitted if proposed departure time is beyond two hours, unless specifically requested by the pilot. Forecast surface temperatures are not available at this time, but may be in the future. However, we can extrapolate surface temperatures from current data. Because the METAR database is normally reloaded just after the hour, to obtain the latest reports avoid, if possible, calling just prior to the hour.

5. En route forecast. The en route forecast will be summarized in a logical order (climbout, en route, and destination) from appropriate forecasts (FAs, TWEBs, weather advisories, and prog charts). The briefer will interpret, translate, and summarize expected conditions along the route.

6. Destination forecast. Using the TAF where available, or appropriate portions of the FA or TWEB forecast, the briefer will provide a destination forecast, along with significant changes from one hour before until one hour after ETA.

7. Winds aloft forecast. The briefer will summarize forecast winds aloft for the proposed route. Normally, temperatures will only be provided on request. Request temperatures aloft. We want to know if we're going to be below, at, or above the freezing level. Temperature at our flight-planned altitude is an indicator of icing severity, as well as aircraft performance.

8. Notices to Airmen (NOTAMs). The briefer will review and provide applicable NOTAMs for the proposed flight that are on hand, and not already carried in the Notices to Airmen publication. This information consists of NAVAID status, airport conditions, temporary flight restrictions, changes to instrument approach procedures, and flow control information. In the briefing, the term NOTAMs is all-inclusive. I briefed a student one day, and as is my practice, informed this aviator there were no NOTAMs for the route. There was a pause. I asked if he knew what NOTAMs were, he didn't.

   The United States Notam System (USNS) is computerized and occasionally fails. When this occurs, briefers will include the statement: "Due to temporary NOTAM system outage, en route and destination NOTAM information may not be current. Pilots should contact FSSs en route and at destination to ensure current NOTAM information."

9. Other services and items provided on request. At this point in the briefing, briefers will normally inform the pilot of the availability of flight plan, traffic advisory, and Flight Watch services,

and request pilot reports. Upon request, the controller will provide information on military training route (MTR) and military operation area (MOA) activity, review the Notices to Airmen publication, check Loran or GPS NOTAMs, and provide other information requested.

It's not necessary to copy all the information provided because much is supplementary and provides a background for other portions of the briefing. Pertinent information should be noted and it's often advantageous to copy this data. There are many forms available. It's often helpful to have a map containing weather advisory plotting points and jot down significant information, such as the form shown in Fig. 11-3.

Abbreviated Briefing

Briefers provide abbreviated briefings when a pilot requests specific data, information to update a previous briefing, or supplement an FAA mass dissemination system (Transcribed Weather Broadcast, Telephone Information Briefing Service, or Pilot's Automatic Telephone Weather Answering Service).

Requests for Specific Information

When all that's required is specific information, a pilot should state this fact and request an abbreviated briefing. Because the briefer must normally make a request for each individual item, it's extremely helpful to request all items at the beginning of the briefing, thus reducing delays. The briefer will then provide the information requested. When using this procedure, the responsibility for obtaining all necessary and available information rests with the pilot, not the briefer. Pilots must realize that the briefer is still required to offer adverse conditions. Pilots sometimes become irritated when the briefer mentions weather advisories, however, this is a Flight Services handbook requirement.

Requests to Update a Previous Briefing

Pilots requesting an update to a previous briefing must provide the time the briefing was received and necessary background information.

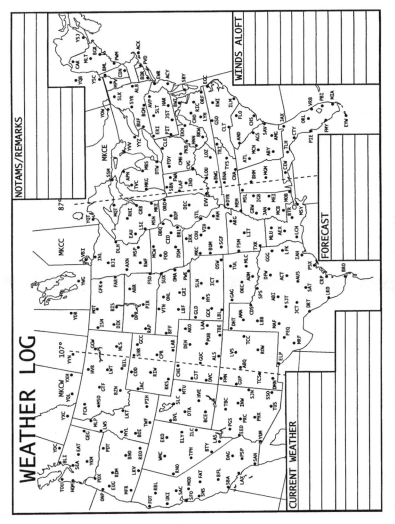

Fig. 11-3 It's often helpful to note significant items on a form, such as this weather log, during a briefing.

The briefer will then, to the extent possible, limit the briefing to appreciable changes. An alarming number of pilots when asked the time of their previous briefing respond, "I got the weather last night." Needless to say, this practice does not comply with regulations. These individuals should be requesting a standard briefing.

Requests for Information to Supplement FAA Mass Dissemination Systems

Again, the briefer must have enough background information and the time the recording was obtained to provide appropriate supplemental data. The extent of the briefing will depend on the type of recording and the time received.

Outlook Briefing

With a proposed departure time beyond six hours, an outlook briefing will normally be provided. The briefing will contain available information applicable to the proposed flight. The detail will depend on the proposed time of departure. The farther in the future, the less specific. As a minimum the outlook will consist of a synopsis and route/destination forecast.

Outlooks beyond FA, TWEB, and TAF valid times are available using significant weather prognosis charts. A last word on outlooks, pilots should not overlook the weather section of the newspaper, the Weather Channel, or local TV programs. Often these sources contain local detail not available in aviation outlook products. Regardless of source, the outlook forecast axiom remains: The weather tomorrow is going to be what the weather is tomorrow, no matter what anybody says.

In-Flight Briefing

Although discouraged, unless unavoidable, briefings once airborne will be conducted in accordance with a standard, abbreviated, or outlook briefing as requested by the pilot. As with any briefing, sufficient background information must be made available.

FAA's Pilot Weather Briefing Service

Briefings can be obtained in person, over the telephone, or by radio. The preferred methods are to obtain a weather briefing in person or by telephone. Initial briefings by radio are discouraged, except where there is no other means. The reasons are simple. The cabin of an aircraft plunging into the wild gray yonder is no place to plan a flight. Attention must be diverted from flying the aircraft to the briefing. Especially with marginal weather, certain pilots have a tendency to push on, regardless of conditions, not to mention the fact that it usually unnecessarily ties up already-congested radio frequencies.

Flight Service Station controller training begins at the FAA Academy, in Oklahoma City, with the equivalent of a college year in basic meteorology and briefing techniques—the weather portion taught by NWS meteorologists. At field facilities, "developmentals" receive training in Area Knowledge (local weather, terrain features, weather reporting locations) and must be certified by both the FAA and National Weather Service. Briefers, like pilots, at some point must get hands-on training. From time to time, pilots will encounter this situation; the briefing might not be clear or concise, but use the same patience that briefers use with student pilots.

The briefing is supposed to be presented in a clear, concise manner. Ambiguous terms, such as "looks bad, scuzzy," and even generalizations like "VFR" are to be avoided.

The point is made that FSS briefers are not meteorologists—a point usually made by meteorologists. These individuals call attention to the problem that when a forecast goes bad, the quality of the briefing falls apart and the pilot is left on the proverbial limb. This is not often the case. Briefers are trained to recognize forecast variance, a difference between the forecast for a given time and existing

CASE STUDY

An FSS friend of mine received a one-liner briefing from Salinas to Sacramento, California. "It's VFR." What does that mean? It could range from clouds almost to the ground and one-mile visibility, to clear and 100.

conditions. A briefer might suggest the pilot wait for a new forecast or coordinate with a forecaster for resolution. In any case, the pilot is made aware of the problem.

Pilots will have less and less access to NWS personnel. The NWS for most practical purposes is out of the weather briefing business. However, telephone numbers are available in the *Airport/Facility Directory* or from the local FSS. Pilots will not necessarily talk to a forecaster.

Many FSS specialists are excellent interpreters of the weather, familiar with local weather patterns and terrain, and pass on their knowledge and experience to the pilot.

The biggest complaint about the FAA's pilot briefing service is delays. An Aviation Safety Reporting Service (ASRS) study states: "The inability to reach flight service by telephone was the complaint...." in a number of incidents. "Reporters relate waits as long as 20 to 45 minutes on hold and then being disconnected. Reporters allege that, because of the inability to reach flight service, many pilots in their area depart without preflight weather briefings or take off and contact en route flight advisory service." Flight Watch is not for an initial briefing; pilots who elect to use this procedure must call an FSS on the station's discrete frequency for an initial briefing.

It's no big mystery why delays are so lengthy. Let's take a large FSS with a Flight Plan Area that serves about 30,000 pilots. At any one time, there might be from four to eight briefers during peak periods. Guess what happens when more than eight pilots call? The longest

CASE STUDY

A rather new flight instructor brought his novice student into a National Weather Service (NWS) office colocated with an FSS. The instructor explained that if the student wants a really good briefing, always go to the NWS. Unfortunately, for this young instructor, a rather crusty old met tech (Meteorological Technician) was on duty. The met tech, quite unceremoniously, admonished the instructor, explaining that many NWS specialists are not meteorologists, nor engaged in aviation, that for aviation, the FSS was the place to go for the weather.

delays occur when weather is marginal; during these periods, the average briefing might take five to eight minutes, whereas during good weather briefs only average two or three minutes. Add to this that after initial checkout, the FAA provides little training to help briefers become more productive.

Pilots complain about the deluge of superfluous information provided by certain briefers, and the difficulty of getting information from others. These complaints result from poor briefer training and perceived paranoia about accident investigations.

Pilots are equally guilty of tying up briefing lines. Pilots inhibit the system by not being prepared for the briefing nor prepared to file a flight plan, and some have unrealistic expectations. This begins with the flight instructor who fails to properly prepare a student for the briefing, to pilots (who should know better) who call to file an IFR flight plan but haven't looked at the charts yet. Usually these people complain the loudest about delays. I have had, on many occasions, students call for a briefing and to file a flight plan with zero knowledge of how to accomplish either. Instructors must take the responsibility to prepare their students, and instructors still have students call for practice briefings during peak periods.

Pilots need to be specific about the information they require. Ambiguous statements such as, "Is it VFR? I'm looking for some soft IFR. Where is it good? Just tell me what I need to know. Is there anything significant?" Such statements have no place in the pilot briefing environment. Is that VFR in controlled or uncontrolled airspace, above or below 10,000 feet, or special VFR? Try finding soft IFR in the Pilot Controller Glossary. "Good" to one briefer could be "1000-foot ceiling and three miles visibility." "Significant" falls into the same category as "good." Some pilots will still simply ask the briefer, "Are there any AIRMETs and SIGMETs for the route?" These individuals might miss significant information.

There are a number of techniques that pilots can use when dealing with air traffic and Flight Service Station controllers.

Patience is a virtue. It's certainly no fun holding on the telephone for 20 or 30 minutes. But, the briefer may have been at it steadily for up to six hours. There are very few reasons for departing without a briefing, or requesting an initial briefing en route; there are lots of excuses. A good pilot realizes the problems of other pilots, controllers, briefers, and forecasters. They are patient with training controllers and briefers because they remember when they were student pilots. These pilots would no more lose control with a controller or briefer than control of the aircraft.

A good pilot seldom blunders into situations and occasionally cancels or discontinues trips because of the weather. A pilot knows the limitations of weather reports and forecasts, and plans accordingly. Based on their experience and the capabilities of the aircraft, they know when the weather answer is "no-go."

A good pilot has the homework done; routes have been reviewed and a partial flight plan completed. These pilots are ready for the briefing and to file a flight plan; they don't guess at the route, trying to file from memory. As required by the practical test standards, these pilots are organized.

Part of the "complete picture" is having more than one way out. When only one out is left, it's exercised. This might mean canceling a flight, circumnavigating weather, avoiding hazardous terrain, or an additional landing en route. The 180-degree turn is made before entering clouds. If the situation becomes uncertain, assistance is obtained before an incident becomes an accident.

A good pilot will never be caught on top or run out of fuel. These pilots combine mental attitude and skill to update weather en route, devise a plan based on this information, and coordinate the action before the situation becomes critical.

Perhaps as important as patience is courtesy. A briefer that's been briefing for four to six hours on a marginal weather day is in no mood for pilot sarcasm. Briefers do not have to put up with obnoxious, rude, or profane pilots; that's the purpose of the telephone release button. Courtesy is a two-way street, however. Pilots don't have to put up with obnoxious or rude briefers. If you don't think you're being treated in a courteous, professional manner, talk to the supervisor or facility manager, or call the FAA's Hot Line (800) FAA-SURE.

Using the FAA's Weather Briefing Service

The weather briefing is a cooperative effort between the pilot and FSS controller. Preliminary planning should be complete, including a general idea of route, terrain, minimum altitudes, and possible alternates. Where available, obtain preliminary weather from one of the recorded services. From the broadcast, determine the type of briefing required—standard, abbreviated, or outlook.

During the briefing, try not to interrupt, unless the briefer is going too fast. Often pilots interrupt with a question that was just about to be answered. This can cause the briefer to lose their train of thought, resulting in the inadvertent omission of information.

Finally, from the "things that bug briefers the most" category: some pilots unintentionally engage in a form of Chinese water torture—after every word the briefer says, they interject "ah ha." This is terribly annoying and distracting. Additionally, if at all possible avoid using a speakerphone. Feedback from these devices is terribly annoying and distracting.

Briefers make mistakes and many are not pilots. At the end of the briefing, don't hesitate to ask for clarification or additional information on any point you do not understand. If conditions are right for turbulence or icing and these phenomena were not mentioned, ask the briefer to verify that there are no weather advisories. Remember that forecasts for light to locally moderate icing do not warrant an advisory, nor locally severe turbulence a SIGMET.

CASE STUDY

I briefed a student one day and about 15 minutes later he called back. I recognized the aircraft and said, "Didn't I just brief you?" "Well, I couldn't make heads or tails of my notes. This time I'm recording it." An outstanding idea, especially those pilots where English is a second language. More students and instructors should adopt this practice. This has the added advantage that the pilot can listen without taking his or her attention from the briefing to write, or requesting the briefer to repeat information.

Forecasts for these conditions can be overlooked. On the other hand, don't expect the freezing level on a clear day—have to watch out for that "clear air icing."

With this as a background and FSS staffing being further reduced, the question becomes how can a pilot best use the services available?

Become familiar with recorded weather information in your area: TWEB, TIBS, and PATWAS. These programs have been established to help reduce delays. They provide a general weather picture, with usually enough information to determine if further checking is warranted. If the weather is IFR or beyond a pilot's limits, there's no need to tie up a briefer. Additionally, pilots can determine if, on a particular day, a flight to the coast, the desert, or the mountains would be best. Briefers can be on the line for 10 minutes or more with pilots looking for a place to fly. This could be eliminated if these individuals would use the recordings. This also applies to student pilots looking for suitable cross-country routes.

Recordings provide much of the information in a standard briefing. Normally these services contain the synopsis, adverse conditions, route, and winds aloft forecasts through 12,000 feet, and selected surface weather reports. Forecasts are normally available 24 hours, although, surface weather reports may be suspended between 10 p.m. and 5 a.m. Depending on the broadcast, other information, such as TAFs, NOTAMs, and military training activity are not available. These broadcasts do not meet regulatory requirements for IFR. However, often the information will be sufficient for a VFR flight. If any clarification or additional information is required, the FSS should be consulted.

There are additional uses of the FAA's recorded weather systems. Knowing when the broadcasts are updated, pilots can obtain an outlook for the following day. Broadcast updates usually coincide with FA and TWEB forecast issuance times. Pilots can check with their FSS for broadcast update times; most FSSs publish these times in Letters to Airmen or Pilot Bulletins. Student and low-time pilots can use broadcast systems to learn aviation weather terminology. I always recommended this to students. In this way, they can become familiar with the terms and phrases used in weather briefings. Anything they don't understand can be discussed with their instructor.

Pilots have a say in the content of these services. Although the FAA prescribes the general content and format, the exact items of information, such as individual weather reports, is left to the discretion of the facility. Facility managers are supposed to solicit comments from users—pilots—about their content. If pilots want a particular item on the broadcast, they should contact the facility.

Finally, pilots should know where to complain. As far as broadcasts go, this usually means it was intelligible or read too fast. If there's a problem, contact the supervisor or manager, or use the FAA's Hot Line (800) FAA-SURE. If pilots don't make the FAA aware of a problem, whose fault is it if it doesn't get fixed?

Commercial Weather Briefing Services/DUAT

The FAA authorized Data Transformation and Contel in February 1990 to provide Direct User Access Terminal (DUAT) service to pilots within the contiguous United States. This computerized system, available at airports and through personal computers, allows direct access to weather briefing and flight plan services. DUAT, and virtually all other commercial services use National Weather Service products, which contradicts the misconception that computer briefings somehow provide a different product than available through an FSS. Graphic products may differ. However, again, they are derived from NWS products and are, typically, less detailed.

When using these services, it's essential to know what information is available. Pilots using a commercial system must check with the vendor to determine how their system handles aviation products. Certain products, for example TWEBs, might not be available on some systems, none provide local NOTAMs. Know your service, and check with an FSS for any additional information required, or to clarify anything you don't understand—remember the disclaimer.

Let's review a DUAT aviation briefing, planning a flight in a Cessna 182 from Livermore, California (LVK), to Salt Lake City, Utah (SLC).

The briefing filled nine complete pages and the weather was good. The briefing contains:

- The Area Forecast

- SIGMETs

- Convective SIGMETs

- Center Weather Advisories

- The AIRMET Bulletin

- METARs

- Pilot Reports

- Radar weather reports

- Terminal Aerodrome Forecasts

- Winds Aloft

- Notice to Airmen

The pilot is presented with the same products—except charts and local NOTAMs—available at the Flight Service Station. The pilot must then decode, translate, and interpret the information to determine which reports and forecasts apply. This briefing took about 15 minutes to obtain and print, and an additional 10 minutes to analyze and apply. After a little practice, you should be able to scan the material as it is displayed and only print significant portions for further review.

A decode function is now available to translate standard contractions, but the pilot is left with interpretation and application. Occasionally, incorrect contractions are used. One synopsis read: "AN UPPER LEVEL LAKE ONTARIO IS OFF NORTHERN BAJA CALIFORNIA." (The forecaster had used the contraction "LO," which decodes as "Lake Ontario," to indicate a low-pressure area.

An FSS briefing would go something like this:

There are weather advisories for moderate turbulence over California. There is a strong northerly flow aloft over California, with an upper-level trough over the Rockies moving eastward.

Livermore's reporting 15,000 thin broken, visibility two zero, wind calm. Over Stockton at 7500, a Baron reports light turbulence with northerly winds 35 to 40 knots. En route, broken to overcast cirroform clouds and unrestricted visibilities becoming, by the Elko, Salt Lake City portion of the route, scattered clouds based around 6000 to 7000. Salt Lake surface winds zero two zero at one one, with standing lenticular altocumulus southeast through west. A Gulfstream two during climbout of Salt Lake southbound reports smooth, tops of scattered clouds 9000 to 10,000. Conditions forecast to remain the same en route, with Salt Lake 6000 scattered, a slight chance of ceilings 5500 broken in light rain showers, surface winds three five zero at one five peak gusts two zero. Winds aloft forecast at 11,500, northwesterly at two five knots. There are no NOTAMs for the route.

The advantages of computer briefings are the relatively prompt access and the capability of a personal copy. With these advantages come the responsibility to decode, translate, interpret, and apply information to a flight. The pilot will have to sift through the mountains of written data, formally reserved for the FSS specialist, to determine if a particular flight is feasible under existing and forecast conditions, and aircraft/pilot capability.

The sheer amount of information might be overwhelming, especially for long distance flights. A pilot might have to study several pages for a single sentence that applies. Flight instructors and pilot examiners might wish to save briefings for training and flight tests. Finally, if you have a problem with one of these services you'll have to contact the vendor.

As so elegantly stated by John Hyde, an ex-Army aviator, Kit Fox owner, and Oakland FSS controller. When obtaining a briefing from an FSS or other source, keep in mind that they're in "sales, not production." In other words, don't blame the messenger for the message.

Updating Weather

A pilot's responsibility does not end with an understanding of forecast products and limitations, and the means of collecting meteorological and aeronautical information. Due to the dynamic character of the atmosphere, data must be continually updated. Surprisingly, many pilots have not been taught, or learned, the importance of updating weather reports, forecasts, and NOTAMs en route. Failure to exercise this pilot-in-command prerogative can have disastrous results.

The importance of updating weather and NOTAMs en route cannot be overemphasized. The primary focal point for these services are the FAA's Flight Service Stations, through FSS communications, broadcasts, and Flight Watch. Secondary sources of information are Automatic Terminal Information Service (ATIS) and automated weather observation (AWOS/ASOS) broadcasts, and Air Route Traffic Control Center (ARTCC) and terminal (tower/approach control) controllers.

Flight Service Station (FSS) Communications

With FSS consolidation, correct, concise, and accurate communications become more important. FSS frequencies are busier than ever, with fewer specialists providing communications over larger areas. Correct communications technique, a seemingly simple task, will take on a greater significance. Towers, approach controls, and centers have specific frequencies for specific purposes (ground control, local control, clearance delivery, ATIS, etc.). Flight Service Stations also have different frequencies for specific services. Normally available are the common FSS, local airport advisory, facility discrete, and emergency frequencies. FSSs also have voice capability over many VORs. A pilot's first task is to select the appropriate frequency for the service desired.

A new service called Ground Communication Outlet (GCO) has recently been established. This is a remotely controlled, ground-to-ground communications facility. Pilots at uncontrolled airports may contact the FSS via VHF radio to a telephone connection to update a weather briefing prior to takeoff. Pilots use six "key clicks" to contact the FSS. The GCO system is intended to be used only on the ground. Available location are advertised in the *Airport/Facility Directory*.

FSS Common Frequency

The FSS common frequency is 122.2 MHz simplex (transmit and receive on the same channel) and is available at virtually every FSS. It is normally not published on aeronautical charts, unless available at a remote site. Prior to FSS consolidation, when pilots were unsure of the appropriate FSS frequency, 122.2 MHz was recommended—although it was likely to be congested, especially over flat terrain or when used at high altitudes. With the completion of FSS consolidation, a common FSS frequency is virtually outdated. It's ironic that with satellite communication and navigation, the FAA holds on so staunchly to the past. Under normal circumstances, pilots should use the appropriate frequency published for their vicinity on aeronautical charts.

Local Airport Advisory Frequency

Local Airport Advisory (LAA) is a terminal service provided by designated facilities located at airports without an operating control tower. LAA is another relic of the past. Even where an FSS is located at a nontower or part-time tower airport, few facilities provide this service. Where available, frequency 123.6 MHz (123.62 or 123.65 MHz at some locations) is used. This service provides wind, altimeter setting, favored or designated runway, and known traffic. Local weather conditions can also be included. At airports where part-time towers are collocated with an FSS, Local Airport Advisory, where available, will be provided on the tower local control frequency when the tower is closed. VFR flights should monitor the frequency when within 10 miles of the airport. IFR flights will be instructed to contact the advisory frequency by the control facility.

The FAA's position remains that Automated Flight Service Stations will not provide LAA. This seems to be a waste of a valuable resource. An FAA group has proposed a similar service for AFSSs. LAA for local or remote airports would be considered on an individual basis. Wind and altimeter would be provided either from direct-reading instruments or the local weather report. If the local weather report were used, the time of observation would be included. The inclusion of time will alert the pilot that wind direction is true, rather than magnetic, as reported from direct-reading instruments.

Discrete Frequency

Routine communications (weather information, flight plan services, position reports, etc.) should be accomplished on the station's discrete frequency. These frequencies are unique to individual facilities, and remote locations. Their use will usually avoid frequency congestion with aircraft calling adjacent stations.

FSS frequencies can be found on aeronautical charts as illustrated in Fig. 11-4 and in the *Airport/Facility Directory*. A heavy line box indicates standard FSS frequencies, 122.2 MHz, and the emergency frequency 121.5 MHz. Other frequencies, such as the station discrete and Local Airport Advisory, are printed above the box. If a frequency is followed by the letter R (122.15R), the FSS has receiver capability only on that frequency. The pilot must receive transmissions from the FSS on another frequency, usually the associated VOR; this duplex communication requires the pilot to ensure the volume is turned up on the VOR receiver.

For example, refer to the Remote Communications Outlet/NAVAID portion of Fig. 11-4. Rancho Murietta FSS, noted below the box, has a remote receiver at the VOR site on 122.1 MHz, noted above the box. A pilot wishing to communicate through the VOR would tune the transmitter to 122.1 MHz, and select Friant, 115.6 MHz, on the VOR receiver. The pilot must remember to turn up the volume on the VOR receiver because "Rancho Radio" will transmit on that frequency. A thin-line box indicates a Remote Communications Outlet. The frequency or frequencies available are printed above the box with the name of the controlling FSS below. After selecting the frequency for the service desired, correct communications technique must be used. By following the procedures below, pilots will realize faster, more efficient service and decrease the chance of error or delay.

1. Monitor the frequency before transmitting. Monitoring the frequency before transmitting is paramount to effective communications. How many times have we heard someone transmit over someone else? We've all done it; select the frequency and press the transmit button. All this does is add to the congestion of already crowded frequencies. This basic procedure should be followed when contacting any facility.

2. Use the complete aircraft identification. The FSS needs the full aircraft call sign.

FSS COMMUNICATIONS

HEAVY LINE BOX indicates FSS. Normally **122.2** and **121.5** are available.

122.35   122.5

HAWTHORNE HHR

122.35 (Simplex) FSS Primary Discrete Frequency.
122.5 (Simplex) FSS Secondary Discrete Frequency.

REMOTE COMMUNICATIONS OUTLET/NAVAID
(Duplex) "FRIANT" is the name of the RCO and NAVAID. RANCHO MURIETTA is the controlling FSS.

122.1R

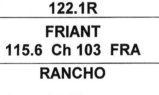

FRIANT
115.6 Ch 103 FRA

RANCHO

122.1R (Duplex) FSS has receiver ONLY. *Pilot must transmit on 122.1 and listen on the VOR frequency 115.6.*

An underlined frequency (i.e. <u>109.4</u>) indicates NAVAID only. NO FSS communications.

HEAVY LINE BOX indicates FSS. Normally **122.2** and **121.5** are available. Square, inside lower right corner, indicates **HIWAS** or a circle with a "T" indicates **TWEB** available on the VOR frequency.

122.6
123.65 VOR/DME

ARCATA
110.2 Ch 39 ACV

122.6 (Simplex) FSS discrete frequency.
123.65 (Simplex) FSS Local Airport Advisory.

REMOTE COMMUNICATION OUTLET
(Simplex) "BURBANK" is the name of the RCO with a frequency of **122.35**.

122.35

BURBANK RCO

HAWTHORNE

HAWTHORNE is the controlling FSS.

Fig. 11-4 FSSs communication frequencies are depicted on aeronautical charts; pilots should select the appropriate frequency for the service desired.

3. Advise the FSS on which frequency you expect a response and your general location. Most FSSs monitor from between five and 10 different frequencies. With FSS consolidation, this practice has become increasingly important for efficient communications. Figure 11-5 shows the in-flight console at the McAlester, Oklahoma AFSS. Each light on the panel represents one receiver.

4. Establish communications before proceeding with your message. The controller might be busy with other aircraft on other frequencies or other duties. Then, listen to what the controller says.

Fig. 11-5 Correct techniques are imperative for effective communications; pilots should always advise the FSS on which frequency they expect a response and their general location.

A classic failure occurs when a pilot calls to file a flight plan. The controller, busy with another aircraft on another frequency, advises the pilot to stand by. The pilot proceeds with the flight plan. The controller has no option, but to mute the receiver and conclude the contact with the other aircraft. The pilot wishing to file is somewhat miffed when the controller says, "Go ahead with your flight plan."

En Route Flight Advisory Service (Flight Watch)

The objective and purpose of Flight Watch is to enhance aviation safety by providing en route aircraft with timely and meaningful weather advisories. This objective is met by providing complete and accurate information on weather as it exists along a route pertinent to a specific flight, provided in sufficient time to prevent unnecessary changes to a flight plan, but when necessary, to permit the pilot to make a decision to terminate the flight or alter course before adverse conditions are encountered.

Flight Watch is not intended for flight plan services, position reports, initial, or outlook briefings, nor is it to be used for aeronautical information, such as NOTAMs, center or navigational frequencies, or for single or random weather reports and forecasts. The altimeter setting may only be provided on request. Pilots requesting services not within the scope of Flight Watch will be advised to contact an FSS.

Using all sources, Flight Watch provides en route flight advisories, which include any hazardous weather, presented as a narrative summary of existing flight conditions—real-time weather—along the proposed route of flight, tailored to the type of flight being conducted.

The purpose of Flight Watch is to provide meteorological information for that phase of flight that begins after climbout and ends with descent to land, therefore the specialist can concentrate on weather trends, forecast variance, and hazards. Flight Watch is specifically intended to update information previously received, and, serve as focal point for system feedback in the form of PIREPs. ARTCC and tower controllers do accept PIREPs, but weather is a secondary duty and, unfortunately, PIREPs aren't always passed along; if possible, PIREPs should be reported directly to Flight Watch. The effectiveness of Flight Watch is to a large degree dependent on this two-way exchange of information.

CASE STUDY

A Bonanza pilot approached an area of thunderstorms in California's Central Valley. The pilot received the latest weather radar and satellite information, as well as PIREPs and surface observations from Flight Watch. The pilot safely traversed the area with minimum diversion or delay.

This is not a very exciting story, but that's the purpose of Flight Watch, to assist pilots in conducting uneventful flights. En route Flight Advisory Service has been around for more than 20 years. In spite of this, its function, and the best way to use this important service, is misunderstood by many pilots.

En route Flight Advisory Service (EFAS), originally En route Weather Advisory Service (radio call Eee'waas, which no one could pronounce), began on the West Coast in 1972 originally as a 24-hour service; Flight Watch now normally operates from 6 a.m. until 10 p.m. local time. Flight Watch is not available at all altitudes in all areas. The service provides communications generally at and above 5000 ft AGL. Although, in areas of low terrain and closer to communication outlets, service will be available at lower altitudes. Figure 11-6 shows the Los Angeles Flight Watch position circa 1976.

The system expanded in 1976 and a network of 44 Flight Watch Control Stations became operational in 1979. The common frequency 122.0 MHz immediately became congested, especially from aircraft at high altitudes. A discrete high-altitude frequency was assigned Flight Watch stations in the Southwest in 1980, to help resolve the problem. With Flight Service Station consolidation Flight Watch responsibility has been assigned the FSSs associated with the Air Route Traffic Control Centers (Oakland FSS-Oakland Center, Hawthorne FSS-Los Angeles Center, etc.). A discrete high-altitude frequency, for use at and above Flight Level 180, has been assigned each Flight Watch Control Station to cover the associated center's area.

Fig. 11-6 Flight Watch began on the West Coast in 1972 when specialists only had Teletype reports and forecasts, and pilot weather reports.

Establishing communications is the first step. Because only one frequency is available for low altitudes, pilots must exercise frequency discipline. In addition to the basic communications technique already discussed, the following procedures should be used when contacting Flight Watch.

1. When known, use the name of the associate Air Route Traffic Control Center (ARTCC) followed by "Flight Watch" (Salt Lake Flight Watch). If not known, simply calling Flight Watch is sufficient.

2. State the aircraft position in relation to a major topographical feature or navigation aid (near Fresno, over the Clovis VOR, etc.).

    Exact positions are not necessary, but the general aircraft location is needed. Flight Watch facilities cover the same geographical areas as the ARTCCs. With numerous outlets, on a single frequency, the specialist needs to know which transmitter serves the pilot's area. This will eliminate interference with aircraft calling other facilities, garbled communications, and repeated transmissions. Failure to state the aircraft position on initial contact is the single biggest complaint from Flight Watch specialists.

3. When requesting weather or an en route flight advisory, provide the controller with cruising altitude, route, destination, and IFR capability, if appropriate.

    The controller needs sufficient background information to provide the service requested.

Flight Watch controllers are required to continually solicit reports of turbulence, icing, temperature, wind shear, and upper winds regardless of weather conditions. This information, along with PIREPs of other phenomena, is immediately relayed to other pilots, briefers, and forecasters. Together with all sources of information, the controller has access to the most complete weather picture possible.

ARTCC controllers are helpful relaying reports of turbulence and icing, and providing advice on the location of convective activity, but the information is limited by equipment, and usually to immediate and surrounding sectors. Their primary responsibility is the separation of aircraft. On the other hand, Flight Watch has only one responsibility, weather. Flight Watch—with real-time National Weather Service weather radar displays, satellite pictures, and the latest weather and pilot reports—provides specific real-time conditions, as well as the big picture. Additionally, Flight Watch controllers have direct communications with Center Weather Service Unit personnel and NWS aviation forecasters.

Getting a hold of Flight Watch is usually a simple matter, even for single-pilot IFR operations. ATC will usually approve a request to leave the frequency for a few minutes, but don't wait until the last minute. Trying to find an alternate airport in congested approach airspace is no fun for anyone. I routinely use this procedure and have never been denied the request from en route controllers.

The early days of airline flying were plagued by thunderstorms as well as icing, turbulence, widespread low ceilings and visibilities, and the limited range of the aircraft. Today's jets have virtually overcome these obstacles. More and more pilots of general aviation aircraft, equipped with turbochargers and oxygen or pressurization, are encountering the same problems as yesterday's airline captains. The only difference is a vastly improved air traffic and communication system. Among one of the FAA's best-kept secrets is the implementation of high-altitude Flight Watch.

Continually updating the weather picture is the key to managing a flight, especially at high altitude in aircraft without ice protection and storm avoidance equipment, and with relatively limited range. Winds aloft can be a welcome friend eastbound or a terrible foe westbound. With limited range, even a small change in winds at altitude can have a disastrous result. At the first sign of unexpected winds, Flight Watch should be consulted, if for no other reason than to provide a pilot report. A significant change in wind direction or speed is often the first sign of a forecast gone sour. A revised flight plan might be required. Flight Watch can provide needed additional information on current weather, PIREPs, and updated forecasts upon which to base an intelligent decision.

A primary reason for high-altitude flying is to avoid mechanical, frontal, and mountain wave turbulence; however, the flight levels have their own problems—wind shear or Clear Air Turbulence. When problems are encountered, Flight Watch can help find a smooth altitude or alternate route. If the pilot elects to change altitude, an update of actual or forecast winds aloft is often a necessity.

Icing is normally not a significant factor in the flight levels, except around convective activity or in the summer when temperatures can range between 0 degrees C and –10 degrees C. However, icing can be significant during descent, especially when destination temperature is at or below freezing. Flight Watch can provide information on tops, temperatures aloft, reported and forecast icing, and current surface conditions.

Many aircraft are equipped with airborne weather radar and lightning detection equipment. However, these systems are plagued by low power, attenuation, and limited range. A pilot might pick his or her way through a convective area only to find additional activity beyond. Flight Watch has the latest NWS weather radar information. Well before engaging any convective activity, a pilot should consult Flight Watch to determine the extent of the system, its movement, intensity, and intensity trend. Armed with this information, the pilot can determine whether to attempt to penetrate the system or select a suitable alternate. ATC prefers issuing alternate clearances compared to handling emergencies in congested airspace and severe weather.

Finally, there is destination and alternate weather. The preflight briefing provided current and forecast conditions at the time of the briefing. This information should be routinely updated en route; the airlines do it, often through Flight Watch. Are updated reports consistent with the forecast? If not, why? Flight Watch controllers through their training are in an excellent position to detect forecast variance. Whether the forecast was incorrect or conditions are changing faster or slower than forecast, the pilot needs to know and plan accordingly. Knowledge of forecast issuance times is often helpful. Forecasts might not be amended if the next issuance time is close. Flight Watch is in the best position to provide the latest information and suggest possible alternatives.

Updates must be obtained far enough in advance to be acted upon effectively. This must be done before critical weather is encountered or fuel runs low. Hoping a stronger-than-forecast head wind will abate, or arriving over a destination that has not improved as forecast, is folly. At the first sign of unforecast conditions, Flight Watch should be consulted and, if necessary, an alternate plan developed. This might mean an additional routine landing en route, which is eminently preferable to, at best a terrifying flight, or at worst an aircraft accident.

High-altitude Flight Watch frequencies for individual ARTCCs are provided in Fig. 11-7. Frequencies and outlets can also be found on the inside back cover of the *Airport/Facility Directory*. Standard frequency 122.0 MHz can be used when a pilot is unsure of the discrete frequency.

Using the System

With the increased availability of automated weather observation systems, AWOS/ASOS has become a significant weather resource. This is especially true for uncontrolled fields. By monitoring AWOS/ASOS, as well as sky conditions, visibility, and altimeter setting, we receive surface wind information. From this, we can often determine favored runway. By checking the *Airport/Facility Directory*, and now available on aeronautical charts, we establish traffic direction for that runway. This allows us to more effectively enter the traffic pattern.

Some final thoughts about the "complete picture" and personal minimums and risk management.

The "complete picture" is knowledge of weather systems for a proposed flight that includes the synopsis, current, and forecast conditions. It includes the nearest area of good weather, should the forecast go sour. The "complete picture" begins with a standard briefing and continues throughout the flight with weather updates from Flight Watch, or other available sources (ATIS, HIWAS, AWOS/ASOS, and pilot observations).

Personal minimums are directly related to risk assess and management. Aeronautical decision making is defined as the ability to obtain all available, relevant information, evaluate alternate courses of actions, then analyze and evaluate their risks, and determine the results. First, evaluate all the factors for a particular flight and decide if the risk is worth the mission. This can be extremely simple or extremely complex. There are three elements in risk assessment and management. They are: planning, aircraft, and pilot. Planning is the

HIGH-ALTITUDE FLIGHT WATCH

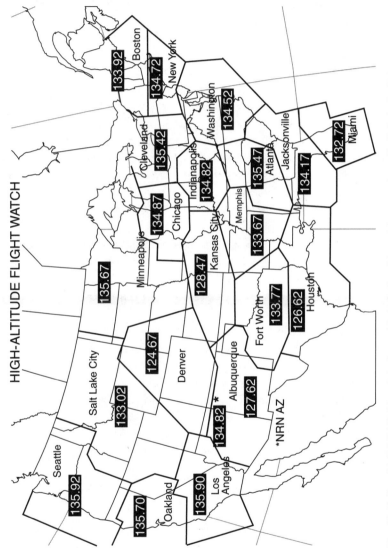

135.92 Seattle

135.70 Oakland

135.90 Los Angeles

133.02 Salt Lake City

134.82 *

127.62 Albuquerque

124.67 Denver

128.47 Kansas City

135.67 Minneapolis

134.87 Chicago

135.42 Cleveland

134.82 Indianapolis

134.52 Washington

133.92 Boston

134.72 New York

135.47 Atlanta

134.17 Jacksonville

132.72 Miami

133.67 Memphis

133.77 Fort Worth

126.62 Houston

*NRN AZ

Fig. 11-7 Discrete high-altitude Flight Watch frequencies have been commissioned nationwide to eliminate much frequency congestion, especially with aircraft at low altitudes.

CASE STUDY

The Weather Channel reported a fast moving cold front, with strong surface wind, approaching Palm Springs. Due to the large amount of traffic for the 1998 AOPA convention, there were no tie-downs available. (They did, however, offer to sell us a set of commemorative chalks. Hum?) With our business concluded, we decided to leave on Saturday. I received a briefing and filed a VFR flight plan to Lancaster's Fox field—plan A.

It was a beautiful flight, smooth air with a high overcast. With plenty of fuel, we decided to continue on to Harris Ranch in the San Joaquin Valley. I updated weather and revised our flight plan with Riverside Radio—plan B.

Over Bakersfield I made a position report to Rancho Radio and received updated weather. Navy Leemore, adjacent to Harris Ranch, was reporting visibility three-quarters of a mile in blowing dust, wind gusting to 35 knots! Well, we knew where the front was. We check the weather at Visalia, and again amended our flight plan— plan C.

As we proceeded toward Visalia we could see the billowing dust storm approaching from the northwest. Fortunately, Visalia had an ASOS. We were only 10 miles south of Visalia when the ASOS reported the arrival of the storm. I contacted Rancho Radio, advised them of the situation, canceled the flight plan, and descended into the traffic pattern at Tulare—plan D. We got the airplane tied down about five minutes before the storm hit.

This is a good example of using the system—FSS and ASOS, evaluating and managing risk, and the decision-making process. You may ask why I used flight service and not Flight Watch. Since flight plan revisions were required, Flight Watch was not appropriate. Also, I only needed specific weather reports. I was able to accomplish both tasks with one radio contact.

"homework" part of the flight, which we've previously mentioned. We study terrain, altitude requirements, and the environment. The environment includes the weather, our personal minimums, and alternatives. Now we evaluate the aircraft. Does it have the performance and equipment for the mission? If the answer is yes, we preflight the aircraft and determine that it is airworthy. Assuming the pilot is "fit for flight," we're ready to go. Simple, huh?

The decision can be as simple as my friend John and his Kit Fox looking at an afternoon flight in the traffic pattern—or, as complex as one of NASA's shuttle missions.

Let's start with John's decision. Planning: Airport elevation 397 feet, runway 25L 2699 feet; pattern altitude 1400 feet; the environment—clear, cool, winds calm, alternate runway 25R. Aircraft: Performance of the Kit Fox OK; airplane equipped for flight in Class D airspace. Pilot: Fit for flight. Decision: GO!

Don't worry. We're not going to evaluate a space shuttle mission. Instead let's take an actual flight situation. We were flying from Oklahoma City to Palm Springs for the 1998 AOPA convention. We made it as far as Santa Rosa, New Mexico before the weather closed in. Hal Marx (USMC retired), the Santa Rosa airport manager, fueled our airplane and gave us a lift into town, where we remained overnight. The next day wasn't any better and we spent another night.

We had been trying to get to Albuquerque for two days without success. The following morning wasn't much better, but forecast to improve.

Planning. Santa Rosa has a field elevation of 4782 feet. Along I-40 the high plateau of eastern New Mexico rises to over 7000 ft, with the pass through the Sandia Mountains at about the same elevation. Terrain is slightly lower to the north and south, but still over 6000 ft. Because of the mountains IFR MEAs vary from about 10,000 to 12,000 ft. Minimum altitudes would range from 6500 to 8500 VFR or 10,000 to 12,000 ft IFR. Although we were flying a Cessna 172 we still had the option of going IFR or VFR.

Environment. Upslope due to rising terrain was, and continued to be, the culprit. MVFR to IFR ceilings, generally good visibility, high tops, freezing level at about 10,000 ft, conditions forecast to slowly improve during the day. When evaluating risk: Flying toward or in improving weather is better than flying toward or in deteriorating conditions.

With my training and experience I have different personal minimums depending on the environment. I also have confidence in my ability to make the decision to turn around. As John Hyde puts it,

"Cowardice is the better part of valor." (Undoubtedly, an axiom he learned from his Army aviator days.)

When we talk about personal minimums there are a number of factors to consider. We've touched on some of them thus far.

- Training

- Experience

- Currency

- Aircraft

- Weather

- Time of day

- Physical condition

- Psychological condition

When establishing personal minimums first consider your level of training. Are you a student, private, commercial, instrument, or airline transport pilot? Our Air Force Aero Club and my flight school at Livermore have specific limits of wind, visibility, and ceiling for each certificate and rating.

As our level of experience increases we may wish to consider different minimums. As a flight instructor I tailored student minimums to their training and experience. For example, I had a student flying out of Lancaster's Fox Field, in the Mojave Desert of California. We trained in strong, gusty surface winds. When the student was proficient I would increase the minimums. Some pilots obtain an instrument rating without ever having flown in the clouds. Do they have the experience to operate in actual instrument conditions? A prudent pilot would have another qualified, experience pilot or flight instructor along until they became familiar with flight in clouds.

Currency with the type of operation is another personal minimums factor. Here again, legal does not necessarily mean safe. If we've been recently qualified to fly at night, we would certainly want to gain experience before tackling weather close to, either VFR or IFR, minimums during this time of day.

How familiar are we with the aircraft. If we've just check out in a high performance aircraft, especially without previous experience, are we ready to fly it in minimum weather? Probably not. Low ceilings and visibilities, even when technically legal, are often an unacceptable risk. Depending on training and experience low ceilings with good visibilities may be acceptable.

Time of day is another factor to consider. There is no question that flying at night introduces additional challenges and risk.

Physical and psychological conditions have already been discussed. If we're not fit, we shouldn't go. Here's a good example of the application of personal minimums. One of our local Flight Standards Operations Inspectors had a flight in a Mooney 252 from Hayward to Ukiah in California. There was a low stratus layer over the San Francisco Bay. This individual had thousands of hours as a Navy P3 pilot. Although this individual was qualified and current, he was not comfortable conducting this IFR operation. I volunteered to fly with him and we had an uneventful flight.

IFR flight. High-minimum altitudes, low-freezing level, I did not have approach charts for Albuquerque. The airplane would be at the limit of its performance envelope. The airplane was equipped for IFR operations, except not certified for flight in known icing. We would be at the MEA in probable icing conditions, unable to climb, over mountainous terrain. What alternates were available? None! Risk high. Decision: NO GO.

VFR flight: Plan A—Climb to VFR on top and fly to Albuquerque and descend through broken clouds—forecast anyway. Plan B—Fly under the clouds and land at Albuquerque. Plan C—Fly south, along the railroad to Albuquerque. (For some reason railroad engineers always select the lowest terrain.) Plan D—Return to Santa Rosa. Risk, yes, but plenty of options. For me this was a "go take a look" situation. Why? The area was sparsely populated, good visibility, good weather at the departure airport. On the negative side, I was not familiar with the area; familiarity has led many a pilot to disaster. It was daylight. A night flight, either IFR or VFR under these conditions would have resulted in a NO-GO decision.

Airplane performance and equipment was GO for the VFR plan. The pilot was fit for flight. Decision: GO.

Risk assessment and management does not stop with a GO decision. We must reevaluate conditions throughout the operation, from preflight inspection to determining that a particular airport is suitable for landing. Should the airplane be unairworthy—this includes equipment—the decision is NO GO. If conditions at the destination (wind, weather, surface conditions, etc.) change, we may have to divert. If we don't have an alternate plan risk is too high, resulting in a NO GO decision.

With the preflight complete, and four-and-a-half hours of fuel, we departed and opened our VFR flight plan to Albuquerque. (A VFR flight plan, especially under these conditions, is part of risk management.) Ceilings were low, but visibility was excellent. It soon became apparent that plan A, over the clouds, was not going to work. This was confirmed through a conversation with Albuquerque Radio advising that their weather had not improved. Plan A: NO GO.

Plan B—fly under the clouds. Approaching Clines Corners, terrain rises to about 7000 ft. The clouds went right down to the ground! Don't push the weather, your aircraft, or yourself; turn around and wait it out. We initiated a 180-degree turn. We would have been flying from poor to worse weather. Risk too high. Decision: NO GO.

At this point I had resigned myself to returning to Santa Rosa—plan D. However, my wife said, "What about plan C?" An increased risk accompanied plan C. There were only a couple of dirt strips with high elevations and short runways for alternates. The terrain was lower, ceilings low, but visibility remained excellent. For navigation we had the "iron compass" (railroad). I called Albuquerque Radio changed our route and ETA. As is my practice I made position reports and updated weather with flight service—another part of risk management. We always had the option of returning to Santa Rosa should the weather deteriorate. Albuquerque did not improve and we landed short at Alexander, New Mexico. With the weather now improving from the west we continued on to Palm Springs.

There are many excuses for getting caught in weather, but few if any reasons!

Abbreviations

Many contractions are used on aviation weather reports and forecasts to save space on telecommunication circuits, in computer equipment, and on charts. The contractions will normally be used for any derivative of the root word. If confusion would result, variations might be shown by adding the following letters to the contraction of the root word.

able	BL
al	L
ally, erly, ly	LY
ary, ery, ory	RY
ance, ence	NC
der	DR
ed, ied	D
ening	NG
er, ier, or	R
ern	RN
ically	CLY
ive	V
iest, est	ST

iness, ness	NS
ing	G
ity	TY
ment	MT
ous	US
s, es, ies	S
tion, ation	N
ward	WD

The following contractions are normally used on aviation weather reports, PIREPs, forecasts, charts, and Notices to Airmen. The appendix is divided into two sections: weather and international. To avoid duplication and save space, redundant contractions have been eliminated. Therefore, it may be necessary to check more than one section to decode a particular contraction.

Weather

ABNDT	Abundant
ABNML	Abnormal
ABT	About
ABV	Above
AC	Convective Outlook; Altocumulus
ACC	Altocumulus Castellanus
ACCUM	Accumulate
ACFT	Aircraft
ACLT	Accelerate
ACLTD	Accelerated
ACLTG	Accelerating
ACLTS	Accelerates
ACPY	Accompany
ACRS	Across
ACSL	Altocumulus Standing Lenticularus

ACTV	Active
ACTVTY	Activity
ACYC	Anticyclone
ADJ	Adjacent
ADL	Additional
ADQT	Adequate
ADQTLY	Adequately
ADRNDCK	Adirondack
ADVCT	Advect
ADVN	Advance
ADVNG	Advancing
ADVY	Advisory
ADVYS	Advisories
AFCT	Affect
AFDK	After dark
AFOS	Automated Field Operations System
AFT	After
AFTN	Afternoon
AGL	Above ground level
AGN	Again
AGRD	Agreed
AGRMT	Agreement
AHD	Ahead
AK	Alaska
AL	Alabama
ALF	Aloft
ALG	Along
ALGHNY	Allegheny
ALQDS	All quadrants
ALSTG	Altimeter setting
ALTA	Alberta

ALTHO	Although
ALTM	Altimeter
ALUTN	Aleutian
AMD	Amend
AMDD	Amended
AMDG	Amending
AMDT	Amendment
AMP	Amplify
AMPG	Amplifying
AMPLTD	Amplitude
AMS	Air mass
AMT	Amount
ANLYS	Analysis
ANS	Answer
AOA	At or above
AOB	At or below
AP	Anomolous Propagation
APCH	Approach
APLCN	Appalachian
APLCNS	Appalachians
APPR	Appear
APRNT	Apparent
APRX	Approximate
AR	Arkansas
ARND	Around
ARPT	Airport
ASAP	As soon as possible
ASL	Above Sea Level
ASMD	As amended
ASSOCD	Associated
ATLC	Atlantic

ATTM	At this time
ATTN	Attention
AVBL	Available
AVG	Average
AVN	Aviation Model
AWT	Awaiting
AZ	Arizona
AZM	Azimuth
BACLIN	Baroclinic
BAJA	Baja California
BATROP	Barotropic
BC	British Columbia
BCH	Beach
BCKG	Backing
BCM	Become
BDA	Bermuda
BDRY	Boundary
BFDK	Before dark
BFR	Before
BGN	Begin
BHND	Behind
BINOVC	Breaks in overcast
BKN	Broken
BLD	Build
BLDG	Building
BLDS	Builds
BLDUP	Buildup
BLKHLS	Black Hills
BLKT	Blanket
BLKTG	Blanketing
BLKTS	Blankets

BLO	Below
BLZD	Blizzard
BND	Bound
BNDRY	Boundary
BNDRYS	Boundaries
BNTH	Beneath
BOOTHEEL	Bootheel
BR	Branch
BRG	Branching
BRS	Branches
BRF	Brief
BRK	Break
BRKG	Breaking
BRKHIC	Breaks in higher clouds
BRKS	Breaks
BRKSHR	Berkshire
BRM	Barometer
BTN	Between
BYD	Beyond
C	Celsius
CA	California
CAA	Cold Air Advection
CARIB	Caribbean
CASCDS	Cascades
CAVOK	Ceiling and visibility OK
CAVU	Ceiling and visibility unlimited
CB	Cumulonimbus
CC	Cirrocumulus
CCLDS	Clear of clouds
CCLKWS	Counterclockwise
CCSL	Standing lenticular cirrocumulus

CDFNT	Cold front
CDFNTL	Cold frontal
CFP	Cold front passage
CG	Cloud-to-ground
CHC	Chance
CHG	Change
CHSPK	Chesapeake
CI	Cirrus
CIG	Ceiling
CLD	Cloud
CLDNS	Cloudiness
CLKWS	Clockwise
CLR	Clear
CLRS	Clears
CMPLX	Complex
CNCL	Cancel
CNDN	Canadian
CNFDC	Confidence
CNTR	Center
CNTRD	Centered
CNTRLN	Centerline
CNTRL	Central
CNTY	County
CNTYS	Counties
CNVG	Converge
CNVGG	Converging
CNVGNC	Convergence
CNVTN	Convection
CNVTV	Convective
CNVTVLY	Convectively
CO	Colorado

COMPAR	Compare
COND	Conditions
CONT	Continue
CONTD	Continued
CONTLY	Continually
CONTG	Continuing
CONTRAILS	Condensation Trails
CONTS	Continues
CONTDVD	Continental Divide
CONUS	Continental U.S.
COORD	Coordinate
COR	Correction
CPBL	Capable
CRC	Circle
CRCLC	Circulate
CRCLN	Circulation
CRNR	Corner
CRS	Course
CS	Cirrostratus
CSDR	Consider
CST	Coast
CSTL	Coastal
CT	Connecticut
CTGY	Category
CTSKLS	Catskills
CU	Cumulus
CUFRA	Cumulus Fractus
CVR	Cover
CYC	Cyclonic
CYCLGN	Cyclogenesis
DABRK	Daybreak

DALGT	Daylight
DBL	Double
DC	District of Columbia
DCR	Decrease
DE	Delaware
DEG	Degree
DELMARVA	Delaware-Maryland-Virginia
DFCLT	Difficult
DFNT	Definite
DFRS	Differs
DFUS	Diffuse
DGNL	Diagonal
DGNLLY	Diagonally
DIGG	Digging
DIR	Direction
DISC	Discontinue
DISRE	Disregard
DKTS	Dakotas
DLA	Delay
DLT	Delete
DLY	Daily
DMG	Damage
DMNT	Dominant
DMSH	Diminish
DNDFTS	Downdrafts
DNS	Dense
DNSLP	Downslope
DNSTRM	Downstream
DNWND	Downwind
DP	Deep
DPND	Deepened

DPNS	Deepens
DPNG	Deepening
DPTH	Depth
DRFT	Drift
DRZL	Drizzle
DSCNT	Descent
DSIPT	Dissipate
DSND	Descend
DSNT	Distant
DSTBLZ	Destabilize
DSTC	Distance
DTRT	Deteriorate
DURG	During
DURN	Duration
DVLP	Develop
DVRG	Diverge
DVV	Downward vertical velocity
DWNDFTS	Downdrafts
DWPNT	Dew point
DX	Duplex
E	East
EBND	East bound
EFCT	Effect
ELNGT	Elongate
ELSW	Elsewhere
EMBDD	Embedded
EMERG	Emergency
ENCTR	Encounter
ENDG	Ending
ENE	East-northeast
ENELY	East-northeasterly

ENERN	East-northeastern
ENEWD	East-northeastward
ENHNC	Enhance
ENTR	Entire
ERN	Eastern
ERY	Early
ERYR	Earlier
ESE	East-southeast
ESELY	East-southeasterly
ESERN	East-southeastern
ESEWD	East-southeastward
ESNTL	Essential
ESTAB	Establish
ESTS	Estimates
ETA	Eta model
ETC	Et cetera
ETIM	Elapsed time
EVE	Evening
EWD	Eastward
EXCLV	Exclusive
EXCP	Except
EXPC	Expect
EXTD	Extend
EXTN	Extension
EXTRAP	Extrapolate
EXTRM	Extreme
EXTSV	Extensive
F	Fahrenheit
FA	Aviation area forecast
FAH	Fahrenheit
FAM	Familiar

FCST	Forecast
FCSTD	Forecasted
FCSTG	Forecasting
FIG	Figure
FILG	Filling
FIRAV	First available
FL	Florida
FLG	Falling
FLRY	Flurry
FLRYS	Flurries
FLT	Flight
FLW	Follow
FLWG	Following
FM	From
FMT	Format
FNCTN	Function
FNT	Front
FNTL	Frontal
FNTGNS	Frontogenesis
FNTLYS	Frontolysis
FORNN	Forenoon
FPM	Feet per minute
FQT	Frequent
FRM	Form
FROPA	Frontal passage
FROSFC	Frontal surface
FRST	Frost
FRWF	Forecast wind factor
FRZ	Freeze
FRZN	Frozen
FRZG	Freezing

FT	Feet
FTHR	Further
FVRBL	Favorable
FWD	Forward
FYI	For your information
G	Gust
GA	Georgia
GEN	General
GEO	Geographic
GEOREF	Geographical reference
GICG	Glaze icing
GLFALSK	Gulf of Alaska
GLFCAL	Gulf of California
GLFMEX	Gulf of Mexico
GLFSTLAWR	Gulf of St. Lawrence
GND	Ground
GNDFG	Ground fog
GRAD	Gradient
GRDL	Gradual
GRDLY	Gradually
GRT	Great
GRTLKS	Great Lakes
GSTS	Gusts
GSTY	Gusty
GV	Ground visibility
HAZ	Hazard
HCVIS	High clouds visible
HDFRZ	Hard freeze
HDSVLY	Hudson Valley
HDWND	Head wind
HGT	Height

HI	High
HIER	Higher
HIFOR	High-level forecast
HLF	Half
HLTP	Hilltop
HLSTO	Hailstones
HLYR	Haze layer aloft
HND	Hundred
HR	Hour
HRS	Hours
HRZN	Horizon
HTG	Heating
HURCN	Hurricane
HUREP	Hurricane report
HV	Have
HVY	Heavy
HVYR	Heavier
HVYST	Heaviest
HWVR	However
HWY	Highway
IA	Iowa
IC	Ice
ICG	Icing
ICGIC	Icing in clouds
ICGIP	Icing in precipitation
ID	Idaho
IL	Illinois
IMDT	Immediate
IMPL	Impulse
IMPT	Important
INCL	Include

INCR	Increase
INDC	Indicate
INDEF	Indefinite
INFO	Information
INLD	Inland
INSTBY	Instability
INTCNTL	Intercontinental
INTL	International
INTMD	Intermediate
INTMT	Intermittent
INTMTLY	Intermittently
INTR	Interior
INTRMTRGN	Intermountain region
INTS	Intense
INTSFCN	Intensification
INTSFY	Intensify
INTSTY	Intensity
INTVL	Interval
INVRN	Inversion
IOVC	In overcast
INVOF	In vicinity of
IPV	Improve
IPVG	Improving
IR	Infrared
ISOL	Isolate
ISOLD	Isolated
JCTN	Junction
JTSTR	Jet stream
KFRST	Killing frost
KLYR	Smoke layer aloft
KOCTY	Smoke over city

KS	Kansas
KT	Knots
KY	Kentucky
LA	Louisiana
LABRDR	Labrador
LAT	Latitude
LCL	Local
LCTD	Located
LCTN	Location
LCTMP	Little change in temperature
LEVEL	Level
LFM	Limited Fine Mesh Model
LFTG	Lifting
LGRNG	Long range
LGT	Light
LGTR	Lighter
LGWV	Long wave
LI	Lifted Index
LK	Lake
LKS	Lakes
LKLY	Likely
LLJ	Low-Level Jet
LLWS	Low-Level Wind Shear
LLWAS	Low-level wind shear alert system
LMTD	Limited
LN	Line
LN	Lines
LO	Low
LONG	Longitude
LONGL	Longitudnal
LRG	Large

LST	Local standard time
LTD	Limited
LTG	Lightning
LTGCC	Lightning cloud-to-cloud
LTGCG	Lightning cloud-to-ground
LTGCCCG	Lightning cloud-to-cloud cloud-to ground
LTGCW	Lightning cloud-to-water
LTGIC	Lightning in cloud
LTL	Little
LTLCG	Little change
LTR	Later
LTST	Latest
LV	Leaving
LVL	Level
LVLS	Levels
LWR	Lower
LYR	Layer
MA	Massachusetts
MAN	Manitoba
MAX	Maximum
MB	Millibars
MCD	Mesoscale discussion
MD	Maryland
MDFY	Modify
MDFYD	Modified
MDFYG	Modifying
MDL	Model
MDT	Moderate
ME	Maine
MED	Medium
MEGG	Merging

MESO	Mesoscale
MET	Meteorological
METRO	Metropolitan
MEX	Mexico
MHKVLY	Mohawk Valley
MI	Michigan
MID	Middle
MIDN	Midnight
MIL	Military
MIN	Minimum
MISG	Missing
MLTLVL	Melting level
MN	Minnesota
MNLND	Mainland
MNLY	Mainly
MO	Missouri
MOGR	Moderate or greater
MOV	Move
MPH	Miles per hour
MRGL	Marginal
MRNG	Morning
MRTM	Maritime
MS	Mississippi
MSG	Message
MSL	Mean sea level
MST	Most
MSTR	Moisture
MT	Montana
MTN	Mountain
MULT	Multiple
MULTILVL	Multilevel

MXD	Mixed
N	North
NAB	Not above
NAT	North Atlantic
NATL	National
NAV	Navigation
NB	New Brunswick
NBND	Northbound
NBRHD	Neighborhood
NC	North Carolina
NCWX	No change in weather
ND	North Dakota
NE	Northeast
NEB	Nebraska
NEC	Necessary
NEG	Negative
NELY	Northeasterly
NERN	Northeastern
NEWD	Northeastward
NEW ENG	New England
NFLD	Newfoundland
NGM	Nested Grid Model
NGT	Night
NH	New Hampshire
NIL	None
NJ	New Jersey
NL	No layers
NLT	Not later than
NLY	Northerly
NM	New Mexico
NMBR	Number

NMC	National Meteorological Center
NML	Normal
NMRS	Numerous
NNE	North-northeast
NNELY	North-northeasterly
NNERN	North-northeastern
NNEWD	North-northeastward
NNW	North-northwest
NNWLY	North-northwesterly
NNWRN	North-northwestern
NNWWD	North-northwestward
NNNN	End of message
NOAA	National Oceanic and Atmospheric Administration
NOPAC	Northern Pacific
NPRS	Nonpersistent
NR	Near
NRN	Northern
NRW	Narrow
NS	Nova Scotia
NTFY	Notify
NV	Nevada
NVA	Negative vorticity advection
NW	Northwest
NWD	Northward
NWLY	Northwesterly
NWRN	Northwestern
NWS	National Weather Service
NY	New York
NXT	Next
OAT	Outside Air Temperature
OBND	Outbound

OBS	Observation
OBSC	Obscure
OCFNT	Occluded front
OCLD	Occlude
OCLN	Occlusion
OCNL	Occasional
OCR	Occur
OFC	Office
OFP	Occluded frontal passage
OFSHR	Offshore
OH	Ohio
OK	Oklahoma
OMTNS	Over mountains
ONSHR	On shore
OR	Oregon
ORGPHC	Orographic
ORIG	Original
OSV	Ocean station vessel
OTLK	Outlook
OTP	On top
OTR	Other
OTRW	Otherwise
OUTFLO	Outflow
OVC	Overcast
OVNGT	Overnight
OVR	Over
OVRN	Overrun
OVRNG	Overrunning
OVTK	Overtake
OVTKG	Overtaking
OVTKS	Overtakes

PA	Pennsylvania
PAC	Pacific
PBL	Planetary boundary layer
PCPN	Precipitation
PD	Period
PDMT	Predominant
PEN	Peninsula
PERM	Permanent
PGTSND	Puget Sound
PHYS	Physical
PIBAL	Pilot balloon observation
PIBALS	Pilot balloon reports
PIREP	Pilot weather report
PLNS	Plains
PLS	Please
PLTO	Plateau
PM	Post meridian
PNHDL	Panhandle
POS	Positive
POSLY	Positively
PPINE	PPI no echoes
PPSN	Present position
PRBL	Probable
PRBLTY	Probability
PRECD	Precede
PRES	Pressure
PRESFR	Pressure falling rapidly
PRESRR	Pressure rising rapidly
PRIM	Primary
PRIN	Principal
PRIND	Present indications are

PRJMP	Pressure jump
PROC	Procedure
PROD	Produce
PROG	Forecast
PROGD	Forecasted
PROGS	Forecasts
PRSNT	Present
PRSNTLY	Presently
PRST	Persist
PRSTNC	Persistence
PRSTNT	Persistent
PRVD	Provide
PS	Plus
PSBL	Possible
PSG	Passage
PSN	Position
PTCHY	Patchy
PTLY	Partly
PTNL	Potential
PTNS	Portions
PUGET	Puget Sound
PVA	Positive vorticity advection
PVL	Prevail
PVLT	Prevalent
PWR	Power
QN	Question
QPFERD	NMC excessive rainfall discussion
QPFHSD	NMC heavy snow discussion
QPFSPD	NMC special precipitation discussion
QSTNRY	Quasistationary
QUAD	Quadrant

QUE	Quebec
RADAT	Radiosonde observation data
RAOB	Radiosonde observation
RAOBS	Radiosonde observations
RCH	Reach
RCKY	Rocky
RCKYS	Rockies
RCMD	Recommend
RCRD	Record
RCV	Receive
RDC	Reduce
RDGG	Ridging
RDR	Radar
RDVLP	Redevelop
RE	Regard
RECON	Reconnaissance
REF	Reference
REPL	Replace
REQ	Request
RESP	Response
RESTR	Restrict
RES	Reserve
RGL	Regional Model
RGT	Right
RI	Rhode Island
RGD	Ragged
RGLR	Regular
RGN	Region
RH	Relative Humidity
RIOGD	Rio Grande
RLBL	Reliable

RLTV	Relative
RLTVLY	Relatively
RMN	Remain
RNFL	Rainfall
ROT	Rotate
RPD	Rapid
RPLC	Replace
RPLCD	Replaced
RPRT	Report
RPT	Repeat
RQR	Require
RS	Receiver station
RSG	Rising
RSN	Reason
RSTR	Restrict
RSTRG	Restricting
RSTRS	Restricts
RTRN	Return
RUF	Rough
RUFLY	Roughly
RVS	Revise
S	South
SASK	Saskatchewan
SATFY	Satisfactory
SBND	Southbound
SBSD	Subside
SBSDD	Subsided
SBSDNC	Subsidence
SBSDS	Subsides
SC	South Carolina
SCND	Second

SCNDRY	Secondary
SCSL	Standing lenticular stratocumulus
SCT	Scatter
SCTR	Sector
SD	South Dakota
SE	Southeast
SEC	Second
SELY	Southeasterly
SEPN	Separation
SEQ	Sequence
SERN	Southeastern
SEWD	Southeastward
SFC	Surface
SFERICS	Atmospherics
SGFNT	Significant
SHFT	Shift
SHLD	Shield
SHLW	Shallow
SHRT	Short
SHRTWV	Shortwave
SHUD	Should
SHWR	Shower
SIERNEV	Sierra Nevada
SIG	Signature
SIGMET	Significant meteorological information
SIMUL	Simultaneous
SKC	Sky clear
SKED	Schedule
SLD	Solid
SLGT	Slight
SLO	Slow

SLP	Slope
SLT	Sleet
SLY	Southerly
SM	Statute mile
SMK	Smoke
SML	Small
SMRY	Summary
SMS	Synchronus meteorological satellite
SMTH	Smooth
SMTM	Sometime
SMWHT	Somewhat
SNBNK	Snowbank
SND	Sand
SNFLK	Snowflake
SNGL	Single
SNOINCR	Snow increase
SNOINCRG	Snow increasing
SNST	Sunset
SNW	Snow
SNWFL	Snowfall
SOP	Standard operating procedure
SPCLY	Especially
SPD	Speed
SPDS	Speeds
SPENES	Satellite precipitation estimate statement
SPKL	Sprinkle
SPKLS	Sprinkles
SPLNS	Southern Plains
SPRD	Spread
SPRL	Spiral
SQAL	Squall

SQLN	Squall line
SR	Sunrise
SRN	Southern
SRND	Surround
SRNDG	Surrounding
SS	Sunset
SSE	South-southeast
SSELY	South-southeasterly
SSERN	South-southeastern
SSEWD	South-southeastward
SSW	South-southwest
SSWLY	South-southwesterly
SSWRN	South-southwestern
SSWWD	South-southwestward
ST	Stratus
STAGN	Stagnation
STBL	Stable
STBLTY	Stability
STD	Standard
STDY	Steady
STFR	Stratus fractus
STFRM	Stratiform
STG	Strong
STLT	Satellite
STM	Storm
STN	Station
STNRY	Stationary
SUB	Substitute
SUBTRPCL	Subtropical
SUF	Sufficient
SUFLY	Sufficiently

SUG	Suggest
SUP	Supply
SUPG	Supplying
SUPR	Superior
SUPS	Supplies
SUPSD	Supersede
SVG	Serving
SEV	Severe
SVRL	Several
SW	Southwest
SWD	Southward
SWWD	Southwestward
SWLG	Swelling
SWLY	Southwesterly
SWOMCD	SELS Mesoscale Discussion
SWRN	Southwestern
SX	Stability index
SXN	Section
SYNOP	Synoptic
SYNS	Synopsis
SYS	System
TCNTL	Transcontinental
TCU	Towering cumulus
TDA	Today
TEMP	Temperature
THD	Thunderhead
THDR	Thunder
THK	Thick
THKNG	Thickening
THKNS	Thickness
THKST	Thickest

THN	Thin
THR	Threshold
THRFTR	Thereafter
THRU	Through
THRUT	Throughout
THSD	Thousand
THTN	Threaten
TIL	Until
TMPRY	Temporary
TMW	Tomorrow
TN	Tennessee
TNDCY	Tendency
TNGT	Tonight
TNTV	Tentative
TOPS	Tops
TOVC	Top of overcast
TPG	Topping
TRBL	Trouble
TRIB	Tributary
TRKG	Tracking
TRML	Terminal
TRNSP	Transport
TROF	Trough
TROFS	Troughs
TROP	Tropopause
TRPCD	Tropical continental
TRPCL	Tropical
TRRN	Terrain
TRSN	Transition
TRW	Thunderstorm
TRW+	Thunderstorm with heavy rain shower

TSFR	Transfer
TSHWR	Thundershower
TSHWRS	Thundershowers
TSNT	Transient
TSQLS	Thundersqualls
TSTM	Thunderstorm
TSTMS	Thunderstorms
TURBC	Turbulence
TURBT	Turbulent
TWD	Toward
TWI	Twilight
TWRG	Towering
TX	Texas
UDDF	Up and down drafts
UN	Unable
UNAVBL	Unavailable
UNEC	Unnecessary
UNKN	Unknown
UNL	Unlimited
UNRELBL	Unreliable
UNRSTD	Unrestricted
UNSATFY	Unsatisfactory
UNSBL	Unseasonable
UNSTBL	Unstable
UNSTDY	Unsteady
UNSTL	Unsettle
UNUSBL	Unusable
UPDFTS	Updrafts
UPR	Upper
UPSLP	Upslope
UPSTRM	Upstream

URG	Urgent
USBL	Usable
UT	Utah
UVV	Upward vertical velocity
UVVS	Upward vertical velocities
UWNDS	Upper winds
VA	Virginia
VARN	Variation
VCNTY	Vicinity
VCOT	VFR conditions on top
VCTR	Vector
VDUC	VAS Data Utilization Center (NSSFC)
VFY	Verify
VLCTY	Velocity
VLNT	Violent
VLY	Valley
VMC	Visual meteorological conditions
VOL	Volume
VORT	Vorticity
VR	Veer
VRG	Veering
VRBL	Variable
VRISL	Vancouver Island, BC
VRS	Veers
VRT MOTN	Vertical Motion
VRY	Very
VSB	Visible
VSBY	Visibility
VSBYDR	Visibility decreasing rapidly
VSBYIR	Visibility increasing rapidly
VT	Vermont

VV	Vertical velocity
W	West
WA	Washington
WAA	Warm Air Advection
WBND	Westbound
WDLY	Widely
WDSPRD	Widespread
WEA	Weather
WFO	Weather Forecast Office
WFOS	Weather Forecast Offices
WFP	Warm front passage
WI	Wisconsin
WIBIS	Will be issued
WINT	Winter
WK	Weak
WKDAY	Weekday
WKEND	Weekend
WKNG	Weakening
WKNS	Weakens
WKR	Weaker
WKN	Weaken
WL	Will
WLY	Westerly
WND	Wind
WNDS	Winds
WNW	West-northwest
WNWLY	West-northwesterly
WNWRN	West-northwestern
WNWWD	West-northwestward
WO	Without
WPLTO	Western Plateau

WRM	Warm
WRN	Western
WRMR	Warmer
WRMFNT	Warm front
WRMFNTL	Warm Frontal
WRNG	Warning
WRNGS	Warnings
WRS	Worse
WSHFT	Wind shift
WSHFTS	Wind shifts
WSFO	Weather Service Forecast Office
WSFOS	Weather Service Forecast Offices
WSO	Weather Service Office
WSOS	Weather Service Offices
WSTCH	Wasatch Range
WSW	West-southwest
WSWLY	West-southwesterly
WSWRN	West-southwestern
WSWWD	West-southwestward
WTR	Water
WTRS	Waters
WTSPT	Waterspout
WUD	Would
WV	West Virginia
WVS	Waves
WW	Severe Weather Watch
WWAMKC	Status Report
WWD	Westward
WWS	Severe Weather Watches
WX	Weather
WY	Wyoming

XCP	Except
XPC	Expect
XPLOS	Explosive
XTND	Extend
XTRM	Extreme
YDA	Yesterday
YKN	Yukon
YLSTN	Yellowstone
ZN	Zone
ZNS	Zones

International

AAL	Above aerodrome level
ABT	About
ABV	Above
ACC	Area Control Center or area control
ACCID	Notification of an aircraft accident
ACK	Acknowledge
ACPT	Accept or accepted
ACT	Active or activated or activity
AD	aerodrome
ADA	advisory area
ADDN	Addition or additional
ADR	Advisory route
ADVS	Advisory service
ADZ	Advise
AFT	After...(time or place)
AGL	Aboveground level
AGN	Again
ALT	Altitude
AMSL	Above mean sea level

AP	Airport
APR	April
APSG	After passing
ARFOR	Area forecast
ARR	Arrive or arrival
AS	Altostratus
ASC	Ascent to or ascending to
ATP...	At...(time or place)
AUG	August
AVG	Average
B	Blue
BA	Braking action
BASE	Cloud base
BCFG	Fog patches
BDRY	Boundary
BECMG	Becoming
BFR	Before
BKN	Broken
BL...	Blowing
BLO	Below clouds
BLW	Below...
BR	Mist
BRKG	Braking
BTL	Between layers
C	Center (runway identification) or Degrees Celsius
CAT	Category or Clear Air Turbulence
CCA	Corrected meteorological message
CI	Cirrus
CLA	Clear type of ice formation
CM	Centimeter
CNL	Cancel or canceled

COM	Communications
CONS	Continuous
COOR	Co-ordinate or co-ordination
COR	Correct or correction or corrected
COT	At the coast
COV	Cover or covered or covering
CUF	Cumuliform
CW	Continuous wave
DEC	December
DEG	Degrees
DEP	Depart or departure
DES	Descend or descending to
DEV	Deviation or deviating
DIF	Diffuse
DIST	Distance
DIV	Divert or diverting
DOM	Domestic
DP	Dew point temperature
DR	Low drifting
DRG	During
DS	Duststorm
DTG	Date-time group
DTRT	Deteriorate or deteriorating
DU	Dust
DUC	Dense upper cloud
DUR	Duration
DZ	Drizzle
EB	Eastbound
ELEV	Elevation
EMBD	Embedded in a layer
ENE	East northeast

ENRT	En route
ER	Here...or herewith
EST	Estimate or estimated or estimate
ETA	Estimated time of arrival
ETD	Estimated time of departure
EV	Every
EXC	Except
EXER	Exercises or exercising or to exercise
EXP	Expect or expected or expecting
FAX	Facsimile transmission
FBL	Light (e.g., FBL RA = light rain)
FC	Funnel cloud (tornado or water spout)
FEB	February
FG	Fog
FIC	Flight information center
FIR	Flight information region
FIS	Flight information service
FL	Flight level
FLD	Field
FLG	Flashing
FLT	Flight
FLUC	Fluctuating or fluctuation or fluctuated
FLW	Follow(s) or following
FLY	Fly or flying
FM	From
FPM	Feet per minute
FREQ	Frequency
FRI	Friday
FST	First
FU	Smoke
FZ	Freezing

FZDZ	Freezing drizzle
FZFG	Freezing fog
FZRA	Freezing rain
G	Green
GEN	General
GR	Hail
GRID	Processed meteorological data in the form of grid-point values
GS	Small hail and/or snow pellets
HDG	Heading
HEL	Helicopter
HGT	Height or height above
HJ	Sunrise to sunset
HN	Sunset to sunrise
HOL	Holiday
HPA	Hectapascal
HURCN	Hurricane
HVY	Heavy
HYR	Higher
HZ	Haze
IAO	In and out of clouds
IC	Diamond dust (very small ice crystals in suspension)
ICE	Icing
ID	Identifier or identify
IFR	Instrument Flight Rules
IMC	Instrument meteorological conditions
IMPR	Improve or improving
IMT	Immediate or immediately
INBD	Inbound
INC	In cloud
INFO	Information
INOP	Inoperative

INP	If not possible
INPR	In progress
INSTL	Install or installed or installation
INTL	International
INTRP	Interrupt or interruption or interrupted
INSTF	Intensify or intensifying
INTST	Intensity
IR	Ice on runway
ISA	International standard atmosphere
JAN	January
JTST	Jet stream
JUL	July
JUN	June
KG	Kilograms
KM	Kilometers
KMH	Kilometers per hour
KPA	Kilopascal
KW	Kilowatts
LAM	Logical acknowledgment (message type designator)
LAN	Inland
LAT	Latitude
LDG	Landing
LEN	Length
LGT	Light or lighting
LGTD	Lighted
LMT	Local mean time
LOC	Local or locally or location or located
LONG	Longitude
LSQ	Line squall
LTD	Limited
LV	Light and variable (relating to wind)
M	Mach number (followed by figures)

M	Meters (preceded by figures)
MAP	Aeronautical maps and charts
MAR	March
MAX	Maximum
MAY	May
MCW	Modulated continuous wave
MET	Meteorological or meteorology
METAR	Aviation routine weather report
MIFG	Shallow fog
MIL	Military
MIN	Minutes
MNM	Minimum
MNT	Monitor or monitoring or monitored
MOD	Moderate
MON	Above mountains
MON	Monday
MOV	Move or moving or movement
MS	Minus
MSG	Message
MSL	Mean sea level
MT	Mountain
MTU	Metric units
MTW	Mountain waves
MWO	Meteorological watch office
MX	Mixed type of ice formation
NAT	North Atlantic
NAV	Navigation
NB	Northbound
NBFR	Not before
NC	No change
NE	Northeast
NEB	North-eastbound

NEG	No or negative or permission not granted or that is not correct
NGT	Night
NIL	None or I have nothing to send to you
NM	Nautical miles
NML	Normal
NOSIG	No significant change
NOTAM	A notice to airmen
NOV	November
NR	Number
NS	Nimbostratus
NSC	Nil significant cloud
NSW	Nil significant weather
NWB	North-westbound
NXT	Next
OAC	Oceanic area control center
OBS	Observe or observe or observation
OBSC	Obscure or obscured or obscuring
OBST	Obstacle
OCNL	Occasional or occasionally
OCT	October
OHD	Overhead
OPA	Opaque, white type of ice formation
OPMET	Operational meteorological (information)
OPN	Open or opening or opened
OPR	Operator or operate or operative or operating or operational
OPS	Operations
OTLK	Outlook
OTP	On top
OUBD	Outbound
PARL	Parallel
PCD	Proceed or proceeding

PL	Ice pellets
PLVL	Present level
PO	Dust devils
POSS	Possible
PRI	Primary
PROB	Probability
PROC	Procedure
PS	Plus
PSG	Passing
PSN	Position
PWR	Power
QBI	Compulsory IFR flight
QFE	Atmospheric pressure at aerodrome elevation
QUAD	Quadrant
R	Red or right or restricted area
RA	Rain
RAFC	Regional area forecast center
RAG	Ragged
RCH	Reach or reaching
RE	Recent
REP	Report or reporting or reporting point
REQ	Request or requested
RL	Report leaving
RMK	Remark
ROBEX	Regional OPMET bulletin exchange (scheme)
ROC	Rate of climb
ROD	Rate of descent
ROFOR	Route forecast
RPLC	Replace or replaced
RR	Report reaching
RRA	Delayed meteorological message

RTD	Delayed
RTE	Route
RTN	Return or returned or returning
RVR	Runway Visual Range
RWY	Runway
SA	Sand
SAP	As soon as possible
SARPS	Standards and Recommended Practices (ICAO)
SAT	Saturday
SB	Southbound
SEB	Southeast bound
SEC	Seconds
SEP	September
SEV	Severe
SFC	Surface
SG	Snow grains
SH	Showers
SIGMET	Information concerning en route weather phenomena which may affect the safety of aircraft operations
SIGWX	Significant weather
SIMUL	Simultaneous or simultaneously
SKC	Sky clear
SKED	Schedule or scheduled
SLW	Slow
SN	Snow
SPECI	Aviation selected special weather report
SPECIAL	Special meteorological report
SPOT	Spot wind
SQ	Squall
SR	Sunrise
SRY	Secondary
SS	Sandstorm or sunset

STD	Standard
STF	Stratiform
STN	Station
STNR	Stationary
SUN	Sunday
SWB	Southwest bound
T	Temperature
TAF	Aerodrome forecast
TAS	True airspeed
TC	Tropical cyclone
TDO	Tornado
TEMPO	Temporary or temporarily
TEND	Trend forecast
THR	Threshold
THRU	Through
THU	Thursday
TIL	Until
TIP	Until past...(place)
TL...	Till TO To...(place)
TOP	Cloud top
TR	Track
TROP	Tropopause
TS	Thunderstorm
TT	Teletypewriter
TUE	Tuesday
TURB	Turbulence
TYP	Type of aircraft
TYPH	Typhoon
UAB	Until advised by...
UFN	Until further notice
UIR	Upper-flight information region

UNA	Unable
UNL	Unlimited
UNREL	Unreliable
U/S	Unserviceable
UTC	Coordinated Universal Time
VA	Volcanic Ash
VAL	In valleys
VC	Vicinity of the aerodrome
VCY	Vicinity
VER	Vertical
VFR	Visual flight rules
VHF	Very high frequency (30 to 300 MHz)
VIP	Very important person
VIS	Visibility
VMC	Visual meteorological conditions
VOLMET	Meteorological information for aircraft in flight
VOR	VHF omnidirectional radio range
VRB	Variable
VSA	By visual reference to the ground
W	White
WAC	World Aeronautical Chart ICAO 1:1,000,000
WAFC	World area forecast center
WB	Westbound
WDI	Wind direction indicator
WDSPR	Widespread
WED	Wednesday
WI	Within
WID	Width
WIE	With immediate effect or effective immediately
WILCO	Will comply

WINTEM	Forecast upper wind and temperature
WIP	Work in progress
WKN	Weaken or weakening
WO	Without
WRNG	Warning
WS	Wind shear
WTSPT	Waterspout
WX	Weather
X	Cross
XNG	Crossing
XS	Atmospherics
Y	Yellow
YR	Your

Forecast and Report Locations

Weather Advisory Plotting Chart Locations

ABI	ABILENE	TX
ABQ	ALBUQUERQUE	NM
ABR	ABERDEEN	SD
ABY	ALBANY	GA
ACK	NANTUCKET	MA
ACT	WACO	TX
ADM	ARDMORE	OK
AEX	ALEXANDRIA	LA
AIR	BELLAIRE	OH
AKO	AKRON	CO
ALB	ALBANY	NY
ALS	ALAMOSA	CO
AMA	AMARILLO	TX
AMG	ALMA	GA
ANW	AINSWORTH	NE
APE	APPLETON	OH
ARG	WALNUT RIDGE	AR
ASP	OSCODA	MI

Weather Advisory Plotting Chart

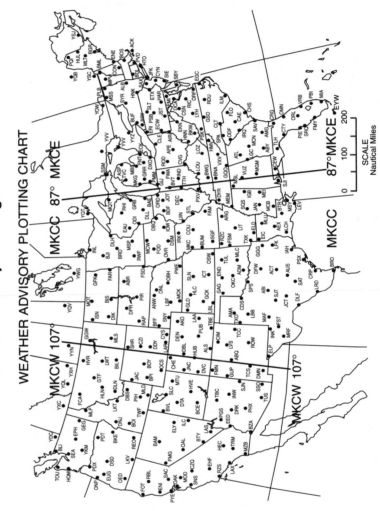

WEATHER ADVISORY PLOTTING CHART

MKCC   87° MKCE

MKCW 107°

MKCW 107°

87°MKCE

MKCC

SCALE
Nautical Miles

0   100   200

ATL	ATLANTA	GA
AUS	AUSTIN	TX
BAE	MILWAUKEE	WI
BAM	BATTLE MOUNTAIN	NV
BCE	BRYCE CANYON	UT
BDF	BRADFORD	IL
BDL	WINSOR LOCKS	CT
BFF	SCOTTSBLUFF	NE
BGR	BANGOR	ME
BIL	BILLINGS	MT
BIS	BISMARK	ND
BJI	BEMIDJI	MN
BKE	BAKER	OR
BKW	BECKLEY	WV
BLI	BELLINGHAM	WA
BNA	NASHVILLE	TN
BOI	BOISE	ID
BOS	BOSTON	MA
BOY	BOYSEN RESV.	WY
BPI	BIG PINEY	WY
BRD	BRAINERD	MN
BRO	BROWNSVILLE	TX
BTR	BATON ROUGE	LA
BTY	BEATTY	NV
BUF	BUFFALO	NY
BUM	BUTLER	MO
BVL	BOONEVILLE	UT
BVT	LAFAYETTE	IN
BWG	BOWLING GREEN	KY
BZA	YUMA	AZ
CAE	COLUMBIA	SC

CDS	CHILDRESS	TX
CEW	CRESTVIEW	FL
CHE	HAYDEN	CP
CHS	CHARLESTON	SC
CIM	CIMARRON	NM
CLE	CLEVELAND	OH
CLT	CHARLOTTE	NC
CON	CONCORD	NH
COU	COLUMBIA	MO
CRG	JACKSONVILLE	FL
CRP	CORPUS CHRISTI	TX
CSN	CASSANOVA	VA
CTY	CROSS CITY	FL
CVG	COVINGTON	KY
CYN	COYLE	NJ
CYS	CHEYENNE	WY
CZI	CRAZY WOMAN	WY
CZQ	FRESNO	CA
DBL	EAGLE	CO
DBQ	DUBUQUE	IA
DBS	DUBOIS	ID
DCA	WASHINGTON	DC
DDY	CASPER	WY
DEC	DECATUR	IL
DEN	DENVER	CO
DFW	DALLAS-FT WORTH	TX
DIK	DICKINSIN	ND
DLF	LAUGHLIN AFB	TX
DLH	DULUTH	MN
DLL	DELLS	WI
DLN	DILLON	MT

DMN	DEMING	NM
DNJ	MC CALL	ID
DPR	DUPREE	SD
DRK	PRESCOTT	AZ
DSD	REDMOND	WA
DSM	DES MOINES	IA
DTA	DELTA	UT
DVC	DOVE CREEK	CO
DXO	DETROIT	MI
DYR	DYERSBURG	TN
EAU	EAU CLAIRE	WI
ECG	ELIZABETH CITY	NC
ECK	PECK	MI
EED	NEEDLES	CA
EHF	BAKERSFIELD	CA
EIC	SHREVEPORT	LA
EKN	ELKINS	WV
ELD	EL DORADO	AR
ELP	EL PASO	EX
ELY	ELY	NV
EMI	WESTMINSTER	MD
END	VANCE AFB	OK
ENE	KENNEBUNK	ME
ENI	UKIAH	CA
EPH	EPHRATA	WA
ERI	ERIE	PA
ETX	EAST TEXAS	PA
EUG	EUGENE	OR
EWC	ELLWOOD CITY	PA
EYW	KEY WEST	FL
FAM	FARMINGTON	MO

FAR	FARGO	ND
FCA	KALISPELL	MT
FLO	FLORENCE	SC
FMG	RENO	NV
FMN	FARMINGTON	NM
FMY	FT MEYERS	FL
FNT	FLINT	MI
FOD	FT DODGE	IA
FOT	FORTUNA	CA
FSD	SIOUX FALLS	SD
FSM	FT SMITH	AR
FST	FT STOCKTON	TX
FWA	FT WAYNE	IN
GAG	GAGE	OK
GCK	GARDEN CITY	KS
GEG	SPOKANE	WA
GFK	GRAND FORKS	ND
GGG	LONGVIEW	TX
GGW	GLASGOW	MT
GIJ	NILES	MI
GLD	GOODLAND	KS
GQO	CHATTANOOGA	TN
GRB	GREEN BAY	WI
GRR	GRAND RAPIDS	MI
GSO	GREENSBORO	NC
GTF	GREAT FALLS	MT
HAR	HARRISBURG	PA
HBU	GUNNISON	CO
HEC	HECTOR	CA
HLC	HILL CITY	KS
HLN	HELENA	MT

HMV	HOLSTON MOUNTAIN	TN
HNK	HANCOCK	NY
HNN	HENDERSON	WV
HQM	HOQUIAM	WA
HTO	EAST HAMPTON	NY
HUL	HOULTON	ME
HVE	HANKSVILLE	UT
HVR	HAVRE	MT
IAH	HOUSTON INTERNATIONAL	TX
ICT	WICHITA	KS
IGB	BIGBEE	MS
ILC	WILSON CREEK	NV
ILM	WILMINGTON	NC
IND	INDIANAPOLIS	IN
INK	WINK	TX
INL	INTERNATIONAL FALLS	MN
INW	WINSLOW	AZ
IOW	IOWA CITY	IA
IRK	KIRKSVILLE	MO
IRQ	COLLIERS	SC
ISN	WILLISTON	ND
JAC	JACKSON	WY
JAN	JACKSON	MS
JCT	JUNCTION	TX
JFK	NEW YORK/KENNEDY	NY
JHW	JAMESTOWN	NY
JNC	GRAND JUNCTION	CO
JOT	JOLIET	IL
JST	JOHNSTOWN	PA
LAA	LAMAR	CO
LAR	LARAMIE	WY

LAS	LAS VEGAS	NV
LAX	LOS ANGELES INTL	CA
LBB	LUBBOCK INTERNATIONAL	TX
LBF	NORTH PLATTE	NE
LBL	LIBERAL	KS
LCH	LAKE CHARLES	LA
LEV	GRAND ISLE	LA
LFK	LUFKIN	TX
LGC	LA GRANGE	GA
LIT	LITTLE ROCK	AR
LKT	SALMON	ID
LKV	LAKEVIEW	OR
LOU	LOUISVILLE	KY
LOZ	LONDON	KY
LRD	LAREDO	TX
LVS	LAS VEGAS	MN
LWT	LEWISTOWN	MT
LYH	LYNCHBURG	VA
MAF	MIDLAND	TX
MBS	SAGINAW	MI
MCB	MC COMB	MS
MCK	MC COOK	NE
MCN	MACON	GA
MCW	MASON CITY	IA
MEI	MERIDIAN	MS
MEM	MEMPHIS	TN
MGM	MONTGOMERY	AL
MIA	MIAMI	FL
MKC	KANSAS CITY	MO
MKG	MUSKEGON	MI
MLC	MC CALESTER	OK

MLD	MALAD CITY	ID
MLP	MULLAN PASS	ID
MLS	MILES CITY	MT
MLT	MILLINOCKET	ME
MLU	MONROE	LA
MOD	MODESTO	CA
MOT	MINOT	ND
MPV	MONTPELIER	VT
MQT	MARQUETTE	MI
MRF	MARFA	TX
MSL	MUSCLE SHOALS	AL
MSP	MINNEAPOLIS	MN
MSS	MASSENA	NY
MSY	NEW ORLEANS	LA
MTU	MYTON	UT
MZB	MISSION BAY	CA
OAK	OAKLAND	CA
OAL	COALDALE	NV
OBH	WOLBACH	NE
OCS	ROCKSPRINGS	WY
ODF	TOCCOA	GA
ODI	NODINE	MN
OED	MEDFORD	OR
OKC	OKLAHOMA CITY	OK
OMN	ORMOND BEACH	FL
ONL	O'NEIL	NE
ONP	NEWPORT	OR
ORD	O'HARE INTERNATIONAL	IL
ORF	NORFOLK	VA
ORL	ORLANDO	FL
OSW	OSWEGO	KS

OVR	OMAHA	NE
PBI	WEST PALM BEACH	FL
PDT	PENDLETON	OR
PDX	PORTLAND	OR
PGS	PEACH SPRINGS	AZ
PHX	PHOENIX	AZ
PIE	SAINT PETERSBURG	FL
PIH	POCATELLO	ID
PIR	PIERRE	SD
PLB	PLATTSBURGH	NY
PMM	PULLMAN	MI
PQI	PRESQUE ISLE	ME
PSB	PHILLIPSBURG	PA
PSK	DUBLIN	VA
PSX	PALACIOS	TX
PUB	PUEBLO	CP
PVD	PROVIDENCE	RI
PWE	PAWNEE CITY	NE
PXV	POCKET CITY	IN
PYE	POINT REYES	CA
RAP	RAPID CITY	SD
RBL	RED BLUFF	CA
RDU	RALEIGH-DURHAM	NC
REO	ROME	OR
RHI	RHINELANDER	WI
RIC	RICHMOND	VA
ROD	ROSEWOOD	OH
ROW	ROSWELL	NM
RWF	REDWOOD FALLS	MN
RZC	RAZORBACK	AR
RZS	SANTA BARBARA	CA

SAC	SACRAMENTO	CA
SAT	SAN ANTONIO	TX
SAV	SAVANNAH	GA
SAX	SPARTA	NJ
SBY	SALISBURY	MD
SEA	SEATTLE	WA
SGF	SPRINGFIELD	MO
SHR	SHERIDAN	WY
SIE	SEA ISLE	NJ
SJI	SEMMNES	A;
SJN	ST JOHNS	AZ
SJT	SAN ANGELO	TX
SLC	SALT LAKE CITY	UT
SLN	SALINA	KS
SLT	SLATE RUN	PA
SNS	SALINAS	CA
SNY	SIDNEY	NE
SPA	SPARTANBURG	SC
SPS	WICHITA FALLS	TX
SQS	SIDON	MS
SRQ	SARASOTA	FL
SSM	SAULT STE MARIE	MI
SSO	SAN SIMON	AZ
STL	ST LOUIS	MO
SYR	SYRACUSE	NY
TBC	TUBA CITY	AZ
TBE	TOBE	CO
TCC	TUCUMCARI	NM
TCS	TRUTH OR CONSEQUENCES	NM
TLH	TALLAHASSEE	FL
TOU	NEAH BAY	WA

TRM	THERMAL	CA
TTH	TERRE HAUTE	IN
TUL	TULSA	OK
TUS	TUCSON	AZ
TVC	TRAVERSE CITY	MI
TWF	TWIN FALLS	ID
TXK	TEXARKANA	AR
TXO	TEXICO	TX
UIN	QUINCY	IL
VRB	VERO BEACH	FL
VUZ	VULCAN	AL
VXV	KNOXVILLE	TN
YDC	PRINCETON	BC
YKM	YAKIMA	WA
YOW	OTTAWA	ON
YQB	QUEBEC	QB
YQL	LETHBRIDGE	AB
YQT	THUNDER BAY	ON
YQV	YORKTON	SK
YSC	SHERBROOKE	QB
YSJ	ST JOHN	NB
YVV	WIARTON	ON
YWG	WINNIPEG	MB
YXC	CRANBROOK	BC
YXH	MEDICINE HAT	AB
YYN	SWIFT CURRENT	SA
YYZ	TORONTO	ON

TWEB Routes

TWEB ROUTE FORECASTS

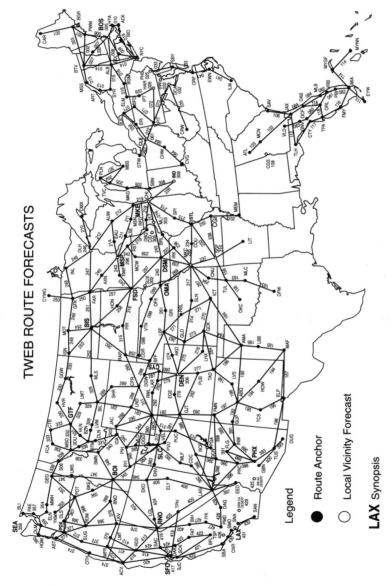

Legend

● Route Anchor

○ Local Vicinity Forecast

LAX Synopsis

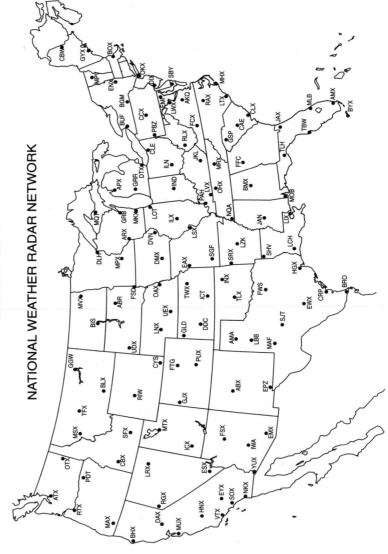

NWS Weather Radar

NATIONAL WEATHER RADAR NETWORK

NWS Weather Radar Site Locations

ALABAMA

BMX - Birmingham/Alabaster WSR-88D/WFO

MOB - Mobile Regional Airport, Mobile WSR-88D/WFO

ARKANSAS

LZK - Little Rock WSR-88D/WFO

SRX - Ft. Smith WSR-88D

ARIZONA

EMX - Tucson WSR-88D

FSX - Flagstaff WSR-88D

IWA - Williams Gateway Airport, Phoenix WSR-88D

YUX - Yuma WSR-88D

CALIFORNIA

BHX - Eureka WSR-88D

DAX - Davis WSR-88D

EYX - Edwards AFB WSR-88D

HNX - San Joaquin/Hanford WSR-88D/WFO

MUX - San Francisco WSR-88D

NKX - Miramar Naval Air Station, San Diego WSR-88D

SOX - Santa Ana Mountains WSR-88D

VTX - Los Angeles WSR-88D

COLORADO

FTG - Front Range Airport, Denver WSR-88D

GJX - Grand Junction WSR-88D

PUX - Pueblo WSR-88D

FLORIDA

AMX - Richmond Heights (Miami) WSR-88D/WFO

BYX - Key West WSR-88D

JAX - Jacksonville International Airport WSR-88D/WSO

MLB - Melbourne International Airport WSR-88D/WSO

TBW - Tampa Bay-Ruskin WSR-88D/WSO

TLH - Tallahassee Regional Airport WSR-88D/WSO

IDAHO

CBX - Boise WSR-88D

SFX - Pocatello WSR-88D

GEORGIA

FFC - Peachtree City/Falcon Field Airport (Atlanta)
WSR-88D/WSO

ILLINOIS

ILX - Central Illinois WSR-88D/WFO, Lincoln

LOT - Lewis University Airport, Chicago/Romeoville
WSR-88D/WFO

INDIANA

IND - Indianapolis International Airport, Indianapolis
WSR-88D/WFO

IWX - North Webster WSR-88D

IOWA

DMX - Des Moines/Johnston WSR-88D/WFO

DVN - Davenport Municipal Airport, Davenport WSR-88D/WFO

KANSAS

DDC- Dodge City Regional Airport, Dodge City WSR-88D/WFO

GLD - Renner Field (Goodland Municipal) Airport, Goodland WSR- 88D/WFO

ICT - WiCHIta Mid-Continent Airport, WiCHIta WSR-88D/WFO

TWX - Topeka WSR-88D

KENTUCKY

JKL - Julian Carroll Airport, Jackson WSR-88D/WFO

LVX - Fort Knox WSR-88D

PAH - Barkley Regional Airport, Paducah WSR-88D/WFO

LOUISIANA

LCH - Lake Charles Regional Airport, Lake Charles WSR-88D/WFO

LIX - New Orleans/Slidell WSR-88D/WFO

SHV - Shreveport Regional Airport, Shreveport WSR-88D/WFO

MAINE

CBW - Houlton/Hodgton WSR-88D

GYX - Portland/Gray WSR-88D/WSO

MASSACHUSETTS

BOX - Taunton (Boston) WSR-88D/WSO

MICHIGAN

APX - Green Township, Alpena County WSR-88D/WFO

DTX - Detroit/White Lake WSR-88D/WFO

GRR - Kent County International Airport, Grand Rapids WSR-88D/WFO

MQT - Marquette County Airport, Marquette WSR-88D/WFO

MINNESOTA

DLH - Duluth International Airport, Duluth WSR-88D/WFO

MPX - Minneapolis/Chanhassen WSR-88D/WFO

MISSISSIPPI

JAN - Jackson International Airport, Jackson WSR-88D/WFO

MISSOURI

EAX - Kansas City/Pleasant Hill WSR-88D/WFO

LSX - St Louis/Weldon Spring WSR-88D/WFO

SGF - Springfield Regional Airport, Springfield WSR-88D/WFO

MONTANA

BLX - Billings WSR-88D

GGW - Glasgow International Airport, Glasgow WSR-88D/WFO

MSX - Missoula WSR-88D

TFX - Great Falls WSR-88D/WFO

NEBRASKA

LNX - North Platte WSR-88D

OAX - Omaha/Valley WSR-88D/WFO

UEX - Blue Hill (Hastings) WSR-88D/WFO

NEVADA

ESX - Las Vegas WSR-88D

LRX - Elko WSR-88D

RGX - Reno WSR-88D

NEW JERSEY

DIX - Wrightstown (Philadelphia) WSR-88D

NEW MEXICO

ABX - Albuquerque WSR-88D

EPZ - Santa Teresa (El Paso) WSR-88D

NEW YORK

BGM - Binghamton WSR-88D/WSO

BUF - Buffalo WSR-88D/WSO

ENX - State University of New York/East Berne (Albany)
WSR-88D/WSO

OKX - Brookhaven National Laboratory, New York City
WSR-88D/WSO

NORTH CAROLINA

LTX - Shallotte (Wilmington) WSR-88D

MHX - Morehead City/Newport WSR-88D/WSO

RAX - Raleigh/Durham WSR-88D

NORTH DAKOTA

BIS - Bismarck Municipal Airport, Bismarck WSR-88D/WFO

MVX - Grand Forks WSR-88D

OHIO

CLE - Cleveland-Hopkins International Airport WSR-88D/WSO

ILN - Wilmington Airborne Airpark Airport WSR-88D/WSO

OKLAHOMA

INX - Inola (Tulsa) WSR-88D

TLX - Twin Lakes/Midwest City (Oklahoma City) WSR-88D

OREGON

MAX - Medford WSR-88D

PDT - Eastern Oregon Regional at Pendleton Airport, Pendleton WSR- 88D/WFO

RTX - Portland WSR-88D

PENNSYLVANIA

CCX - Centre County (State College) WSR-88D

PBZ - Corapolis (Pittsburgh) WSR-88D/WSO

SOUTH CAROLINA

CAE - Columbia WSR-88D/WSO

CLX - Charleston WSR-88D

GSP - Greenville/Spartenburg WSR-88D/WSO

SOUTH DAKOTA

ABR - Aberdeen Regional Airport, Aberdeen WSR-88D/WFO

FSD - Joe Foss Field Airport, Sioux Falls WSR-88D/WFO

UDX - Rapid City WSR-88D

TENNESSEE

MRX - Knoxille/Morristown WSR-88D/WFO

NQA - Millington Municipal Airport, Millington (Memphis) WSR-88D

OHX - Old Hickory (Nashville) WSR-88D/WFO

TEXAS

AMA - Amarillo International Airport, Amarillo WSR-88D/WFO

BRO - Brownsville/South Padre Island International Airport, Brownsville WSR-88D/WFO

CRP - Corpus Christi International Airport, Corpus Christi WSR- 88D/WFO

EWX - San Antonio/New Braunfels WSR-88D/WFO

FWS - Fort Worth Spinks Airport, Fort Worth WSR-88D

HGX - Dickinson (Houston) WSR-88D/WFO

LBB - Lubbock International Airport, Lubbock WSR-88D/WFO

MAF - Midland International Airport, Midland WSR-88D/WFO

SJT - Mathis Field Airport, San Angelo WSR-88D/WFO

UTAH

ICX - Cedar City WSR-88D

MTX - Salt Lake City WSR-88D

VIRGINIA

AKQ - Wakefield (Richmond) WSR-88D/WSO

FCX - Roanoke WSR-88D

LWX - Sterling (Washington D.C.) WSR-88D/WSO

WASHINGTON

ATX - Everett WSR-88D

OTX - Spokane WSR-88D

WEST VIRGINIA

RLX - Charleston WSR-88D/WSO

WISCONSIN

ARX - LaCrosse Ridge WSR-88D/WFO

GRB - Austin Straubel International Airport, Green Bay WSR-88D/WFO

MKX - Milwaukee/Sullivan Township WSR-88D/WFO

WYOMING

CYS - Cheyenne Airport, Cheyenne WSR-88D/WFO

RIW - Riverton Regional Airport, Riverton WSR-88D/WFO

Area Designators

Area Forecast Areas of Coverage, States

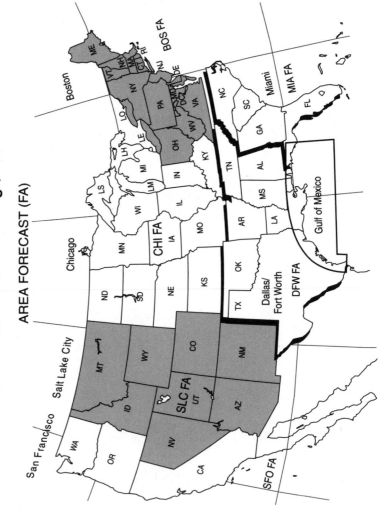

AREA FORECAST (FA)

Area Forecast Designators (NW)

COMMON GEOGRAPHICAL DESIGNATORS (NORTHWEST)

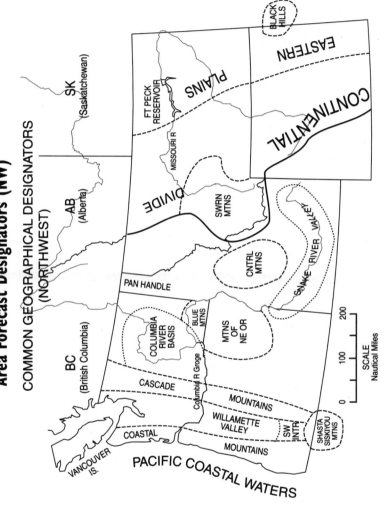

SK (Saskatchewan)

AB (Alberta)

BC (British Columbia)

BLACK HILLS

EASTERN

PLAINS

FT PECK RESERVOIR

MISSOURI R

CONTINENTAL

DIVIDE

SWRN MTNS

SNAKE RIVER VALLEY

CNTRL MTNS

PAN HANDLE

COLUMBIA RIVER BASIS

BLUE MTNS

MTNS OF NE OR

CASCADE

MOUNTAINS

Columbia R Groge

WILLAMETTE VALLEY

SW INTR

SHASTA SISKIYOU MTNS

COASTAL

MOUNTAINS

VANCOUVER IS.

PACIFIC COASTAL WATERS

SCALE
Nautical Miles

0   100   200

439

Area Forecast Designators (SW)

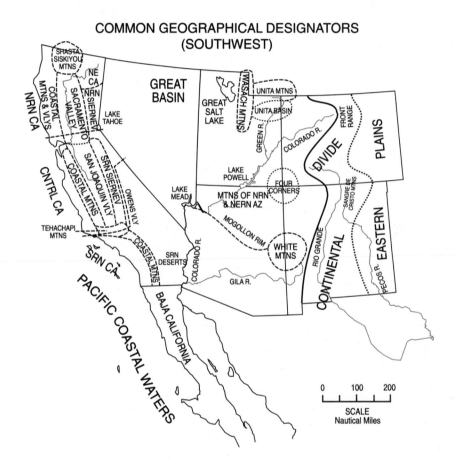

COMMON GEOGRAPHICAL DESIGNATORS
(SOUTHWEST)

Area Forecast Designators (C)

COMMON
GEOGRAPHICAL
DESIGNATORS
(CENTRAL)

Area Forecast Designators (NE)

COMMON GEOGRAPHICAL DESIGNATORS (NORTHEAST)

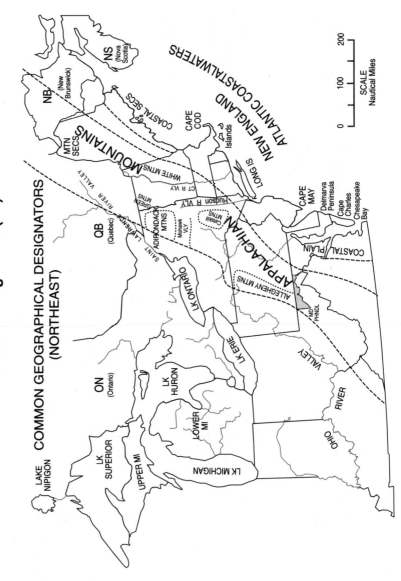

SCALE
Nautical Miles

0   100   200

Area Forecast Designators (SE)

COMMON
GEOGRAPHICAL
DESIGNATORS
(SOUTHEAST)

Alaskan and Hawaiian Area Forecast Designators

COMMON GEOGRAPHICAL DESIGNATORS

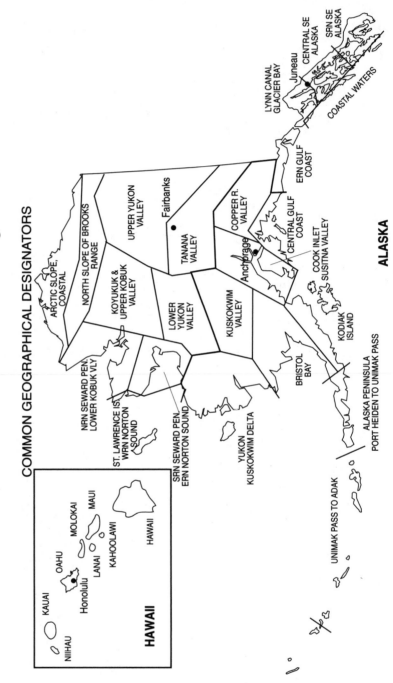

ALASKA

CENTRAL SE ALASKA
SRN SE ALASKA
LYNN CANAL GLACIER BAY
Juneau
COASTAL WATERS
ERN GULF COAST
Fairbanks
UPPER YUKON VALLEY
COPPER R. VALLEY
CENTRAL GULF COAST
TANANA VALLEY
Anchorage
COOK INLET SUSITNA VALLEY
ARCTIC SLOPE, COASTAL
NORTH SLOPE OF BROOKS RANGE
KOYUKUK & UPPER KOBUK VALLEY
LOWER YUKON VALLEY
KUSKOKWIM VALLEY
KODIAK ISLAND
NRN SEWARD PEN. LOWER KOBUK VLY
ST. LAWRENCE IS. WRN NORTON SOUND
SRN SEWARD PEN. ERN NORTON SOUND
YUKON KUSKOKWIM DELTA
BRISTOL BAY
ALASKA PENINSULA PORT HEIDEN TO UNIMAK PASS
UNIMAK PASS TO ADAK

HAWAII

NIIHAU
KAUAI
OAHU
Honolulu
MOLOKAI
MAUI
LANAI
KAHOOLAWI
HAWAII

Atlantic, Caribbean, and Gulf or Mexico Area Forecast Areas of Coverage

ATLANTIC, CARIBBEAN, AND GULF OF MEXICO

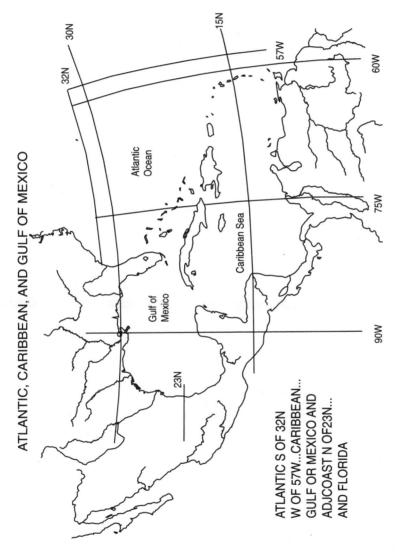

ATLANTIC S OF 32N
W OF 57W...CARIBBEAN...
GULF OR MEXICO AND
ADJCOAST N OF23N...
AND FLORIDA

Glossary

absolute instability   A condition of the atmosphere where vertical displacement is spontaneous, whether saturated or unsaturated.

absolute stability   A condition of the atmosphere that resists vertical displacement whether a parcel is saturated or unsaturated.

accretion   The deposit of ice on aircraft surfaces in flight as a result of the tendency of cloud droplets to remain in a liquid state at temperatures below freezing.

adiabatic process   A thermodynamic change of state with no transfer of heat or mass across the boundaries, where compression always results in heating, expansion in cooling.

advection   The process of moving an atmospheric property from one location to another. Advection usually refers to the horizontal movement of properties (temperature, moisture, vorticity, etc.).

air mass   A widespread body of air whose homogeneous properties were established while that air was over a particular region of the Earth's surface, and undergoes specific modifications while moving away from its source region.

air-to-air visibility   The visibility aloft between two aircraft or the aircraft and clouds.

air-to-ground visibility   See slang range visibility.

AIRMET Bulletin   An in-flight weather advisory program intended to provide advance notice of potentially hazardous, weather to small aircraft.

altimeter setting   A value of atmospheric pressure used to correct a pressure altimeter for nonstandard pressure.

anti-icing   Prevention of ice from forming on aircraft surfaces.

anticyclonic   Having a clockwise rotation in the northern hemisphere, associated with the circulation around an anticyclone (high-pressure area).

arc cloud   See arc line.

arc line   An arc-shaped line of convective clouds often observed in satellite imagery moving away from a dissipating thunderstorm area.

atmospheric phenomena   As reported on METAR, atmospheric phenomena is weather occurring at the station and any obstructions to vision. Obstructions to vision are only reported when the prevailing visibility is less than seven miles.

atmospheric property   A characteristic trait or peculiarity of the atmosphere such as temperature, pressure, moisture, density, and stability.

atmospheric phenomena   As reported on METAR, atmospheric phenomena is weather occurring at the station and any obstructions to vision. Obstructions to vision are only reported when the prevailing visibility is less than seven miles.

augmented   When referring to a surface weather observation, means someone is physically at the site monitoring the equipment and has overall responsibility for the observation.

AUTO   When used in METAR and SPECI indicates the report comes from an automated weather observation station that is not augmented.

automated observation   An automated report indicates the observation was derived without human intervention.

Automated Surface Observing System   ASOS is a computerized system similar to AWOS but developed jointly by the FAA, NWS, and Department of Defense; in addition to standard weather elements the system encodes climatological data at the end of the report.

Automated Weather Observing System   AWOS is a computerized system that measures sky condition, visibility, precipitation, temperature, dew point, wind, and altimeter setting. It has a voice synthesizer to report minute-by-minute observations over radio frequencies, telephone lines, or local displays.

Automatic Terminal Information Service (ATIS)   A recorded service provided at tower-controlled airports to provide the pilot with weather, traffic, and takeoff and landing information.

arc cloud   An arc-shaped line of convective clouds often observed in satellite imagery moving away from a dissipating thunderstorm area.

backscatter device   An instrument used to measure surface visibility at an automated weather observing station.

backup   See augmentation.

baroclinic   A state of the atmosphere where isotherms—lines of equal temperature—cross contours, temperature and pressure gradients are steep, and temperature advection takes place. A baroclinic atmosphere enhances the formation and strengthens the intensity of storms. It is characterized by an upper-level wave one-quarter wave length behind the surface front.

barotropic   Barotropic is an absence of, or the opposite of baroclinic. Theoretically, an entirely barotropic atmosphere would yield constant pressure charts with no height or temperature gradients or vertical motion.

berm   A raised bank, usually frozen snow, along a taxiway or runway.

Bjerknes, Vilhelm   Norwegian meteorologist who developed the polar front theory at the beginning of the twentieth century.

bleed air   Small extraction of hot air from turbine engine compressor.

blocking high   An upper-level area of high pressure that blocks approaching weather systems. See omega block.

boundaries   Zones in the lower atmosphere characterized by sharp gradients or discontinuities of temperature, pressure, or moisture and often accompanied by convergence in the wind field. Examples include surface fronts, dry lines, and outflow boundaries. In the latter case, the boundary is produced by a surge of rain-cooled air flowing outward near the surface from the originating area of convection. In an unstable air mass, thunderstorms tend to develop along these zones and especially at intersections of two or more boundaries.

bridging   A formation of ice over the deicing boot that is not cracked by boot inflation.

BWER/WER/LEWP   Bounded Weak Echo Region/Weak Echo Region/Line Echo Wave Pattern. All of these weather radar terms are indicators of strong thunderstorms and the development of severe weather.

Calorie   A unit of heat required to raise the temperature of one gram of water one degree Celsius.

carburetor ice   Ice formed in the throat of a carburetor due to the effects of lowered temperature by decreased air pressure and fuel vaporization.

celestial dome   That portion of the sky that would be visible provided, due to the absence of human-made structures, there was an unobstructed view of the horizon in all directions.

Celsius   A temperature scale where 0 is the melting point of ice and 100 the boiling point of water.

Chinook   An American Indian name given to a foehn wind on the eastern side of the Rockies.

chop   Reported with turbulence, chop refers to a slight, rapid, and somewhat rhythmic bumpiness without appreciable changes in altitude or attitude.

clear air turbulence (CAT)   Nonconvective, wind shear, turbulence occurring at or above 15,000 feet, although it usually refers to turbulence above 25,000 feet.

clear ice   A glossy, clear, or translucent ice formed by relatively slow freezing of large supercooled droplets; the large droplets spread out over the airfoil prior to complete freezing, forming a sheet of clear ice.

closed low   An area of low pressure aloft completely surrounded by a contour.

closed cell stratocumulus   Common over water, this term is used to describe satellite viewed oceanic stratocumulus associated with an inversion. They are associated with high pressure.

cloud band A nearly continuous cloud formation with a distinct long axis, a length-to-width ratio of at least four to one, and a width greater than one degree of latitude (60 nm).

cloud element The smallest cloud form that can be resolved on satellite imagery from a given satellite system.

cloud line A narrow cloud band in which individual elements are connected and the line is less than one degree of latitude in width. Indicates strong winds, often 30 knots or greater over water.

cloud shield A broad cloud formation that is not more than four times as long as it is wide. Often it is formed by cirrus clouds associated with a ridge or the jet stream.

cloud streets A series of aligned cloud elements that are not connected. Several cloud streets usually line up parallel to each other and each street is not more than 10 miles wide.

coalescence The merging of two water drops into a single larger drop.

Coefficient of Friction The ratio of the tangential force needed to maintain uniform relative motion between two contacting surfaces (aircraft tires to the pavement surface) to the perpendicular force holding them in contact (distributed aircraft weight to the aircraft tire area). The coefficient is often denoted by the Greek letter MU. It is a simple means used to quantify the relative slipperiness of pavement surfaces. Friction values range from 0 to 100 where zero is the lowest friction value and 100 is the maximum frictional value obtainable.

cold-core low A low pressure area that intensifies aloft. When this type of low contains closed contours at the 200-mb level, its movements tend to be slow and erratic.

cold pool Generally refers to an area at 500 mbs in which the air temperature is colder than adjacent areas. Other atmospheric conditions being equal, thermodynamic instability is greater beneath cold pools, thus making thunderstorm development more likely.

comma cloud system A cloud system that resembles the comma punctuation mark. The shape results from differential rotation of the cloud border and upward and downward moving air.

comma head   The rounded portion of the comma cloud system. This region often produces most of the steady precipitation.

comma tail   The portion of the comma cloud that lies to the right of, and often nearly parallel to, the axis of maximum winds.

conditional instability   A condition of the atmosphere where a parcel will spontaneous rise as a result of it becoming saturated when forced upward.

conduction   The process of transferring energy by means of physical contact.

confluence   A region where streamlines converge. The speed of the horizontal flow will often increase where there is confluence. It is the upper-level equivalent of surface convergence.

Coordinated Universal Time   Formerly Greenwich Mean Time, also known as Z or ZULU time, Coordinated Universal Time (UTC) is the international time standard. UTC is used in all aviation time references.

convergence   Air flowing together near the surface is forced upward due to convergence. It is a vertical motion producer that tends to destabilize the atmosphere near the surface.

convergence zone   An area when surface convergence is occurring, often associated with a large body of water.

Coriolis force   An apparent force that causes winds to blow across isobars at the surface.

Coriolis, Gaspard de   A French mathematician, in 1835 he developed the theory of an apparent deflection force produced by angular rotation.

COR   In a METAR/SPECI report indicated that the original was transmitted with an error, that has now been corrected.

cumuliform   Cumuliform describes clouds that are characterized by vertical development in the form of rising mounds, domes, or towers, and an unstable air mass.

cut-off low   See closed low.

cyclongenesis   The development or strengthening of a cyclone.

cyclonic   Having a counterclockwise rotation in the northern hemisphere, associated with the circulation around a cyclone or low-pressure area.

deformation zone   An area within the atmospheric circulation where air parcels contract in one direction and elongate in the perpendicular direction. The narrow zone along the axis of elongation is called the deformation zone. Deformation is a primary factor in frontogenesis and frontolysis.

dendritic pattern   This branchy, saw tooth, pattern identifies areas of snow cover. Mountain ridges above the tree line are essentially barren and snow is visible; in the tree-filled valleys, most of the snow is hidden beneath the trees.

density   The weight of air per unit volume.

density altitude   Density altitude is pressure altitude corrected for nonstandard temperature.

dew point   The temperature to which air must be cooled, water vapor remaining constant, to become saturated.

dew point front   See dry line.

diabatic   A process that involves the exchange of heat with an external source, or nonadiabatic; the loss may occur through radiation resulting in fog or low clouds, or conduction through contact with a cold surface.

dig or digging   Indicates a trough with a strong southerly component of motion. These troughs contain considerable strength and are difficult to forecast accurately.

difulence   The spreading apart of adjacent streamlines. The speed of horizontal flow often decreases with a difluent zone. It is the upper air equivalent of surface divergence and activates or perpetuates thunderstorm development.

Direct User Access Terminal (DUAT)   A computer terminal where pilots can directly access meteorological and aeronautical information, plus file a flight plan without the assistance of an FSS.

divergence   Subsiding air diverges, or spreads, at the surface. Divergence is a downward motion producer that tends to stabilize the atmosphere near the surface.

drainage wind   A wind directed down the slope of an incline and caused by greater air density near the slope than at the same levels some distance horizontally from the slope.

dry adiabatic lapse rate   The rate at which unsaturated air cools or warms when forced upward or downward (3 degrees C per 1000 feet).

dry snow   Snow which has insufficient free water to cause cohesion between individual particles; generally occurs at temperatures well below 0 degrees C.

dry line   An area within an air mass that has little temperature gradient, but significant differences in moisture. The boundary between the dry and moist air produces a lifting mechanism. Although not a true front, it has the potential to produce hazardous weather. It is also known as a dew point front.

dry slot   A satellite meteorology term used to describe a cloud feature associated with an upper-level short-wave trough. Generally speaking, the cloud system is shaped like a large comma. As the system develops, sinking air beneath the jet stream causes an intrusion of dry, relatively cloud-free air on the upwind side of the comma cloud. The air of the intrusion is the dry slot. It is commonly the location where lines of thunderstorms subsequently develop.

embedded thunderstorm   A thunderstorm that occurs within nonconvective precipitation. A thunderstorm that is hidden in stratiform clouds.

Enhanced Infrared (IR) Imagery   A process by which infrared imagery is enhanced to provide increased contrast between features to simplify interpretation. This is done by assigning specific shades of gray to specific temperature ranges.

enhanced V   A cloud top signature sometimes seen in enhanced infrared imagery in which the coldest cloud top temperatures form a V shape. Storms that show this cloud top feature are often associated with severe weather.

Eutectic Temperature/Composition   A deicing chemical that melts ice by lowering the freezing point.

eye   An area of clear skies that develops in the center of a tropical storm.

eye wall   The area of thunderstorms that surrounds the eye of a tropical storm.

Fahrenheit   A temperature scale where 32 degrees is the melting point of ice and 212 degrees the boiling point of water.

fall streaks   Fall streaks are ice crystals or snowflakes falling from high clouds into dry air where they sublimate directly from a solid to a gas.

fine line/thin line   At times weather radar picks up dust or debris that appear as a fine or thin line caused by a dry front or gust front. It indicates the presence of low-level wind shear.

Flight Level   Pressure altitude read off an altimeter set to standard pressure of 29.92; altitude used in the United States above 17,999 feet.

foehn wind   A warm, dry wind on the lee side of a mountain range.

freezing level   As used in aviation forecasts the level at which ice melts.

freezing point depressant   A fluid that combines with supercooled water droplets forming a mixture with a freezing temperature below the ambient air temperature.

front   A boundary between air masses of different temperatures, moisture, and wind.

frontal zone   See front.

frontogensis   The process by which frontal systems are formed.

frontolysis   The process of frontal system dissipation.

general circulation   See planetary scale.

Geostationary Operational Environmental Satellite   See GOES

glaciation   The transformation of liquid cloud particles to ice crystals.

global circulation   See planetary scale.

Global Positioning System (GPS)   A network of Earth satellites that provides high-accuracy position, velocity, and time information to ground-based or airborne receivers.

GOES   Geostationary Operational Environmental Satellites, normally located about 22,000 nm above the equator at 75 degrees W and 135 degrees W. The satellites provide half-hourly visible and infrared imagery.

gravity wind   See drainage wind.

ground clutter   Interference of the radar beam due to objects on the ground.

ground icing Structural icing that occurs on an aircraft on the ground, usually produced by snow or frost.

Great Basin The area between the Rockies and Sierra Nevada mountains, consisting of southeastern Oregon, southern Idaho, western Utah, and Nevada.

gust front A low-level windshift line created by the downdrafts associated with thunderstorms and other convective clouds. Acting like a front, these features might produce strong gustiness, pressure rises, and low-level wind shear.

Hadley Cell A circulation theory describing how low pressure at the equator rises, moves toward the pole, and sinks in high pressure at the pole, then moves toward the equator.

Hadley, George In 1735, George Hadley was the first to propose a direct thermally driven and zonally symmetric circulation as an explanation for the trade winds.

hail shaft A shaft of hail detected on weather radar.

heat The total energy of the motion of molecules—with the ability to do work.

heat burst A rapid, but brief, temperature jump associated with a thunderstorm.

heat capacity The amount of heat required to raise the temperature of air, or the amount of heat lost when air is cooled.

hectopascal The international unit of atmospheric pressure is the hectopascal (hPa), equivalent to the millibar (mb).

high Area of high pressure completely surrounded by lower pressure

hook echo A bona fide hook echo indicates the existence of a mesolow associated with a large thunderstorm cell. Such mesolows are often associated with severe thunderstorms and tornadoes. Hook echoes are not seen on ATC radars.

horizontal extent The horizontal distance of an icing encounter.

hydroplaning A condition where a thin layer of water between the wheel and runway causes the tires to lose contact with the runway.

ice The solid form of water consisting of a characteristic hexagonal symmetry of water molecules.

ice protection equipment   Equipment required for an aircraft to be certified for flight into known icing conditions.

icephobic liquid   A spray that reduces the adhesion of ice to the deicing boot surface improving deicing.

impulse   A weak, mid- to upper-level and fast-moving shortwave feature, that can kick off thunderstorms.

inches of mercury   For aviation purposes we commonly relate atmospheric pressure to inches of mercury (in. Hg)—altimeter setting.

indicated airspeed   The airspeed read of the airspeed indicator uncorrected for temperature and pressure.

indicated altitude   The altitude read of the altimeter uncorrected for temperature and pressure.

in-flight visibility   See air-to-air visibility.

infrared   Satellite imagery that measures the relative temperature of clouds or the Earth's surface.

instrument flight rules (IFR)   Federal regulations that govern flight in instrument meteorological conditions—flight by reference to aircraft instruments.

intermountain region   The area of the western United States, west of the Rocky Mountains and east of the Sierra Nevada Mountains, which includes Idaho and Arizona.

International Standard Atmosphere (ISA)   A hypothetical vertical distribution of atmospheric properties (temperature, pressure, and density). At the surface, the ISA has a temperature of 15 degrees C (59 degrees F), pressure of 1013.2 mb (29.92 in.), and a lapse rate of approximately 2 degrees C in the troposphere.

intertropical convergence zone (ITCZ)   The dividing line between the southeast trade winds and the northeast trade winds of the southern and northern hemispheres respectively.

inversion   A lapse rate where temperature increases with altitude.

isobars   Lines connecting equal values of surface.

isohumes   Lines of equal relative humidity.

isopleths   Lines of equal number or quantity.

isotachs   Used on charts and graphs, lines of equal wind speed.

isothermal   A constant lapse rate.

isotherms   Used on charts and graphs, lines of equal temperature.

jet streaks   See jet stream.

jet stream   A segmented band of strong winds that occur in breaks in the tropopause.

jetlets   See jet stream.

katabatic wind   Any wind blowing down an incline.

Kollsman, Paul   A German-born aeronautical engineer, invented the method to correct the altimeter for nonstandard pressure in 1928.

lapse rate   The decrease of an atmospheric variable with height, usually temperature.

lee-side low   Low-pressure areas that develop east of mountain barriers.

latent heat   The amount of heat exchanged (absorbed or released) during the processes of condensation, fusion, vaporization or sublimation.

liquid water content (LWC)   The total mass of water contained in all the liquid cloud droplets within a unit volume of cloud. Units of LWC are usually grams of water per cubic meter of air (g/m3).

level of free convection (LFC)   The level at which a parcel of air lifted adiabatically until saturation would become warmer than its surrounding air, and become unstable.

LEWP   See BWER/WER/LEWP

lifted index   A measure of atmospheric instability that is computed on a thermodynamic chart by lifting a parcel of air near the surface to the 500 mb level and subtracting the temperature of the parcel from the temperature of the environment. A negative index means the lifted parcel is buoyant at 500 mb and will continue to rise, which is an unstable condition.

lifted condensation level (LCL)   The level at which a parcel of air lifted adiabatically would cool and become saturated. The level at which clouds would form.

location identifier   Consisting of three to five alphanumeric characters, location identifiers are contractions used to identify geographical locations, navigational aids, and intersections.

long wave   See Rossby wave.

low   An area of low pressure completely surrounded by higher pressure.

low-level wind shear (LLWS) See wind shear.

manual observation The term manual refers to the fact that a human has overall responsibility for the observation.

mean effective diameter (MED) The droplet diameter that divides the total water volume present in the droplet distribution in half; half the water volume will be in larger drops and half the volume in smaller drops.

median volumetric diameter (MVD) The droplet diameter that divides the total water volume present in the droplet distribution in half; half the water volume will be in larger drops and half the volume in smaller drops.

mean wind vector The mean wind vector is the direction and magnitude of the mean winds from 5000 feet AGL to the tropopause. It can be used to estimate cell movement.

melting level The temperature at which ice melts, often referred to as the freezing level.

mesolow Also known as mesocyclone, a mesolow is a small area of low pressure within a severe thunderstorm. Tornadoes can develop within the vortex.

mesoscale Small-scale meteorological phenomena that can range in size from that of a single thunderstorm to an area the size of the state of Oklahoma.

mesoscale convective complex (MCC) A large homogeneous convective weather system on the order of 100,000 square miles. They tend to form during the morning hours.

METAR Meteorological Aviation Routine surface weather report.

micron (μm) One millionth of a meter.

microscale See sub synoptic scale.

millibar For aviation purposes we commonly relate atmospheric pressure to inches of mercury or in millibars (mb).

mixed icing conditions An atmospheric environment where supercooled liquid water and ice crystals coexist.

mixing ratio The ratio of water vapor to dry air, expressed in grams of water vapor per kilogram of dry air.

microburst A small-scale, severe, storm downburst less than two-and-half miles across. Reaching the ground, the burst continues as an expanding outflow producing severe wind shear.

moisture convergence An objective analysis field combining wind flow convergence and moisture advection. Under certain circumstances, this field is useful for forecasting areas of thunderstorm development.

mixing layer The layer of the atmosphere, usually within several thousand feet of the surface, where wind speed and direction are affected by friction with the Earth's surface—in which the air is thoroughly mixed by convection.

negative tilt Refers to troughs with an axis in the horizontal plane tilting from northwest to southeast. These systems tend to cause more weather in California because they bring in warm, moist air.

negative vorticity advection Area of low values of vorticity producing downward vertical motion.

neutral stability An atmospheric condition that after a parcel is displaced it remains at rest—even when the displacing force ceases.

NEXRAD The next generation Doppler weather radar system.

nucleation In meteorology, the initiation of either of the phase changes from water vapor to liquid water, or from liquid water to ice.

omega block A blocking high that on weather charts resembles the Greek letter omega.

open cell On satellite imagery a pattern of clear air surrounding individual convective cells.

orographic A term used to describe the effects caused by terrain, especially mountains, on the weather,.

outflow boundary An outflow boundary is a surface boundary left by the horizontal spreading of thunderstorm-cooled air. The boundary is often the lifting mechanism needed to generate new thunderstorms.

overrunning A condition in which air flow from one air mass is moving over another air mass of greater density. The term usually applies to warmer air flowing over cooler air as in a warm frontal situation. It implies a lifting mechanism that can trigger convection in unstable air.

parcel A parcel is a small volume of air arbitrarily selected for study; it retains its composition and does not mix with the surrounding air.

Pascal, Blaise Blaise Pascal (1623–1662) was a French philosopher and mathematician for whom the international unit of atmospheric pressure, the hectopascal (hPa), is named.

patchy conditions Areas of bare pavement showing through snow and/or ice covered pavements. Patches normally show up first along the centerline in the central portion of the runway in the touchdown areas.

partial obscuration In MRTAR/SPECI is reported when between one-eighth and seven-eighths of the sky is hidden by a surface-based obscuring phenomena.

planetary boundary layer The frictional layer between the surface and the atmosphere.

planetary scale Planetary scale, also called global or general circulation, consists of the jet stream, subtropical high, polar front, and intertropical convergence zone.

polar front A semipermanent, semicontinuous front separating air masses of tropical and polar origin.

polar jet The jet stream located at the break between the polar tropopause and subtropical tropopause.

positive tilt Refers to troughs with an axis in the horizontal plane tilting from northeast to southwest.

positive vorticity advection (PVA) Positive vorticity advection, usually applies to the 500 mb level and refers to areas where the wind flow implies advection from higher values of absolute vorticity to lower ones. These areas are presumed to mark zones where upward vertical motion will be supported or enhanced. A vertical motion producer.

precipitation Any or all of the forms of water particles, whether liquid or solid, that fall from the atmosphere and reach the ground.

pressure Pressure is force per unit area.

pressure altitude The altitude above the mean sea level constant pressure surface; indicated altitude with the altimeter set to 29.92 in Hg.

prevailing visibility Visibility reported in manual observations— the greatest distance that can be seen throughout at least half the horizon circle, which need not be continuous.

QFE   Altimeter setting used so that the altimeter will read zero when the aircraft is on the ground.

QNE   Altimeter setting used to obtain pressure altitude.

QNH   Altimeter setting used to obtain indicated altitude.

radiation   The process of transferring energy through space without the aid of a material medium.

Rapid Update Cycle (RUC)   A high-speed computer model that updates every three hours, designed for short-term forecasting.

relative humidity   The ratio, expressed as a percentage, of water vapor present in the air compared to the maximum amount the air could hold at its present temperature.

ridge   An elongated area of high pressure.

rime   A white or milky and opaque granular deposit of ice.

rime ice   A rough, milky, opaque ice formed by the instantaneous freezing of small, supercooled droplets as they strike the aircraft.

Rossby waves   Also known as major waves, planetary waves, or long waves, they are characterized by their large length and significant amplitude. They tend to be slow moving.

runback   Icing that occurs when local heating of accumulated ice melts, water runs back to unheated areas, and refreezes.

Santa Ana   The local name given to a foehn wind that occurs in late fall, winter, and early summer in Southern California.

saturated adiabatic lapse rate   The rate at which saturated air cools or warms when forced upward or downward.

scud   Shreds of small detached clouds moving rapidly below a solid deck or higher clouds.

severe thunderstorm   A thunderstorm that produces winds of 50 knots or more, or hail $3/4$ in. in diameter or greater.

severe wind shear   See wind shear.

shear axis   An axis indicating maximum lateral change in wind direction, as in an elongated circulation. This lateral change or shear might be either cyclonic or anticyclonic.

short wave   With wave lengths shorter than long waves, they tend to move rapidly through the long-wave circulation. They can intensify or dampen weather systems.

showers   Showers are characterized by the suddenness with which they start and stop, and rapid changes of intensity.

SIGMET   A significant meteorological advisory that warns of phenomena that affects all aircraft.

slant range visibility   The visibility between an aircraft in the air and objects on the ground.

slush   Snow that has a water content exceeding its freely drained condition such that it takes on fluid properties (e.g., flowing and splashing).

Sonora storm   Local name given to storms that approach Southern California from the southeast.

snow   A porous, permeable aggregate of ice grains that can be predominately single crystals or close groupings of several crystals.

SPECI   A special surface aviation weather report.

squall line   An organized line of thunderstorms.

stability   The property of an airmass to remain in equilibrium—its ability to resist displacement from its initial position.

stagnation point   The point on a surface where the local free-stream velocity is zero; the point of maximum collection efficiency for a symmetric body at zero degrees angle of attack.

Standard Atmosphere   See International Standard Atmosphere.

storm detection equipment   This term refers to airborne access to real-time weather radar or lightning detection equipment.

stratiform   Stratiform describes clouds of extensive horizontal development, and a stable air mass.

stratosphere   The atmospheric layer above the tropopause. It is characterized by a slight increase in temperature with height and the near absence of water vapor. Occasionally severe thunderstorms will break through the tropopause into the stratosphere.

streamlines   A line that represents the wind flow pattern, and is parallel to the instantaneous velocity. Streamlines indicate the trajectory of the flow.

subsynoptic scale   Small, microscale events that often are not within the detection system currently available—tornadoes and microbursts.

sublimation   The process by which ice changes directly to water vapor, or water vapor directly to ice. The sublimation of ice to vapor is a cooling process, and water vapor to ice is a warming process.

subsidence   Downward vertical motion of the air.

subtropical jet   The jet around 20 degrees to 30 degrees north latitude at approximately 39,000 feet, located in the break between the midlatitude and tropical tropopause.

supercell   A thunderstorm where updrafts and downdrafts coexist prolonging the life of the cell, often producing a severe thunderstorm and tornadoes.

supercooled   Liquid water or water vapor that exists at temperatures below freezing is called supercooled.

surface visibility   The visibility at and along the surface of the Earth.

synoptic scale   Large-scale weather patterns the size of the migratory high- and low-pressure systems of the lower troposphere with wave lengths on the order of 1000 miles.

TAF   Terminal Aerodrome Forecast.

temperature   A measurement of the average speed of molecules.

thermal high   An area of high atmospheric pressure caused by the cooling of air by a cold surface. It remains relatively stationary over the cold ground.

thermal low   An area of low atmospheric pressure caused by intense surface heating. It is common to the continental subtropics in summer, remains stationary, and cyclonic circulation is generally weak and diffuse.

thin line   See fine line/thin line.

Torricelli, Evangelista   The Italian inventor of the mercurial barometer in 1643.

total air temperature   The result of ambient air temperature and aerodynamic heating.

towering cumulus   Growing cumulus that resembles a cauliflower, but with tops that have not yet reached the cirrus level.

transverse cirrus banding   Irregularly spaced bandlike cirrus clouds that form nearly perpendicular to a jet stream axis. They indicate turbulence associated with the jet.

tropical cyclone   A general term applied to any low-pressure area that originates over tropical oceans.

tropopause The boundary between the troposphere and the stratosphere is called the tropopause. It consists of several discrete overlapping leaves, rather than a single continuous surface, and acts as a lid trapping almost all water vapor in the troposphere. It is marked by a decrease in wind speed, and constant temperature with an increase in height.

troposphere The lower layer of the atmosphere, extending from the surface to an average of seven miles. Temperature normally decreases with height, and winds increase with height. It is the layer of the atmosphere where almost all weather occurs.

trough An elongated area of low pressure.

true altitude Indicated airspeed corrected for temperature and pressure.

upslope The orographic effect of air moving up a slope, which tends to cool adiabatically.

vertical motion Upward or downward motion in the atmosphere.

VIP Video Integrator and Processor used in six levels to indicate precipitation intensity on the Radar Summary Chart.

virga Virga is rain that evaporates before reaching the surface.

visible moisture Moisture in the form of clouds or precipitation.

visual flight rules (VFR) Federal regulations that govern flight in visual meteorological conditions—flight by reference to the natural horizon and surface.

vort lobe A contraction for vorticity lobe. It usually applies to the 500-mb level and identifies an area of relatively higher values of vorticity. It is synonymous with short-wave trough or upper-level impulse. Generally speaking, there is rising air ahead of the vort lobe and sinking air behind.

vort max A contraction for vorticity maximum. It usually applies to the 500-mb level and refers to a point along a vorticity lobe where the absolute vorticity reaches a maximum value.

vortex In the most general use, any flow possessing vorticity. More often the term refers to a flow with closed streamlines.

vorticity Indicates a circulation or rotation within the atmosphere.

wall cloud See eye wall.

warm air advection A condition in the atmosphere characterized by air flowing from a relatively warmer area to a cooler area. It is often accompanied by upward vertical motion that in the presence of sufficient instability leads to thunderstorm development.

warm core low   An area of low pressure that is warmer at its center than at its periphery. Thermal lows and tropical cyclones are examples.

warm nose   A prominent northward bulge of relatively warm air.

water vapor   The invisible water molecules suspended in the air.

wave   A pattern of ridges and troughs in the horizontal flow as depicted on upper-level charts. At the surface, a wave is characterized by a break along a frontal boundary. A center of low pressure is frequently located at the apex of the wave.

WER   See BWER/WER/LEWP.

wet ice   An ice surface covered with a thin film of moisture caused by melting, insufficient to cause hydroplaning.

wet snow   Snow that has grains coated with liquid water that bonds the mass together but has no excess water in the pore spaces.

whiteout   An atmospheric optical phenomenon in which the pilot appears to be engulfed in a uniformly white glow. Neither shadows, horizon, or clouds are discernible; sense of depth and orientation is lost.

wind chill factor   The cooling effect of temperature and wind.

wind field   Winds plotted at a specified level in the atmosphere are referred to as a wind field (surface, 5000 feet, 300 mb, etc.). Wind fields show areas of convergence, divergence, and advection, which provide meteorologists with a valuable forecast tool.

wind shear   Any rapid change in wind direction or velocity. Low-level wind shear (LLWS) is generally shear that occurs within about 2,000 feet of the surface. LLWS is classified severe when a rapid change in wind direction or velocity causes an airspeed change greater than 15 knots or vertical speed change greater than 500 feet per minute.

zonal flow   A wind flow that is generally in a west to east direction.

Index

About the Author

Terry T. Lankford has been a Weather Specialist with the FAA for nearly 30 years, and is the author of three titles in McGraw-Hill's *Practical Flying Series*: *Understanding Aeronautical Charts*, 2nd Edition, *Cockpit Weather Decisions*, and all three editions of this book. He also wrote *Aircraft Icing*. A pilot since 1967, he also holds single-engine, multiengine, and instrument ratings, as well as an FAA Gold Seal Instructor certificate. An FAA accident prevention counselor, he earned the Flight Safety Award in 1979. Lankford also contributes articles to pilot periodicals.